The Right Thing to Do, The Smart Thing to Do
Enhancing Diversity in the Health Professions

Summary of the Symposium on Diversity in Health Professions
in Honor of Herbert W. Nickens, M.D.

Brian D. Smedley and Adrienne Y. Stith
Institute of Medicine

Lois Colburn
Association of American Medical Colleges

Clyde H. Evans
Association of Academic Health Centers

INSTITUTE OF MEDICINE

NATIONAL ACADEMY PRESS
Washington, D.C.

**NATIONAL ACADEMY PRESS • 2101 Constitution Avenue, N.W. •
Washington, DC 20418**

NOTICE: The project that is the subject of this report was approved by the Governing Board of the National Research Council, whose members are drawn from the councils of the National Academy of Sciences, the National Academy of Engineering, and the Institute of Medicine. The members of the committee responsible for the report were chosen for their special competences and with regard for appropriate balance.

Support for this project was provided by The Robert Wood Johnson Foundation, The Henry J. Kaiser Family Foundation, the W.K. Kellogg Foundation, the Bureau of Health Professions, Division of Health Professions Diversity and Bureau of Primary Health Care of the Health Resources and Services Administration, and the Office of Minority Health, U.S. Department of Health and Human Services. The views presented in this report are those of the Institute of Medicine and are not necessarily those of the funding agencies.

International Standard Book Number 0-309-07614-5

Additional copies of this report are available for sale from the National Academy Press, 2101 Constitution Avenue, N.W., Box 285, Washington, D.C. 20055. Call (800) 624-6242 or (202) 334-3313 (in the Washington metropolitan area), or visit the NAP's home page at **www.nap.edu.** The full text of this report is available at **www.nap.edu.**

For more information about the Institute of Medicine, visit the IOM home page at: **www.iom.edu.**

The serpent has been a symbol of long life, healing, and knowledge among almost all cultures and religions since the beginning of recorded history. The serpent adopted as a logotype by the Institute of Medicine is a relief carving from ancient Greece, now held by the Staatliche Museen in Berlin.

*"Knowing is not enough; we must apply.
Willing is not enough; we must do."*
—Goethe

INSTITUTE OF MEDICINE

Shaping the Future for Health

THE NATIONAL ACADEMIES

National Academy of Sciences
National Academy of Engineering
Institute of Medicine
National Research Council

The **National Academy of Sciences** is a private, nonprofit, self-perpetuating society of distinguished scholars engaged in scientific and engineering research, dedicated to the furtherance of science and technology and to their use for the general welfare. Upon the authority of the charter granted to it by the Congress in 1863, the Academy has a mandate that requires it to advise the federal government on scientific and technical matters. Dr. Bruce M. Alberts is president of the National Academy of Sciences.

The **National Academy of Engineering** was established in 1964, under the charter of the National Academy of Sciences, as a parallel organization of outstanding engineers. It is autonomous in its administration and in the selection of its members, sharing with the National Academy of Sciences the responsibility for advising the federal government. The National Academy of Engineering also sponsors engineering programs aimed at meeting national needs, encourages education and research, and recognizes the superior achievements of engineers. Dr. Wm. A. Wulf is president of the National Academy of Engineering.

The **Institute of Medicine** was established in 1970 by the National Academy of Sciences to secure the services of eminent members of appropriate professions in the examination of policy matters pertaining to the health of the public. The Institute acts under the responsibility given to the National Academy of Sciences by its congressional charter to be an adviser to the federal government and, upon its own initiative, to identify issues of medical care, research, and education. Dr. Kenneth I. Shine is president of the Institute of Medicine.

The **National Research Council** was organized by the National Academy of Sciences in 1916 to associate the broad community of science and technology with the Academy's purposes of furthering knowledge and advising the federal government. Functioning in accordance with general policies determined by the Academy, the Council has become the principal operating agency of both the National Academy of Sciences and the National Academy of Engineering in providing services to the government, the public, and the scientific and engineering communities. The Council is administered jointly by both Academies and the Institute of Medicine. Dr. Bruce M. Alberts and Dr. Wm. A. Wulf are chairman and vice chairman, respectively, of the National Research Council.

NICKENS SYMPOSIUM ADVISORY COMMITTEE

FITZHUGH MULLAN, M.D. (Chair), Contributing Editor, *Health Affairs*, Bethesda, MD

MAXINE BLEICH, President, Ventures in Education, New York, NY

ROGER J. BULGER, M.D. (ex-officio), President, Association of Academic Health Centers, Washington, D.C.

LAURO F. CAVAZOS, Ph.D., Professor, Tufts University School of Medicine, Department of Community Health, Boston, MA

JORDAN J. COHEN, M.D. (ex-officio), President, Association of American Medical Colleges, Washington, D.C.

CLYDE H. EVANS, Ph.D., Vice President, Association of Academic Health Centers, Washington, D.C.

VANESSA NORTHINGTON GAMBLE, M.D., Ph.D., Vice President, Division of Community and Minority Programs, American Association of Medical Colleges, Washington, D.C.

MARILYN H. GASTON, M.D., Assistant Surgeon General and Director, Bureau of Primary Health Care, Health Resources and Services Administration, U.S. Department of Health and Human Services, Bethesda, MD

MI JA KIM, R.N., Ph.D., Chicago, IL

MARSHA LILLIE-BLANTON, Dr.P.H., Vice President, Health Policy, Henry J. Kaiser Family Foundation, Washington, D.C.

SUSANNA MORALES, M.D., Department of Medicine, Weill Medical College of Cornell University, New York, NY

ROBERT G. PETERSDORF, M.D., Distinguished Professor of Medicine, University of Washington School of Medicine, Seattle, WA

VINCENT ROGERS, D.D.S., M.P.H., HRSA Northeast Cluster, Philadelphia, PA

REVIEWERS

This report has been reviewed in draft form by individuals chosen for their diverse perspectives and technical expertise, in accordance with procedures approved by the NRC's Report Review Committee. The purpose of this independent review is to provide candid and critical comments that will assist the institution in making its published report as sound as possible and to ensure that the report meets institutional standards for objectivity, evidence, and responsiveness to the study charge. The review comments and draft manuscript remain confidential to protect the integrity of the deliberative process. We wish to thank the following individuals for their review of this report:

Mary Lou de Leon Siantz, Georgetown University School of Nursing

Susan C. Scrimshaw, University of Illinois at Chicago

Curtis C. Taylor, Institute of Medicine

Although the reviewers listed above have provided many constructive comments and suggestions, they were not asked to endorse the conclusions or recommendations nor did they see the final draft of the report before its release. The review of this report was overseen by **M. Alfred Haynes**. Appointed by the Institute of Medicine, he was responsible for making certain that an independent examination of this report was carried out in accordance with institutional procedures and that all review comments were carefully considered. Responsibility for the final content of this report rests entirely with the institution.

ACKNOWLEDGMENTS

The Advisory Committee to the "Symposium on Diversity in Health Professions in Honor of Herbert W. Nickens, M.D.," wishes to thank a number of individuals and organizations whose hard work and support contributed to the success of the symposium and publication of this volume. The symposium and this publication would not be possible without the generous financial support of The Robert Wood Johnson Foundation, The Henry J. Kaiser Family Foundation, the W.K. Kellogg Foundation, the Bureau of Health Professions, Division of Health Professions Diversity and Bureau of Primary Health Care of the Health Resources and Services Administration, and the Office of Minority Health, U.S. Department of Health and Human Services. Representatives of these organizations served on the Advisory Committee, which was chaired by Fitzhugh Mullan, M.D., Contributing Editor of *Health Affairs*. The Advisory Committee would also like to thank Jordan J. Cohen, M.D., Roger J. Bulger, M.D., and Kenneth I. Shine, M.D., the presidents of the three sponsoring organizations and ex-officio members of the Advisory Committee, for their leadership and support of the symposium.

Many individuals labored hard to plan and provide staff support for the symposium. In addition to the Advisory Committee members, staff of the Association of American Medical Colleges (AAMC), including Vanessa Northington Gamble, Lois Colburn, Carol Savage, and Ella Cleveland; Clyde Evans of the Association of Academic Health Centers (AHC); Brian Smedley and Adrienne Stith of the Institute of Medicine (IOM); and Faith Mitchell of the Division of Behavioral, Social Sciences, and Education (DBASSE) of the National Research Council were actively involved in planning, organizing, and preparing the summary of the event. Amelia Cobb and Parthenia Purnell of AAMC and Thelma Cox and Geraldine Kennedo of IOM provided logistical support during the symposium. Carol Savage of AAMC deserves special acknowledgment for her hard work to shepherd the entire symposium process, including commissioning of papers and inviting speakers.

The Advisory Committee also wishes to thank the speakers and discussants who contributed to the symposium. These individuals are listed in the program agenda that appears in the appendix of this volume.

Table of Contents

The Right Thing to Do, The Smart Thing to Do: Enhancing Diversity in the Health Professions

Brian D. Smedley and Adrienne Y. Stith
Institute of Medicine

Lois Colburn
Association of American Medical Colleges

Clyde H. Evans
Association of Academic Health Centers

INTRODUCTION

Newspaper headlines underscore the challenges that the health professions face in this period of dramatic change in the American health care enterprise: critical shortages of nurses and other health professionals, tight budgets and rising health care costs, increasing public concern about patient safety and medical errors, and rising criticism of the quality of care that Americans receive, to name a few. Indeed, the health professions and health care industry are fighting to retain the public's confidence that the U.S. health care system can continue to be the world's best.

Compounding these problems is the future viability of the U.S. health care workforce. The health professions are becoming less appealing to many U.S. high school and college students, as applications for slots in many health professions training programs, such as medical, nursing, and dental schools, have declined over the last decade. Desperate for well-trained nurses and other health professionals, hospitals are recruiting worldwide to fill needed shortages. These trends raise the questions: Will we have the health care workforce we need in the 21st century? Where will future health professionals come from? And what will the U.S. health care workforce look like in the near future?

Demographic trends indicate that future U.S. workers will increasingly be persons of color: by the year 2050, in fact, one of every two U.S. workers will be African American, Hispanic, Asian American, Pacific Islander, or Native American (see Figure 1). In three states and the District of Colombia, these populations already constitute a majority, and in thirteen other states, minorities

1

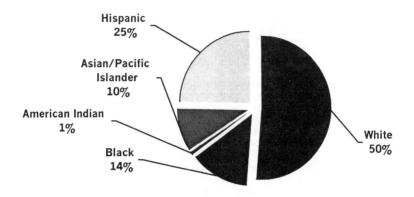

FIGURE 1 U.S. Population Aged 16–64, Year 2050 (percentages).
SOURCE: U.S. Bureau of the Census, Population Projections Program, based on 1990 Census.

constitute at least 30% of the populace. In many other locales, current K–12 enrollment suggests that the talent pool for the next generation of professionals is largely composed of children of color. With growing numbers of "baby boomers" and a longer-living population of seniors, today's youth will be increasingly relied upon to supply the skills and labor needed to maintain a sufficient health care workforce.

Many minority groups, however, including African Americans, Hispanics, and Native Americans, are poorly represented in the health professions relative to their proportions in the overall U.S. population. These groups also tend to be less healthy than the U.S. majority, experience greater barriers to accessing health care, and often receive a lower quality and intensity of health care once they reach their doctor's office. Further, the proportion of these groups within the U.S. population is growing rapidly, increasing the need to respond to their public health and health care needs. This disparity presents a significant challenge to the health professions and to educators, as they must garner all available resources to meet future health care demands.

Increasing the diversity of health professionals has been an explicit strategy of the federal government and many private groups to address these needs. Yet the policy context for efforts to increase diversity within the health professions has shifted significantly over the past decade. Several events—including public referenda, judicial decisions, and lawsuits challenging affirmative action policies in 1995, 1996, and 1997 (notably, the Fifth District Court of Appeals finding in *Hopwood* v. *Texas*, the California Regents' decision to ban race or gender-based preferences in admissions, and passage of the California Civil Rights Initiative [Proposition 209] and Initiative 200 in Washington State)—have forced many higher education institutions to abandon the use of race and ethnicity as factors in admissions decisions. To compound this problem, the "pipeline" of elementary, secondary, and higher education that prepares students for careers in health professions continues to rupture with respect to underrepresented minority (URM) students. In particular, the math and science achievement gap between URM and non-URM students persists, and in some cases, has widened, frustrating efforts to increase minority preparation and participation in health professions careers.

Given these problems—an increasing need for minority health professionals, policy challenges to affirmative action, and little progress toward enhancing the numbers of URM students prepared to enter health professions careers—three health policy and professional organizations met to consider a major symposium that would explore challenges and strategies to achieving diversity among health professions. Representatives of the Association of American Medical Colleges (AAMC), the Association of Academic Health Centers (AHC), and the Institute of Medicine (IOM) and Division of Behavioral, Social Sciences, and Education (DBASSE) of the National Academy of Sciences met in the early spring of 1999 to consider such a national symposium. Among those in attendance at this meeting was Herbert W. Nickens, M.D., Vice President and Director of Community and Minority Programs at AAMC and a longtime advocate for focused efforts to enhance URM representation in health professions (see text box).

Herbert W. Nickens
1947–1999

Until his death on March 22, 1999, Herbert W. Nickens, M.D., M.A., served as the first vice president and director of the Division of Community and Minority Programs at AAMC. AAMC created this division to focus its commitment on an expanded role for minorities in medicine and improving minority health status.

Before coming to the AAMC, Dr. Nickens was the first director of the Office of Minority Health, U.S. Department of Health and Human Services. In that role, he was pivotal in crafting the programmatic themes for that office—many of which continue to this day. Prior to that he served on the staff of the landmark Secretary's Task Force on Black and Minority Health, was director of the Office of Policy, Planning, and Analysis of the National Institute on Aging (NIA), and before that was Deputy Chief, Center on Aging, National Institute of Mental Health (NIMH).

Dr. Nickens received his A.B. in 1969 from Harvard College, and a M.D. and M.A. (in Sociology) from the University of Pennsylvania in 1973. He served his residency in psychiatry at Yale and the University of Pennsylvania. At the University of Pennsylvania he was also a Robert Wood Johnson Clinical Scholar, and a member of the faculty of the School of Medicine.

Dr. Nickens' vision for the symposium was clear and persuasive. Noting that many efforts to enhance minority student preparation and participation in health professions careers had become fragmented, he urged that leading health policymakers, health professions educators, K–12 educators, and higher education policymakers be convened to share strategies and develop a comprehensive plan to address the many political, legal, and educational challenges to greater diversity among health professionals. He also saw such a symposium as an important vehicle to revitalize the case for diversity among health professionals, and as a corollary, to improve public support for and understanding of diversity as a tool to address the nation's health needs.

Tragically, Dr. Nickens passed away before the symposium could be convened. His leadership in promoting diversity and addressing the health needs of communities of color, however, continues to be felt among the many students who have benefited from his efforts to open doors to heath professions careers, and the many faculty and administrators of health professions schools whose work he influenced. To acknowledge his leadership and contributions as a champion of efforts to diversify the health professions, the symposium was named in his honor.

These proceedings summarize presentations and discussion during the March 16–17, 2001, "Symposium on Diversity in the Health Professions in Honor of Herbert W. Nickens, M.D." Consistent with Dr. Nickens' vision, the symposium was convened to:

1. re-examine and revitalize the rationale for diversity in health professions, particularly in light of the rapid growth of racial and ethnic minority populations in the United States;
2. identify problems in underrepresentation of U.S. racial and ethnic minorities in health professions, and discuss the strategies that are being developed to respond to underrepresentation;
3. assess the impact of anti-affirmative action legislative and judicial actions on diversity in health professions and health care service delivery to ethnic minority and medically underserved populations;
4. identify effective short-term strategies for enhancing racial and ethnic diversity in health professions training programs (e.g., in the admissions process, in pre-matriculation and summer enrichment programs); and
5. identify practices of health professions schools that may assist in improving the preparation of racial and ethnic minority students currently underrepresented in health professions, thereby enhancing the long-term likelihood of greater diversity in health professions.

To accomplish these goals, symposium organizers invited nearly two dozen leaders in health policy, higher education, secondary education, education policy, law, health professions education, and minority health to provide presentations at the symposium. Some of these presentations were offered in plenary sessions, while others were delivered in small discussion groups during the second day of the symposium, to encourage dialogue and the development of new alliances and strategies. A list of speakers and paper topics are provided in the appendix of these proceedings. Selected papers from the symposium are published in this volume.

THE CASE FOR DIVERSITY IN HEALTH PROFESSIONS

"The Right Thing to Do ... The Smart Thing to Do"

Several presenters argued for a re-examination of the rationale for diversity in health professions, and, more specifically, the value of affirmative action as a tool for achieving diversity in health professions training settings. Mark Smith, president and CEO of the California Health Care Foundation, noted in a keynote address that the two traditional arguments presented in support of affirmative action, *fairness* and *function*, must be updated if advocates seek to overcome objections of some policymakers and the prevailing public sentiment.

Issues of *fairness*, Smith stated, have traditionally been at the heart of arguments in support of affirmative action, based on the fact that many racial and ethnic minorities have been traditionally excluded from economic and professional opportunities. Affirmative action policies were therefore established as a mechanism for redress and expanded opportunity. The contemporary challenge, he noted, is to update this understanding of fairness and make the mechanisms of redress more sophisticated to reflect social, economic, and demographic changes that have occurred since affirmative action policies were first implemented. For example, Smith noted that by pointing to minority individuals who have attained success and broken traditional economic and employment barriers, opponents of affirmative action argue that minorities now have equal, if not greater opportunities to succeed. Increasingly, he added, African Americans, Native Americans, and Hispanics have ascended to middle- and upper-class status, creating a perception that affirmative action is no longer needed. Opportunity, however, is still inequitably distributed, according to Smith—a point that will be lost should proponents of affirmative action not acknowledge the economic, political, and educational gains that minorities have made, he added.

Proponents of affirmative action must also address the perception that "merit" can be fairly and objectively assessed, according to Smith. This perception is bolstered, he noted, by the heavy reliance among some administrators on test scores in admissions processes. Test scores, Smith stated, create an aura of scientific precision without necessarily predicting the outcomes of interest—such as the kinds of skills necessary to be a good nurse. A silent form of "pseudo precision," he argued, is conferred when quantitative measures are used without a clear understanding of how and when these data are useful. Such misunderstandings are a "constant threat" to notions of fairness that have been central to efforts to increase diversity, according to Smith.

Arguments in support of affirmative action that focus on the *functional utility* of a diverse workforce must also be updated, according to Smith. Noting that some research and anecdotal evidence supports the argument that a diverse health care workforce helps to improve access to care for minority communities and enhance trust and communication, Smith called for more critical analysis and research. Not all racial and ethnic minority health care providers will "click" with minority patients, he noted; similarly, one should not assume that non-minority providers cannot adequately serve minority patients. Research must better assess the key variables that affect the patient-provider relationship, such as trust, being treated with dignity, and mutual respect, and consider how the race and ethnicity of patients and providers influence these variables, he noted.

Smith concluded by drawing an analogy to common myths about the pyramids and other great artifacts of ancient Egypt. He noted that a common misperception about the pyramids is that their construction involved highly technical scientific achievements that were once thought unavailable to the Egyptians. This was not the case, he stated—in fact, much of the construction conformed to basic understandings, and was not "rocket science." Much the same can be said about efforts to diversify health professions, Smith said, in that basic efforts such as mentoring, developing a critical mass of URM health professions students and faculty, focal and consistent support from leadership, and social and psychological support can all help to enhance diversity. "These are not sophisticated concepts," he noted.

Another myth about the pyramids, Smith stated, is that stone materials used in their construction were brought in from miles away, across desert and waterways. In fact, he noted, the pyramids were built using materials that were readily available. Similarly, we need not look far for sources of future health professionals—tomorrow's dentists, doctors, nurses, pharmacists, and other health professionals are all around us, he said.

Finally, Smith related that the famous Sphinx was not planned, but, rather, was an artifact of another major construction effort that yielded a fortunate discovery. Ancient Egyptians were building a causeway, Smith stated, and came upon a large rock formation that blocked the causeway. Rather than try to remove the rock, the Egyptians carved the Sphinx into its surface. Similarly, proponents of diversity and affirmative action often encounter obstacles and political challenges, but these challenges must be addressed, Smith said. He noted that opponents who cannot be convinced of the need for diversity on political grounds can often be swayed on scientific grounds, heightening the need for creative and well-supported arguments. When "you've got lemons, you make lemonade," he stated, adding that opponents can be swayed that affirmative action is not only "the right thing to do . . . [but also] the smart thing to do."

The Necessity of Sustained Efforts

Lee Bollinger, president of the University of Michigan, delivered a theme similar to that of Smith in a keynote address that focused on Michigan's efforts to defend its affirmative action policies against two lawsuits that questioned the constitutionality of affirmative action. Bollinger, a constitutional law scholar, argued that the U.S. Supreme Court's ruling in the landmark 1978 *Bakke* case, which remains the preeminent ruling on affirmative action as of this writing, refutes the notion that race, ethnicity, and color cannot and should not be taken into account in admissions processes. To the contrary, the *Bakke* decision points out that U.S. society is not "color-blind," as opponents have argued, borrowing civil rights-era language, according to Bollinger. Combating such arguments has been challenging, he said, in the wake of an increasingly conservative Supreme Court, nationwide efforts to bring suit against universities that have affirmative action policies, state referenda (e.g., Proposition 209), and public attitudes that indicate dwindling support for affirmative action. Bollinger noted that affirmative action proponents are often urged to "move on," or to find some other way to accomplish diversity without explicitly considering race or ethnicity in admissions processes. Under his leadership, however, the University of Michigan won the lawsuit challenging its undergraduate admissions processes, and is appealing a ruling against the school's law school admissions policies. In the process, Bollinger stated, he has learned that: 1) higher education, when organized and ready to address challenges, is "hard to beat;" 2) it is important not to accept the attitudes of the times (e.g., that affirmative action has been beaten, and that other alternatives should be explored); and 3) one must never underestimate the necessity of sustained efforts in dealing with diversity issues.

Michigan's success in defending its affirmative action policies can be linked to two broad-based strategies, said Bollinger. The first was a legal strategy to provide support for the rationale in the *Bakke* decision, which assumes that a racially diverse student body leads to better educational outcomes for all students and serves compelling government interests. Michigan's defense drew from several sources, including social science research indicating that educational and civic outcomes were better for college students educated in more diverse environments. The second strategy, according to Bollinger, was a public education campaign that sought to "make the case, with complete openness and candor," to inform the public about admissions processes and the benefits of diversity. Bollinger and his colleagues actively sought opportunities to present Michigan's rationale for diversity, while continuing to build allies among other higher education leaders, as well as businesses and corporations, such as General Motors.

In the process, Bollinger stated, Michigan was able to identify and debunk several misperceptions about affirmative action:

Race is no longer a factor in American life, and therefore should not be a factor in admissions processes. Bollinger responded to this charge by noting that the vast majority of Michigan students, both minority and non-minority, came from starkly segregated high schools. This suggests that college represents the first opportunity for many of these students to work and live with people from other backgrounds, in effect training them for participation in the working world.

Admissions processes should be based on applicants' credentials, not race. Like many other schools that have affirmative action policies, Michigan's admissions process considers applicants' academic preparation and achievements in conjunction with other factors—such as their geographic location, leadership, socioeconomic status, athletic abilities, and alumni status—to create a diverse student body, said Bollinger. Race and ethnicity are but two of the many factors that must be considered to assemble a class "like a symphony," he said. Noting that the term "affirmative action" is not commonly used when universities consider applicants' "legacy" status (i.e., children of alumni), Bollinger said that people mistakenly believe that applicants' race or ethnicity is somehow given greater emphasis than other attributes when admissions committees attempt to assemble a diverse student body.

Diversity is not central to the educational mission, but rather an add-on. Bollinger refuted this argument, stating that diversity is critical to efforts that help students to "get outside of" their own perceptions and viewpoints and encounter other perspectives. "This why we study history, law ... and literature," he said, noting that undergraduate curricula typically requires study outside of students' major field, to ensure breadth. Similarly, he argued, students should be exposed to other cultures, viewpoints, and perspectives.

Diversity does not work because students self-segregate on campus, nullifying its benefits. Bollinger acknowledged that students of different racial and ethnic backgrounds do segregate themselves, but believes such segregation is less prevalent than commonly believed. In part, this may reflect what students are most comfortable with, given that they arrive on campus with generally limited exposure to other racial and ethnic groups, he said. Further, he argued, such self-segregation occurs in society, but should not be an excuse for failing to encourage students to learn from each other.

College and university admissions committees can achieve diversity by striving for a socioeconomic mix, or by automatically admitting a percentage of the top high school graduates. Bollinger also refuted this argument. Using socioeconomic status alone as a key factor in admissions will not ensure racial and ethnic diversity, he argued, as most poor individuals are white. In addition, automatically admitting a percentage of the top high school graduates removes the discretion and autonomy of universities to choose the type of student body that they feel would create the best learning environment.

Can Diversity Among Health Professionals Decrease Health Disparities?

African Americans and Native Americans, and to a lesser extent Hispanics, experience rates of mortality and disability from disease and illness that are significantly higher than rates for white Americans. The excess burden of illness in these populations is due to many complex factors, including socioeconomic inequality, environmental and occupational exposures, direct and indirect consequences of discrimination, health risk factors such as overweight, cultural and psychosocial factors such as health-seeking behavior, biological differences, and less access to health insurance and health care. Because many racial and ethnic minority communities have a shortage of physicians, increasing the numbers of health professionals—and in particular, providers who are themselves racial and ethnic minorities—to serve in these communities has been proposed as one means of addressing the excess burden of illness among minorities.

Raynard Kington, Diana Tisnado, and David Carlisle explored this hypothesis in a symposium presentation, noting that the question of training minority health providers to serve in minority communities extends back at least to the 1910 Flexner report, which advocated that "Negro" doctors be trained exclusively to serve the African-American population (see Kington, Tisnado, and Carlisle, this volume). Kington and colleagues explored the impact of diversity among health professionals via three pathways: the effect of practice choices of minority providers; the quality of communication between minority patients and providers; and the quality of training in health professions training settings as a result of increasing diversity in these settings. Kington et al. addressed these questions using data for physicians, because these data are generally more available and reliable than data for other health professionals.

Kington and colleagues noted that African-American and Hispanic patients are less likely than whites to have a regular physician, to have health insurance, to have routine visits with a physician, and to receive some preventive and screening services. After gaining access to health care, however, minorities still do not fare as well as their white counterparts; African Americans, and to a lesser extent Hispanics, receive fewer diagnostic and therapeutic procedures than whites, even after controlling for clinical, co-morbid, and sociodemographic factors.

Not surprisingly, Kington and his colleagues note, physician supply is inversely related to the concentration of African Americans and Hispanics in health service areas, even after adjusting for community income levels. A consistent body of research, however, indicates that African-American and Hispanic physicians are more likely to provide services in minority and underserved communities, and are more likely to treat poor (e.g., Medicaid-eligible) and sicker patients. Some studies, according to Kington and his co-authors, indicate that on average, minority physicians treat four to five times the numbers of minority patients than white physicians do. These practice patterns appear to be by choice, according to the authors; studies of new minority medical graduates, for example, indicate a greater preference to serve in minority and underserved communities.

Kington and his colleagues also reviewed several studies that examine the quality of patient-provider communication across and within racial and ethnic groups. These studies indicate that for some minority patients, having a minority physician may result in better communication, greater patient satisfaction with care, and greater use of preventive services. However, the authors caution, there is little empirical evidence that cultural competence influences patient outcomes, or that increasing the numbers of minority physicians to serve patients of color improves outcomes through culturally appropriate care. In addition, although many speculate that increased diversity in medical training may expose physicians to a wider range of cultural backgrounds and improve their interactions with patients, there is little evidence that diversity within health care training settings (e.g., greater numbers of URM students in medical school) improves training for all medical students, according to Kington et al. The authors noted, however, that this question has not been subject to consistent, rigorous study.

Kington and colleagues concluded that increased diversity among physicians appears to be valuable for increasing access to care in minority communities. Minority providers, they argue, are more likely to seek to serve individuals of their own racial and ethnic backgrounds, and tend to positively influence minority patients' satisfaction with clinical encounters. Further, these providers are more likely to provide preventive and primary care services that are most needed among less healthy populations. Kington and his co-authors caution, however, that while the evidence supports increasing the numbers of minority physicians to meet health needs of minority communities, we must guard against the notion that minority providers should be trained primarily to serve racial and ethnic minorities, or that white physicians cannot adequately serve minority patients. Given the disproportionately low representation of minorities among the ranks of health professions, such simplistic assumptions are likely to widen the gap in access and quality of care for minority patients.

The Impact of Diversity in Health Professions Education

As Kington and colleagues noted, a potentially important aspect of the case for diversity in health professions is the impact of diversity within health professions education settings. Lisa Tedesco, Vice President and Secretary of the University of Michigan, explored the theoretical and empirical evidence for this argument. Tedesco cited a growing number of studies indicating that diversity in higher education settings is associated with positive academic and social outcomes for students, and argued that such benefits extend to health professions training, as well.

One such landmark study, said Tedesco, was described in *The Shape of the River*, a book by William Bowen and Derek Bok (1998). Bowen and Bok studied educational and career outcomes for two cohorts of white and minority students who attended 28 selective colleges and universities in the 1970s and 1980s. They found that minority graduates of these institutions attained levels of academic achievement that were on par with their non-minority peers (e.g., minority and non-minority students attained graduate degrees at approximately equivalent rates). Further, minority graduates of these schools obtained professional degrees in fields such as law, medicine, and business at rates far higher than national averages for all students. African-American students from selected schools in the 1976 cohort, for example, were seven times more likely to receive degrees in law and five times more likely to receive degrees in medicine compared with the general college population, according to Tedesco. Similarly, African-American students in the 1989 cohort of students in this study were only slightly less likely to earn doctorates than were white students. Significantly, Tedesco noted, civic engagement and community activity was higher among minorities from the selected schools than their white counterparts.

Similar findings were obtained by Patricia Gurin, said Tedesco. Gurin, a professor of psychology at the University of Michigan, studied academic and civic outcomes of college students who attended racially and ethnically diverse colleges, and those who attended less diverse institutions. Gurin found that students at diverse institutions were more likely to be involved in community and civic activities, and were "better able to participate in an increasingly heterogeneous and complex democracy," according to Tedesco. These students, she added, were better able to understand and consider multiple perspectives, deal with the conflicts that different perspectives sometimes create, and "appreciate the common values and integrated forces that harness differences in pursuit of the common good." Gurin concluded that students can best develop the capacity to understand the ideas and feelings of others in an environment characterized by a diverse study body, equality among peers, and discussion of the rules of civil discourse.

"These factors are present on a campus with a racially diverse student body," Tedesco stated. "Encountering students from different racial and ethnic groups enables students to get to know one another and appreciate both similarities and differences." Significantly, Tedesco noted, diversity was also associated with a range of better cognitive and intellectual outcomes. Gurin found, according to Tedesco, that "interactions with peers from diverse racial backgrounds, both in the classroom and informally, is cognitively associated with a host of what are called learn-

> "Students who experience the most racial and ethnic diversity in classroom settings and in informal interactions with peers show the greatest engagement in active thinking processes, growth in intellectual engagement and motivation and growth in intellectual and academic skills."
> Lisa Tedesco

ing outcomes. Students who experience the most racial and ethnic diversity in classroom settings and in informal interactions with peers show the greatest engagement in active thinking processes, growth in intellectual engagement and motivation and growth in intellectual and academic skills."

Tedesco noted that parallel data linking the benefits of diversity in graduate health professions training are not available. Nonetheless, she stated, the research by Gurin, Bowen and Bok, and others suggests that the rich learning environments associated with diversity in undergraduate settings probably extend to health professions education settings. In the best case, she noted, students from diverse undergraduate settings enter health professions schools with a growing sense of cultural competence and experience interacting across racial and ethnic boundaries, as peers and as students. These students can be expected to engage in rich and lively discussions, would likely be vigorous contributors to tutoring and mentoring programs, and would add a dimension of intellectual and social complexity to areas in the curriculum that require social analysis and clinical judgment. In addition, students learning in diverse health professions training settings would likely extend the reach of health professions schools into the community for preventive care and youth services. Tedesco added that research should be done to assess the contributions of diversity in health professions training, for "it would be an opportunity lost not to study what our students are bringing to us."

Finally, Tedesco noted, students trained in diverse health professions education settings are likely to help improve the delivery of health care to minority and medically underserved communities. Observing that mistrust of the medical establishment has been linked to poor patient compliance, lack of participation in clinical trials, and low rates of patient satisfaction, Tedesco argued that diversity experiences can help health care providers and the patients they serve to develop bonds of understanding that will improve trust. Building an infrastructure of trustworthy health care professionals and health care institutions, she stated, has great potential to increase the health and well-being of individuals and the community, thus extending the benefits of diversity. In addition, noting that a lack of cultural competence among providers has become a barrier to care, Tedesco argued that diversity in health professions training settings is a step toward enhancing providers' understanding of cultural dimensions of care and their ability to work with diverse patient populations. Without this cultural skill, she stated, health care providers contribute institutionally and in other ways to patient non-compliance, premature end to treatment, and less than optimal treatment outcomes.

IS AFFIRMATIVE ACTION DEAD?

Lee Bollinger's presentation highlighted the strategies that the University of Michigan has developed in response to legal challenges regarding its admissions policies. Thomas Perez, formerly the director of the Office of Civil Rights of the U.S. Department of Health and Human Services, further described the current legal status of affirmative action programs, and suggested ways that the health professions can comply with current law and meet legal challenges (Perez, this volume). Perez noted that while courts and legal scholars disagree about the meaning of the landmark *Bakke* decision, little disagreement exists regarding the current constitutional standard in affirmative action cases. This standard dictates that courts must apply strict scrutiny in evaluating race-conscious admissions plans, and that institutions adapting these plans must demonstrate that the plan serves a "compelling government interest" and is narrowly tailored to achieve this goal.

"Compelling government interest," Perez noted, has traditionally been argued from the standpoint of either remedial justification or a diversity rationale. Remedial justification arguments have typically been advanced as a means of addressing the contemporary effects of past discrimination. This argument has met with limited success, Perez stated, as courts have held that higher education institutions (or in the case of state-supported institutions, state governments) must show complicity in prior discrimination, and must clearly demonstrate how its prior discrimination is linked to present inequality. The diversity rationale, on the other hand, has met with greater success in court challenges, according to Perez. As articulated by Bollinger and Tedesco, this argument poses that the state holds a compelling interest in enhancing students' educational experiences through a diverse student body. Perez cited recent court decisions, such as the Ninth Circuit Court ruling in a case challenging race-conscious admissions at the University of Washington's Law School and the district court ruling in the University of Michigan's undergraduate admissions case, as evidence that narrowly tailored, race-conscious admissions constructed on the basis of the diversity rationale can withstand court scrutiny. While this rationale has not survived court scrutiny in some cases (such as the Michigan law school admissions case), Perez argued that the rationale has survived enough challenges that "commentators' depiction of affirmative action as dead is at odds with the empirical evidence."

Perez concluded by noting that higher education institutions and the health professions can assist in the legal battle to preserve affirmative action in several ways. Following the University of Michigan's lead, he stated, institutions can help to build the case for diversity as a compelling interest by developing the evidence base supporting the benefits of diversity in higher education. Similarly, the health professions should work to enhance the "operational necessity" argument, which links the state's interest in facilitating the health care of its citizens via a racially and ethnically diverse health care workforce, Perez stated. This argument, he noted, has met with success in some legal challenges to affirmative action in the context of police and corrections hiring. In

> "The reality is that the current affirmative action landscape in higher education is quite unsettled, but by no means dead."
> Thomas Perez

addition, health professions education institutions should assess whether race-neutral policies, such as reduced reliance on test scores, could help in the effort to increase diversity. If not, he argued, institutions should be prepared to show why these practices are insufficient as part of a thorough defense of the use of race-conscious admissions practices.

REDEFINING EDUCATIONAL MERIT

Standardized Testing and Educational Opportunity

Noting that "tests and assessments are the most powerful levers of opportunity to higher status education and employment," Michael Nettles and Catherine Millett analyzed trends in the performance of African-American and Hispanic students on standardized tests, and discussed the implications of group differences in test performance for the participation of URM students in higher education (Nettles and Millet, this volume). In particular, they explored how test performance has become associated with "educational merit," and discussed the use of additional criteria to provide a more complete assessment of applicants' intellectual capital. The authors concluded with an analysis of student demographic and school factors associated with higher test performance among URM students.

The central question posed by Nettles and Millet is: "What do we need to do to achieve greater diversity in American society at every level?" Diversity, they argued, is especially needed in the higher levels of a meritocracy. Standardized tests, however, have become a core indicator of merit in this country, serving as the gateway through which opportunity is allocated. The higher a student's score, according to Nettles and Millet, the more access she/he has to high-quality curricula, colleges, and professional schools, which translates into higher status employment and a better quality of life. In order to reverse the underrepresentation of minorities in higher education, the authors stated, their participation in and performance on the principal mediums of meritocracy—test scores and grades—must be improved.

Colleges and universities use a variety of criteria (e.g., test scores, GPA, class rank, essays, parental alumni status) when making decisions about admissions, Nettles and Millet noted, and use a variety of weighting schemes to assign relative importance to these criteria. Test scores, they asserted, represent the biggest challenge for African-American and Hispanic students in admissions to both undergraduate and graduate institutions. Nettles and Millet noted that many schools have begun to de-emphasize test scores—for example, some institutions have amended tests and still others have made them optional. However, test score data generally remain a key component in admissions. African-American, Hispanic, and Native American students generally perform poorly on standardized tests relative to their white and Asian-American peers, according to the authors. Data from the Scholastic Aptitude Test (SAT), for example, reveal that

80% of African Americans and 66% of Hispanics score below 1,000, while whites are fairly evenly distributed across the range of scores, with about 39% scoring below 1,000. The distribution of American College Test (ACT) and the Medical College Admissions Test (MCAT) reveals a similar pattern.

Racial and ethnic gaps in high school and college test scores begin very early in students' careers, Nettles and Millet noted. Data from the National Assessment of Educational Progress (NAEP), which is administered in a variety of subjects, reveal that a large number of minority students are not achieving even basic levels of performance in early grades. By the fourth grade, Nettles and Millet stated, more than 65% of African-American and 60% of Hispanic children are performing below basic levels in math. These data are in contrast to the 22% of white students who perform below basic level on the NAEP. Nettles and Millet pointed out that these gaps do not tend to narrow as students advance, as indicated by the continued gap in SAT, ACT, and MCAT scores.

Several factors correlate with minority student performance on standardized tests, according to Nettles and Millett. Not surprisingly, they noted, the concentration of minority students in schools is inversely associated with students' test performance. For example, data from the NAEP illustrate that, in general, the greater the African-American and Hispanic enrollment of the school, the lower the 4th grade math scores of students in that school. Interestingly, they noted, NAEP data reveal that some schools with predominantly African-American and Hispanic student populations scored above the white mean, and some predominantly white schools scored at or below the African-American mean. The schools in the survey are anonymous, but Nettles and Millet argued that if more can be learned from these schools, greater insight could be gained into factors related to teacher quality, curriculum, family involvement, and other influences, that may help raise scores for minority children.

Nettles and Millet also examined demographic and student characteristics and their relationship to standardized test scores. For all racial and ethnic groups, parents' socioeconomic status (levels of education and income) and the type and number of courses taken (particularly honors classes) were positively associated with student test performance. Students whose first language was English, who intended to major in a natural science field, and who attended private schools (and/or schools that offer Advanced Placement courses) were also more likely to have higher test scores. For African-American students, attending a high school where the majority of students are white and attending private school were associated with higher test performance. Further, for African-American males, participation in extracurricular athletic activities was associated with higher test scores. For white males, public versus private school and involvement in athletics did not predict test scores.

Nettles and Millett concluded that the strongest criteria available to potentially supplant or complement standardized test data are related to school curricula. "Students who experience the most rigorous curricula in school," they noted, "and earn relatively high grades are the most promising prospects for success in college, graduate and professional school." Public and private initiatives that enhance the academic preparation of minority students and expose them to an enriched curricula, they argued, should help to improve the performance of minority students on standardized tests, and subsequently, improve their educational options.

Strategies to Enhance Diversity in Health Professions:
An International Perspective

New perspectives to address the underrepresentation of racial and ethnic minorities among health professionals in the United States can be gained by understanding how other nations deal with similar diversity questions, according to Alan Herman, M.D., Ph.D., Dean of the National School of Public Health at the Medical University of Southern Africa (MEDUNSA), who delivered an afternoon keynote address. Herman has a bicontinental perspective regarding diversity and education. He was born and educated in South Africa, and came to the United States in the 1980s, where he worked and taught at the National Institutes of Health. He was recruited back to South Africa in the mid-1990s to start the first American-style school of public health at MEDUNSA.

South Africa is a country of contrasts that is still in the grips of its own racism, stated Herman. Education, he noted, especially health professions education, is still defined and shaped by that racism. When founding the National School of Public Health, Herman stated, two fundamental principles had to be addressed. The first was equity, a term Herman prefers to affirmative action. According to Herman, equity is a fundamental principle that is intrinsic to the principles of liberty. "Equity is not important because it will close the gap between blacks and whites," he stated. Rather, "It's important because it's important." The second fundamental principle, according to Herman, is that the probability of success in health professions education for black South Africans is poorly predicted by quantitative metrics, such as standardized tests. "If you take my score from high school in mathematics," Herman stated, "there was no way you could predict that I would become a methodologist." He added, "... I did come from a slum and my cognitive ability was in fact clouded by the racism of my society. Until, I think, we move to that understanding, we won't be able to create equity in education nor will we be able to create equity in health care."

> "I did come from a slum and my cognitive ability was in fact clouded by the racism of my society. Until, I think, we move to that understanding, we won't be able to create equity in education nor will we be able to create equity in health care."
> Alan Herman

MEDUNSA was created in 1980 by the apartheid regime to educate "second class doctors" to care for "second class people," Herman stated. Since the end of apartheid, however, enrollment in MEDUNSA's medical school has increased, while enrollment in other medical schools (which are majority white) has decreased. The most recently admitted class at MEDUNSA comprised 300 students, while other medical schools had 120 to 130 students. Through its history, MEDUNSA has trained 70% of South Africa's black physicians, 90% of its black dentists, 100% of the country's black veterinarians, 50% of South Africa's black M.P.H. degree holders, 100% of the nation's black doctorates in public health, and between 40 and 100% of South Africa's black physician specialists, said Herman.

In admissions decisions, preference is given to disadvantaged students. "We will go to the poorest schools to find the smartest kids to bring them into medicine," Herman stated. MEDUNSA's success in retaining and graduating these students, he noted, can be attributed to the faculty and administration's understanding of the needs of disadvantaged students. Remedial courses and mentoring are offered to help address gaps in students' prior academic preparation, and students are not removed from the university if they have difficulty successfully completing coursework. As an example, Herman noted that 15% of MEDUNSA's students fail in the first year. These students are placed into a supplementary program, however, and are able to repeat the first year. Most of these students are able to return and complete school. While this practice has been criticized, it has paid off, Herman argued, in that many of the students who take the longest time to complete their education practice in some of the most remote areas of the country.

MEDUNSA offers a formal academic mentoring program that is managed by senior students and faculty. Although the mentoring program is focused on students who do not complete the first year, informal mentoring is offered to all new students. MEDUNSA has also developed initiatives to assist secondary schools, such as academic outreach programs and a science mentoring program for high school students in physics, chemistry, biology, and math, that is organized and managed by the MEDUNSA student government. Outreach efforts, Herman stated, are enhanced by the creation of a "science bus" that tours the countryside with two science faculty members, teaching from school to school. MEDUNSA also helps to upgrade the skills of high school science and math teachers with refresher courses and university "open days."

The end result of these outreach efforts, Herman stated, is that MEDUNSA has been able to make strides toward addressing South Africa's need for a diverse health care workforce. While many students of color choose to attend majority white schools because they have more resources, he stated, MEDUNSA has the advantage of being committed to helping students stay enrolled.

"Working the Demand Side of the Problem":
Algebra and Opportunity

Robert Moses expanded on the theme of improving educational opportunities for racial and ethnic minority children as he discussed the importance of math and science literacy in an increasingly globalized, high-tech economy. Moses, a mathematician, founded the Algebra Project 20 years ago to help minority children gain access to better-quality mathematics curricula than that typically provided in poor, predominantly minority school districts. After becoming frustrated because his daughter's school did not offer algebra, Moses was invited by her teacher to provide instruction for several advanced students. According to Moses, children must master algebra, as it is the gateway to college-preparatory curriculum and subsequently to higher education and increased opportunity in life. In the process of participating in the project, Moses stated, children gain a better appreciation of why math and science training is essential to help them become full participants in an expanding economy. The project also helps children recognize that this training can help them shape the technological advancements that will ultimately affect their lives. In this way, he argues, students and communities that have been traditionally left out of the economic and political mainstream gain a significant voice. "This is working the demand side of the problem," he noted.

Moses began his career as a math teacher and was drawn to the south in 1960 to become a full-time worker in the struggle for civil rights. In Mississippi, he helped to organize the poor rural population, register thousands of voters, and train organizers in freedom schools. Moses drew analogies between the Civil Rights movement's goal to bring disenfranchised groups into the political mainstream, and the Algebra Project's effort to bring disadvantaged children into the economic and intellectual mainstream. Previously, he noted, industrial technology and physical labor was the driving economic engine of the country. Today, however, computer-based technology and intellectual labor drive the economy, and minority children must be prepared to participate.

"The new technology has brought with it a new requirement for literacy for citizenship," Moses stated. "For example, in earlier days if people couldn't read or write they were the designated serfs of our industrial technology." He contended that in the current era, people need a fundamental math literacy in addition to reading and writing skills. "Without that," he says, "we are growing designated serfs."

Unfortunately, Moses stated, today's schools still teach children—especially minority children—based on artifacts of the older technology, in effect dooming them to poorer career

> "The national discussion that we're having is misplaced. We're having a national discussion about education as a selection process—who is going to go where. What we need is a national discussion about education as an opportunity structure."
>
> Robert Moses

opportunities and second-class citizenship. He noted that the average student is graduating with the equivalent of an 8th-grade education, making it difficult to obtain a job that will lead to a dignified life in this country. "The national discussion that we're having is misplaced," Moses said. "We're having a national discussion about education as a selection process—who is going to go where." As an example, he stated that the tendency is to not "fix" schools, but move students around, through voucher programs, busing, and charter schools. "What we need," he challenged, "is a national discussion about education as an opportunity structure. It's the difference between discussing the ceiling and the floor. We need a discussion about the floor. What's the floor out here for everyone to stand on, so that if we provide this floor and they get on it then they have a real opportunity to be citizens."

TRENDS IN ADMISSION, ENROLLMENT, AND RETENTION OF URM STUDENTS IN THE HEALTH PROFESSIONS EDUCATION PIPELINE

Lost Opportunities: The Journey to Higher Education for URM Students

Noting large disparities in educational outcomes between underrepresented minority (URM) and non-URM students, Patricia Gandara discussed points along the education pipeline where opportunities to improve minority achievement are lost (Gandara, this volume). Gandara pointed to large discrepancies in higher education achievement, such as the fact that white students are twice as likely as black students to earn a college degree, and that Asian students are more than five times as likely as Hispanics to earn a college degree. As the U.S. population is expected to become increasingly diverse, she noted, disparities in educational attainment are also expected to increase between underrepresented minorities and white and Asian-American students.

Gaps in educational opportunity can be noted as early as the preschool level, according to Gandara. African-American and Hispanic children are more likely than white children to have multiple risk factors for school failure (i.e., living in poverty or in single-parent households, having a mother with less than 12 years of education, speaking a primary language other than English, and/or having a mother who is unmarried at the time of her child's birth). Further, Gandara noted that high-quality preschool programs, which have demonstrated positive effects on children's cognitive functioning, health status, and socioemotional development, are less available for those who cannot afford to pay. Some evidence suggests that the beneficial effects of preschool programming for at-risk students diminish when the program ends. However, other studies indicate that if intervention programs are applied early and intensively over a long period of time, intellectual gains for at-risk children may be sustained, she said.

Kindergarten and elementary schooling presents another opportunity to intervene to raise the achievement of URM students, according to Gandara, because data indicate that achievement gaps between URM and non-URM students begin to widen at this stage. African-American, Hispanic, and Native American children are more than twice as likely as Asian and white children to be in the lowest quartile in reading and math skills during their kindergarten year. By elementary school, for example, 39% of white students score at or above proficiency in reading, while only 10% of African-American and 13% of Hispanic children do so, according to 1998 NAEP data. Gandara noted that it is during this stage that a process of "disengagement" begins, in which low-income and minority students who are initially high performers experience a decline in grades one through six.

Middle school, Gandara noted, presents another stage at which URM students face educational risks, as this is a stage when curriculum tracking begins. Children who are held back in basic math courses, she stated, will have difficulty catching up and may not be able to complete college preparatory courses in high school. Compared to their representation in the K–12 population, African-American, Native American and Hispanic children are underrepresented in programs for "gifted and talented" students, according to Gandara. These programs are important because they predict placement in high-level math courses in middle school, and subsequently, high school. In addition, she stated, white and Asian-American students are much more likely to be assigned to algebra in grade 8 than African-American and Hispanic students. Not all of these differences can be explained by test scores, she noted, particularly for Hispanic students. Further, URM middle school students, independently of their families' socioeconomic status, are more likely to be taught by teachers with lower test scores and less academic preparation than white children. There is some evidence, Gandara noted, that higher-quality teachers (as assessed by test scores, the quality of the institution where teachers obtained their degree, and certification) are associated with higher student performance.

By high school, according to Gandara, URM students who face academic difficulty are often permanently lost to the educational pipeline. Dropout rates are higher for URM students. Persistence in high school, she noted, is related to social and academic integration. Students who are more active and involved in their schools and communities are at lower risk for dropping out. High residential mobility, a system that is indifferent to the needs of URM students, outside peer influences, and leaving school for employment all influence the likelihood that minority students will leave school prematurely, she said. Those students who do stay, according to Gandara, have varied academic experiences. URM students have lower GPAs and SATs scores than white and Asian-American students, even when controlling for family income.

Students' chances of achieving in high school are often limited by the quality of the school they attend. For minority students, these schools are likely to be less rigorous than schools in white and upper-income communities, according to Gandara. In low-income schools, for example, only 52% of classes meet college prep requirements, as opposed to 63% of classes in higher-income schools. Further, she noted, minority students are often locked in schools that are inferior and highly segregated by race. In 1997, for example, over one-third of Hispanic students attended schools that were 90%–100% minority. Even within nominally desegregated schools, she noted, minority students are more likely to be segregated in vocational and general education tracks. Furthermore, high school students with limited English proficiency are more likely to have teachers with inadequate training, to be in classrooms that do not take their language into account, and to be provided with poor-quality curriculum, according to Gandara. These students perform less well on achievement tests, even when compared with students from similar socioeconomic backgrounds.

Given the multiple barriers that URM students face in K–12 education, Gandara noted, it is not surprising that a lower percentage of URM students participate in higher education relative to white students. URM students are poorly represented in four-year colleges. Despite making up nearly one-quarter of the U.S. population, URM students attained only 14% of bachelor's degrees conferred in 1997, according to Gandara. Further, URM students are less likely to be enrolled in biological/life sciences or health professions, further diminishing the supply of potential health professionals.

Gandara concluded by noting that these disparities in educational attainment are projected to increase, particularly between Hispanics and all other groups. By one projection, she noted, Mexican-American adults in the United States, who were three times more likely than white adults to have fewer than 12 years of education in 1990, will be four times more likely to have this low level of education by 2015. By any measure, she argued—whether one assesses the public benefits of a well-educated workforce or the costs to the nation of unemployment, social welfare, and increased taxes—education is cost-effective.

The Impact of Reversing Affirmative Action

"Percent Plans" in California and Texas

In 1996, the passage of Proposition 209 in California and the *Hopwood* decision in the Fifth Circuit Court produced sweeping changes in the state-supported California and Texas university systems. Noting that because these two states are home to over half of the nation's college-aged Hispanic population and nearly 20% of the nation's African-American college-aged population, Marta Tienda argued that developments in these states will have a significant impact on the pool of URM students who will attain health professions degrees (Tienda, this volume). Both state university systems have attempted to compensate for bans on the use of race or ethnicity in admissions decisions. Texas, for example, has implemented a plan to admit students to its universities who graduate in the top ten percent of their high school class, while California has recently adapted a similar policy to admit state residents who graduate in the top four percent of their high school class. Tienda stated that while long-term trends cannot be adequately assessed at this point, neither state appears to have improved the representation of URM students in their flagship state universities. Rather, URM matriculation in these states generally has declined, a trend that is even more disturbing considering the large increases of URM students among the school-age population in these states.

Tienda analyzed undergraduate enrollment in the two states' flagship institutions (the University of California at Berkeley and the University of California at Los Angeles in California, and University of Texas at Austin and Texas A&M University in Texas) pre- and post-policy changes in admissions. She noted that while both the *Hopwood* decision and passage of Proposition 209 occurred in 1996, the states' responses to these events varied significantly. In California, Proposition 209 became law but did not fully affect admissions decisions until after 1997. In Texas, the state legislature responded to *Hopwood* by passage of the above-mentioned bill that guaranteed admission to state universities to all of the state's top decile high school graduates; California did not implement a compensatory policy or other strategy ("four percent solution") in response to Proposition 209 until 2000. Thus, it is not possible to fully assess the impact of California's percent solution, Tienda noted, although the states' differing responses to the ban on the use of race or ethnicity in admissions produced notably different results.

Tienda noted sharp initial declines in the enrollment of URM students at the four flagship campuses in both states. In Texas, URM enrollment dropped sharply between 1996, prior to the *Hopwood* decision, and 1998, the first year that applicants' race and ethnicity were banned in admissions considerations. At UT Austin, African-American freshman enrollment declined by one-third between 1996 and 1998, from 4.8% to 3.2%; this decline is even more dramatic considering the African American freshmen enrollment at UT Austin peaked at 6% in 1994. Similarly, Hispanic enrollment declined 15%, from 14.9% in 1996 to 12.6% in 1998. At Texas A&M, similar declines were observed for both African Americans (25% between 1996 and 1998) and Hispanics (19% decline between 1996 and 1998). As was the case at UT Austin, this decline was even more dramatic considering that freshman enrollment for these groups peaked just one year prior to the *Hopwood* decision, at nearly 5% among African Americans and nearly 15% among Hispanics in 1995, to a decade-long low of less than 3% enrollment of African Americans and less than 10% of Hispanics post-*Hopwood*.

UT Austin, however, has recently rebounded from this initial decline, according to Tienda, as both African-American and Hispanic freshman enrollment increased by one percent for each group in 1999. In contrast, Texas A&M has not recovered; in 1999, Hispanic representation among enrolled freshmen declined to 8.5%, approximately half of the peak enrollment for this group in 1995. African-American freshman enrollment has remained below 3%. Tienda attributed this decline to significant differences between the two institutions in their response to *Hopwood*; at UT Austin, university officials conducted significant outreach efforts to encourage URM students to apply to the university, and increased scholarship support to ensure that admitted URM students would be able to clear financial barriers and matriculate.

California, in contrast to Texas, did not immediately implement an alternative policy to address its prohibition on the use of race and ethnicity in admissions decisions, according to Tienda. While the effects of the recently implemented "four percent solution" cannot be assessed for several years, it is clear that Proposition 209 continues to have dramatic effects on the representation of URM students at Berkeley and UCLA, she stated. From 1996, when Proposition 209 was approved by California voters, and 1998, when the law was fully implemented, African-American and Hispanic freshman enrollment declined by more than one-third. Relative to the peak enrollment of URM freshmen in 1995, the numbers of African-American and Hispanic freshmen declined by approximately half for each group by 1998. At UCLA, African-American freshman enrollment slid from 7.3% in 1995 to 3.4% in 1998; at Berkeley, 7.2% of entering freshmen in 1997 were African American, but this percentage declined to only 3.4 % in 1998. Hispanic enrollment at Berkeley declined from a high of 15.6% in 1995 to 7.3% in 1998. At UCLA, Hispanic freshmen enrollment slid from a high of 21.6% in 1995 to 10.5% in 1998.

Tienda concluded that the ban in Texas and California on the use of race and ethnicity in admissions represents a "31-year setback." Texas' more immediate response to these policy shifts has stemmed these reversals only slightly, she added. Texas' "ten percent solution" plan represents a significant step, she noted, in that these policies shift the foundation of admissions decisions to academic performance measures (e.g., high school academic performance) rather than standardized test score data. Test score data, Tienda stated, are less reliable than high school grades as a predictor of collegiate performance. Such policies, however, are not likely to succeed in the long run, according to Tienda. In part, "percent solution" plans rely on racial and ethnic segregation in high schools to achieve racial and ethnic diversity at state universities, as it is assumed that heavily minority high schools will produce eligible graduates for admission. However, these students are also more likely to attend schools with the fewest academic resources and the poorest quality instruction (Gandara, this volume). In addition, the "ten percent" plan in Texas appears to have stemmed the decline in

> "If swelling numbers of Hispanic college-age youth are not accompanied by commensurate increases in college attendance and graduation, education inequality will rise dramatically in the foreseeable future."
>
> Marta Tienda

URM enrollment only slightly, according to Tienda. This trend promises only to increase the achievement gap between URM and non-URM students, as demographic shifts indicate that in California and Texas, Hispanic and African-American school-aged children are already a majority. "If swelling numbers of Hispanic college-age youth are not accompanied by commensurate increases in college attendance and graduation," Tienda noted, "education inequality will rise dramatically in the foreseeable future."

Trends in URM Participation in Health Professions

Kevin Grumbach and his colleagues (Grumbach, Coffman, Rosenoff, and Munoz, this volume) assessed trends in the participation rates of URM students in a variety of health professions training programs (i.e., allopathic and osteopathic medicine, nursing, public health, dentistry, pharmacy, and veterinary medicine). Using data obtained from associations representing these health professions, Grumbach et al. assessed trends in application, admission, and matriculation of URM students from 1990–2000, with a specific focus on trends in Texas and California, given policy changes in these states that limit the use of applicants' race or ethnicity in admissions decisions.

Data on numbers of applicants, admission rates, and matriculation patterns were not consistently available across health professions. Grumbach and his colleagues, however, found that no single trend characterizes URM participation rates. While some health professions appear to be improving the percentages of URM students enrolled in training programs, others appear to be losing ground. In the fields of allopathic medicine, osteopathic medicine, dentistry, and veterinary medicine, for example, the authors found that the gap between URM and non-URM student participation in health professions has expanded in recent years, with URM students declining as an overall percentage of students in these fields.

URM student participation did not reach population parity (26%) for any of the seven health professions studied. Three fields, however—nursing, public health, and pharmacy—saw modest but steady increases in the proportion of URM students enrolled in training programs, with URM participation greatest in public health (nearly 20% of all matriculants in public health programs were URM students by 1997, a rise of almost 4% since 1989). Dental schools, in contrast, observed a steady decline in URM participation over the last decade. Schools of veterinary medicine had the lowest rates of URM participation, as slightly fewer than 6% of matriculants in these programs were URM students.

Allopathic medicine experienced a sharp increase in URM matriculants in the mid-1990s, reaching a high of 15.5% in 1994, according to Grumbach and his colleagues, before falling to 13.8% in 2000. The numbers of URM applicants to allopathic medical schools peaked in 1996 and 1997, but has declined since then, mirroring trends among the larger population. URM applicants achieved acceptances to allopathic medical schools at rates as high or higher than non-URM applicants by the early 1990s, but this trend, the authors noted, began to reverse in 1995. As a result, the growth in the proportion of URM students entering allopathic medical schools seen in the early 1990s was reversed by the late 1990s. In fact, since 1999, non-URM applicants have experienced a growing likelihood of acceptance while URM applicants face a declining likelihood of acceptance.

Grumbach and his colleagues' analysis also indicated that allopathic medical schools in California and Texas experienced more substantial decreases in URM matriculants than schools in other states in the late 1990s. In Texas, URM matriculants declined from 21% of entering allopathic medical school classes in 1996 to 15.6% in 2000, while California schools observed a similar decline. The authors concluded that "much of the overall decline in URM matriculation in medical schools in the United States is accounted for by the decreases in California and Texas." This is not surprising, Grumbach et al. noted, as these states, because of their large African-American and Hispanic populations, have traditionally enrolled a disproportionately large share of minorities in health professions training programs.

Osteopathic medicine has traditionally been less successful than allopathic medicine in attracting URM students, as the proportion of URM students entering these schools is approximately half that of URM participation in allopathic medical schools. Overall, applications to osteopathic medical schools increased by 168% between 1990 and 1999, but URM applications increased less dramatically. While data on acceptance rates were not available, Grumbach and colleagues found that URM matriculation rates lagged behind that of non-URM students in the early 1990s, then exceeded that of non-URM students in 1995 and 1996, only to decline nearly 6% below that of non-URM students by 1998. In that year, the last year for which matriculation data are available, URM matriculants represented 8% of all osteopathic medical school students, a decline of 20% from 1995. Similarly, data for dentistry are limited to numbers of applicants and matriculants, but these data indicate patterns similar to those seen for osteopathic medicine. Matriculation rates for URM dental students fell below that of non-URM dental students in 1997, declining to the point where URM students represented slightly less than 10% of all dental students by 1999. In California and Texas, the percentage of URM students matriculating in dental schools declined precipitously over the decade of the 1990s, with California URM dental school matriculation rates falling to 3.6% by 1999. This percentage, Grumbach et al. noted, is 10 times below that of the population of African Americans, Hispanics, and Native Americans in the state.

Pharmacy, public health, and nursing programs enjoyed greater success than other health professions in the 1990s in attracting and enrolling URM students, according to the authors. URM participation in pharmacy programs (including both B.S. and Pharm.D.) increased 19% between 1990 and 1999, to the point where 13.8% of pharmacy matriculants were URM students. Nursing programs, which offer the greatest diversity of entry points into the profession via two-year, four-year, and graduate degree programs, saw the greatest sustained growth in URM student participation. Grumbach et al.'s analysis of nursing programs, which was limited to baccalaureate degree programs, revealed that URM participation increased 48% between 1991 and 1999. By 1999, URM students represented 16% of matriculants in baccalaureate nursing programs. Public health programs have the highest proportion of URM enrollees of any of the health professions analyzed by Grumbach and his colleagues; as with nursing and pharmacy programs, public health saw a steady increase in URM student participation during the 1990s, increasing from 15.3% of all matriculants in 1990 to 19.5% in 1999.

Noting that a decreasing proportion of URM students are enrolling in medical schools in California and Texas, Grumbach and his colleagues concluded that "recent legislative and judicial decisions limiting the consideration of race and ethnicity in health professions' schools admissions decisions may be contributing to diverging trends for URM and non-URM acceptance rates." For other health professions such as public health, nursing, and pharmacy, they noted, trends in URM matriculation rates in California and Texas are consistent with the rest of the nation. Grumbach et al. speculated that in part, these schools may be able to maintain or increase levels of URM participation because they are under less public scrutiny than fields such as medicine, or may be less affected by policy changes in admissions processes.

Improving Access to Quality Education and Health Careers for Minority Students

Addressing Educational Inequality in the United States

Efforts to enhance the pipeline of URM students prepared to enter health professions careers must address the structural and economic problems of schools that educate these students, stated Linda Darling-Hammond, who discussed the implications of inequities in funding of public schools on the quality of education for racial and ethnic minority students (Darling-Hammond, this volume). Inequities in the quality of teaching and schooling in the United States, she noted, are striking. While European and Asian nations fund schools centrally and equally, in the United States, the wealthiest ten percent of school districts spend almost 10 times more than the poorest 10 percent. Poor and minority students attend the least well-funded schools, which have fewer resources than schools serving mostly white students. The consequences of these inequities are tragic for students of color, according to Darling-Hammond: as an example, she noted that in 1993 African-American dropouts had only a 25% chance of being employed, compared with a 50% chance for white dropouts.

Darling-Hammond argued that educational inequality is fueled by the increasing segregation of minority students. Almost two-thirds of minority students attend predominantly minority schools, and one-third of African-American students attend intensely segregated schools (90% or more minority enrollment), most of which are located in central cities. These schools have difficulty competing for the most qualified teachers, which is a major contributor to the achievement gap, according to Darling-Hammond. As an example, she cited a study of 900 school districts in Texas, which found that, after controlling for students' socioeconomic background, the wide variability in teachers' qualifications accounted for almost all of the variation in black and white students' test scores.

Darling-Hammond also contended that school funding systems and tax policies result in fewer resources allocated to urban districts compared with suburban districts. In general, she noted, urban schools suffer from lower expenditures of state and local dollars per pupil, higher student-teacher ratios and student-staff ratios, larger class sizes, lower teacher experience, and poorer teacher qualifications. These inequities have prompted legal action in some areas. In New York State, for example, the supreme court ruled that the funding system was unconstitutional because it denied students in high-need and low-spending districts the opportunities to learn material required by state standards, and failed to provide well-qualified teachers and curriculum supports.

Three factors, according to Darling-Hammond, are important in determining the quality of teaching for low-income and minority students—access to good teaching, the distribution of teachers, and access to high-quality curriculum. Problems in *access to teaching*, Darling-Hammond stated, include the fact that policymakers are frequently willing to lower standards in order to fill teaching vacancies. Poorly prepared teachers, however, are less skilled at implementing instruction, are less able to anticipate students' potential difficulties, and are more likely to blame students if their teaching is not successful, she stated. Most importantly, their students learn at lower levels. In terms of the *distribution of teachers*, unqualified and underprepared teachers are found disproportionately in schools servicing greater numbers of low-income or minority students. This is due in part, she said, to real shortages, but also to hiring practices in urban districts that are highly bureaucratic and poorly managed. The *quality of curriculum* is another critical variable in teaching, according to Darling-Hammond. Schools that serve primarily low-income and minority students offer few advanced and more remedial courses, and have smaller academic tracks and larger vocational programs. Darling-Hammond cited as an example a study in New Jersey finding that 20% of 11th and 12th grade students in a wealthy suburb participated in Advanced Placement courses, while none were offered in nearby poor and predominantly African-American communities. In addition, the practice of tracking students within schools rations challenging curricula to a very small proportion of students, she said.

Darling-Hammond suggested three policy initiatives to equalize educational opportunities for minority and low-income students: resource equalization, changes in curriculum and testing, and increasing the supply of highly qualified teachers. *Resources*, she stated, should be equalized between states, among districts, among schools within districts, and among students within schools. Many of the problems with schools attended by low-income and minority students begin with district and state policies and practices that provide inadequate funding and "incompetent" staff, and require inordinate attention to arcane administrative requirements, Darling-Hammond stated. Initiatives should improve the core practices of schooling, she added, rather than layering additional programs onto an already faulty base. Another important goal, Darling Hammond added, is to equalize the hiring of high-quality teachers across urban and suburban areas.

Changes in curriculum and testing, Darling-Hammond maintained, should include the development of "opportunity to learn" standards that would define a floor of core resources and provide incentives for schools to work toward professional standards of practice. Curriculum, she noted, should move away from a focus on lower-order rote skills and move toward independent analysis and problem solving, research and writing, use of technology, and accessing and using resources in new situations, or "thinking curriculum." Similarly, the types and uses of achievement tests should be steered toward more performance-oriented (e.g., analysis, writing) objectives, and should not be used to punish students and schools, but as a tool for identifying strengths and needs. Tests should improve teaching and learning, and should not, as Darling-Hammond stated, "serve to reinforce tendencies to sort and select those who will get high quality education from those who will not."

Finally, according to Darling-Hammond, *quality teaching* can be achieved through providing all teachers with a greater knowledge base and ensuring mastery of this knowledge in areas that include how children learn and develop, how curricular and instructional strategies can help them, and how changes in classroom and school practices can support achievement. This, she says, will help eliminate the practice of allowing poorly trained personnel to teach in underserved schools in disproportionate numbers and will raise the knowledge base for the occupation.

Darling-Hammond called on the federal government to serve as a leader in providing an adequate supply of qualified teachers, citing similar action on behalf of physicians with the passage of the 1963 Health Professions Education Assistance Act. This provision supported and improved the caliber of medical training and teaching hospitals, provided scholarships and loans for medical students, and created incentives for physicians to train in certain specialties and practice in underserved areas. Darling-Hammond also stated that federal initiatives should be implemented that would help to recruit new teachers, strengthen and improve teachers' preparation, and improve teacher retention and effectiveness.

> "Tests should improve teaching and learning, and should not, "serve to reinforce tendencies to sort and select those who will get high quality education from those who will not."
> Linda Darling-Hammond

Rethinking Admissions Processes

With recent challenges to affirmative action policies, increasing numbers of institutions of higher learning are re-examining the processes by which they identify and select underrepresented and disadvantaged applicants. The challenge has been difficult for many, forcing the reevaluation of standards of merit and concepts of fairness, according to Filo Maldonado, Assistant Dean for Admissions at Texas A&M College of Medicine (Maldonado, this volume). Maldonado discussed the importance of diversity in health professions and examined the issues involved in race-neutral admissions in Texas, which has been barred from considering applicants' race or ethnicity in admissions as a result of the *Hopwood* decision.

Maldonado contended that a lack of adequate access to health care—particularly for those who live in inner cities and rural areas—and the erosion of trust between patients and doctors are significant problems that health professions schools must address. He argued that because physicians from underrepresented minority groups are more likely to practice in minority and poor communities, diversity among health professionals will help to ensure that the needs of these communities are met. "Enrolling more qualified underrepresented and disadvantaged applicants to medical schools," Maldonado stated, "not only promotes better access to health care—and in all probability, improved health—but helps fulfill in large part medicine's social obligation to serve society's needs."

Maldonado argued for the importance of using both cognitive and non-cognitive criteria in selecting applicants. Most medical schools, he stated, do, in fact, value non-cognitive traits (e.g., motivation, knowledge of profession through experience, leadership skills, resilience) when making admissions decisions. He also indicated that there is evidence of a significant relationship between both cognitive and non-cognitive variables and performance in medical school. Some schools, he said, have begun to track the performance of students who possess strong non-cognitive traits and less strong GPAs and MCAT scores. According to Maldonado, there is some evidence that successful at-risk students are more focused on academics and less likely to scatter their attention in school. While some of these studies have limitations, findings indicate that MCAT scores were predictive of success for at-risk white students but not for at-risk African-American students. In addition, he cited evidence that using MCAT scores along with other pre-admission data improved prediction of clerkship grades over the use of MCATs alone. This was particularly true for African Americans and Hispanics.

As an illustration of the importance of both cognitive and non-cognitive factors, Maldonado cited the AAMC's Predictive Validity Research Study, which indicated that 34% of the variation in students' medical school GPAs can be explained by undergraduate GPA, and that 41% of students' medical school GPAs can be explained by MCAT scores (58% variance explained by both).

However, 42% of the variance was not explained by these factors. These other factors, he posits, may include educational achievements or experiences, major, additional degrees, community services activities, or character and motivation.

The Texas A&M College of Medicine and other Texas medical and dental schools have begun to develop a race-neutral admissions process in the aftermath of *Hopwood*, said Maldonado, that administrators hope will help to achieve the goal of diversity. According to Maldonado, the new admissions plan calls for: 1) a mindfulness of the vision and mission of the institution in assessing and selecting students; 2) a more inclusive approach in assessing cognitive abilities; 3) a broad-minded scrutiny of applicants' non-cognitive characteristics at the pre-interview and interview phase of the evaluation; 4) enhanced interview techniques; 5) improved protocol for admissions committee deliberations; and 6) frequent self-monitoring. As an initial step, MCAT and GPA scores are weighted, and applicants sorted. This is completed in a manner that will jeopardize neither the integrity of academic criteria nor the breadth of qualified applicants, according to Maldonado. The admissions committee then screens between 900 and 1,000 applicants for interviews. In addition to consideration of academic scores, a screening form has been created to "widen the field of vision." Items on the screening instrument fall into four categories including: 1) academic performance and intellectual capacity, 2) humanism, dedication to service, and capacity for effective interactions, 3) special life experiences, and 4) other compelling factors (including supportive letters of evaluation, areas of interest within medicine, area where applicant lives, and awareness of and knowledge about the impact of cultural factors on heath care).

While the implementation of this new admissions process at Texas A&M has improved the number of underrepresented minority students being interviewed and offered acceptances following the *Hopwood* decision, the number of these students enrolling is still low (3% in 2000, compared to 15.6% in 1996 before *Hopwood*). Changing the perspective of a medical institution, Maldonado said, from an insular and narrow one to one that examines unique qualities of students is difficult work that may often prove frustrating and produce discouraging results. In order to increase diversity, however, schools must critically assess themselves and commit to redesigning their admissions processes, he stated.

Retaining URM Students in Health Professions Programs

While the most popular strategy to increase the number of underrepresented minorities in health professions has been to increase admissions to health professions schools, minorities are more likely than non-minority students to experience academic problems that result in a change in their academic status and delayed graduation, according to Michael Rainey, Acting Associate Dean for Academic Affairs at SUNY-Stony Brook School of Medicine (Rainey, this volume). He indicated that URM students in medical schools are dismissed six times more frequently than white students, withdraw three times more frequently, and are three times more likely to still be enrolled in medical school in the sixth year.

Rainey discussed five reasons for difficulties in retaining underrepresented minorities in the health professions—admissions policies, faculty, curriculum, support services, and remedial strategies used by schools. He cited several problems related to admissions. Although some medical schools' deans have provided vital leadership in the effort to attain a diverse student body, recent turnover in the medical education leadership makes it difficult to maintain strong and consistent support for increasing admissions and retention of URM students. However, Rainey noted that some schools are increasingly interested in considering non-cognitive factors (e.g., students' knowledge of their ways of learning, openness to seek out help, time management skills, family support) during the admissions process in order to better predict what types of students are likely to succeed in future years.

The curricula of many health professions training programs pose another challenge to the retention of URM students. Rainey argued that there is a heavy reliance on content delivery (e.g., lecture format) rather than focusing on student learning, particularly in the first year. He cited one study suggesting that URM students may prefer a more interactive style of teaching, compared to white students, who in general prefer a lecture format. In addition to issues of content, Rainey stated that the standard curriculum is fast-paced, with little time to ask questions, and that there is a "boot camp" atmosphere in schools. "The word 'survival' is common when students talk about the first semester," he stated. Because of these factors, he said, it is the least-prepared students who will have the most difficulty. URM students are at greater risk for attrition than non-minority students given their generally poorer academic preparation and lack of familiarity with the culture and fast-paced environment of medical school, according to Rainey.

Faculty, Rainey maintained, are under increased pressure to engage in research and generate income through clinical practice. Teaching is not valued or rewarded in tenure and salary increase decisions. In addition, Rainey stated, the shortage of URM faculty in health professions "marginalizes" underrepresented minority students because they have little contact with faculty with whom they can identify. As an example, Rainey cited results from the 2000 AAMC Medical School Graduation Questionnaire, in which 20% of students indicated they were mistreated during medical school. Of this group, 12% said they were denied opportunities for training or rewards because of their race/ethnicity one or more times during their schooling, and 16% indicated they had been subjected to racially/ethnically offensive remarks directed towards them. The source of this mistreatment was typically faculty in clinical settings and interns/residents.

The lack of support services for underrepresented minorities also presents a significant obstacle to the retention of URM students, according to Rainey. For example, he reported that of the 120 predominately white medical schools in the United States, 57% indicate having a minority affairs officer. Only one in four of these is an M.D. or Ph.D. with senior rank, which means that they are less likely to be a voting member of admissions, promotions, or curriculum committees. In addition, he noted that underrepresented minority students are more reliant on loans and scholarships than non-minority students (these students receive 6% of their education costs from families, as compared with 20% for non-minority students). Financial aid officers therefore need to be an active and involved member of the support team for URM students, according to Rainey, but this is often not the case.

Lastly, Rainey contended that some remedial strategies employed by health professions schools may be inappropriate for many URM students. For instance, some schools identify at-risk students and intervene shortly after classes start. However, many minority students resist this and feel stigmatized. Alternatively, many students with academic difficulty are simply given more time to learn material, which may be a mistake for underrepresented minority students, according to Rainey. Rather than additional time, he stated, more focus may be needed on learning techniques. In some cases students having academic difficulty are granted a leave of absence. However, this removes them from sources of support, their classmates, and learning assistance. It is important, he added, to keep students in an academic environment whenever possible.

In conclusion, Rainey offered 34 recommendations for institutions to increase the admission and retention of underrepresented minority students, in the areas of admissions, curriculum, faculty, and support services. In admissions, for example, Rainey suggested that the word "diversity" be part of the mission statement of every medical school accredited by LCME, and that institutions should deploy senior URM faculty, residents, and students to serve on admissions committees as recruiters, interviewers, and voting committee members. With regard to curriculum, Rainey advised that orientation be at least two weeks long and should include an orientation to the curriculum, learning styles, testing strategies, and small group work as well as an introduction to the medical school and the community. In addition, an extended orientation program should be instituted, during which some classes should cover prerequisite material. Material should be tested in the same way the first semester courses are tested. Feedback should be provided to students that identifies areas of strength and weakness. Rainey also advocated exploring ways to help URM faculty earn tenure and promotion at the same rate as non-minority faculty, and address the issues of clinical faculty and resident/intern discrimination and harassment directed at URM students in school. Finally, as an example of strategies to help improve support services, he recommended that the institutions' office of minority affairs be staffed with high-ranking, visible, and available staff and have resources to provide support services to URM students.

DISCUSSION AMONG SYMPOSIUM PARTICIPANTS

As noted earlier, a major goal of the symposium was to foster discussion among individuals representing a range of disciplines and perspectives, including primary and secondary school educators and policymakers, health professions educators, professional associations, and others. To further this goal, several small discussion sections were convened during the second day of the symposium to allow participants to react to paper presentations summarized above. These small discussion sections were asked to generate recommendations regarding strategies to improve minority student preparation and achievement in primary and secondary schools, to enhance the representation of URM students in higher education, to improve health professions' schools admissions processes to achieve greater diversity in these settings, and to better retain URM students in health professions. These recommendations are summarized below.

Improving URM Student Achievement in Primary and Secondary Schools

Two small discussion groups reacted to presentations focused on improving the achievement of URM students in K–12 education. Rapporteurs for these groups stated that health professions must "de-isolate" themselves from communities, particularly minority communities that may serve as the source of future health professionals. Health professions organizations should advocate to improve the quality of teaching, one stated, by urging additional funding to help better prepare teachers, particularly in math and science. This rapporteur also noted that health professions should seek roles in assisting school reform, such as converting large urban schools into smaller segments (e.g., "schools within schools") to develop more supportive relationships with students. Support for teaching should also include advocacy to ensure that all students have access to high-quality curriculum. Health professions should take a lead role, another rapporteur noted, in assisting teachers and providing them with effective resources, such as tools to improve students' analytical reasoning and literacy skills. These interventions should not be focused solely at one or a handful of schools, the rapporteur stated, but rather toward coalitions or regional alliances of schools.

Another discussion group considered the impact of high-stakes standardized testing on URM student achievement in K–12 settings. The rapporteur for this group urged that the health professions education and policy communities should carefully consider the messages that are conveyed in their use of test data, such as MCAT scores. The community should consider what these tests measure and how they are used in admissions processes, as educational leaders will be influenced by how health professions view and use such tests. Health professions should also highlight important issues in high-stakes testing, such as differences in teaching, curricula, and educational resources across schools that can have an impact on student performance.

Recruiting, Admitting, and Retaining URM Students in Health Professions Education

Three discussion groups explored strategies to recruit, admit, and retain URM students in health professions education programs. Sustaining URM students in undergraduate pre-medical and pre-health career tracks, one rapporteur noted, can be accomplished with a variety of academic, peer, and economic supports. Health professions organizations should invest in education and professional development for health careers advisors, and reward faculty for serving as advisors and mentors for pre-health career URM students. This can be accomplished by providing financial and logistical support to faculty advisors, considering such work in tenure decisions, and developing networks for advisors to share strategies and provide junior advising staff with resources and supports, the rapporteur stated. Additional financial supports should be provided to pre-health students so that they can be less reliant on outside jobs; in addition, economic barriers to applying to health professions schools (e.g., costs of MCAT and other tests, application fees, travel) should be addressed. Finally, health professions should tap pools of URM students who are "nontraditional" or mature students. These students may require remediation, child care, and/or economic support, and could benefit from post-baccalaureate programs or other initiatives that consider their special circumstances.

New admissions strategies can be successfully developed that address the need for racial and ethnic diversity in health professions training settings while acknowledging the shifting policy contexts regarding affirmative action, another rapporteur noted. Drawing on Maldonado's example of new admissions strategies and criteria used at the Texas A&M College of Medicine, the rapporteur urged that all health professions schools adopt admissions criteria that give greater consideration to applicants' non-cognitive attributes, such as life experiences and commitment to serving poor and minority communities. Changing admissions criteria, however, will require integration of these changes into institutions' mission and goals. Faculty, administrators, and staff must "buy in" to new admissions processes and the consequences of such changes, such as the fact that new students may be admitted who flourish under different learning conditions and different teaching styles. Finally, the rapporteur noted that because admissions efforts are limited by the quality of the pool of applicants, greater outreach efforts are needed to "beat the drums a little more loudly to get people to start thinking about health professions careers" earlier than college.

Similarly, retaining URM students in health professions training settings will require a re-examination of the institution's goals and priorities, according to another rapporteur. Institutions must conduct honest assessments to determine how the climate of the institution affects progress and learning for both URM and non-URM students. Research is also needed to better understand the reasons why students withdraw from health professions schools. Some research has focused on the difficulties that medical students face in the first year, for example, but little is known about the third and fourth year, when evaluation is more subjective. The rapporteur suggested that greater support be provided for mentoring, particularly where URM faculty currently offers informal mentoring. These roles could be more formalized and institutional support provided so that minority faculty are not disproportionately burdened. Finally, the rapporteur urged that health professions educators revisit the way that students are trained. The style of teaching and grading typically used in these settings may disproportionately affect URM students, as Rainey noted above, and should be re-evaluated to improve learning for all students.

A closing panel discussion on the first day of the symposium featured reactions and commentary from several leaders in health, public health, and education. One of the panel members, Vanessa Northington Gamble, Vice President of the Division of Community and Minority Programs at AAMC, noted that efforts to enhance diversity in health professions must be expanded to address educational inequities beginning at primary school levels. These effects will be enhanced by building coalitions and educating the public about the importance of diversity in all levels of education and in the health professions. "We have to really raise the expectations of our children, and also raise expectations of other people for children and of our communities," she stated, noting, "This is not a minority issue—this is an American issue."

> "This is not a minority issue—this is an American issue."
> Vanessa Northington Gamble

CONCLUSION

The Symposium on Diversity in the Health Professions in Honor of Herbert W. Nickens, M.D., was convened to provide a forum for health policymakers, health professions educators, education policymakers, researchers, and others to address three significant, and at times, contradictory challenges: the continued underrepresentation of African Americans, Hispanics, and Native Americans in health professions; the growth of these populations in the United States and subsequent pressure to address their health care needs; and the recent policy, legislative, and legal challenges to affirmative action that may limit access among URM students to health professions training. The symposium summary and collection of papers from the symposium presented here are intended to help stimulate further discussion and action toward addressing these challenges.

The Role of Diversity in the Training Of Health Professionals

Lisa A. Tedesco[1,2]
University of Michigan

INTRODUCTION

Never has higher education been so pressed to articulate, with both data and argument, the clear and compelling benefits of diversity. Social scientists and policy scholars have noted this need (Alger, 1998; Orfield, 1998; 1999), observing that after Bakke, "affirmative action was hanging by a thread" and instead of providing solid evidence about the benefits of diversity, academic researchers gave greatest attention to "examining the problems that minority students were experiencing on campuses that were racially diverse." Because the benefits of diversity appeared obvious, higher education—and for the most part health professions education—was focused on recruitment, retention, and a full range of ways to encourage diversity (Orfield, 2001; Orfield & Whitla, 2001; Cavazos, 2001; Ready, 2001).

With the most recent challenges to affirmative action, a substantial amount of compelling evidence has emerged that demonstrates the benefits of diversity in education.[3] These data articulate the important role of diversity in undergraduate

---

[1] Dr. Tedesco is Vice President and Secretary of the University and Professor of Dentistry, at the University of Michigan.

[2] Deep appreciation and recognition for assistance and support are given to the following Michigan colleagues: Dr. Patricia O'Connor, Associate Professor Emerita, School of Dentistry; Brenda Henry, doctoral student and researcher, School of Public Health, Patricia F. Anderson, Senior Associate Librarian; and Dr. Sherman James, Professor, School of Public Health.

[3] See, for example, the expert testimony of leading scholars on behalf of the University of Michigan, in *The Compelling Need for Diversity in Higher Education*, available through the Office of the Vice President and General Counsel, University of Michigan, 503 Thompson Street, Ann Arbor, MI, 48109-1340, or online, http://www.umich.edu/~urel/admissions/.

education. While studies on the benefits of diversity in the training of health professionals do not exist on the same parallel, there is a substantial literature to guide our understanding of the benefits of diversity in the health professions.

This paper discusses the educational and civic outcomes of diversity for all students, and how these outcomes are related to students in the health professions. From literature that represents a number of different disciplines, I discuss what we expect to accrue from diversity in the health professions and from cultural competence, and the interdisciplinary connections that will advance teaching, clinical practice, and research. Finally, I provide recommendations for future directions that can be taken collaboratively across our academic health center disciplines.

EDUCATIONAL AND CIVIC OUTCOMES
FROM DIVERSITY

In the last five years, a number of primary and secondary studies have emerged that provide comprehensive analyses on the benefits of diversity in undergraduate education. These benefits span a range of positive outcomes that not only contribute to a graduate's success in life, but also to society's well-being by contributing to forces that create social capital. The sections below summarize the work of Bowen and Bok reported in the *Shape of the River* (1998), as well as the work of Gurin (1999), Light (2001), the Astin group (Astin, 1993a; 1993b; Sax & Astin, 1998) and Orfield and others in legal education (Chambers, Lempert, & Adams, 1999; Syverud, 1999; Orfield & Kurlaender, 2001; Orfield & Whitla, 2001).

Bowen and Bok. The findings in the *Shape of the River* come from a large database constructed between 1994 and 1997 by the Mellon Foundation in cooperation with 28 selective colleges and universities. The outcomes discussed here represent approximately 30,000 graduates in 1976 and 1989, from the larger database. In short, the abilities and performance of minority students admitted to selective colleges and universities where race was important to the creation of a diverse student body have been outstanding.

Minority students have graduated in large numbers. In the 1989 cohort overall the graduation rate for black matriculants was 75%, while the national benchmark for this period was 40%. The graduation rate for Whites during this period was 86%, with the national rate at 59%.

Choice of academic major, as an educational outcome, provides noteworthy information as well. In the 1989 cohort, Blacks and Whites majored in biology, chemistry, mathematics, and engineering to the same degree. In the social sciences, more black students than white students majored in psychology, political science, and sociology. While the science disciplines prepare students in areas that directly tie to our health professions curriculum, it can be argued that the social sciences enhance and shape orientations that lead to civic engagement and the building of community or social capital.

A look at the data on graduate and professional school study is an area of high relevance to the subject of this symposium. In general, the matriculants at the selective schools completed a range of advanced degrees at a higher percentage when compared with other graduates nationally. In the 1976 cohort, 56% of the Blacks and Whites from selective schools earned advanced degrees, while nationally these figures were 34% and 38%, respectively. The data also show that especially large fractions from the selective schools receive professional degrees (law, medicine, business)—40% of all black graduates and 37% of white graduates. The national figures are 8% and 12%, respectively. On closer analysis, Bowen and Bok reported that black graduates from the selective schools were slightly more likely than white graduates to earn degrees in law and medicine. And when compared with the general college population, black graduates were seven times more likely to gain degrees in law and five times more likely in medicine. These patterns were sustained in the 1989 cohort data. As for Ph.D. study, the 1976 data showed that Blacks were less likely to pursue and attain the doctorate than their white cohorts in the selective schools. By 1989, this gap had all but closed by a percentage point (8% of white graduates; 7% of black graduates).

Civic engagement and community service is particularly high among minorities from the selective schools, who undertake these opportunities in greater numbers than their white counterparts. Black men in particular, were especially likely to be involved with community, social service, youth, and educational activities. Bowen and Bok reported that one-third of the black men from the selective schools participated in community or neighborhood improvement groups, and about one-third participated in youth and religious organizations. About 25% were involved with K–12 activities. For each type of activity, black involvement was several percentage points higher than white involvement. Bowen and Bok went on to emphasize that in every type of community or volunteer activity in their study, the ratio of black male leaders to white male leaders is even higher than that of black to white male participants. When these data were examined for differences within advanced degree groups, black leadership exceeded white leadership across the board, with the largest differences in law, medicine, business, and at the doctoral degree level.

One final analysis from *Shape of the River* must be emphasized. Bowen and Bok examined what society would have lost if race-conscious admissions had not been used at the schools in their study. They used a methodology of "retrospectively rejecting" students to see what would happen if the schools had employed race-neutral approaches. Using the 1976 cohort of matriculants, they estimated that 700 students would have been rejected. More than 225 members of the groups of retrospectively rejected black matriculants went on to attain professional degrees or doctorates. Approximately 70 are physicians and 60 are lawyers. There are about 125 business executives in the group and well over 300 are reported to be leaders of civic activities. It is clear that denying our institutions the benefit of this diversity would have been at great expense to individual development and social capital.

The Michigan Casebook-The Gurin Analyses. Another body of work from Gurin and her colleagues provides an additional focus on academic-intellectual benefits, as well as interpersonal group relations benefits. The studies summarized in this section are from the expert testimony provided by Gurin (1999) as part of the University of Michigan's defense of race-conscious admissions.

Based in part on classical theory in adolescent development and the now classic findings on the importance of discontinuity and discrepancy for cognitive development, Gurin uses contemporary analyses to demonstrate understanding that there are multiple views of the world, and understanding what it means to have a different life experience than your own is essential to a complete education. Equally essential is learning again and again to test your assumptions about how people view the world, and that although sometimes you expect someone to think differently, in fact they may not. Thinking through your own perceptions, becoming reflective and capable of characterizing another view when it is not your own view, and engaging in effective problem solving and critical thinking are the important, valuable benefits from an education where diversity exists in the classroom. Briefly stated, Gurin's research shows that students with diversity experiences during college become more active and thoughtful learners and are better prepared to participate in a heterogeneous society.

With existing survey data from three different investigations, Gurin examined the impact of student racial and ethnic diversity on educational outcomes. The work included a multi-institutional analysis from data supplied by the Cooperative Institutional Research Program (CIRP) of over 9,000 students entering 184 colleges and universities in 1985; the Michigan Student Study (MSS), an extensive study of the University of Michigan entering undergraduate class of 1994 (participants included 187 African American students and 1,134 white students); and another study of University of Michigan students from a class in the Intergroup Relations Community and Conflict Program (IRCCP) with a matched group of students as controls.[4]

---

[4] Data from an evaluation of the introductory course taken by students in 1990 in The Intergroup Relations Community and Conflict Program (IRCCP) were part of the third analyses reported by Gurin. Among other topics, the course covered the history of group experiences in the United States, a contemporary analysis of group inequalities in economic, educational and political arenas, analysis of political issues and policies, and theories of conflict and conflict management. Importantly for the work reported here, all students participated in 10 weeks of dialogue with diverse peers. The explicit goals of the dialogues were to help students understand viewpoints on contested issues, examine differences within groups on issues, identify and negotiate conflicts that arise, and challenge the groups to find a basis for coalition. Special emphasis was placed on understanding, perspective taking, complex thinking, and socio-historical thinking. The IRGCCP combines two kinds of diversity, classroom diversity content and interaction with diverse peers. A non-participant group of students was matched on a number of variables and served as controls for comparison.

Gurin studied diversity on three dimensions: structural diversity, classroom diversity, and interactional diversity. In a college or university, structural diversity is determined by the racial and ethnic composition of the student body. Because most students still come from fairly segregated high schools, a degree of diversity on this dimension provides an essential ingredient for creating a learning environment that includes difference and discrepancy.[5] Classroom diversity refers to the incorporation of knowledge about diverse groups in the curriculum. Classroom content and research on diverse groups engages and encourages a wide range of discussion when coupled with structural diversity. The third dimension—informal interactional diversity—is represented by the opportunity students from diverse backgrounds have to interact in a variety of social settings.

Structural diversity serves as the foundation or starting point but cannot, in isolation from classroom and interactional diversity, ensure that a more complete academic and social experience will occur that will contribute to the student's overall development. The core purpose of the work was to determine the effect of diversity on the following outcome measures: learning outcomes measured by growth in intellectual and academic skill; engagement in active thinking processes; growth in intellectual engagement and motivation; and democracy outcomes, such as the preparation of students for meaningful participation in a pluralistic society. It is important to note that a number of variables, including those represented by reports of behavior and attitudes, comprised the composite outcome measures defined as learning outcomes and democracy outcomes above.

Results showed strong evidence for the impact of diversity on *learning outcomes* across analyses. Students who had experienced the most diversity in classroom settings and in informal interactions with peers showed the greatest engagement in active thinking processes, growth in intellectual engagement, and motivation and growth in intellectual and academic skills. For *democracy outcomes* results strongly supported the value of experiencing diversity in classroom and informal interactions on engagement of various kinds of citizenship and engagement with people of other races or ethnicities. Students who had experienced more diversity were also more likely to acknowledge that group differences are compatible with the interests of the broader community. As was the case with learning outcomes, there was a striking consistency across studies and across a broad range of democracy outcomes that included both values and reported behavior.

In addition to the data reported across the three analyses above, it is important to note findings from the follow-up surveys of CIRP studies, administered five years after college. Attending a college high in structural diversity and being white was positively associated with reports of diversity among current

---

[5] High structural diversity was a designation assigned to institutions with 25 percent or more students of color; low structural diversity designated those institutions with 9 percent or fewer students of color.

friends, neighbors, and co-workers. Informal interaction diversity, including participation in racial/cultural awareness workshops, discussion of racial ethnic issues and interracial socializing, and having diverse close friends in college were especially influential in accounting for later patterns of social and worklife integration. Enrollment in an ethnic studies course in college was also related to diversity among friends and neighbors five years after college.

Similarly, effects of diversity observed at the time of graduation were sustained over a five-year period for both learning outcomes and diversity outcomes. Students who had experienced the greatest classroom diversity and informal instructional diversity during college continued to show the strongest academic motivation and growth in learning. They also placed the greatest value on intellectual and academic skills as part of their post-college lives and believed they were most prepared for graduate school.

For white graduates, both classroom diversity and informal interaction diversity in college were positively associated with having discussed racial/ethnic issues and having socialized with someone of another racial/ethnic group. Informal interaction diversity was associated with feeling that their undergraduate education prepared them for their current job. Students of color reported that interaction with diverse peers during college was also related to interaction with people from diverse backgrounds. Overall, the results of the post-college study show that the positive impact of racial and ethnic diversity experienced in college has lasting—rather than ephemeral—influence. As Gurin observed, the analyses confirm that the "long term pattern of racial separation noted by many social scientists can be broken by diversity experiences in higher education" (1999, p. 101).

Astin. Other in-depth analyses by Astin and his colleagues (Astin, 1993a; 1993b; Sax & Astin, 1998) provide findings related to those described above and support academic and civic benefits from diversity gained by white and black students alike. Interestingly, positive changes in areas related to cultural awareness, such as, "promoting racial understanding" and "influencing social values," were associated with academic concentrations in the social sciences and humanities more so than in the basic sciences, engineering, nursing, or business. All of these outcomes are more prevalent on campuses that have a higher degree of institutional commitment to diversity, faculty whose teaching and research reflect diversity and multiculturalism, and student diversity experiences, such as taking courses in race and ethnicity.

Light. In a recently released publication, entitled *Making the Most of College, Students Speak Their Minds*, Richard Light (2001) described the results of carefully designed qualitative studies that included interviews of more than 400 Harvard students about contemporary college experiences. The data include some emphasis on the impact of racial and ethnic diversity. Among a number of findings, students from public high school experiences reported that diversity before coming to college was negative and disappointing, in that efforts were not made to build a sense of community or shared culture. From classroom experiences in small groups to a range of social experiences outside the classroom, white students reported that their Harvard classmates who were racially and ethnically different had taught them things that they would not have learned or otherwise thought about.

Orfield, Kurlaender, and Associates. Adding to these studies is a very recent volume edited by Orfield and Kurlaender (2001). *In Diversity Challenged: Evidence on the Impact of Affirmative Action,* a number of authors add to the growing body of evidence about the positive impact of increasing diversity in student enrollment in higher education. From policy analyses and social science and educational data, a number of similar positive outcomes are addressed, including broadened educational experience, democracy outcomes, and enhanced preparation for graduate study in the professions. A range of findings are discussed in this volume and include the fact that greater social interaction is promoted by diversity, and that with inter-racial socialization there is more discussion of controversial issues, higher retention in college, and increased satisfaction with the college experience (Chang, 2001). Other findings are that with increased diversity, faculty tend to use a greater variety of teaching methods, including active learning (Milem, 2001), and that there are more and different opportunities for leadership, increased awareness of other cultures, and increased ability to work collaboratively (Hurtado, 2001). Orfield and associates assert that "the basic results of these studies are that diversity does make a difference, but that the differences are neither automatic or uniform (p. 7)." Campus leadership, mindful programming, adequate resources, and development opportunities for faculty are equally important.

Legal Education. Extending and echoing the findings in undergraduate education are recent data from legal education. In his expert testimony on behalf of the University of Michigan, Syverud (1999) explained how racial and ethnic heterogeneity in the classroom produces an examination of assumptions and frank discussion about the law that cannot be achieved in environments without such diversity. One example he provided is from his teaching in civil procedure, where students engage in role play for jury selection procedures. Syverud described students as shocked and enlightened when unexpected differences in assumptions about human nature, experience, and the law are analyzed in relation to jury composition.

In more formal analyses, conducted through Gallup Poll surveys at Michigan and Harvard law schools, in informal Internet studies at seven similarly competitive law schools, and in studies of graduates, equally positive results were found, supporting the educational and professional benefits of diversity (Chambers, Lempert, & Adams, 1999; Orfield & Whitla, 2001). For example, a great majority of students at Michigan and Harvard reported that conflicts related to racial differences challenged them to rethink their values, and well over half of these same students believed that conflict because of racial differences ultimately produces positive learning experiences (Orfield & Whitla, 2001). The need for increased diversity among the faculty was also noted in these studies to further the educational benefits for all students, especially those coming from more homogeneous living and learning environments. Other studies of law graduates at Michigan (Chambers, Lempert, & Adams 1999) have shown that while all graduates, over a 27-year period, provided significant community service and pro bono work, minority graduates tended to average twice the number of hours of their white counterparts.

Amicus Briefs. A number of significant amicus briefs were filed on behalf of the University of Michigan in support of its defense for the use of race as one of several factors in the admissions process. To date, these briefs represent approximately 80 organizations, including higher education associations and academic societies, Fortune 500 corporations, and government and industry-related entities. They strongly support the University's use of race in admissions. Citing case law, classical writings on democracy, empirical data from higher education, and business venue demographics, the briefs outlined in clear terms the necessity of diversity for a more complete education and for experiences that will foster a talented, successful workforce in an increasingly global marketplace.[6]

A Strengths Orientation. When taken together, there is a crucial underpinning in the new data and new argument on diversity in higher education. The discussions and discourse are framed from an orientation of strength rather than one of disadvantage and deficiency (Trickett et al., 1994). By understanding the benefits of diversity, our awareness necessarily moves away from a focus on remediation and disadvantage. Instead, cultural pluralism and cultural identity are positive elements that contribute to equally positive outcomes based on diversity in the classroom and curriculum. Diversity brings the benefit of intellectual and social growth, trust, and enriched cultural experience and understanding, with renewed meaning for a wide range of social and higher education policy (ACE/AAUP, 2000; Palmer, 2001).

Further, a strengths orientation is consistent with social science data, from multiple sources. Described most clearly by Gurin (2001a, 2001b), students who had the most experience with a diverse group of their peers, formally or informally, whether through classes, relationships, multicultural events, and intergroup dialogues, indicated a stronger sense of commonality with students not like them, racially or ethnically. Most importantly, Gurin stated, "the students with the greatest experience with diverse peers were more, not less, committed to understanding the points of view of other students (Gurin, 2001b, p. 2). These

---

[6] These briefs are available through the University of Michigan, Office of the Vice President and General Counsel, or online at the addresses below.

http://www.umich.edu/~urel/admissions/gra_amicus/
http://www.umich.edu/~urel/admissions/legal/gratz/amici.html
http://www.umich.edu/~urel/admissions/gra_amicus/gra_ace.html
http://www.umich.edu/~urel/admissions/gra_amicus/gra_now.html

educational outcomes can only be seen as strengths, compelling and of great benefit, in light of society's increasing social and demographic diversity, and the essential skills for future health care providers, and professional commitment to high-quality care.

EDUCATIONAL AND CIVIC OUTCOMES FOR HEALTH PROFESSIONS STUDENTS

In the absence of parallel studies on the benefits of diversity for health professions students, what might all these findings suggest for health professions education? Assume for purposes of this discussion that there is a match for high level diversity experiences between the schools students come from as undergraduates and those they go to for health professions school, be it medicine, dentistry, nursing, or pharmacy.

Imagine how rich and lively the discussions would be in classrooms and in clinical seminars. It is also likely that these students would participate in community outreach projects, and design new opportunities to extend school-community partnerships. We might even expect the academic health center to have a vigorous HPPI (Health Professions Partnership Initiative) program with health professions students highly involved in tutoring and mentoring middle school and high school students interested in science and health careers. We might also expect these same students to engage in other forms of service learning that are health-related and community-based providing an enhanced educational experience (Seifer, 1998, 2001). And, through all these activities and orientations, we might expect these students to add a dimension of intellectual and social complexity to all those areas in the curriculum that require social analysis and clinical judgment.

The students we select for admission from undergraduate institutions with high degrees of structural diversity, classroom diversity, and interactional (informal) diversity will be those students who will provide enriched and appropriately complex approaches to patient-centered care and evidence-based practice. I would predict that these students would extend the reach of our schools into the community for preventive programs, health care, and youth services. And I would predict that it is these students who will be the best recruiters for future classes.

These examples are the ones that we would hope to capture through more formal study. Recall that in both the Gurin analyses and the Bowen and Bok studies, the effects of diversity in college carried over into later life. Civic engagement continued on in the lives of selective college graduates and attending a diverse college was associated with more diverse friends, neighbors, and work associates almost a decade after entering college.

Clearly, more questions than answers emerge when discussing the benefits of diversity in health professions education. What other benefits might we observe in our academic health centers and communities from students who fit the educational and experiential profile described in the undergraduate studies? Even if the entering classes of students across health disciplines represented structural diversity at our institutions, would the attendant classroom (curricular) diversity and interactional (informal/social) diversity exist to benefit the maturing health care providers, their patients, and the community's health? With incomplete or weak diversity along the dimensions studied in the work of Gurin and others, do health professions schools attenuate, or even squander, the investment made at the undergraduate level?

DIVERSITY, SOCIAL CAPITAL, AND TRUST

There is a substantial and poignant literature on health disparities and the positive contributions that are made by increasing diversity in the health professions (Nickens, 1992; Diez-Roux, 1998; Nickens & Ready, 1999; Yen & Syme, 1999; Berkman & Kawachi, 2000; Fiscella, et al., 2000; Stoddard, Back, & Brotherton, 2000; Carlisle, Tisnado, & Kington, 2001). Because of the relationship of health status with social, economic, and environmental influences, the construct of social capital adds to the discussion of benefits from diversity in ways that could enhance our understanding and thereby our teaching, clinical practice, and research when it comes to benefits from diversity in the health professions.

Social capital has been defined (Cohen & Prusak, 2001) as "the stock of active connections among people; the trust, mutual understanding, and shared values and behaviors that bind the members of . . . communities and make cooperative action possible." Berkman and Kawatchi (2000) defined social capital as "those features of social structures—such as levels of interpersonal trust and norms of reciprocity and mutual aid—which act as resources for individuals and facilitate collective action." James, Schulz, and van Olphen (2000) suggested that most agree that the construct "connotes mutual trust, a sense of reciprocal obligation, and civic participation aimed at benefiting the group or community as a whole." A fair amount of work is emerging that connects social capital to the health of communities and those characteristics that can be used to describe successful public health interventions to improve the health of communities.

With each student we graduate from programs that have maximized diversity experiences, in either the classroom, in social interactions, or in the composition of our classes, we enhance and extend the democracy outcomes discussed earlier. Can these student outcomes then in turn contribute, over a longer term, to the creation of social capital? While a great deal of research remains to be done to understand social capital and its role in interventions to remove health disparities, it seems reasonable to also place the benefits of educational benefits of diversity somewhere in the explanatory mix. Does the undergraduate diversity experience create an orientation or a pattern that is strengthened and extended in medical school or dental school to contribute to the health of diverse communities, and to communities of the unserved and underserved? What are our schools doing to capitalize on or to diminish this orientation? Should we extend or disrupt the arc of engagement that our undergraduates bring to our programs?

If diversity experiences can build social capital, then by definition diversity experiences are building trust. Building the trustworthiness of our health professions and institutions has great potential to increase the health and well-being of individuals and communities, thus extending the benefit of diversity in health professions. Low rates of patient satisfaction, regimen compliance, low rates of service utilization, and non-participation in clinical research have all been linked to medical mistrust (Gamble, 1993, 1997; Crawley, 2000; LaViest, Nickerson, & Bowie, 2000; Cohen & Prusak, 2001). Crawley (2000), writing on participation in clinical trials, urged us to resituate the issue of trust—from the individual who does not trust to the institution that has bred the mistrust. From the literature in organizational studies, we know that social trust and civic engagement are strongly correlated (Cohen & Prusak, 2001). Extending this notion then, we should expect that our students will bring with them readiness, sensitivities, and skills to help our institutions become more uniformly trustworthy.

In summary, the benefits of diversity in the undergraduate experience create an expectation of similar benefits that can and should extend to health professions education. From an accumulation of diversity experiences, including civic engagement and other democracy outcomes, our students would be expected to contribute to social capital and trustworthiness and to further the well being and health of individuals and communities.

ENHANCING CULTURAL COMPETENCE

Learning how to provide care and serve communities across a broad range of racial and ethnic diversity is a lifetime's work. Beyond the traditional disciplines in anthropology, sociology, and psychology, an amazing wealth of information has emerged across all the health professions. Between the Internet and traditional print sources, the literature on cultural competence in health care is abundant (Leininger, 1995; Mason, Braker, & Williams-Murphy 1995; Talabere, 1996; AMA, 1999; Cohen & Goode, 1999; Nash, 1999; Salimbene, 1999; Goode et al., 2000; Goode & Harrisone, 2000). Interestingly, except for nursing and social work, this literature has matured only during this last decade.

I have repeatedly suggested that students are entering our programs with more and more diversity experiences. As they acquire the cultural rules and cultural identities of their chosen health profession, their earlier diversity experiences will no doubt influence their development in some way. In terms of access and use of health care, lack of cultural competence on the part of service providers has become a barrier to care. In particular, mental health services and child health services have documented (Satcher, 1999) the growing need for cultural competence in care delivery. Broadly, there is an acknowledged need to include cultural competence knowledge and skills in the regular and in the continuing education curriculum for students as well as faculty to contribute to addressing health disparities. Through our own lack of crosscultural knowledge and skills, we can contribute to patient noncompliance, premature ends to treatment, poor followup, and non-optimal treatment outcomes. Increased attention is also being given to language needs in the clinical encounter as well as to linguistic competence (AMA, 1999; Goode et al., 2000).

Among the health professions there are a number of opportunities for gaining experience and the skills needed for cultural competence. Programs that place students in community-based primary or general care settings are increasingly important (Mullan, 1992; Zwiefler, 1998). From these settings and with supporting, curriculum students quickly learn about the connections that exist among cultural competency, public health, and primary care.

Definitions and Approaches. The American Medical Association has prepared an extraordinary resource, the Cultural Competence Compendium (AMA, 1999). This rather powerful volume calls on the reader to understand the special needs of patients along a number of dimensions—patients as women, men, children, seniors, African Americans, Hispanics, Asians, Whites, people with disabilities, and those facing chronic illnesses, end of life illnesses, and socioeconomic constraints (AMA, 1999, p. iii). The text provides resources, bibliographies, lists of agencies and professional societies, virtual resources, patient support and education materials, and information on practices complementary to traditional medicine. The nursing profession is acknowledged for having devoted a great deal of attention over many years to cultural competence, more than most other professions, and these resources can be readily used or adapted for teaching across health disciplines. The volume is designed to support the ultimate long-term goal of eliminating racial and ethnic disparities in health with competence representing an important milestone in reaching this goal.

The literature is vast, and there are any number of definitions and lists defining cultural competence. Communication skills, listening skills, and understanding stereotyping, power, dominance, social identity, and privilege, and familiarity with a number of cultures and histories are but a few of the characteristics described as aspects of cultural competence.

Interdisciplinary Necessities. Three concepts in clinical psychology suggested by Stanley Sue (1998) are particularly helpful in framing some basics to define cultural competency. In his approach to "uncovering the essence of cultural competency," he promotes three critical ingredients: scientific mindedness, skills in dynamic sizing, and culture-specific expertise. By scientific mindedness he is referring to hypothesis-forming skills rather than coming to quick conclusions about the status of a patient who is culturally different from his or her health care provider. Scientific mindedness is accomplished by awareness and checking for the potential of cultural meaning attached to symptoms. For example, do other symptoms match? Are other individuals in the culture unfamiliar with the symptom? Can experts in the culture indicate that the symptom is unusual for that culture? Dynamic sizing, like the fluctuating cache in computers, is a concept that can be applied to cultural competence. This concept suggests that appropriate skills are needed in knowing when to generalize and to be inclusive, and when to individualize and to be exclusive, or "flexibly generalizing in a valid manner." This skill defends against stereotyping on the one hand, and on the other hand, while not ignoring cultural group characteristics that may be helpful in understanding the patient or clients' condition. It works to avoid stereotypes for individuals while appreciating the importance of culture. The third ingredient Sue describes is culture-specific expertise. This expertise requires helping professionals to have knowledge and understanding of their own worldviews, specific knowledge about cultural groups with which they work, possess an understanding of the social and political influences faced by culturally different groups, and have specific skills for interventions and therapeutic strategies needed when working with culturally different groups.

Social Epidemiology and Clinical Social Work. There are two disciplines crucial to providing a more complete education for our health professions students along the dimension of cultural competence—social epidemiology and clinical social work. Both disciplines represent distinct knowledge bases, providing a wide array of intellectual and behavioral skills that have been used by a number of researchers and teachers to define aspects of cultural competence.

Public health experts assert that the the the driving question of "social epidemiology—how social conditions give rise to patterns of health and disease in individuals and populations—has been around since the dawn of public health" (Berkman & Kawachi, 2000). But with the maturing of work in physiology, social and preventive medicine, medical sociology, and health psychology, new and different connections have been made that have added to a rediscovery of social epidemiology. Berkman and Kawatchi listed a number of public health researchers, who from the late 1960s and 1970s through to the present "began to develop a distinct area of investigation centered on the health impact of social conditions, particularly cultural change, social status, and status inconsistency (for example, social class, race, power, and control), and life transitions" (Berkman & Kawachi, 2000, p. 4). A dizzying collaboration of areas comes into play with emphasis on a number of social phenomena such as social class, social networks and support, discrimination, racial and ethnic bias, work demands, and control and disease. From health psychology and the companion disciplines, behaviors are no longer viewed as exclusively within the realm of individual choice. Instead, choices are understood as occurring in a social context that constrains or enhances health-protective behavior. And because of the ever-broadening diversity in the "social context," the discipline of social epidemiology must be at the center for preparing the culturally competent health professional. Research and teaching in social epidemiology is necessarily collaborative and interdisciplinary, offering yet another opportunity for diversity, both intellectual and academic, to emerge.

Clinical social work, as a discipline, endeavors to define cultural competence in a similar way. From the varying literature on cultural competence, there seems to be none as coherent and clear as that in clinical social work. Just as social epidemiology provides a framework for understanding health and illness in a social context, clinical social work provides a framework for clinical interactions that are sensitive to social conditions and context.

From adaptations of clinical social work practice, we know that health professions students can be exposed to a number of constructs critical to working with people in their social environments (Glover-Reed et al., 1997; Ewalt et al., 1999). Age, race, sexual orientation, ethnicity, gender, social class, and disability status define social groupings for the patient/client and for the practitioner. Throughout work in this discipline, special attention is paid to power imbalances and the influence they might have on treatment outcomes. Of critical importance is how difference and dominance come together in the clinical relationships. We are called on to recognize that each individual has a complex self-definition based on multiple social identities, and that reducing the patient or client's identity to a singular dimension can influence the quality of the doctor-patient relationship and the effectiveness of treatment.

As mentioned earlier, a number of our students are coming to our programs with substantial diversity experience, and extending these experiences should be related to developing cultural competence as a health care provider. Students, through more formal instruction, observation, reflection, and practice must come to understand their new social role and the added dimension of "power" and "position" that inextricably comes as a part of their health care provider role. As critical consciousness develops and through careful reflection, students understand how we are advantaged and disadvantaged by aspects related to social identities. Learning how one can be privileged by location along one social identity dimension but disadvantaged because of another is essential for culturally competent interactions in the course of the patient/client and provider relationship. For example, there are status privileges to being a physician or dentist or pharmacist, but in certain social contexts, this status may be diminished by gender and race.

The language and constructs of clinical social work are complex, specific, and different, in part, from some of the other cultural competence literature. At the same time, the discipline has a coherent approach, developed over a 30-year period, to understanding and modeling cultural competence (Green, 1995). Part of what makes this discipline so appealing for greater adaptation in health professions education is the emphasis it places on race and ethnicity and power in relationships, social privilege, and the development of critical consciousness for cultural competence (Glover-Reed et al., 1977).

Critical consciousness creates the ability to undergo a process of continual self-reflection and examination of how an individual's position in society and his or her viewpoint shapes and impacts how he or she engages with others and views others. Through this examination, people are better able to understand their status in society and how their position influences how they treat and are treated by others. In many ways, critical consciousness skills extend and deepen understandings essential to the popularized approaches in patient-centered care (Laine & Davidoff, 1996).

Supporting Pedagogy. Clearly, social epidemiology and clinical social work provide strong content bases that would be useful in the design of a curriculum for cultural competence. Content- and discipline-based information in the curriculum is clearly necessary, but not sufficient. The curriculum must be presented within an appropriate pedagogy.

The importance of an appropriate pedagogy cannot be overstated. As described above, cultural competence is not simply about an individual's ability to know behaviors and practices specific for a cultural or ethnic group. Instruction focused on teaching specific practices and behaviors will lead only to stereotyping of individuals and groups. Rather, cultural competence strives to develop and make mature an individual's ability to be sympathetic and knowledgeable of differences that exist between practitioner and patient/client and to deal with such differences in culturally relevant ways (Glover-Reed, Newman, Suarez, & Lewis, 1997).

One of the more important elements contributing to the needed pedagogy links to the ideas and data presented by Gurin (1999), Light (2001), and others (Morey & Kitano, 1997; Hurtado, 2001; Orfield, 2001). An obvious and quite tangible element for pedagogy in support of cultural competence is the diversity of students in the classroom. Diverse classroom settings provide a unique contribution to learning, discussion, and understanding that is not necessarily attainable elsewhere. It is equally important to have an instructor who can facilitate the discussions, analyses, and examination of conflicting ideas that will necessarily arise, and to maximize interaction among learners. An interactive pedagogy will maximize exposure of all individuals to the full range of thinking, experience, and perspectives from the students' lives.

Another teaching skill that enhances cultural competence is the instructor's ability to foster critical thinking among students. Encompassed in this skill is the conscious uncovering of causes or relationships among differences that may be based on individual and group characteristics. For example, when speaking about African Americans in the United States having poorer health outcomes when compared with Whites, a discussion of factors that may have contributed to this disparity being observed must follow. Such critical examination allows individuals to see that there are underlying processes or causes for the observed circumstances. It is also important that each phenomenon observed is often influenced by a multitude of factors, often outside the control of the group or individual.

Pedagogy designed to develop critical thinking is an important tool. When used with discipline knowledge represented by social epidemiology and the other process skills from clinical social work, such as critical consciousness, a more complex and more complete examination of data or background information for understanding health and illness would emerge. Coupled with the instructor's ability to model skills for critical thinking and critical consciousness, students are better prepared to think about their own prejudices and position in society and their influence on how they view and interact with others (Glover-Reed et al., 1997).

There is a mature literature on pedagogy for critical thinking, and it emerges out of teaching approaches that encourage active learning (Astin, 1973; Hurtado, et al., 1999; 2001; Guitierrez & Alvarez, 2000; Milem, 2001). Active learning is characterized by teaching methods that minimize lecturing, with greater emphasis placed on cooperative learning, group projects, student critiques and evaluations of other students' work, experiential learning, and reflection. Common to all these approaches are discussion and dialogue that are rich with complexity and difference.

TRANSFORMATION AND POTENTIAL: MODEST RECOMMENDATIONS

In *Diversity Challenged*, Gudeman (2001) cited the work of Martha Nussbaum (1977) on narrative imagination and its role in the cultivation of humanity. As one of the essential abilities of the citizen, narrative imagination is "the ability to think what it might be like to be in the shoes of a person different from oneself, to be an intelligent reader of that person's story, and to understand the emotions and wishes and desires that someone so placed might have" (Gudeman, 2001, p. 252).

Within the context of the Nickens Symposium, this passage carries an urgency and poignancy for the benefits of diversity in health professions education. With the practitioner-patient relationship as a constant, Nussbaum's statement is filled with implication and purpose. The modest recommendations below are related to the ideas presented in this paper.

Behavioral Sciences. It would be impossible to become a researcher in molecular genetics without rich exposure and understanding of a number of basic sciences, like biochemistry, for example. It is only reasonable then, to expect that effective clinical practice in areas of health care, cannot be achieved without a rich exposure and understanding of a number of social sciences. Working collaboratively across the behavioral science disciplines is essential to investing in the benefits of diversity and to providing high-quality care to a diverse population of patients.

There is extraordinary potential for new learning and new ways of teaching and working that resides in the experiences of our entering students. By creating classroom and clinical encounters that reflect the relevant content from public health, social work, and social sciences, and by including community outreach, an investment in the entering students' diversity will have great and positive impact for our institutions and for those people our institutions serve. What is crucial, though, is that the diversity represented among students and our faculty (viz., structural diversity) create the fundamental conditions for the diversity that must be mindfully planned in the curriculum and in clinical education teaching and learning contexts (Gurin, 1999, 2001a, 2001b). As such, these conditions lead to further benefit in terms of cultural competence, increased quality of patient care, and community well-being. National initiatives, through academic and clinical societies in the health professions and social sciences, would have the natural agency to design and disseminate materials for teaching both students and faculty.

External Standards, National Guidelines. While consensus on definitions for cultural competence may be a distant goal, a mindful dialogue on creating curriculum, supportive materials, and training for faculty must have higher priority and increased focus. For example, accreditation standards in social work and clinical psychology (APA, 1996; CSWE, 2001) can serve as a basis for revising and enhancing cultural competence in medicine, dentistry, and pharmacy. National guidelines, in a less formal format than accreditation standards, would be useful for institutions to draw on as they design programs for students and faculty. These guidelines for education programs could include best practices and facilitation through collaborations with behavioral scientists.

Benefits of Diversity Task Force. As the data emerge on the benefits of diversity in health professions education, it will be important to synthesize and disseminate the information widely. Where efforts are started on these studies, they should be continued; and in the places where efforts are needed, they should be programmatically defined and supported through start-up funding. This work should be designed to examine the broad range of benefits, shaped from the findings in undergraduate education, that extend to a number of areas particularly relevant to health care and community wellness.

REFERENCES

American Council on Education and American Association of University Professors. (2000). Does diversity make a difference? Three research studies on diversity in college classrooms. Washington, DC: ACE/AAUP.

Alger, J.R. (1998). Unfinished homework for universities: Making the case for affirmative action. Journal of Urban and Contemporary Law, 54, 73–91.

American Medical Association, (1999). Cultural competence compendium. Chicago, IL: AMA.

American Psychological Association, (1996). Guidelines and principles for accreditation of programs in professional psychology. Committee on Accreditation. Washington, DC: APA. (see also, http://www.apa.org/ed/g&p.html).

Astin, A.W. (1993a). What matters in college? Four critical years revisited. San Francisco, CA: Jossey-Bass Inc.

Astin, A.W. (1993b). Diversity and multiculturalism on the campus: How are students affected? Change, March/April, 44–49.

Berkman, L.F., & Kawachi, I. (2000). Social epidemiology. New York: Oxford University Press, Inc.

Bowen, W.G., & Bok, D. (1998). The shape of the river: Long-term consequences of considering race in college and university admissions. Princeton, NJ: Princeton University Press.

Carlisle, D., Tisnado, D., & Kington, R. (2001). Increasing racial and ethnic diversity among health professionals: An intervention to address health disparities. Symposium on Diversity in the Health Professions in Honor of Herbert W. Nickens, M.D. Washington, DC: National Academy of Sciences/Institute of Medicine and Association of American Medical Colleges (in press).

Cavazos, L.F. (2001). Strategies for enhancing the diversity of the oral health profession. Journal of Dental Education, 65, 269–272.

Chambers, D.L., Lempert, R.O., & Adams, T.K. (Summer, 1999). Doing well and doing good: The careers of minority and white graduates of the University of Michigan Law School, 1970–1996. Law Quadrangle Notes. Ann Arbor: University of Michigan Law School.

Chang, M.J. (2001). The positive educational effects of racial diversity on campus. In: G. Orfield & M. Kurlaender (Eds.). Diversity challenged: Evidence on the impact of affirmative action, pp. 175–186. Cambridge, MA: Harvard Education Publishing Group.

Cohen, D., & Prusak, L. (2001). In good company: How social capital makes organizations work. Boston: Harvard Business School Press.

Cohen, E., & Goode, T.D. (1999, Winter). Rationale for cultural competence in primary health care. Georgetown University Child Development Center–National Center for Cultural Competence, Policy Brief 1. Washington, DC: Georgetown University. (see also http://gucdc.georgetown.edu/nccc/.

Crawley, L.M. (2000, November). African American participation in clinical trials: Situating trust and trustworthiness. In For the health of the public: Ensuring the future of clinical research, 2, 17–21. Washington, DC: Association of American Medical Colleges Task Force on Clinical Research.

CSWE (2001). Educational policy and accreditation standards. Alexandria, VA: Council on Social Work Education.

Diez-Roux, A. (1998). Bringing context back into epidemiology: Variables and fallacies in multilevel analysis. American Journal of Public Health, 88, 216–222.

Ewalt, P.L., Freeman, E.M., Fortune, A.E., Poole, D.L., & Witkin, S.L. (1999). Multicultural issues in social work: Practice and research. Washington, DC: National Association of Social Workers, NASW Press.

Fiscella, K., Franks, P., Gold, M.R., & Clancy, C.M. (2000). Inequality in quality: Addressing socioeconomic, racial and ethnic disparities in health care. Journal of the American Medical Association, 283, 2579–2584.

Gamble, V.N. (1993). A legacy of distrust: African Americans and medical research. American Journal of Preventive Medicine, 9, 35–38.

Gamble, V.N. (1997). Under the shadow of Tuskegee: African Americans and health care. American Journal of Public Health, 87, 1773–1778.

Glover-Reed, B., Newman, P.A., Suarez, Z.E., & Lewis, E.A. (1997). Interpersonal practice beyond diversity and toward social justice: The importance of critical consciousness. In: C.D. Garvin & B.A. Seabury (Eds.). Interpersonal Practice in Social Work: Promoting competence and social justice. Needham Heights, MA: Allyn & Bacon.

Goode, T., & Harrisone, S. (2000, Summer). Cultural competence in primary healthcare: Partnerships for a research agenda. Georgetown University Child Development

54   THE RIGHT THING TO DO, THE SMART THING TO DO

Center-National Center for Cultural Competence, Policy Brief 3. Washington, DC: Georgetown University. (see also http://gucdc.georgetown.edu/nccc/).

Goode, T., Sockalingam, S. Brown, M., & Jones, W. (2000, Winter). Linguistic competence in primary healthcare systems: Implications for policy. Georgetown University Child Development Center-National Center for Cultural Competence, Policy Brief 2. Washington, DC: Georgetown University. (see also http://gucdc.georgetown.edu/ nccc/).

Green, J. (1995). Cultural awareness in the human services: A multi-ethnic approach. Boston: Allyn & Bacon.

Gudeman, R.H. (2001). Faculty experience with diversity: A case study of Macalester College. In: G. Orfield & M. Kurlaender (Eds.). Diversity challenged: Evidence on the impact of affirmative action, pp. 251–276. Cambridge, MA: Harvard Education Publishing Group.

Gurin, P. (1999). Expert report of Patricia Gurin, *Gratz, et al., v. Bollinger, et al.,* No. 97– 75321 (E.D. Mich.; *Grutter, et al. v. Bollinger, et al.,* No. 97–75928 (E.D. Mich.). In: The compelling need for diversity in higher education, pp. 99–234. Ann Arbor: University of Michigan, Office of the Vice President and General Counsel.

Gurin, P. (2001a). Evidence for the educational benefits of diversity in higher education: Response to the critique by the National Association of Scholars of the Expert Witness Report of Patricia Gurin, *Gratz, et al, v. Bollinger, et al.,* No. 97–75321 (E.D. Mich.; *Grutter, et al. v. Bollinger, et al.,* No. 97–75928 (E.D. Mich.). Ann Arbor: University of Michigan, Office of the Vice President and General Counsel. (see also, http://www.umich.edu/~urel/admissions/new/gurin.html)

Gurin, P. (2001b). Evidence for the educational benefits of diversity in higher education: An addendum, *Gratz, et al, v. Bollinger, et al.,* No. 97–75321 (E.D. Mich.; *Grutter, et al. v. Bollinger, et al.,* No. 97–75928 (E.D. Mich.). Ann Arbor: University of Michigan, Office of the Vice President and General Counsel. (see also http://www.umich.edu/~urel/admissions/new/gurin_add.html).

Gutierez, L., & Alvarez, A.R. (2000). Educating students for multicultural community practice. Journal of Community Practice, 7, 39–56.

Hurtado, S. (2001). Linking diversity and educational purposes: How diversity affects the classroom environment and student development. In: G. Orfield & M. Kurlaender (Eds.). Diversity challenged: Evidence on the impact of affirmative action, pp. 187– 204. Cambridge, MA: Harvard Education Publishing Group.

James, S.A., Schulz, A.J., & van Olphen, J. (2001, in press). Social capital, poverty, and community health: An exploration of linkages. In: S. Saegert, P. Thompson, & M. Warren (Eds). Building and using social capital in poor communities.

Laine, C., & Davidoff, F. (1996). Patient-centered medicine: A professional evolution. Journal of the American Medical Association, 275, 152–156.

LaViest, T.A., Nickerson, K.J., & Bowie, J.V. (2000). Attitudes about racism, medical mistrust, and satisfaction with care among African American and white cardiac patients. Medical Care Research and Review, 57, 146–161.

Leininger, M. (1995). Transcultural nursing: Concepts, theories, research and practices. New York: McGraw Hill Publishers.

Light, R. (2001). Making the most of college: Students speak their minds. Cambridge, MA: Harvard University Press.

Mason, J.L., Braker, K., & Williams-Murphy, T.L. (1995). An introduction to cultural competence principles and elements. An annotated bibliography. Portland, OR: Portland State University, Research and Training Center on Family Support and Children's Mental Health.

Milem, J.F. (2001). Increasing diversity benefits: How campus climate and teaching methods affect student outcomes. In: G. Orfield & M. Kurlaender (Eds.), Diversity challenged: Evidence on the impact of affirmative action, pp. 233–250. Cambridge, MA: Harvard Education Publishing Group.

Morey, A.I., & Kitano, M.K. (1997). Multicultural course transformation in higher education: A broader truth. Needham Heights, MA: Allyn & Bacon.

Mullan, F. (1992). Community-oriented primary care. New England Journal of Medicine, 307, 1076–1078.

Nash, K.A. (1999). Cultural competence: A guide for human service agencies. Washington, DC: Child Welfare League of America, Inc., CWLA Press.

Nickens, H.W. (1992). The rationale for minority-targeted programs in medicine in the 1990s. Journal of the American Medical Association, 267, 2390, 2395.

Nickens, H.W., & Ready, T. (1999). A strategy to tame the "savage inequalities." Academic Medicine, 74, 310–311.

Nussbaum, M. (1997). Cultivating humanity: A classical defense of reform in liberal education. Cambridge, MA: Harvard University Press.

Orfield, G. (1998). Campus resegregation and its alternatives. In: G. Orfield & E. Miller (Eds.). Chilling admissions: The affirmative action crisis and the search for alternatives, 1–16. Cambridge, MA: Harvard Education Publishing Group.

Orfield, G. (1999). Affirmative action works—But judges and policy makers need to hear that verdict. The Chronicle of Higher Education, December 10, 1999, Washington, DC.

Orfield, G. (2001). Introduction. In: G. Orfield & M. Kurlaender (Eds.), Diversity challenged: Evidence on the impact of affirmative action, pp. 1–30. Cambridge, MA: Harvard Education Publishing Group.

Orfield, G., & Kurlaender, M., Eds. (2001). Diversity challenged: Evidence on the impact of affirmative action. Cambridge, MA: Harvard Education Publishing Group.

Orfield, G., & Whitla, D. (2001). Diversity in legal education: Student experiences in leading law schools. In: G. Orfield & M. Kurlaender (Eds.), Diversity challenged: Evidence on the impact of affirmative action, pp. 143–174. Cambridge, MA: Harvard Education Publishing Group.

Palmer, S.R. (2001). A policy framework for reconceptualizing the legal debate concerning affirmative action in higher education. In: G. Orfield & M. Kurlaender (Eds.), Diversity challenged: Evidence on the impact of affirmative action, pp. 49–80. Cambridge, MA: Harvard Education Publishing Group.

Ready, T. (2001). The impact of affirmative action on medical education and the nation's health. In: G. Orfield & M. Kurlaender (Eds.), Diversity challenged: Evidence on the impact of affirmative action, pp. 205–219. Cambridge, MA: Harvard Education Publishing Group.

Salimbene, S. (1999). Cultural competence: A priority for performance improvement action. Journal of Nursing Care Quality, 13, 23–35.

Satcher, D. (1999). Surgeon General's report on mental health. Washington, DC, (see also http://www.surgeongeneral.gov/library/mentalhealth/home.html).

Sax, L.J., & Astin, A.W. (1998). Developing "civic virtue" among college students. In: J.N. Gardner, G. VanderVeer, & Associates (Eds.), The senior year experience: Facilitating integration, reflecting closure, and transition, pp. 133–151.

Seifer, S.D. (1998). Service-learning: Community-campus partnerships for health professions education. Academic Medicine, 73, 273–277.

Seifer, S.D. (2001, March). The Center for Health Professions newsletter: From the director. San Francisco.

Stoddard, J.J., Back, M.R., & Brotherton, S.E. (2000). The respective racial and ethnic diversity of U.S. pediatricians and American children. Pediatrics, 105, 27–31.

Sue, S. (1998). In search of cultural competence in psychotherapy and counseling. American Psychologist, 53, 440–448.

Syverud, K.D. (1999). Expert report of Kent D. Syverud, *Grutter, et al.* v. *Bollinger, et al.,* No. 97–75928 (E.D. Mich.). In: The compelling need for diversity in higher education, pp. 265–267. Ann Arbor: University of Michigan, Office of the Vice President and General Counsel.

Talabere, L.R. (1996). Meeting the challenge of culture care in nursing: Diversity, sensitivity, competence, and congruence. Journal of Cultural Diversity, 3, 53–64.

Trickett, E.J., Watts, R.J., Birman, & Birman, D. (1994). Toward an overarching framework for diversity. In: E.J. Trickett, R.J. Watts, & D. Birman (Eds.). Human diversity: Perspectives on people in context, pp. 7–26. San Francisco: Jossey-Bass Inc.

Yen, I.H., & Syme, S.L. (1999). The social environment and health: A discussion of the epidemiologic literature. Annual Review of Public Health, 20, 287–308.

Zweifler, J., & Gonzalez, A.M. Teaching residents to care for culturally diverse populations. Academic Medicine, 73, 1056–1061.

Increasing Racial and Ethnic Diversity Among Physicians: An Intervention to Address Health Disparities?

Raynard Kington[1]
Associate Director of NIH for Behavioral and Social
Sciences Research

Diana Tisnado
UCLA School of Public Health

David M. Carlisle[2]
Director, Office of Statewide Health Planning and Development,
State of California

INTRODUCTION

Health disparities across racial and ethnic groups in the United States have been well documented for over a century and have remained remarkably persistent in spite of the changes in many facets of the society over that period. Despite dramatic improvements in overall health status for the U.S. population in the 20th century, members of many racial and ethnic minority populations experience worse health status along many dimensions compared with the majority white population. These disparities are the result of multiple root causes. Social inequalities resulting directly from discrimination and indirectly from structural factors have led to inequalities in socioeconomic position, health insurance status, and environmental and occupational exposures, all of which influence health status (Kington & Nickens, 2001). Health disparities are associated with cultural and psychosocial factors related to patient perceptions of health, illness, and the health care system, all of which influence health care-seeking behavior and are also influenced by structural characteristics of our health care system.

Because many minority neighborhoods have a shortage of physicians (Komaromy, 1996) and less access to medical care, increasing the supply of minority physicians has been proposed as an intervention that may help to ameliorate differences in health status. Programs to increase the numbers of underrepresented minority physicians have been the subject of much debate in recent years.

---

[1] The opinions expressed are those of the author and do not necessarily reflect the official position of the U.S. Department of Health and Human Services or the National Institutes of Health.

[2] The opinions expresssed do not necessarily reflect the State of California or the Office of Statewide Health Planning and Development.

Efforts of colleges and universities to increase the enrollment of minority students also have increasingly become the focus of sharp criticism (Bowen, 1998). While empirical evidence of the impact of diversity in colleges and universities has become a core part of the debate about college admission policies, little attention has been given to rigorously assessing the scientific evidence about the likely impact of increasing the numbers of underrepresented minority physicians, especially as an intervention to improve health care for minority populations and, ultimately, to reduce health disparities in the United States.

The goals of this paper are to present a brief overview of racial and ethnic disparities in health and the potential causes of these differences, primarily related to health care, and then to review the conceptual underlying bases and the evidence about the likely pathways by which increasing the diversity of physicians might decrease disparities. We focus on three hypothesized pathways. The first pathway is through the practice choices of minority physicians, which may lead to increased access to care in underserved communities. The second pathway is through improvements in quality of health care due to better physician-patient communication and greater cultural competency. The third hypothesized pathway is through improvements in the quality of medical education that may accrue to medical students as a result of increasing diversity in medical education.

BACKGROUND

Disparities in Health Status Across Racial and Ethnic
Groups in the United States

Differences in health status across racial and ethnic groups in the United States have been described for a wide array of diseases, conditions, and outcomes (NCHS, 2000). Despite overall improvements in life expectancy in the past century, African Americans still experience a lower average life expectancy at birth and higher average age-adjusted all-cause death rates than Whites. African Americans also experience higher death rates for many conditions, including coronary disease, stroke, and cancer, and infant morality rates are higher among both African-American and American Indian/Alaska Native populations than among Whites and most Hispanic subpopulations. Mexican Americans experience a higher rate of uncontrolled hypertension than white Americans. Asian and Pacific Islander Americans, African Americans, and Hispanic Americans all have an elevated incidence of tuberculosis compared with the white population. African Americans, Hispanics, and Native Americans have surpassed Whites in the incidence of HIV infection, and die at higher rates than Whites from diabetes mellitus, homicide, and unintentional injuries (NCHS, 2000). With respect to health-related quality of life, higher percentages on African Americans and Hispanics report that they are in fair or poor health as compared to Whites (NCHS, 1994).

Differences in health status between white and minority populations may arise from many causal factors. These include patient-level risk factors, such as differences in education and economic resources, health behaviors, nutrition, genetic predisposition, and environmental exposures. Health care system characteristics that influence access to appropriate health care services and the quality of care also contribute to health status. These factors are especially important because they may be directly effected by public policy.

Racial and Ethnic Differences in Access to Health Care

An individual's access to health care may be conceptualized in terms of a model that groups factors into those affecting: 1) the predisposition to use services as suggested by demographic and social characteristics as well as beliefs about health services (predisposing characteristics); 2) the ability to secure services as indicated by personal resources and availability of services in the community (enabling characteristics); and 3) health status, as perceived by the patient and evaluated by a professional (need characteristics) (Andersen, 1978). Access to health care is monitored and evaluated using a number of different indicators, including health insurance status and having a usual source of medical care; rates of utilization of different types of services; rates of negative health outcomes thought to be preventable such as certain diagnoses, complications, and types of utilization such as hospitalization; and structural indicators such as the availability of physicians, clinics, and other types of health services.

Three common indicators of access to care are health insurance status, having a usual source of health care, and having a regular physician. While health insurance alone cannot ensure that patients will obtain all needed services, it can help protect individuals and families from the costs of illness and routine health maintenance. Lack of health insurance coverage and a usual source of care have both been associated with lower utilization of preventive and disease-management health services, even when controlling for patient health status (Freeman et al., 1990; Moy, 1995). Having a regular source of care has been shown to be an independent predictor of access to care rather than merely a result of access to care (Kuder, 1985).

Usual Source of Care

African-American and Hispanic patients have been found to be less likely to have a regular physician than Whites, even after controlling for sociodemographic characteristics (Gray, 1997). In an analysis of nationally representative household surveys over a 20-year period, Hispanics were found to be nearly twice as likely to lack a usual source of care as Whites (Zuvekas & Weinick, 1999). This gap widened over the study period and could not be explained solely by changes in health insurance status over the period studied. In

fact, health insurance status explained only approximately one-fifth of the decline in usual source of care among Hispanics. Similar patterns are observed
among children. African-American and Hispanic children have been shown to
be more likely to lack a usual source of care than white children (Cornelius,
1993; Newacheck, 1996), and may be less likely to obtain as many physician
visits as a result (Lieu et al., 1993).

Health Insurance Status

Lack of health insurance is a barrier to access to health care, and one that is
more prevalent among racial and ethnic minorities than Whites (Freeman et al.,
1990). In a study of the health insurance status of white, black, and Hispanic
Americans in two time periods (1987 and 1996) gaps in coverage were identified between Blacks and Hispanics and Whites (Monheit & Vistnes, 2000). Racial and ethnic minorities continue to be more likely to lack insurance coverage
than Whites. The gap in employment-related coverage between white and Hispanic males actually expanded by 6.4 percentage points over the decade, leaving
Hispanic males with the highest rates of being uninsured of all racial/ethnic
groups (38.9%).

Health Services Utilization

The utilization of a wide range of health care services varies across racial
and ethnic groups. Variations in utilization across subpopulations may be due to
differences in patient health care-seeking behavior, health status, and personal
preferences for different treatment options and willingness to pay for them.
Other reasons for differences in utilization include differences in the availability
of services, individual physician or health care organization preferences and
their propensity to make certain recommendations, patient differences in ability
to pay for desired services, and differences in non-financial factors such as
transportation or child care issues.

Despite having worse health status, rates of utilization of many types of
services—including routine physician visits, preventive services, procedures,
and treatments for illness—have long been shown to be lower for many racial
and ethnic minorities as compared with Whites. Ambulatory service use has
been found to be lower among Blacks and Hispanics as compared with Whites
(Cornelius, 1993). Health screening rates for women of reproductive age have
been shown to be lower among Hispanics, Native Americans, and Asians and
Pacific Islanders (Wilcox, 1993).

After gaining access to the health care system, minority patients have a
lower likelihood of receiving appropriate management of and treatments for
their conditions. Black patients have been found to receive a lower intensity of
hospital services than Whites (Yergan et al.,1987), and to experience higher

rates of post-discharge problems after hospitalizations for several major conditions in a national study of hospital care (Kahn et al., 1994).

Racial variations have been shown in numerous studies of cardiac procedure use and survival after a myocardial infarction. Blacks and Hispanics in New York with angiographically confirmed coronary artery disease were found to be between 36% and 40% less likely to receive bypass surgery than Whites when the surgery was judged medically appropriate, and Blacks were 37% less likely to receive the procedure when judged medically necessary, controlling for disease severity, age, gender, and insurance status (Hannan, 1999). Other studies have found similar results with respect to cardiac care and invasive cardiac procedures, even when controlling for demographic, socioeconomic, and clinical variables (Carlisle et al., 1995; Ferguson et al., 1997). Racial differences have also been observed in the likelihood of receiving care from high-quality cardiac surgeons (Mukamel et al., 2000).

In a study of analgesia practices in the emergency department of a large teaching hospital, Hispanics were less likely to receive adequate analgesia for long bone fractures than white patients and were twice as likely to receive no analgesia whatsoever (Todd et al., 1993). Inadequate pain management has also been found to be significantly more likely among black nursing home patients with cancer compared with Whites (Bernabei, 1998). In multiple studies, Blacks and Hispanics with HIV infection have been found to have lower outpatient utilization and less treatment with antiretroviral medications and prophylactic medications (Andersen et al., 2000; Schwarcz, 1997; Moore et al., 1994; Easterbrook et al., 1991).

Health Outcomes

Patients seek medical care to obtain some improvement or to prevent or delay deterioration in health status. The examination of health outcomes and how they vary across subpopulations is an important tool in the evaluation of the quality of medical care. The health outcomes that can be influenced by health care include physical outcomes (death, complications, and physical functioning), patient satisfaction, and quality of life.

In a study of 1993 administrative data for 26.3 million Medicare beneficiaries over the age of 65, age and sex adjusted mortality rates were higher among black men as compared with white men (O.R = 1.19, $p < 0.001$) and for black women as compared with white women (O.R = 1.16, $p < 0.001$) (Gornick et al., 1996). Studies have shown that minorities experience higher hospitalization and mortality rates due to conditions that many providers and health services researchers agree should be preventable with appropriate outpatient management (Schwartz, 1990). Blacks experience higher rates of uncontrolled hypertension, contributing to major coronary heart disease-related events (Clark, 1999). Age-adjusted mortality rates from cervical cancer were found to be twice as high among Blacks as compared with Whites in a Chicago sample of women, and the differences remained significant even after adjusting for income (Samelson, 1994). In a study of U.S. mortality data, African Americans were found to experience higher standardized mortality rates due to asthma than Whites, controlling for income and educational level (Grant, 2000). African Americans and Hispanics who have been in contact with the health care system also tend to report lower satisfaction with medical care than Whites (Blendon et al., 1989; Morales et al., 1999).

Physician Supply

Other important indicators of access to quality health care include structural characteristics of the health care system, particularly the availability of physician services. Whether the United States as a whole faces a physician oversupply has been a matter of debate for some time (Schwartz, 1988; Ginzberg, 1989). Whether or not there are "too many" physicians in the country overall, many areas remain underserved. Thousands of areas throughout the country are designated as Health Professionals Shortage Areas by the Health Resource Services Administration (HRSA.gov, 2001). In particular, many predominantly minority communities face shortages of health services. In California, research has shown that physician supply is inversely related to the concentration of Blacks and Hispanics in a health service area, even after adjusting for community income level (Komaromy et al., 1996). This relationship was found in both urban and rural areas. Population projections indicate that by the year 2020, the minority populations of many of these regions are likely to increase substantially.

As part of a study to project the numbers of minority physicians needed to achieve a race/ethnicity-specific physician-to-population ratio of 218 per 100,000, Libby and colleagues provide data about the numbers of active physicians in 1990 from the Census Bureau's Equal Employment Opportunity database (1997). A projection model developed by Libby yielded results indicating that in order to reach 218 physicians per 100,000 persons for each racial/ethnic group, the numbers of first year residents would need to roughly double for Hispanic and black physicians, triple for Native American physicians, and be reduced by two-fifths for white and Asian physicians. Although we do not assert that exact racial and ethnic parity in physician-to-population ratios should be an explicit public policy goal, these numbers and projections illustrate the extent to which Blacks, Hispanics, and Native Americans are underrepresented in medicine relative to their numbers in the population. Although underrepresented minority enrollment increased by 43% after 1986, it peaked in 1994, did not increase in 1995, and actually declined by 5% in 1996 (Carlisle et al., 1998). It is likely that gains made in numbers of underrepresented minorities to enter medicine in the early 1990s, a period that saw a 27% increase in underrepresented minority enrollment (Nickens, 1994), are now being reversed by restrictions in affirmative action programs across the country.

TABLE 1 Numbers of Active Physicians per 100,000 Persons, 1990, and Average Annual Increase, 1980–1990, by Race/Ethnicity

Race/ethnicity	1990			1980–1990
	Active physicians	Population in thousands	Active physicians per 100,000 persons	Average annual increase in physicians
Hispanic (all races)	27,620	22,354	124	835
Black	20,032	29,216	69	649
Native American	833	1,794	46	31
Asian	60,988	6,968	875	1,813
White, non-Hispanic	453,295	188,128	241	8,746
Total	562,768	248,710	227	12,074

Based on Libby et al., 1997, with data from the U.S. Bureau of the Census Equal Employment Opportunity File (Washington: U.S. Department of Commerce, 1990) and G. Roback, L. Rudolph, and B. Seidman, *Physician Characteristics and Distribution in the Unites States: 1992 Edition* (Chicago, AMA, 1992).

THE IMPACT ON HEALTH DISPARITIES OF INCREASING THE NUMBER OF UNDERREPRESENTED MINORITY PHYSICIANS: A REVIEW OF THE EVIDENCE

Medical training for African Americans first became a topic of policy debate in the United States in the context of the post-Civil War South as a way to address the health needs of the African-American community. Disparities between the health status of Whites and African Americans had been observed throughout American history. In the antebellum South, slave owners documented health problems that threatened productivity, and pointed out health disparities between African Americans and Whites to reinforce beliefs that biological differences between the races justified slavery (Savitt, 1985). Common health problems ranged from injuries and malnutrition to pneumonia and tuberculosis. Conditions in the South after the Civil War were not dissimilar to other postwar periods, with many people left homeless—refugees in search of a place to live and a way to make a living (Summerville, 1983). Lack of food, water, and sanitation exacerbated what had already been extremely poor living conditions. The result was major outbreaks of pneumonia, cholera, diphtheria, smallpox, yellow fever, and tuberculosis. Yet, very few white physicians were willing to see black patients, and very few African Americans could afford their fees. The education of African-American physicians and other health professionals was seen as a necessary step to improve the health of Blacks and to protect the public health of the communities where African Americans lived, primarily in the South. African-American medical schools were founded to address this need.

Against the backdrop of institutionalized segregation, Flexnor (1910) echoed both social justice and public health arguments for training black physicians in his famous report, with the underlying assumption that the best way to meet the great health needs of black communities in the United States was by providing more black physicians. His recommendation was to concentrate resources on the two black medical schools out of seven that he believed had the best chance of meeting the standards being set for modern medical training programs, Howard and Meharry. The preface to his recommendations reflects the tension between the societal goals of improving access to care by training more physicians and changing requirements to standardize and improve the quality of practicing physicians, while simultaneously an unstated goal and trend was also restricting entry into the profession (Starr, 1982). As recently as 1965, only 2% of all medical students were black, and three-fourths of these students attended Howard or Meharry.

In sum, the social and public policy questions and debates regarding the training of minority physicians have been with us for some time, and are not likely to be resolved in the near future.

Practice Choices of Underrepresented Minority Physicians

Since the 1970s and 1980s, when minority students were first admitted to medical schools in larger numbers, a number of studies have examined the practice patterns of minority physicians as compared with white physicians. These studies have varied in terms of study samples, data sources, and methodologies. These studies have also examined alternative hypotheses through various methods, including statistically controlling for potential confounders and conducting additional analyses to address certain additional questions raised by the main analyses. Despite their differences, empirical analyses regarding the practice locations and patient populations of minority physicians have been remarkably consistent. Minority physicians tend to be more likely to practice in underserved areas and to have patient populations with a higher percentage of minorities than their white colleagues. Some evidence also suggests that minority physicians tend to have a higher percentage of patient populations with lower incomes and worse health status and who are more likely to be covered by Medicaid.

Underserved Practice Locations

A good deal of interest has focused on whether minority physicians are any more likely to practice in underserved areas than white physicians. One of the early studies to describe the practice patterns of black physicians was based on data from the 1975 National Ambulatory Medical Care survey, a nationally representative survey conducted by the federal government. These data confirmed that black physicians practice predominantly in metropolitan areas. The analysis showed that 4,679,145, or (91.8%) of ambulatory visits by black patients to black physicians and 583,491 (94.4%) of ambulatory visits of white patients to black physicians occurred in metropolitan areas. In contrast, 28,842,477 (69.3%) of visits of black patients to non-black physicians and 369,081,473, or 72.6% of visits of white patients to non-black physicians occurred in metropolitan areas (Rocheleau, 1978). The 1975 data set was designed to over-sample black physicians to obtain more information about their practices than had previously been available. However, only crude measures of differences in practice location by race were presented. Race was only available classified as white, black, and other, and practice location was divided only into metropolitan area or non-metropolitan area.

In other studies, Howard University College of Medicine alumni were surveyed about their current or planned practice patterns. The study by Lloyd et al. (1978) surveyed Howard College of Medicine alumni from seven selected classes that had graduated between 1955 and 1975. More recent classes were over-sampled. Of the 729 individuals surveyed, 311 responded (49%). Older individuals were more likely to respond, as were graduates in medical specialties (85% vs. 75%). An additional analysis of the survey data only included data provided by black alumni in the analysis (Lloyd & Johnson, 1982). The additional analyses also explicitly compared the responses regarding practice patterns of earlier graduates (1955–1970) to the planned practice patterns of the more recent graduates (1973–1975).

Black Howard alumni were slightly less likely to respond than were non-black alumni (81% vs. 85%). Statistical tests with respect to characteristics associated with non-response were not reported. The results showed that the majority of respondents (59.9%) reported practicing or planning to practice in a large city (500,000 population or more). Of all respondents, 32% reported practicing or planning to practice in an inner-city area. Interestingly, the authors noted, this figure is higher than the proportion of respondents who reported growing up in an inner-city area (22.1%), attending college in an inner-city area (25.7%), or who planned to work in an inner-city area at the time of applying to medical school (18%). A higher percentage of earlier graduates (1955–1970) reported inner-city practice. The authors speculate that this may be the result of more opportunities outside of inner cities being available to more recent graduates, as well as fewer of the more recent graduates having come from an inner-city background.

Keith and colleagues (1985) sought to examine for minority and non-minority physicians of the "affirmative action era" the choices of practice location, specialty, specialty board certification, and patient population served. The authors examined data collected from class of 1975 medical school graduates by the American Association of Medical Colleges. The class of 1975 was chosen because of the concern that physicians who graduated earlier may have had less freedom of choice regarding practice location and patient populations due to segregation and overt discrimination in many communities.

Of the 13,428 individuals who received M.D. degrees between June 1974 and July 1975, the AAMC provided data on 12,065, including 574 Blacks, 36 Native Americans, 78 Mexican Americans, 27 mainland and Commonwealth Puerto Ricans, 9,467 Whites, and 219 Asians. Whites and Asians were classified as non-minorities. On average, non-minorities were found to have come from higher socioeconomic status (SES) backgrounds, based on parent education and occupation. Non-minorities also had higher scores on a pre-med performance index, which uses undergraduate science GPA and four components of the MCAT and was designed to predict scores on Part II of the NBME test. Therefore, non-minorities that most resembled minorities in terms of these characteristics as well as medical school attended and other pre-admission characteristics were over-sampled. In addition, all non-minority graduates of Howard and Meharry were included in the sampling frame. Nonetheless, differences persisted between the minority and non-minority samples (1.1 S.D. on the performance index and 0.6 S.D. on the SES index). Questionnaires were mailed to all of the sampled individuals for whom the AMA Masterfile or medical schools could provide addresses. Response rates were 77% for the minority sample and 85% for the non-minority sample. Non-respondents did not differ significantly from respondents on the performance index or in terms of SES. Non-minority primary care physicians did respond less frequently than other specialists; however, this was only a 1.1% difference.

The results of this study showed that overall, almost twice the proportion of minority graduates as non-minorities were practicing in federally designated manpower shortage areas (11.6% vs. 6.1%, $p < 0.001$). This trend appeared in each of the eight specialty categories included in the study. One hypothesis is that minority physicians practice in underserved areas because they face more difficulties obtaining work elsewhere when they wish to. However, the authors found this argument to be inconsistent with one measure of potential competitiveness—a performance index score. The mean score on the performance index for minority physicians practicing in manpower shortage areas actually exceeded that of minority physicians who practiced in non-shortage areas. The location of minority physicians in manpower shortage areas was not explained by socioeconomic status. Although lower socioeconomic status was associated with the likelihood of non-minority physicians practicing in shortage areas, SES did not explain the effect of race/ethnicity.

Significantly more underrepresented minority physicians chose primary care specialties as compared with white physicians, and family and general practitioners were the most likely to serve manpower shortage areas for both groups.

A study of graduates of California medical schools assessed whether minority and non-minority physicians differed in terms of practice patterns, particularly in terms of practicing in areas of California with health personnel shortages and serving underserved populations (Davidson & Montoya, 1987). The study examined data collected using a survey of 1974 and 1975 graduates of seven of California's eight medical schools. Alumnae of one school were excluded due to the school's religious medical missionary focus, which leads to many of its graduates going abroad after graduation. The years 1974 and 1975 were selected as the earliest in which significant numbers of minorities graduated from California medical schools. Contact information for minority (black, Mexican American, mainland Puerto Rican, and American Indian) and non-minority graduates was provided by the medical schools. All minority graduates and a sample of non-minority graduates were selected for a final study population of 144 minority and 145 non-minority graduates. Of 289 questionnaires mailed, 138 were returned, for a response rate of 48%. Response rates differed slightly between minority (46%) and non-minority (50%) subjects, but this difference was not significant at the 0.05 level. Response rates did not differ by school, with the exception of one school that required graduate permission before the release of contact information. Respondents and non-respondents did not differ by likelihood of serving underserved areas except for this school, whose respondents were more likely to report serving underserved areas. Since these subjects were given prior information about the nature of the study, it is possible that only the graduates who were most committed to issues of the underserved chose to release their contact information in order to participate in the study.

The study findings revealed that minority physicians were more likely than white physicians to be practicing in or adjacent to areas designated as having a health care personnel shortage (53% vs. 26%). Although the numbers of physicians in the survey were relatively small (45 minorities and 53 non-minorities), the differences were statistically significant at the 0.01 level. These findings were unadjusted for physician characteristics that might have explained the observed effect of physician race/ethnicity on practicing in an underserved area.

A 1996 study examined the racial and ethnic background of physicians in California and the characteristics of the communities in which they practice (Komaromy et al., 1996). This study took a multiple-step approach. Data from the AMA Masterfile and from the U.S. Census were used to explore the geographic distribution of California physicians and the characteristics of the communities they served. To learn about the association between physician race/ethnicity and the characteristics of the patient population served, a sample of California physicians was then surveyed. The questionnaire included items regarding physician racial/ethnic identification, and the racial/ethnic makeup and distribution of health insurance status of the physicians' patient populations.

First, physician shortages were examined in relation to community racial/ethnic makeup. Areas with shortages of physicians were defined as those with fewer than 30 office-based primary care physicians per 100,000 population. Using the AMA Masterfile and the census data, the examination of the distribution of office-based primary care physicians—including family practitioners, general practitioners, general internists, general pediatricians, and obstetricians and gynecologists—revealed that the supply of physicians was more strongly associated with the proportion of black and Hispanic residents in the community area than with the area's income level. In urban communities, areas with high proportions of both black and Hispanic residents had, on average, the lowest ratio of physicians to population. In contrast, urban areas with high levels of poverty and lower concentrations of Blacks or Hispanics had three times as many physicians per capita. This association was similar for communities with low levels of poverty and for rural areas with high and low levels of poverty.

Next, physician survey data were analyzed to learn about the practice patterns of black and Hispanic physicians. Overall, black and Hispanic physicians were more likely to practice in the areas with fewer primary care physicians per capita and in poorer areas as compared with white physicians. Overall, physicians tended to practice in areas with relatively high proportions of residents of their own race/ethnicity.

As in the study led by Keith et al., the authors also attempted to address the question of whether physicians practicing in underserved areas did so by choice. To test this hypothesis, the authors surveyed graduates from the University of California San Francisco (UCSF) Medical School. Because UCSF is a highly competitive medical school, the authors posit that UCSF graduates would have many opportunities available to them in terms of choice of practice location. Among UCSF graduates, the results were consistent with the findings of the physician survey discussed above. Black physicians tended to practice in areas with higher proportions of black residents than other physicians (14% vs. 6 %), and Hispanic physicians practiced in areas with higher proportions of Hispanic residents than other physicians (19% vs. 12%).

One limitation of this study was the lack of objective data or means to validate data about physician's patient populations. The only available source of data about the makeup of individual physicians' patient populations was physician self-report, which may not be accurate. Furthermore, physicians were asked to report on the proportions of patients of different race, ethnicity, and insurance status backgrounds, but the joint distributions of these characteristics at the individual patient level was unknown. Thus, it was not possible to study the independent effects associated with each of these variables.

A number of the aforementioned studies also examined the patient populations of physicians by physician race and ethnicity. The following sections review the evidence regarding service to potentially vulnerable patient populations irrespective of practice location.

Service to Vulnerable Patient Populations

Rochelau's analysis of data from the 1975 National Ambulatory Medical Care Survey (NAMCS) found that a far greater proportion of black patients was seen in the ambulatory care setting by black physicians than by non-black physicians (87% vs. 7.4%) (Rocheleau, 1978). Black physicians also saw a caseload that may have been somewhat sicker, on average, than that of non-black physicians; however, differences were small and statistical tests for differences were not conducted. Black physicians reported caseloads of which they classified 21.6% as having serious or very serious conditions and 34.1% as having slightly serious conditions. In contrast, non-black physicians characterized 18.8% of their caseload as having serious or very serious conditions, and 32.4% as having slightly serious conditions.

The study of Howard University College of Medicine alumni also asked physicians to estimate the proportions of their patients populations that fell into various categories, including racial (black, white, other) and economic status (well to do, comfortably well off, not very well off, very poor) categories. The authors found that black physicians reported caring for or planning to care for a substantially higher proportion of black patients (72%) than all respondents on average (65%). In addition, the 1982 analysis comparing the earlier and later graduation cohorts suggests that more recent graduates reported caring for or planning to care for a higher percentage of black patients than earlier graduates. Very slightly higher proportions of the patients cared for by black respondents were characterized as very poor (23.5% vs. 21.5%) or not very well off (19.0% vs. 18.3%). This trend did not vary notably between the earlier and more recent graduates. Again, statistical comparisons were not made and potential confounding factors, such as the physician's socioeconomic background or age, were not controlled by the study design or in the analysis. However, restricting the study to the graduates of one medical school, while limiting generalizability, also has the effect of minimizing some of the potential differences in the respondents that might have biased these results.

Keith and colleagues also examined the characteristics of the patient populations reported by physician survey respondents. The authors found that physicians were more likely to treat higher proportions of patients from their own racial and ethnic groups. Thus, black physicians saw higher proportions of black patients than other physicians, and Hispanic physicians saw higher proportions of Hispanic patients. Black patients made up 56% of the patient populations of the black physicians, as compared to 8% to 14% of the caseloads of other physicians. Hispanic patients represented 30% of the patient populations of Hispanic physicians, as compared to 6% to 9% of the caseloads of physicians from other racial/ethnic groups.

The service provided by California physicians to patients on Medicaid and to minority patients was studied by Davidson and Lewis (1997). They found that minority physicians had higher percentages of patients covered by Medicaid in their practices than did non-minority physicians. 31% of minority physicians reported that over 40% of their caseloads was made up of patients covered by Medicaid, as compared with 10% of non-minority physicians. At the other extreme, 33% of minority physicians reported that less than 10% of their caseloads comprised Medicaid patients, as compared with 59% of non-minority physicians. A pooled contingency table indicated a statistically significant difference between the minority and non-minority physicians ($p < 0.02$). Minority physicians also saw higher percentages of minority patients than non-minority physicians in the study. Minority graduates treated significantly higher proportions of patients who were black (23.5% vs. 6.7%) and Hispanic (33.1% vs. 12.5%). However, minority physicians did not treat only minority patients. Black physicians also reported that approximately 33% of their patients were non-minorities, and Hispanics reported a patient mix including 42.2% non-minorities. Unfortunately, because no study thus far has combined data from surveyed physicians about their patient case mix as well as patient-level data from individual patients, it is unclear what the joint distribution of medical indigence and minority status among patients is. These findings were unadjusted for other factors that might explain the apparent concordance between physician race/ethnicity and that of the patient case mix. Furthermore, none of the studies that ask physicians about their general patient case mix was able to collect data regarding patients' reasons for selecting their physician.

The study of California physicians conducted by Komaromy and colleagues also examined the relationship between patient and physician characteristics. They also found significant racial/ethnic concordance between physicians and their patient populations. Even after controlling for the racial/ethnic makeup of the communities in which physician respondents reported practicing, the results revealed that black physicians reported caring for significantly more black patients (25%, $p < 0.001$) and Hispanic physicians reported caring for significantly more Hispanic patients (21%, $p < 0.001$) as compared with other physicians. The results also showed that black physicians cared for more patients covered by Medicaid (45% vs. 18%, $p < 0.001$) and Hispanic physicians cared for a higher proportion of uninsured patients (9% vs. 6%, $p < 0.03$) than non-Hispanic white physicians.

Moy et al. (1995) analyzed data from the nationally representative 1987 National Medical Expenditure Survey (NMES) to test the hypotheses that non-white physicians are more likely to provide care for racial and ethnic minority patients, indigent patients, and sicker patients. Their analysis was limited to patients with at least minimal access to the health care system in that they were able to identify a regular physician as their usual source of care, a total of 15,801 respondents to the survey. Respondents provided detailed data regarding their own personal characteristics, health services utilization, physical and mental health status, functional status, and characteristics of their regular physicians including racial/ethnic group.

Patients of minority physicians, including black, American Indian, Asian, and other physicians were compared to patients of white physicians. Patient race/ethnicity was self-reported as either white, non-Hispanic white, non-Hispanic black, Hispanic, American Indian, or Asian/Pacific Islander. Medically indigent patients were defined as those with incomes under 200% of the federal poverty level. Health insurance status was also examined with patients classified as insured by a plan other than Medicaid, insured by Medicaid, or uninsured.

Moy et al. (1995) found that, among patients who reported having a regular physician as their usual source of care, minority patients were over four times as likely to report receiving care from minority physicians as were white patients (O.R. = 4.39, C.I. = 3.36–5.73). Between 19% and 29% of the low-income, Medicaid-covered, and uninsured patients received care from minority physicians, as compared with 13% of the more affluent patients. Patients who were low-income, poor, or near poor were 1.68 times as likely to receive care from a minority physician as a white physician. Among the uninsured, the odds of having a regular physician who was a minority were 1.44 times as great as the odds of having a regular physician who was white. Patients covered by Medicaid were 2.62 times as likely to receive their care from a minority physician as a white physician. Patients with worse health status were also more likely to receive care from minority physicians than white physicians. Adult Americans who identified a nonwhite physician as their regular source of care also tended to be sicker than the patients who reported having white physicians. A significantly higher percentage of patients of non-white physicians reported being in fair or poor health compared to those of white physicians. Furthermore, patients of non-white physicians reported significantly greater numbers of emergency department visits and hospitalizations and reported experiencing more acute complaints, chronic conditions, functional limitations, and psychological symptoms than patients of white physicians.

To control for other characteristics that could potentially explain this relationship, the authors also constructed multiple logistic regression models. The models to predict the likelihood of receiving care from a nonwhite physician controlled for physician sex, specialty (generalist vs. specialist), workplace setting (office, clinic, other), region of the country (Northeast, Midwest, South, West), and urbanicity (MSA vs. non-MSA). None of these covariates explained the relationships between patient characteristics and likelihood of reporting a minority physician as a usual source of care.

In addition, the researchers addressed two other potential confounders: language concordance and how recently the physicians were trained. One concern was that race/ethnicity was a proxy for patient preferences for a physician who speaks the same language as the patient. The analyses were repeated, excluding respondents who reported a first language other than English. Among native English speakers, physician race remained associated with patient race and ethnicity, medical indigence, and severity of illness. Another hypothesis was that the pattern of physician race and patient race/ethnicity and other patient characteristics is associated with how recently physicians were trained. To test whether results varied with the length of time since the physician was trained, the authors split the data set into two samples, one with patients who had been with their physician for over 10 years (with less recently trained physicians, on average) and one with patients who had been with their physician for less than 10 years (with more recently trained physicians, on average). In both groups, physician race remained associated with patient race/ethnicity, medical indigence, and worse health status.

To determine whether underrepresented minority physicians were more likely to serve underserved groups, including poor and Medicaid-covered patients and minority patients, data from the 1987 and 1991 Young Physicians Survey were analyzed (Cantor et al., 1996). The 1991 data were analyzed cross-sectionally to examine these study questions. The longitudinal sample was then used to determine whether service patterns were sustained over a four-year period. Physicians less than age 40 and in practice at least one year were sampled from the AMA Masterfile and invited to participate in the telephone survey. Minority physicians were over-sampled. Physicians without patient care practices, those who reported practicing less than 10 or more than 126 hours per week, and radiologists, pathologists, and anesthesiologists were excluded. Survey response rates were 70% in 1991 and 63% in 1987. The AMA had previously conducted a study of survey non-response and found that non-respondents were similar to respondents in most respects, and sampling weights were used to correct for differential non-response.

The five outcome variables included the percentages of physicians' patient populations that were black, Hispanic, uninsured, or poor, and the percentage of the physician's revenue derived from Medicaid. The principle independent variables were physician race/ethnicity, sex, socioeconomic status (based on the respondent's parental income level on a five-point scale and highest education level achieved by either of respondent's parents), as well as characteristics of training and practice. Additional analyses examined respondent satisfaction with different aspects of their career.

Of 4,581 respondents in 1991, the racial/ethnic distribution was 85.1% white, 3.0% black, 3.4% Hispanic, and 8.5% other. In bivariate analysis, black physicians were found to serve relatively high proportions of black patients, and Hispanic physicians were found to serve relatively high proportions of Hispanic patients. In addition, minority and female physicians served high proportions of patients who were poor and covered by Medicaid. Physicians from low socioeconomic backgrounds reported higher levels of service to black, Hispanic, poor, and Medicaid patients as compared with physicians from higher SES backgrounds.

In multivariate analysis, controlling for physician sex, physician SES did not explain the physician race/ethnicity effect on patient population served. Additional variables related to physician practice choices were then added to this base model, including specialty, practice setting, urban, rural, or suburban practice location, respondent educational debt, participation in a service program, and type of medical school. These mediating variables did not account for the relationship between physician race/ethnicity and patient characteristics. In this multivariate analysis, educational debt and participation in a service payback program showed little relationship with service of underserved groups. In the longitudinal analysis, little change was observed over time. Generally, service to the underserved did not decrease over the four-year study period, indicating that physicians did not serve these vulnerable patient populations on a merely temporary basis. The authors concluded that socioeconomic disadvantage is not a substitute for race/ethnicity in terms of likelihood to serve minority, poor, uninsured, and Medicaid-covered patient groups. Although physicians from lower socioeconomic backgrounds were more likely to serve the underserved, the relationship between such service and physician race/ethnicity was much stronger.

As with much of the extant literature, this study may be subject to measurement error resulting from measuring characteristics of the patient population using only physician self-report. Although some physicians in certain practice settings may be acutely aware of the percentages of patients they serve who are uninsured and covered by Medicaid, many may be likely to over- or underestimate these figures, as well as figures on the racial/ethnic makeup of their patient population.

The most current literature continues to support the findings that minority physicians are more likely to treat minority and underserved patients. In an analysis of data from the 1987 National Medical Expenditure Survey, the same data source used in the study by Moy, Gray and Stoddard (1997) sought to test the hypothesis that minority patients are more likely than white patients to report a minority physician as their regular source of care, independent of socioeconomic status. Like Moy, Gray studied data on access to care from patients who responded to a nationally representative household survey. However, unlike the method employed by Moy, which included only respondents who reported having a particular physician as a usual source of care, Gray jointly modeled the probability of having a regular provider and the race/ethnicity of that provider while controlling for patient socioeconomic status using a bivariate probit model. Minorities included the categories of African American, Hispanic, and other. Whites and Asians were classified as non-minorities. Patient characteristics included age, sex, poverty status, educational level, employment status, type of insurance, region of residence, and urban residence. The unadjusted results reveal disparities in access to having a regular physician. The likelihood that a Hispanic or African American reported having a regular physician was 50%, as compared with 70% for non-minorities. The unadjusted results also suggest that a strong relationship exists between patient and physician race/ethnicity. Conditional on having a regular physician, minorities were more than five times as likely as Whites to identify a minority physician as their regular provider. After controlling for sociodemographic characteristics, the results showed that minority patients were less likely to have a regular physician than Whites. But for those who had a regular physician, minorities were more likely to have a minority physician compared with non-minority patients ($p < 0.001$). Thus, the authors showed that race/ethnicity is independently related with physician-patient pairing after controlling for numerous sociodemographic patient characteristics. They conclude on this basis that physician-patient racial concordance is the result of physician and/or patient preferences. This conclusion, while a plausible hypothesis, may be unwarranted based on the results of this study alone, which did not address physician characteristics that might be associated with serving a particular patient population.

As a result of concerns over shortages of primary care physicians in the United States, a recent study focused specifically on the practice patterns of generalist physicians and the predictors of their providing care to underserved populations (Rabinowitz et al., 2000). As part of a larger study to learn about influences on choice of generalist careers, a survey was conducted among a stratified random sample of generalists (specialists in family practice, general practice, general internal medicine, or general pediatrics without subspecialization) who had graduated between 1983 and 1984. In all, 2,199 (74%) of the 2,955 surveyed physicians responded. Respondents were considered ineligible for the study if they had left general practice or worked for the military (310) or if they failed to provide responses regarding the outcome variable, one or more of the seven predictor variables, or both (185). Results from 1,704 eligible respondents were analyzed.

The authors tested whether seven variables [sex, belonging to a minority group that is underserved (black, Hispanic, American Indian, Alaska Native), family income when growing up (by quintile), growing up in an inner city or rural area, National Health Service Corps participation, strong interest in underserved practice prior to medical school, and clinical experience with the underserved during medical school] were predictive of reporting providing substantial care to underserved populations after medical school. Care of the underserved was not measured merely in terms of relative proportions of physicians' caseloads that were medically indigent. Substantial care to the underserved was defined as 1) self-reported practice in a federally designated underserved area, 2) having a caseload of which 40% or more of the patients are medically indigent (insured by Medicaid or uninsured), or 3) having a caseload in which 40% of patients are poor. Results of a multivariate logistic regression showed that of seven predictor variables tested, four were significantly and independently predictive of providing substantial care to underserved populations: 1) belonging to a minority group that is underserved, 2) participation in the National Health Service Corps, 3) strong interest in practicing in an underserved area prior to medical school, and 4) growing up in an underserved area. Sex, family income while growing up, and curricular exposure to underserved populations were not significantly associated with caring for the underserved in the adjusted model. The authors found a clear and statistically significant monotonic relationship between the number of predictors and the likelihood of serving an underserved population. However, those belonging to a minority group had the greatest increased likelihood of providing substantial care to the underserved, controlling for all other factors (O.R. = 2.9, p < 0.001).

The primary intent of this study was not aimed solely at testing whether or not minority physicians provide more care to the underserved. However, the findings with respect to this study question appear quite robust. By being restricted to generalists, the study controlled for differences in practice patterns between generalists and specialists, although this limits the ability to generalize about minorities in other specialties. It also controlled for sex, family background, and experience with the underserved in medical school. For the purpose of testing whether minority physicians are more likely than others to serve the underserved, the authors may have overcontrolled for confounding by including physician interest in serving the underserved and participation in the National Health Service Corps in the multivariate model. Despite this modeling approach, minority status again emerged as significantly and independently associated with serving a substantial proportion of underserved patients in their caseloads.

TABLE 2 A Summary of Characteristics of Minority Physician Practice Literature Reviewed

Author, Year	Data Source	Controls, Patient unit of analysis	Controls, Physician unit of analysis				Outcomes			
		Patient socio-economic status?	Physician socio-economic status?	Physician medical school/ educational performance?	Physician educational debt/ participation in NHSC?	Did minorities practice in underserved geographic area?	Did minorities serve more minority patients?	Did minorities serve more medically indigent/ poor patients?	Did minorities serve sicker patients?
Rocheleau, 1978	1975 NAMCS	-	No	No	No	Metro area	Yes	-	Yes
Lloyd et al., 1978; 1982	1975 HUCM Alumni Survey	-	No	All Howard alumni	No	Inner city	Yes	Yes	-
Johnson et al., 1989	1985 HUCM Alumni Survey	-	No	All Howard alumni	No	Inner city	Yes	Yes	-
Keith, et al. 1985	National Physician Survey of 1975 graduates	-	Yes	Yes	No	Yes	Yes	Yes	-
Komaromy, et al. 1996	Census, CA physician survey	-	No	Yes, sub-analysis of UCSF alumni	No	Yes	Yes	Yes	-

Study	Data source				All California medical school alumni				
Davidson & Lewis, 1997	CA physician survey	-	No	No	Yes	Yes	Yes	-
Moy et al., 1995	NMES	Yes	-	-	-	Yes	Yes	Yes
Cantor et al., 1996	1987 and 1991 Young Physicians Survey	-	Yes	No	Urban/ rural	Yes	Yes	-
Rabinowitz et al., 2000	National generalist physician survey	-	Yes	No	Yes	-	Yes	-
Gray & Stoddard, 1997	NMES	Yes	-	-	-	Yes	Yes	-

UNDERREPRESENTED MINORITY PHYSICIANS, CULTURAL COMPETENCE, AND THE PHYSICIAN-PATIENT RELATIONSHIP

We now review the evidence for the hypothesis that improving the diversity of the health care workforce might improve disparities in health status by providing more culturally competent care. The foundation of this hypothesis is that for some minority patients, having a minority physician may lead to better health care because minority physicians may communicate better and provide more culturally appropriate care to minority patients. If underrepresented minority physicians provide higher-quality care to minority patients along the interpersonal dimensions of care, including doctor-patient communication and cultural competence, this could result in higher patient trust and satisfaction. This may in turn facilitate better health outcomes.

Cultural Competence

Clinician skills are often divided conceptually into technical skills and interpersonal skills. Clinicians with equivalent skills along the technical dimension of care may still provide differing quality care to patients along the interpersonal dimension. Increasing attention is being devoted to the technical and interpersonal skills of clinicians in cross-cultural environments, or "cultural competence." Cultural competence may affect barriers both to access to care and to the receipt of appropriate treatments.

As the U.S. population has become more diverse, the concept of "cultural competence" has come into focus as a potentially important factor in serving the health care needs of the population. It has been widely hypothesized that culturally and linguistically competent care will result in better clinician-patient communication, and better communication will facilitate more successful patient education efforts. The hypothesis is that this will lead to an increased likelihood of patients modifying health behaviors and avoiding exposure to risk. More culturally competent care may also influence patient health care-seeking behavior and health care preferences by affecting patient familiarity with and trust in the health care system, thus widening the range of possible acceptable treatment options. The benefits may range from more thorough and accurate documentation of medical histories to greater adherence to treatment regimens by improving trust, communication, and continuity of care. Finally, the spread of improvements in cultural competence throughout the health care system may expand patient choice and access to a wider range of providers. Unfortunately, there is no empirical evidence directly supporting or refuting the hypothesis that cultural competence in providing health care affects health outcomes in such a way that leads to reductions in health disparities. Indeed, there is not even agreement on exactly what constitutes cultural competence.

Cultural competence has been defined in various ways. A broad definition put forth by the proposed DHHS Office of Minority Health National Standards of Cultural and Linguistic Competency is "the ability of health care providers to understand and respond to the cultural and linguistic needs brought by patients to the health care encounter" (DHHS OOMH, 2000). Lavizzo-Mourey and Mackenzie (1996) conceptualized cultural competence "as the demonstrated awareness and integration of three population-specific issues: health related beliefs and cultural values, disease incidence and prevalence, and treatment efficacy." We present hypertension as an example illustrating the application of this conceptual model.

With regard to understanding a disease's epidemiology, hypertension in African Americans is more prevalent, occurs at younger ages, and has three to five times the mortality rate in African Americans as compared with Whites. Furthermore, African Americans experience higher rates of cardiovascular and renal damage at each severity level of hypertension than Whites. Since hypertension is a such a common and important risk factor for coronary heart disease-related events in African Americans, risk prediction algorithms that fail to take this into account may have less predictive value in this population than in others. With regard to understanding treatment efficacy, hypertension in African Americans as compared with Whites is, in general, more responsive to monotherapy with diuretics and calcium channel blockers than to beta blockers or ACE inhibitors. If beta blockers or ACE inhibitors are used, treatment guidelines recommend that the differences in efficacy be offset by a reduction in salt intake, higher doses of the drug, or the addition of a diuretic (NHLBI, 1997). With regard to understanding cultural implications, African-American patients may find adherence to recommended dietary and exercise regimens challenging due to financial, environmental and cultural factors, and experience lower satisfaction with their care than other patients (Coleman et al., 2000). Thus, greater attention to education, counseling, and continuity of care with a physician to gain a patient's trust may be indicated to achieve adherence goals.

Physicians with an understanding of these issues as well as greater interpersonal skills, particularly in a cross-cultural physician-patient encounter, may be better equipped to collect a more accurate patient history, to learn about the specific issues each patient faces, and to work with the patient over time to achieve better blood pressure control.

A number of studies of mental health services have attempted to address the role of race in the patient-provider relationship. Psychiatrists point out that the race of the patient and the mental health professional may influence patient transference and may affect the therapist's ability to empathize with the patient to an appropriate degree (Brantley, 1983). The mental health literature provides some mixed findings with respect to the relationship between provider-patient racial/ethnic concordance and patient treatment adherence and outcomes. Some research has found no relationship between provider-patient racial/ethnic pairing and service use or outcomes (Chinman, 2000). Other work in mental health lends some support to the cultural competence hypothesis. Studies have found that black clients paired with white providers had lower program participation and less improvement (Rosenheck et al., 1995), that ethnic pairing is related to length of treatment and, among non-English speakers, with outcomes (Sue et al., 1991), and that changes in a community mental health system, including an increase in the diversity of mental health providers, were associated with an increase in the mean numbers of visit, particularly among minority clients (O'Sullivan et al., 1989). However, many of these studies examined only case management services rather than physician services. Moreover, with the exception of one study that measured linguistic competence, the outcomes of interest were only indirectly associated with racial/ethnic concordance, while details of the provider-patient relationship that might relate to cultural competency were unmeasured. Important factors to measure might include physician communication skills, patient trust, and patient satisfaction.

A study of the role of race and the effectiveness of drug treatment programs examined the racial makeup of the client population, rather than of the medical staff. Results suggested that race is not a predictor of treatment success when other effects of other characteristics of the treatment environment such as socioeconomic status of the organization's service area, organizational factors and treatment practices were controlled in the analysis (Howard et al., 1996).

Another study of the influence of patient-physician racial concordance on the quality of nursing home care found no effect. Among a sample of elderly nursing home residents in the south, African-American patients with hypertension were more likely to receive medication and to adhere to their prescribed medication regimen than white patients, regardless of white-African American or African American-white patient-provider racial concordance (Howard, et al. 2001). Finally, a recent study of Medicare beneficiaries hospitalized for myocardial infarctions found that black patients had lower rates of cardiac catheterization regardless of whether the patient's attending physician was white or black (Chen et al., 2001).

Patient Trust and Satisfaction

Physicians require the trust of their patients in order to treat them effectively. Work by Thom et al. (1999) to measure patient trust has shown that trust can be measured and demonstrated to be a related but distinct construct from patient satisfaction. The authors found that after controlling for age, education, length of relationship with physician, active choice of a physician, and preference for care, trust was highly predictive of continuity with a physician, self-reported adherence to medications, and satisfaction after six months with a physician,. A study by LaVeist and colleagues found that this mistrust is significantly associated with lower satisfaction with care among African-American cardiac patients (2000).

Historically, some minority groups have had negative experiences with the health care system (Thomas et al., 1991; Gamble,1997; White, 2000). Research abuses, racism, and race-related misconceptions and stereotyping contribute to mistrust among African Americans of the U.S. health care system. Native American, Latino, and Asian patients have other historical and cultural experiences contributing to suspicion and skepticism of the U.S. health care system and physicians. Minority mistrust of physicians can prove to be a stumbling block to the development of a productive clinician-patient relationship. Some hypothesize that this may result in sub-optimal quality of care and, ultimately, lower health status.

One small study found no evidence of patient preferences about the race or ethnicity of their physician. In interviews with 66 patients, patients reported being more concerned that physicians were caring, competent, and able to listen and understand what they had to say than they were over the race/ethnicity of their physician. However, this study included a convenience sample of patients of only three physicians in a single clinic, and included too few Latino or Asian patients to analyze (Bertakis, 1981). A more recent investigation used national data from the Commonwealth Fund's Minority Health Survey. In this study, Saha et al. (1999) found that black and Hispanic patients were more likely to rate care as excellent and very good from physicians of the concordant race. Blacks with racially concordant physicians were more likely to rate them as excellent in terms of providing health care, treating them with respect, explaining medical problems, listening to concerns, and being accessible. Black and Hispanic patients reported that they were more likely to choose a physician of their same race because of personal preferences and also because of ability to speak the patient's language. Patients with racially concordant physicians were also more likely to report that they had received preventive services and needed medical care during the previous year.

There is further evidence in support of the hypothesis that racial concordance can be beneficial to the doctor-patient relationship. A study of African-American patient adjustment to vitiligo, a de-pigmentating skin condition, found that patients treated in an outpatient hospital clinic with a predominantly African-American patient population and clinical staff showed better adjustment to their condition than African-American patients who received comparable treatment in a similar clinic with a predominantly white patient population and clinical staff. African-American patients treated in the predominantly African-American clinic were also more likely to report that their doctor adequately explained the disease to them compared with African-American patients treated in the predominantly white clinic. In addition, the patients treated in the predominantly African-American clinic reported more satisfaction with levels of trust, comfort, and feeling that the doctor was interested in and showed concern for the patients (Porter & Beuf, 1994).

Doctor-Patient Communication

Language is naturally a key component of physician-patient communication. Many health care organizations lack effective access to interpreters with an understanding of medical concepts and terminology. When patients speak some English and the need for an interpreter is not readily apparent, misunderstandings often go unrecognized. A study of patient ratings of satisfaction with their physicians (Morales et al., 1999) showed that overall, Hispanics were more dissatisfied with their communications with Whites. Moreover, Hispanic Spanish-language respondents were significantly more dissatisfied with care compared with Hispanics who had responded in English and compared with non-Hispanic Whites when asked about 1) whether medical staff listened to what they had to say, 2) receiving answers to their questions, 3) explanations about prescription medications, 4) explanations about medical procedures and tests, and 5) reassurance and support from medical staff. The multivariate model included controls for potentially confounding differences in demographic (age, sex), socioeconomic (education, income, marital status, household size), health insurance, and physical and mental health status characteristics.

Other studies of the doctor-patient relationship and doctor-patient communication have examined the construct of participatory decision making (PDM) (Kaplan et al., 1995; Cooper-Patrick et al., 1999). Among patients in the Medical Outcomes Study, Kaplan found that higher PDM styles were associated with greater patient satisfaction and less likelihood of switching physicians. She also found that minorities tended to rate their physicians as being less participatory than white patients did. Cooper-Patrick specifically examined the relationship between patient PDM ratings of their physicians and race/ethnicity, including PDM, in race-concordant and -discordant physician-patient dyads. Overall, minority patients rated their physicians as having lower PDM scores than nonminority patients. Patients in race-concordant relationships with physicians reported that their physician visits were significantly more participatory than did patients in race-discordant relationships, although the magnitude of the difference in scores was small (2.2%, $p < 0.02$). Patient satisfaction was higher with higher PDM styles across ethnic groups in the study.

Kaplan also found that PDM score was significantly related to time spent with patients, a variable that was not controlled for in the Cooper-Patrick analysis. Black and Hispanic physicians were found to spend more time on office visits on average in several of the aforementioned studies on physician practice pattern by race. However, this alternative hypothesis does not explain why white patients rated visits with white physicians as more participatory than did black patients of white physicians. Patient PDM ratings also varied with other characteristics that could be related with patient comfort level and willingness to be involved during a physician visit, such as patient education and having been a patient of the same physician for a longer period of time. This suggests that PDM is not merely a proxy for average length of office visit alone. Rather, it seems likely that PDM represents a construct related to trust, familiarity with the health care system, communication style, and satisfaction.

In summary, there is little consistent empirical evidence to support or refute the hypothesis that cultural competence influences patient health outcomes, or that training more minority physicians could improve the quality of care delivered to minority patients through improved cultural competence. Indeed, there is currently little agreement with respect to the definition or measurement of cultural competence. Moreover, we must take care to avoid the erroneous assumption that physician race/ethnicity is a proxy for cultural competence or sensitivity, or that patients of similar cultural backgrounds necessarily have similar expectations and preferences. Models from the fields of medical anthropology and sociology remind us that the provider-patient relationship is influenced by many factors including but not limited to characteristics of the patient and the provider, their respective cultural identities, models of health and illness, expectations of one another, and the social distance between them. More research is needed to define and measure cultural competence and to demonstrate its linkages to patient outcomes.

DIVERSITY AMONG MEDICAL STUDENTS AND THE QUALITY OF MEDICAL EDUCATION

The third hypothesized mechanism by which diversity may improve disparities in health status is through the effect of diversity on medical education. Increasing diversity in medical training may expose physicians-in-training to a wider range of different perspectives and cultural backgrounds among their colleagues in medical school, residency, and in practice. Such exposure may provide physicians with experiences and interactions that will broaden their interpersonal skills and help in their interactions with patients. These skills may increase the effectiveness of health care providers in addressing health disparities. There is suggestive evidence that medical students bring racial prejudices with them to medical school. In a study of the physician contribution to differences in quality of care, medical student perceptions of model actors were examined and compared (Rathore, 2000). Students were randomized to view a video of a black woman or a white man reporting identical symptoms of angina. Non-minority students rated the health state described by the black woman as less severe than that described by the white man, while the ratings provided by minority students did not differ. These results suggest that there is reason to suspect that medical students are not significantly different from the rest of the population in that they bring with them to medical school differing perspectives based upon their preexisting beliefs, values, and experiences, and are challenged in medical school to learn essential skills about interacting with patients and colleagues from differing perspectives. However, the ways in which increasing diversity in medical education might affect the educational environment and the quality of physicians it produces have not been systematically studied, and as a result there is currently no evidence to support or refute the hypothesis that having a diverse student body enriches the education of all medical students, resulting in better-educated, more culturally competent physicians and better health outcomes for minority patients as well as majority patients.

THE COMING CHALLENGE

Variations in medical care by patient race/ethnicity are at least in part attributable to differences in severity of illness and comorbidities. These factors may be influenced by many patient-level characteristics, including genetic factors, health behaviors, and environmental factors. They are also influenced by patient-level variables that affect access to care, such as socioeconomic status and health insurance status. In addition, access to care is influenced by the physical availability of care, the ease of use of care, and the ability to develop a meaningful doctor-patient relationship.

The goal of increasing the diversity of the physician workforce in the United States in a sense dovetails with other efforts to alter medical education by reflecting a greater emphasis on development of core competencies in interpersonal skills that affect the care of patients. As they shape the entering classes of their institutions, admissions committees may increasingly emphasize diversity of background; life experiences, including cross-cultural experiences; and language and interpersonal skills as well as excellence in the classroom. However, evidence is needed to demonstrate whether such efforts have an impact on the overall quality of medical education or the quality of care ultimately delivered by physicians.

Numerous programs have been implemented over the past 20 years aimed at increasing the numbers of underrepresented minority physicians and improving service to underserved communities. Recent limits on affirmative action pose a serious challenge to many such interventions. This threat is of particular concern as the proportion of racial and ethnic minorities in the U.S. population continues to increase. As minority populations grow, the importance of the supply of minority physicians is likely to increase. Keeping up with this need will require premedical education programs, medical school admissions policies, and physician workforce planning to include explicit strategies to increase the supply of underrepresented minority physicians. However, the racial and ethnic composition and life experiences of minority populations in the United States are constantly in flux. Programs and policies should be constantly reassessed in light of these changes.

The goal of this paper has been to review and synthesize the scientific thinking and evidence related to the potential impact of increasing the racial and ethnic diversity of U.S. physicians on racial and ethnic differences in health status. Strong, compelling evidence suggests that minority physicians are indeed more likely to provide precisely those services that may be most likely to reduce racial and ethnic health disparities, namely primary care services for underserved poor and minority populations. It is the opinion of the authors that the strength of that evidence alone is sufficient to support continued efforts to increase the numbers of physicians from underrepresented minority groups. Some evidence also supports the hypothesis that some patients prefer physicians from their own racial or ethnic group, suggesting the possibility that diversity among physicians may provide greater choices for patients to choose physicians with whom they feel most comfortable. Clearly, the low numbers of physicians from underrepresented minority groups will limit choices for patients.

Although we believe that the evidence supports efforts to increase diversity among health providers to address disparities, we also recognize that we must be vigilant against the potentially pernicious effects of creating the expectation that minority physicians are being trained solely to provide health care services to minority patients or to research minority health issues.

Finally, there is a great need to apply rigorous scientific methods to assess the impact of the race and ethnicity of physicians and patients on health outcomes and the impact of diversity on the quality of medical education for all students and on the quality of health care. We must bring these research findings to bear on continued efforts to assure diversity among health care providers.

REFERENCE

Aday, L.A., & Andersen R.M. (1981). Equity of access to medical care: A conceptual and empirical overview. Medical Care; 19(12, supp), pp. 4–27.

Andersen, R.M., & Aday, L.A. (1978). Access to medical care in the U.S.: Realized and potential. Medical Care; 16(7), pp. 533–546.

Andersen, R.M., Bozzette, S.A., Shapiro, M.F. et al. (2000). Access of vulnerable groups to antiretroviral therapy among persons in care for HIV disease in the U.S. Health Services Research;35(2), pp. 389–416.

Bernabei, R.; Gambassi, G.; Lapane, K.; Landi, F.; Gatsonis, C.; Dunop, R.; Lipsitz, L.; Steel, K.; & Mor, V. (1998). Management of pain in elderly patients with cancer. SAGE Study Group. JAMA; 279(23), pp. 1877–1882.

Bertakis, K.D. (1981). Does race have an influence on patients' feelings toward physicians? The Journal of Family Practice. 13(3), pp. 383–387.

Blendon, R.J.; Aiken, L.H.; Freeman, H.E.; & Corey, C.R. (1989). Access to medical care for black and white Americans. A matter of continuing concern. JAMA; 261(2), pp. 278–281.

Bowen, W.G., & Bok, D. (1998). The shape of the river: Long term consequences of considering race in college and university admissions. Princeton University Press, Princeton, NJ.

Brach, C., & Fraser, I. (2000). Can cultural competency reduce racial and ethnic health disparities? A review and conceptual model. Medical Care Research and Review;57 Suppl 1, pp. 181–217.

Brantley, T. (1983). Racism and its impact on psychotherapy. American Journal of Psychiatry. 140, pp. 1605–1608.

Cantor, J.C.; Miles, E.L.; Baker, L.C.; & Baker, D.C. (1996). Physician service to the underserved: Implications for affirmative action in medical education. Inquiry, Summer; 33, pp. 167–180.

Carlisle, D.M.; Gardner, J.E.; & Liu, H. (1998). The entry of underrepresented minority students into US medical schools: An evaluation of recent trends. American Journal of Public Health; 88(9), pp. 1314–1318.

Carlisle, D.M.; Leake, B.D.; & Shapiro, M.F. (1995). Racial and ethnic differences in the use of invasive cardiac procedures among cardiac patients in Los Angeles County, 1986 through 1988. American Journal of Public Health; 85(3), pp. 352–356.

Chen, J., Rathore, S.S., Radford, M.J., Wang, Y., & Krumholz, H.M. (2001). Racial differences in the use of cardiac catheterization after acute myocardial infarction. 344, pp. 1443–1449.

Chinman, M.J.; Rosencheck, R.A.; & Lam, J.A. (2000). Client-case manager racial matching in a program for homeless persons with serious mental illness. Psychiatric Services; 51(10):1265–1272.

Clark, L.T. (1999). Primary prevention of cardiovascular disease in high-risk patients: Physiologic and demographic risk factor differences between African American and white American populations. American Journal of Medicine; 107(2, supp 1), pp. 22–24.

Coleman, M.T., Lott, J.A., & Sharma, S. (2000). Use of continuous quality improvement to identify barriers in the management of hypertension. American Journal of Medical Quality; 15(2): pp. 72–77.

Cooper-Patrick, L., Gallo, J.J., Gonzales, J.J. et al. (1999). Race, gender, and partnership in the patient-physician relationship. JAMA;282, pp. 583–589.

Cornelius, L.J. (1991). Access to medical care for black Americans with an episode of illness. Journal of the National Medical Association;83(7), pp. 617–626.

Cornelius, L.J. (1993). Barriers to medical care for white, black and Hispanic children. Journal of the National Medical Association; 85, pp. 281–288.

Cunningham, W.E., Markson, L.E., Andersen, R.M. et al. (2000). Prevalence and predictors of highly active antiretroviral therapy use in persons with HIV infection in the U.S. Journal of Acquired Immune Deficiency Syndromes;25(2), pp. 115–123.

Davidson, R.C., & Lewis, E.L. (1997). Affirmative action and other special consideration admissions at the University of California, Davis, School of Medicine. JAMA;278(14), pp. 1153–1158.

Davidson, R.C., & Montoya, R. (1987). The distribution of services to the underserved: A comparison of minority and majority medical graduates in California. Western Journal of Medicine;146, pp. 114–117.

Department of Health and Human Services OOMH. (2000). Office of Minority Health national standards on culturally and linguistically appropriate services (CLAS) in health care. Federal Register;65(247).

Easterbrook, P.J., Keruly, J.C., Creagh-Kirk, T., Richman, D.D., Chaisson, R.E., & Moore, R.D. (1991). Racial and ethnic differences in outcome in zidovudine-treated patients with advanced HIV disease. JAMA;266(19), pp. 2713–2718.

Ferguson, J.A.; Tierney, W.M.; Westmoreland, G.R.; Mamlin, L.A.; Segar, D.S.; Eckert, G.J.; Zhou, X.H.; Martin, D.K.; & Weinberger, M. (1997). Examination of racial differences in management of cardiovascular disease. Journal of the American College of Cardiology; 30(7), pp. 1707–1713.

Flexnor, A. (1910). Medical education in the United States and Canada. Carnegie Foundation for the Advancement of Teaching. Merrymount Press: Boston, MA.

Freeman, H.E., Aiken, L.H., Blendon, R.J., & Corey, C.R. (1990). Uninsured working-age adults: Characteristics and consequences. Health Services Research; 24(6), pp. 811–823.

Gamble, V.N. (1997). Under the shadow of Tuskegee: African Americans and health care. American Journal of Public Health.87, pp. 1773–1778.

Ginzberg, E. (1989). Physician supply in the year 2000. Health Affairs; Summer.

Gornick, M.E., Eggers, P.W., Reilly, T.W. et al. (1996). Effects of race and income on mortality and use of services among Medicare beneficiaries. New England Journal of Medicine; 335(11), pp. 791–799.

Grant, E.N., Lyttle, C.S., & Weiss, K.B. (2000). The relation of socioeconomic factors and racial/ethnic differences in U.S. asthma mortality. American Journal of Public Health; 90(12), pp. 1923–1925.

Gray, B., Stoddard, J.J. (1997). Patient-physician pairing: Does racial and ethnic congruity influence the selection of a regular physician? Journal of Community Health; 22(4), pp. 247–259.

Hannan, E.L.; van Ryn, M.; Burke, J.; Stone, D.; Kumar, D.; Arani, D.; Pierce, W.; Rafii, S.; Sanborn, T.A.; Sharma, S.; Slater, J.; & DeBuono, B.A. (1999). Access to coronary artery bypass surgery by race/ethnicity and gender among patients who are appropriate for surgery. Medical Care; 37(1), pp. 68–77.

Holzer, H., & Neumark, D. (2000). Assessing affirmative action. Journal of Economic Literature; 38, pp. 483–568.

Howard, D.L., LaVeist, T.A., & McCaughrin, W.C. (1996). The effect of social environment on treatment outcomes in outpatient substance misuse treatment organizations: Does race really matter? Substance Use and Misuse. 31(5), pp. 617–638.

Johnson, D.G., Lloyd, S.M., & Miller, R.L. (1989). Survey of graduates of a traditionally black college of medicine. Academic Medicine; 64, pp. 87–94.

Kahn, K.L.; Pearson, M.L.; Harrison, E.R.; Desmond, K.A.; Rogers, W.H.; Rubenstein, L.V.; Brook, R.H.; & Keeler, E.B. (1994). Health care for black and poor hospitalized Medicare patients. JAMA; 271(15), pp. 1169–1174.

Kaplan, S.H., Gandek, B., Greenfield, S. et al. (1995). Patient and visit characteristics related to physician's participatory decision-making styles: Results from the Medical Outcomes Study. Medical Care; 33(12), pp. 1176–1187.

Keith, S.N.; Bell, R.M.; Swanson, A.G.; & Williams, A.P. (1985). Effects of affirmative action in medical schools: A study of the class of 1975. New England Journal of Medicine; 313, pp. 1519–1525.

Kindig, D.A., & Yan, G. (1993). Physician supply in rural areas with large minority populations. Health Affairs, Summer.

Kington, R.S., & Nickens, H.W. (2001). Racial and ethnic differences in health: Recent trends, current patterns, future directions. In America becoming: Racial trends and their consequences, NJ Smelser, WJ Wilson, and F Mitchell. (Eds). Washington, DC, National Academy Press.

Komaromy, M.; Grumbach, K.; Drake, M.; Vranizan, K.; Lurie, N.; Keane, D.; & Bindman, A.B. (1996). The role of black and Hispanic physicians in providing health care for underserved populations. New England Journal of Medicine; 334, pp. 1305–1310.

Kuder, J.M., & Levitz, G.S. (1985). Visits to the physician: An evaluation of the usual-source effect. Health Services Research; 20(5), pp. 579–596.

LaVeist, T.A., Nickerson, K.J., & Bowie, J.V. (2000). Attitudes about racism, medical mistrust, and satisfaction with care among African American and white cardiac patients. Medical Care Research and Review;57 Suppl 1, pp. 146–161.

Lavizzo-Mourey, R., & Mackenzie, E.R. (1996). Cultural competence: Essential measurements of quality for managed care organizations. Annals of Internal Medicine;124, pp. 919–921.

Libby, D.L.; Zhou, Z.; & Kindig, D. (1997). Will minority Physician supply meet the U.S. needs? Projections for reaching racial parity of physicians to population. Health Affairs, July/August; 16(4), pp. 205–214.

Lieu, T.A., Newacheck, P.W., McManus, M.A. (1993). Race, ethnicity and access to ambulatory care among U.S. adolescents. American Journal of Public Health; 83(7), pp. 960–965.

Lloyd, S.M., & Johnson, D.G. (1982). Practice patterns of black physicians: Results of a survey of Howard University College of Medicine Alumni. Journal of the National Medical Association;74(2), pp. 129–141.

Lloyd, S.M., Johnson, D.G., & Mann, M. (1978). Survey of graduates of a traditionally black college of medicine. Journal of Medical Education;53, pp. 640–650.

Mayberry, R.M., Mili, F., & Ofili, E. (2000). Racial and ethnic differences in access to medical care. Medical Care Research and Review; 57(1, supp), pp. 108–145.

Monheit, A.C., & Vistnes, J.P. (2000). Race/ethnicity and health insurance status 1987 and 1996. Medical Care Research and Review; 57(Supp 1), pp. 11–35.

Moore, R.D., Stanton, D., Gopalan, R., & Chaisson, R.E. (1994). Racial differences in the use of drug therapy for HIV disease in an urban community. New England Journal of Medicine;330(11), pp. 763–768.

Morales, L.S., Cunningham, W.E., & Brown, J.A. et al. (1999). Are Latinos less satisfied with communication by health care providers? Journal of General Internal Medicine;14, pp. 409–417.

Moy, E.; Bartman, B.A.; & Weir, M.R. (1995). Access to hypertensive care. Effects of income, insurance, and source of care. Archives of Internal Medicine; 155(14), pp. 1497–1502.

Mukamel, D.B., Murthy, A.S., & Weimer, D.L. (2000). Racial differences in access to high-quality cardiac surgeons. American Journal of Public Health.; 90(11), pp. 1774–1777.

National Center for Health Statistics. Health United States, 2000 with adolescent chartbook. Hyattsville, MD: Public Health Service.

National Institutes of Health Heart, Lung and Blood Institute National High Blood Pressure Education Program. (1997). The sixth report of the Joint National Committee on Prevention, Detection, Evaluation and Treatment of High Blood Pressure; NIH Publication No. 98–4080.Bethesda, MD: NIH.

Newacheck, P.W.; Hughes, D.C.; & Stoddard, J.J. (1996). Children's access to primary care: Differences by race, income, and insurance status. Pediatrics; 97(1), pp. 26–32.

Nickens, H.W. (1992). The rationale for minority-targeted programs in medicine in the 1990s. JAMA, 267(17), pp. 2390–2395.

Nickens, H.W.; Ready, T.P.; Petersdorf, R.J. (1994). Project 3000 by 2000: Racial and ethnic diversity in U.S. Medical Schools. New England Journal of Medicine; 331(7), pp. 472–476.

O'Sullivan, M.J,. Peterson, P.D., Cox, G.B., & Kirkby, J. (1989). Ethnic populations: Community mental health services ten years later. American Journal of Community Psychology.;17(1), pp. 17–30.

Petersdorf, R.G.; Turner, K.S.; Nickens, H.W.; & Ready, T. (1990). Minorities in medicine: Past, present, and future. Academic Medicine;65, pp. 663–670.

Porter, J.R., & Beuf, A.H. (1994). The effect of a racially consonant medical context on adjustment of African American patients to physical disability. Medical Anthropology. 16, pp. 1–16.

Rabinowitz, H.K, Diamond, J.J., & Veloski, J.J. et al. (2000). The impact of multiple predictors on generalist physicians' care of underserved populations. American Journal of Public Health;90(8), pp. 1225–1228.

Rathore, S.S.; Lenert, L.A.; Weinfurt, K.P.; Tinoco, A.; Taleghani, C.K.; Harless, W.; Schulman, K.A. (2000). The effects of patient sex and race on medical students' ratings of quality of life. American Journal of Medicine; 108(7), pp. 561–566.

Rocheleau, B. (1978). Black physicians and ambulatory care. Public Health Reports; 93(3):278–282.

Rosenheck, R., Fontana, A., & Cottrol, C. (1995). Effect of clinician-veteran racial pairing in the treatment of posttraumatic stress disorder. American Journal of Psychiatry;152(4), pp. 5550–5563.

Saha, S., Komaromy, M., Koepsell, T.D., & Bindman, A.B. (1999). Patient-physician racial concordance and the perceived quality and use of health care. Archives of Internal Medicine;159, pp. 997–1004.

Samelson, E.J.; Speers, M.A.; Ferguson, M.S.; & Bennett, C. (1994). Racial differences in cervical cancer mortality in Chicago. American Journal of Public Health; 84(6), pp. 1007–1009.

Savitt, T.L. (1985). Black health on the plantation: masters, slaves and physicians. In Sickness and health in America, J. Leavitt & R. Numbers (Eds.) University of Wisconsin Press.

Schwarcz, S.K.; Katz, M.H.; Hirozawa, A.; Gurley, J.; & Lemp, G.F. (1997). Prevention of Pneumocystis carinii Pneumonia: who are we missing? AIDS; 11, pp. 1263–1268.

Schwartz, E.; Kofie, V.Y.; Rivo, M.; & Tuckson, R.V. (1990). Black/White comparison of deaths preventable by medical intervention: United States and the District of Columbia 1980–1986. International Journal of Epidemiology; 19(3), pp. 591–598.

Schwartz, W.B., Sloan, .FA., & Mendelson, D.N. (1988). Why there will be little or no physician surplus between now and the year 2000. New England Journal of Medicine; 318, pp. 892–897.

Summerville, J. Educating Black Doctors: a History of Meharry Medical College. University, Alabama: University of Alabama Press, 1983.

Starr, P. The Social Transformation of American Medicine. New York: Basic Books, 1982.

Sue, S., Fujino, D.C., Hu, L., & Takeuchi, D.T. (1991). Community mental health services for ethnic minority groups: A test of the cultural responsiveness hypothesis. Journal of Consulting and Clinical Psychology;59(4), pp. 533–540.

Taylor, T. (1989). A practice profile of Native American physicians. Academic Medicine;64, pp. 393–396.

Thomas, S.B., & Crouse-Quinn, S. (1991). Public health then and now. The Tuskegee syphilis study, 1932 to 1972: Implications for HIV education and AIDS risk education programs in the black community. American Journal of Public Health;81(11), pp. 1498–1504.

Thom, D.H., Ribisl, K.M., Stewart, A.L. et al. (1999). Further validation and reliability testing of the trust in physician scale. Medical Care;37(5), pp. 510–517.

Thurmond, V.B. & Kirch, D.G. (1998). Impact of minority physicians on health care. Southern Medical Journal; 91(11), pp. 1009–1013.

Todd, K., Samaroo, N., & Hoffman, J.R. (1993). Ethnicity as a risk factor for inadequate emergency department analgesia. JAMA; 269(12), pp. 1537–1539.

Weinick, R.M., & Krauss, N.A. (2000). Racial/ethnic differences in children's access to care. American Journal of Public Health;90(11), pp. 1771–1774.

Weinick, E.M., Zuvekas, S.H., & Cohen, J.W. (2000). Racial and ethnic differences in access to and use of health care services, 1977–1996. Medical Care Research and Review; 57(1, supp), pp. 36–54.

Weissman, J.S., Gatsonis, C., & Epstein, A.M. (1992). Rates of avoidable hospitalization by insurance status in Massachusetts. JAMA; 268(17), pp. 2388–2394.

White, R.M. (2000). Unraveling the Tuskegee Study of Untreated Syphilis. Archives of Internal Medicine;160, pp. 585–598.

Wilcox, L.S., & Mosher, W.D. (1993). Factors associated with obtaining health screening among women of reproductive age. Public Health Reports;108(1), pp. 76–85.

Yergan, J., Flood, A.B., LoGerfo, J.P. et al. (1987). Relationship between patient race and the intensity of hospital services. Medical Care;25(7), pp. 592–603.

Zuvekas, S.H., Weinick, R.M. (1999). Changes to access to care, 1977–1996: the role of health insurance. Health Services Research; 34(1), pp. 271–808.

Current Legal Status of Affirmative Action Programs in Higher Education

Thomas E. Perez
University of Maryland Law School[1]

INTRODUCTION

In recent years, widespread attention has been focused on eliminating racial and ethnic disparities in health. During the Clinton-Gore administration, President Clinton and Donna Shalala, then Secretary of Health and Human Services, committed the nation to the ambitious yet reachable goal of eliminating racial and ethnic disparities by 2010 in six areas of health status while continuing the progress that has been made in improving the overall health of the American people. The six focus areas of the initiative are: 1) infant mortality; 2) cancer screening and management; 3) cardiovascular disease; 4) diabetes; 5) HIV infection/AIDS; and 6) immunizations. This initiative enjoys bipartisan support, and has been endorsed by current HHS Secretary Tommy Thompson.

When President Clinton announced this initiative in 1998, Surgeon General David Satcher assumed a lead role in coordinating efforts within the federal government and among stakeholders outside the federal government. A number of meetings and conferences were convened nationwide with various stakeholders in an effort to gain a better overall understanding of the root causes of these disparities and to identify solutions.

Through this dialogue, a number of proposals emerged for addressing disparities, including: 1) enhancing access to health insurance; 2) addressing numerous gaps in research; 3) educating and training culturally proficient health care practitioners; 4) educating and empowering health care consumers to navi-

---

[1] Assistant Professor of Law and Director of Clinical Law Programs, University of Maryland Law School; Director, Office for Civil Rights, U.S. Department of Health and Human Services, 1999–2001; Deputy Assistant Attorney General for Civil Rights, U.S. Department of Justice, 1998–1999.

gate the health care system more effectively; 5) ensuring aggressive enforcement of civil rights laws; 6) ensuring that health care providers can address the unique needs of expanding immigrant populations, many of whom have limited English skills; and 7) undertaking aggressive efforts to ensure that the health care profession reflects the growing diversity of the population.

Regarding the diversity issue, a number of steps have been taken to increase the pool of minority health practitioners. These measures include aggressive outreach and recruitment, "pipeline" programs that expose minority students at an early age to health sciences, and affirmative action programs that permit the use of race or ethnicity as one factor in the admissions process.[2]

These affirmative action programs have come under substantial attack. This paper focuses on legal issues surrounding efforts taken by the health care profession to expand the racial and ethnic diversity of the profession by employing affirmative action tools. Part one outlines why this affirmative action issue is so important. Part two traces affirmative action in higher education, from the seminal Supreme Court case of *Regents of the University of California* v. *Bakke* to the present. Although many pundits have opined that affirmative action is dead in light of recent court pronouncements and voter initiatives in California and Washington, these declarations ignore a number of significant developments in courtrooms, voting booths, and legislatures.

The reality is that the affirmative action landscape is indeed muddled, but there are plenty of developments that both sides in the debate can point to in making their case. For either side in this debate to declare victory simply ignores the totality of the evidence, and Part two discusses the current affirmative action landscape, including events that have occurred outside the courtrooms. Part three discusses measures that the health professions can take or support to enhance diversity, including but not limited to affirmative action-related interventions. There are a number of useful measures that health professionals can put into place to increase diversity and better ensure that the health profession can meet the needs of our increasingly diverse population.

Affirmative action means different things to different people. For purposes of this paper, affirmative action refers to measures designed to increase the number of qualified minorities in a particular program through a decision making process that includes the consideration of race and ethnicity among a number of factors. Affirmative action does not mean creating or permitting quotas, or providing opportunities for unqualified people.

---

[2] For a further summary of various efforts undertaken by the medical profession to enhance diversity within its ranks, see American Association of Medical Colleges. 1980. *A Plan for the Implementation of the Goals and Recommendations of the Report of the AAMC Task Force on Minority Student Opportunities in Medicine.* Washington, DC: AAMC.

PART ONE: WHY IS DIVERSITY IN GENERAL AND AFFIRMATIVE ACTION IN PARTICULAR IMPORTANT TO THE HEALTH PROFESSION?

A number of trends and studies highlight the importance of the need to ensure a diverse health profession and the critical importance of affirmative action as a tool to enhance diversity. First, census data demonstrate that the nation as a whole has become even more diverse. Surging immigration is transforming both urban and rural America. For instance, between 1990 and 2000, Chicago's population grew four percent, the first growth since 1950.[3] This growth was fueled in large measure by a substantial infusion of Latino and Asian immigrants. In fact, factoring out the influx of Latinos and Asians, Chicago's population decreased 4.4%. New York City's population grew 9.4% from 1990 to 2000. Factoring out the influx of Latinos and Asians, the population increase in New York City was 0.2%.[4] Population increases in Wisconsin and Iowa, states with large rural pockets, were also attributable in large measure to the influx of Latinos and Asians.[5] In terms of percentage increases, Arkansas experienced the largest increase in immigrants of any state in the country.[6] In short, immigration has fueled much of the population growth in both rural and urban areas across the country. The health care system must be in a position to respond to the often unique needs of immigrant populations, including but not limited to language needs.

At the same time minority populations are increasing, data from the American Association of Medical Colleges show a marked decline in the number African Americans and Latinos admitted to medical schools.[7] In 1994, for instance, 1,384 African American and 1,150 Latino students were accepted to American medical colleges, according to AAMC data. In 2000, the figures declined to 1,168 and 1,082, respectively. For the first half of the 1990s, the admissions and enrollment figures for African Americans and Latinos were basically on the upswing. This trend reversed during the second half of the decade. These declines are troubling, especially when juxtaposed with the aforementioned increases in minority populations across the country.

The declines in African-American and Latino enrollment coincided with two significant events. First, in 1995, the United States Court of Appeals for the Fifth Circuit in *Hopwood* v. *Texas*, struck down as unconstitutional an affirmative action program that had been in place in the University of Texas law school. In so doing, the court effectively precluded higher education institutions as well as other entities in the Fifth Circuit, which covers Texas, Louisiana, and Missis-

---

[3] Cohn, D. 2001, March 16. Immigration Surge Fuels Urban Growth. *Washington Post*. p. A.1.

[4] Id.

[5] Sandler, L., Borowski, G. 2001, March 9. Madison, Dane County Lead Growth, *Milwaukee Journal-Sentinel*. p. A.1.

[6] See www.census.gov.

[7] See www.AAMC.org.

sippi, from taking race or ethnicity into account in the admissions process. This case is discussed in greater detail in Part two.

At about the same time, the Regents of the University of California banned the use of race as a factor in admissions. California voters then passed Proposition 209 which, among other restrictions, prevents public higher education institutions in California from implementing programs that allow race or ethnicity to be considered as one factor in the admissions process. California and Texas are two of the principal pipelines for minorities entering the health professions, and these developments have contributed substantially to the decline in enrollment of African-American and Latino medical students from 1994 to 2000. This experience leaves little doubt that the elimination of affirmative action across the country would seriously hamper efforts to ensure the diversity of the health professions.

The significance of this downward trend in minority enrollment is further magnified by a host of studies showing that minority physicians are much more likely to practice in physician shortage areas and to serve minority populations than are non-minority physicians. For example, a number of studies conclude that African-American physicians are more likely to care for African Americans, and Latino physicians are more likely to care for Latino patients.[8] Other studies have shown that African-American patients care for more patients covered by Medicaid, and Latino physicians care for higher proportions of uninsured patients than non-Latino white physicians. Another study found that Latino and African-American physicians were much more likely to choose primary care specialties as compared with non-minority physicians, and that primary care physicians were the most likely to serve in physician shortage areas. Thus, given the shared goal of eliminating racial and ethnic disparities in health, these studies strongly suggest that increasing the pool of minority health professionals would reduce racial and ethnic disparities, as these practitioners are more likely to provide services for underserved poor and minority populations.

Yet, while the numbers of minorities are increasing substantially across the country, the pipeline of minority physicians is shrinking, even though minority physicians are more likely to practice in areas with higher concentrations of minorities. This confluence of forces raises serious concerns that the number of physician shortage areas will grow, and that access to health care for people of color will become even more difficult. Given these realities, the stakes in the affirmative action debate are indeed quite high.

---

[8] For a listing and summary of these studies, see Kington, R. et. al. 2001. *Increasing Racial and Ethnic Diversity Among Health Professionals: An Intervention to Address Health Disparities.* National Academy Press (presented at Nickens Symposium on Diversity in the Health Professions, March 16, 2001).

PART TWO: AFFIRMATIVE ACTION IN HIGHER EDUCATION: DEVELOPMENTS IN THE COURTROOMS AND ELSEWHERE

A. What Is the Legal Standard, and What Does *Bakke* Hold?

An analysis of the legal status of affirmative action in higher education begins necessarily with an understanding of the constitutional standard, what it means, and a discussion of the landmark *Bakke* decision.[9] A considerable amount has been written about *Bakke*, and analysts and courts have disagreed about its meaning. Most recently, for instance, two federal judges in the United States District Court for the Eastern District of Michigan, one of whom was hearing a constitutional challenge to the admissions policy at the University of Michigan undergraduate school, and the other who was hearing a similar challenge to University of Michigan law school admissions policy, reached diametrically opposite conclusions as to the meaning of *Bakke*.[10]

There is no disagreement, however, about the current constitutional standard in affirmative action cases. Courts must employ strict scrutiny when evaluating any racial classifications put into place by a state or other public entity.[11] Thus, in order to justify the use of race or ethnicity in admissions, a state or other public entity (such as a public university) bears the burden of demonstrating that the use of race or ethnicity 1) served a compelling government interest, and 2) was narrowly tailored to the achievement of that goal.[12] In other words, for a university seeking to justify the use of race as a factor in admission, the legal bar is high but not insurmountable.

The analysis of any admissions program that allows for the consideration of race or ethnicity thus begins with a discussion of the compelling government interest that the university is seeking to serve through the use of race-conscious practices. Historically, the two compelling interests that have been advanced

---

[9] *Regents of the University of California* v. *Bakke*, 438 U.S. 265 (1978).

[10] Wilgoren, J. 2001, March 28. U.S. Court Bars Race as a Factor in School Entry. *New York Times*, p. A–1.

[11] *Adarand Constructors, Inc.* v. *Pena*, 515 U.S. 200 (1995)

[12] A frequently asked question is whether private entities are subject to the same standards as public universities, given that they are not state actors and therefore are not subject to the requirements of the Fourteenth Amendment. The short answer is most likely. Pursuant to Title VI of the Civil Rights Act of 1964, as long as a private university or other entity receives federal financial assistance, it would be required to show that the use of race served a compelling interest and that the program was narrowly tailored to the achievement of that goal. While most of the current affirmative action litigation involves public universities, private universities, virtually all of whom receive some form of federal financial assistance and many of whom use race or ethnicity as a factor in admissions, have a vested interest in the affirmative action debate.

most frequently in the higher education context are 1) the so-called remedial rationale, and 2) the diversity rationale.

Proponents of a remedial rationale contend that the university has a compelling interest in remedying the present effects of past discrimination.[13] Proponents of a diversity rationale contend that a university has a compelling interest in ensuring diversity in the classroom because all students enjoy a richer educational experience and develop greater tolerance and racial understanding. It is with this background in mind that it is useful to turn to the *Bakke* decision, which remarkably remains the only Supreme Court case addressing the constitutionality of race by higher education institutions in the admissions process.

Bakke involved a challenge to the admissions program at University of California at Davis Medical School. The university operated a separate application program for minority applicants, with a separate committee that did not rate the minority applicants against the general applicants. A race-based quota was set for applicants under the special admissions program. Two of the stated justifications for this program were 1) countering the effects of societal discrimination, and 2) obtaining the benefits that flow from an ethnically diverse student body.

Allan Bakke, a white male, applied for admission and was rejected. He challenged the program on constitutional grounds and under Title VI of the Civil Rights Act of 1964. The Supreme Court of California upheld his claim, and enjoined the state from taking race into account in its admissions program.

The United States Supreme Court affirmed the judgment of the California Supreme Court, holding unconstitutional the particular program put into place by the medical school. There were a number of different opinions written in this case. A five-member majority of the U.S. Supreme Court explicitly reversed the portion of the California Supreme Court's decision preventing the school from taking race into account in any fashion in its admissions process. This five-member majority further held that it did *not* violate the equal protection clause for the medical school—even in the absence of any proof of a remedial interest—to take race into account in its admissions process, as long as the program is "properly devised" and involves the "competitive consideration of race."[14] In other words, although the U.S. Supreme Court found the particular program in question unconstitutional, it explicitly stated that the school was not precluded from using race in the future, even if there was insufficient evidence of a remedial justification for the use of race-conscious admissions.

Justice Powell, who announced the judgement of the Court, rejected the remedial rationale put forth by the university, noting that "societal discrimination"

---

[13] See, e.g., *Hopwood* v. *Texas*, 78 F.3d 932 (5th Cir.), *cert. denied*, 518 U.S. 1033 (1995); *Podberesky* v. *Kirwan*, 38 F.3d 147 (4th Cir. 1994); *cert. denied*, 115 S.Ct. 2001 (1995).

[14] 438 U.S. at 320.

is an amorphous concept that is maybe "ageless in its reach into the past."[15] The remedial interest must be much more specific to withstand constitutional scrutiny.

Justice Powell's discussion of the diversity rationale has been the portion of the opinion subject to the greatest debate. Justice Powell stated that obtaining the benefits that flow from a diverse student body may be a compelling interest justifying the use of a race-conscious admissions program. Justice Powell found that "an otherwise qualified student with a particular background—whether it be ethnic, geographic, culturally advantaged or disadvantaged—may bring to a professional school . . . experiences, outlooks and ideas that enrich the training of its student body and better equip its graduates."[16] Justice Powell specifically denounced separate or dual-track admissions programs, such as the program implemented by UC-Davis Medical School, noting that these programs focus solely on racial or ethnic diversity and would "hinder rather than further attainment of genuine diversity."[17]

Justice Powell noted that a key to withstanding constitutional scrutiny is individualized consideration, where race is one of a host of factors under consideration, and the individual is considered with all other candidates for the available seats. He cited the undergraduate admissions policy of Harvard University, which considered race as a "plus" in the applicant's file, but looked at other factors and weighed each candidate fairly and competitively. Justice Powell acknowledged that in some circumstances, an applicant's race "may tip the balance in his favor" just as "geographic origin or life spent on a farm may tip the balance in other candidates' favor."[18]

The most critical and hotly debated question surrounding *Bakke* centers on Justice Powell's pronouncements on the diversity rationale. Specifically, does this portion of the opinion command a majority of the Supreme Court? To put it slightly differently, has a majority of the U.S. Supreme Court held that diversity can be a compelling state interest in the higher education context justifying the use of narrowly tailored, race-conscious admissions programs? Courts and commentators disagree vigorously on the answer to this question.

Three things are clear about *Bakke*. First, a majority of the Supreme Court in *Bakke* held that it is permissible for a university to consider race in admissions, even without a history of discrimination by the university. Second, no subsequent Supreme Court decision has overturned this critical aspect of the ruling. In fact, the Supreme Court on two subsequent occasions has cited *Bakke* for the proposition that diversity may constitute a compelling interest in the

---

[15] Id.
[16] Id. at 314.
[17] Id.
[18] Id. at 323.

higher education context.[19] Third, universities across the country have relied on Justice Powell's opinion for almost a quarter century, and race-conscious admissions programs in higher education are commonplace. The United States Department of Education has relied upon Justice Powell in issuing guidance to educational institutions that narrowly tailored affirmative action for purposes of attaining a diverse student body is constitutional and complies with Title VI.[20] The question remains: will this reliance prove to have been justified?

B. Significant Post-Bakke Developments

In the aftermath of *Bakke,* three of the most significant questions that courts have wrestled with are: 1) what are the precise contours of the remedial justification for affirmative action in higher education, 2) is the diversity rationale viable, and 3) what does a narrowly tailored affirmative action program look like?

1. Remedial Rationale for Race-Conscious Programs in Higher Education

It has become increasingly difficult in recent years to justify race-conscious practices as a means of remedying the effects of past discrimination. States certainly have an interest in remedying the effects of present or past discrimination. In fact, a state has a duty to eliminate every vestige of racial segregation and discrimination.[21] In order to be deemed "compelling," the interest must meet two conditions.

First, discrimination must be "identified" discrimination; that is, "they must identify that discrimination, public or private, with some specificity before they may use race-conscious relief."[22] For instance, a state does not have a compelling interest in remedying the present effects of past societal discrimination. Instead, there must be a showing of prior discrimination by the particular government unit involved before a court will permit the use of race-conscious remedies. Despite several Supreme Court opinions, the precise rules for determining how specific and localized the past discrimination must be before a government entity can employ race-conscious measures to remedy the effects of past discrimination remain unclear.

---

[19] *See Metro Broadcasting Inc.* v. *FCC,* 497 U.S. 547, 568 (1990)(quoting *Bakke,* 438 U.S. at 311–313, overruled in part on other grounds, *Adarand Constructors, Inc.* v. *Pena,* 515 U.S. 200 (1995); see also *Adarand,* 515 U.S. 200, 218 (quoting *Bakke,* 438 U.S. at 291).

[20] Department of Education. 1979. Guidance on Permissible Admissions Practices in Higher Education. *Federal Register* 44:58509, 58510–58511.

[21] *United States* v. *Fordice,* 505 U.S. 717 (1992).

[22] *Shaw* v. *Hunt,* 517 U.S. 899, 909 (1996), *quoting Croson* v. *City of Richmond,* 488 U.S. 469, 504 (1989).

Second, there must be a strong evidentiary basis showing the present effects of past discrimination by the relevant entity, and that the effect is of sufficient magnitude to justify the program.[23]

In recent years, courts that have interpreted the remedial rationale have made it increasingly difficult to justify race-conscious decision-making on remedial grounds. *Podberesky* v. *Kirwan* is a case in point which involved the constitutionality of a scholarship program for African-American students established by the University of Maryland at College Park (UMCP).[24] UMCP is the flagship campus of the Maryland higher education system, and was de jure segregated until the late 1950s and segregated as a matter of practice until the late 1970s. The scholarship program was part of the university's plan to eliminate the lasting vestiges of its past discrimination against African Americans. An extensive record was generated regarding the past discrimination by the university, as well as the present-day effects.

The district court judge hearing the case noted that UMCP had made a strong showing of four present effects of past discrimination by the university: 1) UMCP has a poor reputation within the African-American community, particularly among parents and counselors who influence students choices; 2) African Americans are underrepresented in the UMCP student population; 3) African-American students at UMCP have low retention and graduation rates; and 4) the campus atmosphere is perceived as hostile to African-American students.

The district court ruled that the scholarships were constitutional because they were necessary to remedy the present effects of the university's past discrimination. The Court of Appeals for the Fourth Circuit reversed and declared the program unconstitutional. In so doing, the appellate court rejected the reputation and hostile environment rationales outright. Regarding the racial disparities in enrollment, retention, and graduation, the appellate court presumed that the scholarship program was invalid unless the UMCP could prove that the current racial disparities related solely to its own past discrimination. The university, supported by the United States Department of Justice, sought Supreme Court review of this decision and argued that the appellate court had set the legal bar for a remedial race-conscious program too high. The Supreme Court declined to hear the case.

Podberesky is significant in that the state mounted a vigorous defense of the scholarship program premised on the need to remedy the present effects of past discrimination by the state. In other cases discussed below, the state has not advanced the remedial argument. Despite the aggressive defense, the appellate court rejected the claim, and set a very high bar for establishing the remedial justification for race-conscious programs.

---

[23] Id.
[24] 38 F.3d 147 (4th Cir. 1994)(prior and subsequent history omitted).

Hopwood v. *University of Texas* involved a constitutional challenge to the race-conscious admissions policy at the University of Texas Law School.[25] The university put forth both a remedial and a diversity justification for taking race into account in its admissions. The court rejected both rationales. Regarding the remedial rationale, the university put forth present-day effects of past discrimination that were quite similar to those outlined above in *Podberesky*. The Fifth Circuit rejected these justifications as well.

Most recently, plaintiffs have challenged the undergraduate and law school admissions programs at the University of Michigan.[26] In both cases, the university 1) acknowledged that race was one of a number of factors that it took into account in admissions; 2) claimed that diversity was the compelling interest justifying the use of a race-conscious admissions process; and 3) did *not* advance a remedial justification for the use of race. Similarly, in both cases, outside groups were permitted to intervene in the case to defend the use of a race-conscious admissions process, and these groups advanced both the remedial and diversity arguments. In both cases, the district court rejected the claim that the race-conscious admissions program could be justified under a remedial rationale, concluding that the defendant interveners had not met the aforementioned burden.

Johnson v. *Board of Regents of Georgia* involved a challenge to the race-conscious admissions policy at the University of Georgia. The district court in this case rejected the remedial rationale put forth in an effort to justify the use of a race-conscious undergraduate admissions program.[27]

In light of the consistent court rejection of the remedial rationale, proponents of affirmative action in higher education have focused the bulk of their efforts on the diversity rationale, attempting to establish once and for all that *Bakke* remains good law and that race-conscious programs are legal.

2. Diversity as a Compelling Interest

It appears that the future viability of race-conscious admissions in higher education hinges on whether the Supreme Court will rule that *Bakke* remains good law and stands for the proposition that diversity is a compelling interest that justifies the use of narrowly tailored, race-conscious admissions programs. A number of lower courts have addressed this question. The *Hopwood* decision in the Fifth Circuit has garnered the most attention. In that case, the court struck down the race-conscious admissions program at the University of Texas law school, and ruled that diversity is not a compelling interest justifying the use of race-conscious admissions practices. The court concluded that *Bakke* does not

---

[25] 78 F.3d 932 (5th Cir. 1996), *cert denied*, 518 U.S. 1033 (1996).

[26] *Gratz* v. *Bollinger*, 122 F. Supp. 2d 811 (E. D. Mich 2001) (undergraduate case); *Grutter* v. *Bollinger*, 137 F. Supp. 2d 821 (E. D. Mich, 2001) (law school case).

[27] 106 F.Supp. 2d 1362 (S.D. Ga 2000).

stand for the proposition that race can be a compelling interest. The court stated: "there has been no indication from the Supreme Court, other than Justice Powell's lonely opinion in *Bakke*, that the state's interest in diversity constitutes a compelling justification for governmental race-based discrimination."[28] The panel effectively pronounced *Bakke* dead.

Hopwood remains applicable law in the Fifth Circuit, meaning that public universities in Texas, Mississippi, and Louisiana are prohibited from taking race into account in admissions.[29] Coupled with Proposition 209 in California and a voter referendum in Washington State, the ability of public universities in these five states to employ race-conscious admissions programs is quite curtailed. However, the notion put forth by some that affirmative action is now dead across the country is empirically inaccurate. One author has written a lengthy article on affirmative action in employment in which he discusses, among other things, how legal scholarship and the popular press in the post-Hopwood era have inaccurately portrayed affirmative action as dead or almost dead.[30] In fact, the current affirmative action landscape in higher education is quite unsettled, but by no means dead.

The Fifth Circuit is the only appellate court that has rejected diversity as a compelling interest in the higher education context. A federal district judge in Georgia adopted the *Hopwood* rationale in striking down a race-conscious admissions program at the University of Georgia.[31] The United States Department of Justice, in a number of briefs filed during the Clinton administration, has argued that *Hopwood* was wrongly decided, and that *Bakke* and the diversity rationale in higher education remain good law.[32] Other courts have also rejected *Hopwood* or have explicitly refused to declare the *Bakke* diversity rationale dead. The Ninth Circuit, in a case involving a legal challenge to the race-conscious admissions program at the University of Washington Law School, found that diversity is a compelling interest justifying the use of narrowly tailored, race-conscious admissions programs.[33] The court explicitly noted that *Bakke* remains good law and stands for the proposition that diversity can be a compelling interest in the higher education context. The court further noted that the Supreme Court has not returned to the area of university admissions since *Bakke*, and "has not indicated that Justice Powell's decision has lost its vitality."[34]

---

[28] 78 F.3d at 944.

[29] Following a remand, the Fifth Circuit vacated a portion of the original holding, but the critical holding discussed above remains intact. 236 F.3d 256 (5th Cir. 2000). Recently, the Supreme Court again declined to hear the case. 121 S.Ct. 2550 (2001).

[30] Day, J. 2001. Retelling the Story of Affirmative Action: Reflections on a Decade of Federal Jurisprudence in the Public Workplace. *California Law Review*, 89:59.

[31] 106 F.Supp. 2d 1362 (S.D. Ga. 2000).

[32] For a listing of these briefs, see www.usdoj.gov/crt.

[33] *Smith* v. *University of Washington Law School*, 233 F.3d 1188 (9th Cir. 2000). cert. denied. 121 S.Ct. 2192 (2001).

[34] Id. at 1200.

The Second Circuit, in *Brewer* v. *West Irondequoit Cent. School District*, held that reducing racial isolation was a compelling interest justifying the implementation of a race-conscious voluntary interdistrict transfer program in the Rochester, New York-area public school systems.[35] Under the program at issue, minority students were permitted to transfer from schools in the city to schools in the suburbs, and non-minority students were permitted to transfer to city schools from suburban schools. While the case did not involve the higher education context, the discussion of the compelling interest is instructive. The purposes of the program articulated by the school authorities were: "1) preparing students to function in an adult society, in which they will encounter and interact with people from many different backgrounds, 2) making students more tolerant and understanding of others throughout their lives, and 3) eliminating de facto segregation."[36] The court ruled that reducing racial isolation resulting from de facto segregation can constitute a compelling government interest justifying racial classifications.

Although the district court relied on *Hopwood* in striking down the program, the appellate court explicitly declined to follow *Hopwood*, and expressed concern as to whether *Hopwood* is good law. The diversity interest in the higher education context is quite similar to the rationale of reducing racial isolation in the elementary and secondary school context. As a result, *Brewer* is instructive and provides support to proponents of the diversity rationale in the higher education context.

The First Circuit, in *Wessman* v. *Gittens*, discussed efforts to portray the diversity rationale dead, noting: "We think that any such consensus [that diversity is dead] is more apparent than real."[37] *Wessman* was not a higher education case, but, rather, involved race-conscious admissions practices at three Boston public schools. The court explicitly declined to declare one way or the other that *Bakke's* diversity rationale remains good law. Instead, the court noted that "we assume *arguendo*—but we do not decide that some iterations of diversity might be sufficiently compelling in specific circumstances, to justify race-conscious actions."[38] The Fourth Circuit on two occasions, both involving the use of race-conscious policies in the elementary and secondary level, has also explicitly declined to pass judgment on the continuing vitality of *Bakke*.[39] There is a case pending in the United States District Court for the District of Maryland involving a constitutional challenge to the race-conscious admissions program at the

---

[35] 212 F.3d 738 (2nd Cir. 2000).
[36] Id. at 745.
[37] 160 F.3d 790, 795 (1st Cir. 1998).
[38] Id. at 797.
[39] *See Eisenberg* v. *Montgomery County Public Schools*, 197 F.3d 123 (4th Cir. 1999*); Tuttle* v. *Arlington County School Board*, 195 F.3d 698 (4th Cir. 1999).

University of Maryland Medical School.[40] No dispositive ruling has been issued in this case.

The uncertain status of the diversity rationale is perhaps best illustrated by comparing the two pending Michigan higher education cases that involve the law school and the undergraduate university. Both suits allege that the university's race-conscious admissions programs are unconstitutional. In both cases, the university acknowledged the use of race-conscious programs, noting that race is one of a host of factors (e.g., geography, socioeconomic status, alumni status, quality of high school, and quality of high school courses) taken into account in an individualized decision making process.

The university contended that both programs were constitutional under the diversity rationale set forth in *Bakke*. The university developed an extensive record of social science, demographic, and other testimony to support the diversity rationale. For instance, experts testified about the educational benefits of diversity, noting studies demonstrating that students who experienced the most diversity in classroom settings and in other less formal interactions had the most productive learning experiences. These benefits affect minority and non-minority students alike.

In the undergraduate case, the district court ruled that *Bakke* was controlling and stood for the proposition that diversity is a compelling interest justifying the use of a race-conscious remedy. The judge in the undergraduate case explicitly disagreed with the rationale in *Hopwood*, and concluded that the university had met its burden of demonstrating that the educational benefits flowing from a racially and ethnically diverse student body constitute a compelling interest justifying the use of race-conscious admissions practices. The judge further found that the current admission policy was narrowly tailored in that it did not use quotas, ensured individualized consideration, and allowed race to be used as a "plus" in the manner outlined by Justice Powell.[41]

Approximately three months later, the judge in the law school case reached the opposite conclusion. He ruled that diversity is not a compelling state interest and was not recognized as such by a majority of the Supreme Court in *Bakke*. He further ruled that even if diversity was recognized as a compelling state interest, the program is unconstitutional because it is not narrowly tailored and also violates Title VI. The judge found that the law school's current admissions policy was "practically indistinguishable from a quota system."[42] The judge enjoined the law school from taking race into account in its admissions process, effective immediately. The U.S. Court of Appeals for the Sixth Circuit shortly thereafter issued a stay of this injunction pending the appeal, noting that the district court's

---

[40] *Farmer* v. *Ramsay*, 98–1585 (D.Md. 1998).
[41] *Gratz* v. *Bollinger*, 122 F. Supp. at 816–833.
[42] *Grutter* v. *Bollinger*, 137 F. Supp. 2d at 851.

reading of *Bakke* "diverges from other interpretations of the case including that in [the Michigan undergraduate case] currently pending on appeal."[43]

The two district court opinions are irreconcilable, and will have to be resolved by the Sixth Circuit and, perhaps ultimately, by the Supreme Court. It is impossible to predict the outcome of the Michigan or other cases, but contrary to popular belief, there is substantial case support for the proposition that diversity is a compelling interest in the higher education context.

3. Narrow Tailoring

Even if the Supreme Court ultimately decides that diversity is a compelling interest justifying the use of race-conscious programs, this is only half the battle. A university must also show that its program is narrowly tailored. In fashioning a narrowly tailored program within the context of higher education, it is useful to begin with Justice Powell's analysis in *Bakke*.

Justice Powell made reference to the so-called "Harvard Plan" as a program that would withstand constitutional scrutiny.[44] Rather than using racial set-asides, setting quotas, or considering the application of underrepresented minority students separately, the Harvard Plan considers all applicants in one pool. Each applicant is compared with all other candidates, and there is individualized consideration of each candidate. Equally important, a narrowly tailored plan allows for consideration of race and ethnicity, as well as a host of other factors, such as socioeconomic status, geography, a history of overcoming disadvantage, or alumni status, even if not all factors are accorded the same weight. Race in this setting is a plus, just as geography or some other characteristic. But unlike a set-aside or quota arrangement, it does not insulate the applicant from comparison with other candidates. Justice Powell acknowledged that this "plus" may mean that in certain circumstances, race tips the balance, "just as life spent on a farm may tip the balance in other candidates' cases."[45]

Extrapolating from Justice Powell's opinion and subsequent education cases, it is perhaps easier to identify what is *not* a narrowly tailored program. *Bakke* itself involved a racial set-aside for underrepresented minorities, so that these applicants were not considered with the entire pool. The program at issue in *Hopwood* involved African Americans and Mexican Americans being treated differently from all other applicants. The applications were put into separate stacks. The ranges that were used to place them into the three admissions categories (presumptive admit, presumptive reject, discretionary zone) were different, and a separate minority committee reviewed the applications of African Ameri-

---

[43] 247 F. 3d 631 (6th Cir. 2001).
[44] 438 U.S. at 315–16.
[45] Id.

cans and Mexican Americans who were in the discretionary zone. Separate processes with different standards will not withstand the narrow tailoring test. The program at issue in the University of Michigan undergraduate case involved the assignment of numerical points for various factors, such as grades, test scores, curriculum, quality of school, geography, race or ethnicity, outstanding essay, socioeconomic status, unique ability (such as an athlete or a musician), and alumni status. The school used a 150-point system and, in any given case, any one of the aforementioned factors could tip the balance in an applicant's favor. All applicants are considered in one pool, and there is no set-aside for underrepresented minorities and no quota. In 1999 and 2000, a system was added whereby certain applicants, including but not limited to underrepresented minorities, could be "flagged," which meant that they were kept in the review pool, but were not given additional points. The district court ruled that this program met the narrow tailoring standard set forth in *Bakke*.

The Michigan law school case was similar to the undergraduate case, but in a sense there was even more individualized consideration given to the applications because the applicant pool is much smaller. Nonetheless, the district judge held that this program was *not* narrowly tailored. He found "amorphous" the law school's contention that it uses race to the extent necessary to achieve a critical mass of underrepresented minorities. Although the law school did not set a numerical goal, the district judge, as noted earlier, found the program "practically indistinguishable" from a quota system.

Looking at these two cases, as well as other cases in similar contexts, it is quite difficult to say with certainty what will constitute a narrowly tailored program. However, programs that have been deemed narrowly tailored at a minimum tend to have the following characteristics:

- **Exploration of race-neutral alternatives**—At a minimum, a university should seriously explore whether there are race-neutral alternatives to achieving the same end of a diverse student body. In the Michigan undergraduate case, for instance, the university put forth testimony about prior futile efforts to expand diversity through aggressive outreach and recruitment. The university also presented expert testimony discussing the likely effects that prohibiting the consideration of race and ethnicity would have on the enrollment of underrepresented minorities. It is not necessary that a university implement race-neutral alternatives before moving to race-conscious measures.
- **No quotas or set asides**—All applicants must be considered in one pool. To the extent that there is a separate process, or separate standards for underrepresented minorities, or quotas for minority candidates, the program in all likelihood will not withstand narrow tailoring under the diversity rationale.
- **Race or ethnicity as *one* of a number of factors**—Race should be one of a wide panoply of factors taken into account, and there should be individualized consideration of all applicants.

4. Other Recent Activity in the Affirmative Action Context

Those claiming that affirmative action is dead ignore not only the aforementioned case law but also other significant additional developments both within and outside the courtroom. For instance, *Adarand Constructors, Inc.* v. *Pena* is an affirmative action case in the federal contracting context in which the Supreme Court in 1995 applied strict scrutiny to federal contracting for the first time.[46] The diversity rationale was not at issue in this case. Many experts believed that *Adarand* would become another nail in the affirmative action coffin, and that strict scrutiny would prove "fatal in fact," meaning that the new legal hurdle would be insurmountable in practice. To the contrary, the *Adarand* case itself was remanded to the lower court to determine whether the program could withstand strict scrutiny. Last year, the U.S. Court of Appeals for the Tenth Circuit ruled that the program satisfied strict scrutiny, and was constitutional.[47] The Supreme Court has agreed to hear this case again during the upcoming 2001–2002 term.

On a slightly different front, an author recently conducted a survey of constitutional challenges to 49 remedial workplace affirmative action plans.[48] These plans arose out of employment disputes wherein race-conscious practices were put into place to remedy the present effects of past discrimination. Approximately 40 percent of the plans withstood strict scrutiny, leading the author to conclude that 1) carefully crafted affirmative action plans can and do withstand strict scrutiny, and 2) commentators' depiction of affirmative action as dead is at odds with the empirical evidence.

On Capitol Hill, efforts to eliminate affirmative action have been defeated. For instance, in the United States Senate, a bipartisan majority in 1998 soundly defeated (58–37) a proposal to ban the use of affirmative action in federal contracting. Around the same time, the House of Representatives, by a bipartisan vote of 249–171, defeated a proposal to prohibit the receipt of federal funds by any public higher education institution that has affirmative action programs in place. Voter referenda in California and Washington have dealt serious blows to efforts by public entities, including public universities, to put race-conscious programs in place. Voters in Houston, Texas, however, defeated a similar measure that would have banned the use of affirmative action in city contracting.

Overall, proponents and opponents of affirmative action outside the higher education context have both scored major victories in recent years.

---

[46] 515 U.S. 200 (1995).

[47] 228 F.3d 1147 (10th Cir. 2000), cert. granted, 69 U.S.L.W. 3670 (2001).

[48] Day, J. 2001. Retelling the Story of Affirmative Action: Reflections on a Decade of Federal Jurisprudence in the Public Workplace. *California Law Review*, 89:59.

C. What Does All This Mean?

The upshot of the above analysis is that the future of affirmative action in higher education appears to hinge in large measure on whether the Supreme Court will declare once and for all that diversity is a compelling state interest justifying the use of narrowly tailored, race-conscious practices. In the meantime, many health professions schools are asking a simple but difficult question: can we put into place or continue to employ narrowly tailored, race-conscious admissions programs?

For public health professions schools in Texas, Mississippi, and Louisiana, it is clear under *Hopwood* that race-conscious programs cannot be put into place unless the institution can demonstrate that the race-conscious program is necessary to remedy the present effects of past discrimination by the institution. As noted earlier, although a state has a duty to eliminate every vestige of racial segregation and discrimination in education, establishing the remedial justification in the higher education context has proven in practice to be exceedingly difficult. The Fifth Circuit decision in *Hopwood* was based on the Constitution, which raises the issue of whether it applies to private institutions. As noted earlier, private universities who receive federal financial assistance are subject to the anti-discrimination provisions of Title VI. In the affirmative action higher education context, the applicable standards under Title VI and the Fourteenth Amendment are co-extensive. The upshot is that private universities in the Fifth Circuit that receive federal financial assistance and have race-conscious admissions programs in place are vulnerable under Title VI.

Public universities in states such as California, Washington, and Florida, where the use of race-conscious remedies has been limited by voter referenda or action of state officials, are also prohibited from employing race-conscious admissions and related programs, although private universities in these states do not face the same limitation. A federal court in Georgia has struck down the race-conscious admissions program at the University of Georgia, and that case is on appeal. The district court order in the Michigan law school case has been stayed pending appeal, so that the law school can continue to employ its race-conscious admissions program. Health professions schools in the remainder of the country can implement, or continue to implement, race-conscious programs. Given the conflicting interpretations of what *Bakke* means, it is becoming increasingly likely that the Supreme Court will have to confront this question in the near future.

PART THREE: WHAT THE HEALTH PROFESSIONS CAN DO TO ASSIST IN THE EFFORT TO ENHANCE DIVERSITY IN THE HEALTH PROFESSIONS

There are a host of measures that the health professions can put into place to address the critical need for a diverse health profession, and the American Association of Medical Colleges has led the effort to ensure that enhancing diversity remains a top priority. This section outlines various measures, many of which have already been implemented, to enhance diversity.

A. Build the Case for Diversity as a Compelling Interest

Most, if not all, of the current legal marbles are in the diversity basket. As a result, it is extremely important to develop an extensive record supporting the benefits of diversity. Conclusory statements of university officials are not enough. The University of Michigan, in both the undergraduate and the law school cases, has mounted perhaps the most aggressive and comprehensive case supporting diversity in the history of higher education. Any health professions institution seeking to implement narrowly tailored, race-conscious programs using a diversity rationale should examine carefully the record that has been developed in the Michigan case. The university presented social science research documenting the educational benefits of diversity—how the educational experience for students of all races is enriched by having a racially and ethnically diverse class. Additional evidence was presented about the history of segregation in Detroit. One effect of this sad legacy of segregation is that substantial numbers of incoming students at Michigan have had little or no contact with people of different races.[49] This lack of prior contact with people of different backgrounds increases the importance of ensuring diversity in the classroom.

The health professions, foundations, and others can support further research documenting the educational benefits of having a diverse student body. For example, it would be useful to test the hypothesis that a diverse class contributes to the development of a more culturally competent health care profession. For many, the notion that racial and ethnic diversity is critical and compelling is axiomatic; however, it is necessary to build the case using a wide range of data, and institutions should not wait until a lawsuit is filed to compile the information.

B. Examine Whether a Remedial Justification Exists for Race-Conscious Practices

Although it has become considerably more difficult recently in the higher education context to put forth a remedial justification for race-conscious prac-

---

[49] For an example of the types of research that are critical to building the case for diversity as a compelling interest, see Bowen, W. and Bok, D. 1998. *The Shape of the River*. Princeton, NJ: Princeton University Press.

tices, this does not mean that institutions should ignore this interest. It is important and, admittedly, difficult for institutions to examine whether they bear any responsibility for the vestiges of segregation and discrimination in education. Such a review is critical. Even the court in *Hopwood* acknowledged that race-conscious practices can be used to eliminate the present effects of past discrimination. Thus, institutions should examine the extent to which they were participants, active or passive, in discriminatory practices that continue to have present-day effects.

C. Explore New Compelling Interests That May Justify Race-Conscious Practices

In the affirmative action debate, the compelling interest discussion has focused almost exclusively on the remedial and diversity justifications. It is useful to examine other potential justifications for race-conscious programs that may rise to the level of a compelling interest. Specifically, health professions should explore the potential viability of what I call the "operational need" justification. In *Bakke*, one of the justifications put forth by the state to justify its admission program was the need to increase the number of physicians who will practice in communities currently underserved. In this context, Justice Powell acknowledged "that in some situations a state's interest in facilitating the health care of its citizens is sufficiently compelling to support the use of a [race-conscious] classification."[50] In other words, Justice Powell did not reject this interest out of hand, although he did find that the state had not presented sufficient evidence to support this claim.

In the almost quarter century since *Bakke*, a growing body of research indicates that minority physicians are much more likely to practice in areas with fewer primary care physicians per capita and in poorer areas as compared with white physicians.[51] African-American physicians are also more likely to serve African-American patients, and Latino physicians are more likely to serve Latino patients, according to a number of studies.[52]

As discussed earlier, the recent census data confirms that America has become an even greater melting pot. Communities across the country must address how to ensure that vulnerable populations, which are increasing in numbers in both rural and urban America, can access critical health care. The emerging body of research that minority physicians are more likely to serve poor and/or minority

---

[50] 438 U.S. at 310–11.

[51] See footnote 8 for reference to various studies addressing this issue.

[52] In one study, for instance, African-American patients made up 56% of the patient populations of African-American physicians, as compared to 8–14% of the caseload of other physicians. Latino patients made up 30% of the caseload of Latino physicians, and 6–9% of the caseloads of non-Latino physicians. Keith et al., 1985. Effects of Affirmative Action in Medical Schools: A Study of the Class of 1975. *New England Journal of Medicine*, 313:1519–1525.

populations, coupled with the substantial growth in minority populations, potentially supports the proposition that 1) a state has a compelling interest in ensuring access to health for the entire community; and 2) narrowly tailored, race-conscious admissions practices will further that compelling interest. More research must be done before a conclusive determination can be made as to whether the evidence supports the hypothesis. However, it is an issue well worth exploring.

Courts have recognized operational need as a compelling interest in the context of police and corrections.[53] In so doing, courts have permitted race-conscious hiring practices. A rationale underlying these decisions is that in racially and ethnically diverse communities, maintaining a diverse police force or corrections department is critically important to carrying out the core mission of the department. In light of demographic trends and research discussed earlier regarding practice trends of minority physicians, the health professions should examine whether a similar argument can be made in the health context.

D. Conduct Self Assessments

For almost a quarter century, higher education institutions across the country have relied on Justice Powell's opinion in *Bakke* and have put into place race-conscious programs. It is very useful for institutions to examine these programs to ensure that they take race and ethnicity into account in a manner that would withstand judicial scrutiny. Institutions should not wait to be sued before conducting a self assessment in which they ask a host of questions, including but not limited to 1) what is the compelling interest(s) justifying the use of race-conscious programs; 2) what evidence has been marshaled to support the compelling interest(s); 3) are all applicants considered in one pool by the same committee; 4) is race one of a host of factors taken into account; 5) does the program ensure that there are no quotas or set-asides for minority applicants; 6) have race-neutral interventions been considered and/or implemented and, if so, has their success been measured, and 7) is a mechanism in place for periodic review of the program? This is by no means an exhaustive list of questions, but it would be useful for institutions that have race-conscious programs currently in place to review them. While such a self-assessment does not guarantee that litigation can be avoided, it will assist in placing an institution in the best posture to defend against potential litigation.

E. Consider Race-Neutral Alternatives
That Can Increase Diversity

There are a number of race-neutral interventions that health professions schools should consider as they seek to increase racial and ethnic diversity.

---

[53] See *Wittmer* v. *Peters*, 87 F.3d 916, 919 (7th Cir. 1996)(listing cases in law enforcement and corrections).

1. Reduced Reliance on Test Scores

A number of experts have questioned the efficacy of relying on test scores in making admissions decisions.[54] They argue that the SAT and other similar tests predict no more than performance during the first year of school, and are more related to the student's family income than they are to success in school. For example, Richard Atkinson, President of the University of California system, recently proposed dropping the requirement that applicants take the SAT, the most widely used college entrance exam. In his opinion, the SAT is "distorting educational priorities" and he proposed replacing it with a less quantitative, more holistic set of criteria.[55]

This is not the first time that reliance on test scores has been called into question, but it has added energy to the debate about the role of test scores in the admissions process. Heavy reliance on test scores in the admissions process has an adverse impact on underrepresented minorities, as well as poor people of all races. As a result, many higher education institutions have begun to examine whether to reduce or eliminate reliance on standardized tests in the admissions process. As part of the self-assessment recommended above, it may be useful for health professions schools to determine the extent of current reliance on test scores, and consider the option of reduced or no reliance on such scores. For example, Texas A&M's medical school in 1998 dropped the use of the Medical College Admissions Test (MCAT) for students who successfully completed special undergraduate premedical programs.[56]

2. Class-Conscious, Rather than Race-Conscious Affirmative Action

For years, a number of commentators have called for replacing race-conscious programs with class-conscious measures.[57] These commentators contend that race-conscious affirmative action is simultaneously over- and under-inclusive, while class-conscious affirmative action, which would capture people from economically disadvantaged backgrounds—minority and non-minority alike—is more fair and would promote diversity.

Many universities employ both race-conscious and class-conscious measures. The University of Michigan undergraduate admissions process provides a "plus" for applicants who are economically disadvantaged, as well as for applicants who are underrepresented minorities. The university presented expert testi-

---

[54] See, e.g., Lemann, N. 1999. The Big Test: The Secret History of American Meritocracy. Course J., and Trusheim, D. 1988. The Case Against the SAT.

[55] Selingo, J., & Brainard J. 2001, March 2. Call to Eliminate SAT Requirement May Reshape Debate on Affirmative Action. 2001 *The Chronicle of Higher Education*, p. A.21.

[56] Roser, M.A., 1998, February 4. To Draw Minorities, A&M Drops Test. *Austin American Statesman*, p. A.1.

[57] See, e.g., Kahlenberg, R. 1995, April 3. Class, not Race: An Affirmative Action That Works, *The New Republic*, p. 21.

mony that eliminating race as a factor in the admissions process would result in a substantial reduction in the number of underrepresented minorities in the class. While strongly supporting the use of economic disadvantage as one way to promote viewpoint diversity and thereby enhance the educational experience for all, the University of Michigan and others have raised serious concerns about the overall efficacy of eliminating race as a factor in the admissions process.

3. "Ten Percent" and Other Similar Measures

Following the *Hopwood* decision, enrollment of African-Americans and Latinos in the University of Texas higher education system plummeted. In response, Texas adopted the so-called "10 percent solution," which guarantees a seat at the flagship Texas public colleges and universities to all students from all high schools in the state who graduate in the top 10 percent of their class.[58] Proponents of the plan argued that past success, and not test scores, was the best predictor of future success.

Since adoption of this plan, enrollment of African Americans and Latinos at the two flagship undergraduate universities—University of Texas, Austin and Texas A&M—increased. Enrollment of African Americans and Latinos at University of Texas, Austin returned to the pre-*Hopwood* level by the second year, while enrollment at Texas A&M increased, although not to the pre-*Hopwood* levels. Moreover, the pre-*Hopwood* levels were far lower than the actual percentages of African Americans and Latinos graduating from Texas high schools. For example, the pre-Hopwood enrollment level at the University of Texas, Austin was 3.2 percent African American and 15 percent Latino. African Americans represented 12 percent of Texas high school graduates and Latinos represented 29 percent.[59] These disparities prompted University of Texas Law Professor Gerald Torres, an architect of the Ten Percent Plan, to comment, "There is no reason for the pre-*Hopwood* number to be the baseline."

The geographic mix of the students also changed dramatically as a result of the implementation of the Ten Percent Plan. Previously, out of 1,500 public high schools statewide, 50 to 75 schools were providing 90 percent of the students admitted to University of Texas, Austin. These high schools lacked racial, geographic, and economic diversity. Given the Texas program's success in raising minority enrollment, California and Florida have implemented programs modeled after the Texas plan.

Many supporters of the Texas plan, including a number of architects of the plan itself, caution that it should not be interpreted as a substitute for race-conscious affirmative action. For people such as Professor Gerald Torres of the

---

[58] For a detailed discussion of the Texas plan, see Hair, P. March 2001. *Louder than Words: Lawyers, Communities and the Struggle for Justice*, chapter 1.

[59] Id. at p. 30, fn 57.

University of Texas Law School, the plan was the only alternative in a state where race-conscious policies were foreclosed.

A number of concerns have been raised about the Ten Percent Plan and similar efforts elsewhere.[60] It has no application to graduate programs, which is of obvious relevance to the health professions.[61] Critics note that its success in increasing enrollment of underrepresented minorities depends largely upon the maintenance of a segregated system of public education. In addition, it penalizes students at the state's more demanding high schools who may not be in the top 10 percent, and it sets up for potential failure students from other schools who may be unable to handle the rigors of academics in selective institutions of higher learning. As a result, undergraduate institutions such as Michigan have considered and rejected such proposals as inadequate substitutes for the current race-conscious admissions process.

F. Aggressive Outreach, Mentoring, and Retention

Many health professions schools have undertaken aggressive efforts to recruit underrepresented minorities, and these outreach efforts, while usually not a panacea in and of themselves, can be helpful in increasing the pool of underrepresented minorities.[62] In performing the self-assessment described earlier, it would be useful to look at where recruitment efforts are focused. For instance, have meaningful connections been established with historically black colleges and universities, as well as with other institutions that have sizeable minority enrollments? What connections are being made with the pipeline of elementary and secondary students? Are mentoring programs in place to provide role models to high school and college students who may be considering a career in the health professions? In addition to recruitment, it is important to have retention programs in place that will provide the necessary nurturing and guidance for students who are enrolled.

Pipeline programs are a critical intervention that, in the long term, can lead to the expansion of the overall pool of underrepresented minorities seeking to enter the health profession. For those institutions that participate in or fund such programs, it is important to be mindful of the need not to limit participation by race or ethnicity. Public institutions, as well as private institutions that receive federal dollars, are vulnerable to legal challenge under the Constitution and/or Title VI of the Civil Rights Act of 1964 if they limit enrollment by race or eth-

---

[60] See, e.g., Rhodes, F. 1999, December 24. College by the numbers. *The New York Times*, p. A.29.

[61] Enrollment of underrepresented minorities in graduate programs in Texas remains quite low. In the University of Texas Law School, for instance, nine African Americans enrolled in the first-year class in 1999, compared with 31 in 1996.

[62] For a description of 26 pipeline programs for disadvantaged youth, see Thompson, W. and Denk, J. 1999. Educational programs to strengthen the medical school pipeline, Minority theme issue. Vol. 74, No. 4 (can be ordered from AAMC).

nicity. An alternative approach would be to target social and economically disadvantaged students for participation in the program. This race-neutral approach has been employed with some success in a number of contexts.

G. Revise AAMC Definition of
Underrepresented Minority

The AAMC currently defines underrepresented minority as African American, Native American, Mexican American, and non-Mainland Puerto Rican. Many institutions follow the lead of the AAMC in defining under-represented minority this way. AAMC programs targeted to underrepresented minorities frequently limit eligibility to African Americans, Native Americans, Mexican Americans, and non-Mainland Puerto Ricans. This definition appears to reflect an effort to capture minority groups that historically had been victims of discrimination in America. If the remedial rationale were the only compelling interest justifying the use of race-conscious practices, then the definition perhaps would remain more viable.

However, the diversity rationale embodies a different construct, namely that the educational experience for all students is enhanced when there are people from different geographic areas; people from low-income, middle-class and wealthy backgrounds; and people of different races and ethnicities. Under the diversity logic, the current AAMC definition of underrepresented minority is unduly narrow. In addition, as the nation becomes more heterogeneous, and the health needs of underserved minority populations grow, it is important for health professions schools to respond to changing demographics and emerging needs.

For instance, the Hmong population continues to grow in both Wisconsin and Minnesota. As a result, a health professions school in these states may conclude that it is important to recruit from within the Hmong community, so that an applicant of Hmong descent may receive a "plus" in a *Bakke*-type plan that used race as one of a number of factors in the decisionmaking process. The AAMC definition does not prevent a school from considering taking a person's Hmong origin into account, but it does not acknowledge the value of doing so. In addition, a Hmong American, or a Dominican American from New York City would be ineligible to apply for AAMC programs that are limited to underrepresented minorities, because the current definition excludes them. A broader definition of underrepresented minority would reflect the changing demographic landscape, as well the educational underpinnings of the diversity rationale.

H. Participate in Public Education Campaigns About
Affirmative Action and the Benefits of Diversity in the
Health Professions

The debate about the efficacy and legality of race-conscious practices in education and elsewhere is being conducted both within the courtroom and within the court of public opinion. The bulk of this paper has focused on what is taking place within the courtrooms. However, a considerable amount of activity is occurring elsewhere. Opponents of race-conscious practices mounted successful campaigns in California and Washington that resulted in the passage of voter referenda that, among other things, prohibited the use of race as a factor in admissions in public universities. Voters in Houston, Texas, in 1997 defeated a similar initiative that would have banned the use of race in government contracting.

From these and other experiences, educators who support affirmative action are beginning to appreciate the importance of demystifying the admissions process in higher education for the public at large. This is premised on the belief that affirmative action means different things to different people. Once citizens understand what it really means in practice, they are more likely to be supportive of race-conscious practices.

Thus, for example, opponents of affirmative action at the University of Michigan frequently refer to this and race-conscious admissions programs as "race-based" programs or "racial preferences." Proponents of affirmative action point out that the use of these imprecise terms ignores the fact that race is one of a number of factors taken into account. The programs are seldom, if ever, referred to as "geography-based" or "legacy-based," even though geography or alumni status of family members are also factors taken into account at Michigan, and, like race, may tip the balance in a given case. Educating the public about what affirmative action actually means in practice, what affirmative action is *not*, and why narrowly tailored, race-conscious programs are important is crucial to maintaining public support for race-conscious programs.

Enlisting the business community in building a business case for diversity in the health professions can also be useful. In the Michigan undergraduate case, for instance, a number of Fortune 500 companies filed an amicus brief supporting the Michigan admissions program, and its use of race as a matter of business necessity. These companies argued that if universities were not permitted to consider all qualities of each applicant, including race or ethnicity, universities will be "hampered in [the] search for students with the most promise, and graduates will be less likely to possess the skills, experience, and wisdom necessary to work with and serve the diverse populations of the United States and the global community.[63] The health professions can certainly put forth a similar case.

CONCLUSION

It has been almost a quarter century since the Supreme Court in *Bakke* last addressed the constitutionality of race-conscious admissions practices in the higher education context. For many, *Bakke* is to higher education what *Miranda* is to criminal justice and *Roe* v. *Wade* is to reproductive freedom. It has become

---

[63] *Gratz* v. *Bollinger*, Brief of amicus Steelcase, Inc. et al., at p. 7.

part of the American fabric in the sense that institutions and individuals have placed considerable reliance upon *Bakke* in crafting important policies and practices. Like *Miranda* and *Roe*, *Bakke* continues to be the focus of widespread attention, as courts, legal experts, politicians, practitioners, and the public at large debate its meaning and continued vitality. Like *Miranda* and *Roe*, *Bakke* generates passion on both sides of the debate that is seldom paralleled elsewhere.

Many have attempted to paint race-conscious programs in higher education as dead, citing primarily *Hopwood* and Proposition 209 in California. While those two events were certainly noteworthy, the totality of the evidence reveals a quite mixed scorecard on affirmative action in higher education. Those describing affirmative action as dead are simply ignoring significant developments to the contrary. In fact, colleges and universities in the vast majority of the states continue to maintain race-conscious admissions programs in reliance on *Bakke*.

Given the conflicting and seemingly irreconcilable decisions issued by lower courts in recent years, it has become increasingly likely that the Supreme Court in the near future will revisit Bakke and determine once and for all whether diversity is a compelling interest justifying the use of narrowly tailored, race-conscious admissions practices in higher education. In 2001, the Supreme Court has declined to hear two higher education affirmative action cases (*Hopwood* and *Smith* v. *University of Washington*). Nonetheless, as the Michigan and other cases weave their way through the appellate process, it will become more difficult for the court to avoid the issue.

In the meantime, there is a considerable amount that the health professions can do to assist in the effort to promote their own diversity. Successful implementation of measures to enhance diversity will contribute substantially to the overall effort to eliminate racial and ethnic disparities in health.

College Admission Policies and the Educational Pipeline: Implications for Medical and Health Professions[*]

Marta Tienda
Princeton University

INTRODUCTION

Higher education faces a new dilemma in its quest to achieve a diverse student body. On the one hand, rapid growth of minority college-age youth increases the base from which to draw talented students and further expand educational opportunity for historically excluded groups. On the other hand, states with large shares of black, Hispanic, Asian, and Native American youth have led the charge to eliminate race-sensitive college admission policies adopted during the 1960s and upheld by the Supreme Court in the well-publicized suit against the University of California.[1] In reaching an opinion, Justice Powell reasoned that, "The achievement of a diverse student body . . . clearly is a constitutionally permissible goal for an institution of higher education." Justice Blackmun was even more forceful about the need for race-sensitive admission criteria in asserting that, "In order to get beyond racism, we must first take race into account." Since 1978 the *Bakke* ruling has been used to support policies at selective colleges and universities that consider race or national origin in admission decisions. Beginning in 1996 several states either banned or dismantled their affirmative action policies, and several others are reconsidering the treatment of race and national origin in their admission criteria to public colleges and universities.[2]

[*] This research was supported by grants from the Mellon Foundation and the Ford Foundation. Institutional and computational support is provided from center grants to the Office of Population Research (5R01-HD-35301 and P30HD32030 from the National Institute of Child Health and Human Development.
[1] *Regents of the University of California* v. *Bakke*, 438 U.S. 265 (1978).
[2] Although most discussions of race-sensitive admission policies use the term affirmative action, the lack of coherent definition and implementation across campuses renders it almost useless

In hindsight, the affirmative action backlash in college admissions can be traced to the confluence of two master trends beginning in the mid-1970s, namely rising wealth and income inequality and rapid ethno-racial diversification of the school-age population (Tienda, 1999; Danziger & Gottschalk, 1995; Levy, 1998). Before 1950, nonwhites comprised barely 14 percent of the college-age population and this share rose only two percentage points during the 50s and 60s (Tienda, Lloyd, & Zajacova, 2000).[3] Owing partly to the increasing volume of immigration after 1970, partly to higher fertility of minority and especially recent immigrant women, and partly to improved methods used to enumerate minority groups, the diversification of the college-age population accelerated during the 70s. By 1980, combined, Blacks, Hispanics, Asians, and Native Americans comprised almost one-fourth of the college-age population. A decade later the minority share of college-age youth climbed to 30 percent and an additional 3 percentage points by the year 2000 (Tienda, Lloyd, & Zajacova, 2000). During the last half-century, Hispanics and Asians accounted for the lion's share of the minority population growth, rising from less than 2 percent combined, to 15 and 4 percent, respectively. The black share of college-age youth rose only slightly over the same period, from approximately 12 percent in 1950 to 15 percent in 2000.

That changes in the ethno-racial composition of the college-age population disproportionately affect a few large states, notably the primary immigrant-receiving states, helps us understand the origin of recent initiatives to eliminate race-sensitive college admission policies. California, Texas, and Florida have witnessed tremendous absolute and relative growth in their minority populations largely due to immigration. The 2000 census reveals that Blacks, Hispanics, Asians, and Native Americans combined account for slightly over half of California's total population, and are decisive majorities in many counties and cities throughout the state. Nearly half (45 percent) of Texans self-identified as minority in the most recent census, and approximately one in three New York, New Jersey, and Florida residents did so (Tienda, Lloyd, & Zajacova, 2000). Given the profound demographic changes experienced by California and Texas since 1970, it is hardly a coincidence that the charge to end affirmative action in college admissions originated in these states.[4]

---

from an analytical standpoint. However, in keeping with the current discussion, my use of the term affirmative action refers to myriad policies that permit consideration of race as one of many factors used in college admission decisions.

[3] For purposes of this discussion we define the college-age population as persons ages 19–24.

[4] Several other states, including Florida, Georgia, and Washington, have either banned affirmative action in college decisions and/or proposed new guidelines for admitting students. Officials in Pennsylvania's state university system have been discussing a 15-percent class rank admission criterion, but are not prepared to end affirmative action policies yet. Recently the University of Michigan's use of minority status in admission decisions was challenged in two separate lawsuits, with different rulings for the law school and the undergraduate school.

These demographic trends acquire profound social (and now political) content when mapped against higher income and wealth inequality that favored Whites and Asians over Blacks, Hispanics, and Native Americans in recent decades (Danziger & Gottschalk, 1995; Levy, 1998). Moreover, since 1980, the beneficiaries of growing inequality intensified their competition for places at selective four-year colleges and universities (Reich, 2000). As social and political commitment to affirmative action in higher education wanes and alternative admission criteria are hastily put in place, it is crucial to monitor their consequences in maintaining a diverse pipeline, for this will determine the future enrollments in medical and health professions that require post-baccalaureate training.

Because the most competitive post-secondary institutions are primary gateways to the top graduate, professional, and medical schools in the country, their ethno-racial make-up directly influences the pool of candidates eligible for advanced study in medicine and health sciences. According to the American Association of Medical Colleges (AAMC, 2000: p. 25), during the 1950s and 1960s, less than half of one percent of all medical school graduates were from underrepresented minority groups. The minority share of medical school graduates rose more than five-fold during the 1970s—from a trivial .4 percent to a meager 2.2 percent. Since 1980, the minority share of medical school graduates trebled, rising to 6.8 percent by 1998 (AAMC, 2000: p. 25). However, these increases are modest in absolute terms because they derive from a small base.

Although the minority share of medical school graduates is miniscule compared to the size of the college-age population, admission to the top medical schools remains extremely competitive and is becoming increasingly so. Recent actions to disallow consideration of race or national origin in college admission decisions in those states with the largest minority populations can reverse the trend toward greater representation of Blacks, Hispanics, and Native Americans in medical and health professions if declining minority admissions at the key feeder colleges and universities restrict the pool of admissible applicants. In this connection, it is noteworthy that between 1950 and 1998, the undergraduate institutions of Hispanic medical school graduates included 10 public universities located in Florida, Texas, and California—three states that have banned race-sensitive admission policies since 1996 (AAMC, 2000: p. 47).[5]

Large numbers of black medical school graduates have been trained in historically black colleges and universities, and this trend continues. However, the University of Michigan in Ann Arbor, currently the focus of two major lawsuits challenging the consideration of race and national origin in admission decisions, also is among the top 10 feeder institutions to medical school for African Ameri-

---

[5] If universities in Puerto Rico are excluded from the list, seven of the top eight public schools that feed minorities into medical schools are located in these states. Similarly, of the top 12 schools where Native American medical school graduates received their undergraduate degrees, four are public institutions located in states that recently outlawed consideration of race and national origin in college admission decisions (AAMC, 1998: p. 48).

cans (AAMC, 2000: p. 47). Like Hispanics, Asian medical school graduates also hail from California's leading colleges and universities (AAMC, 2000: p. 45). However, in contrast to Hispanics and Blacks, Asians are not underrepresented in higher education or medical schools relative to their population shares.[6] Accordingly, I focus my discussion of changing admission guidelines on the consequences for Blacks and Hispanics, and data permitting, Native Americans.

Anticipating declines in the diversity of their student bodies, several states have considered "percent plans" based on high school rank, to maintain the diversity of their campuses. In this chapter I discuss the consequences of banning affirmative action in college admission decisions and assess the likely success of percent plans in maintaining ethno-racial diversity of undergraduate institutions. First I provide a thumbnail sketch of minority participation in higher education to illustrate how the educational pipeline progressively restricts the pool of African-American and Hispanic students who enroll and graduate from postsecondary institutions. A selective overview of recent legal challenges to "affirmative action practices" serves as a backdrop for assessing the short-term consequences of changed admission guidelines in California and Texas. Both states banned the use of race-sensitive college admissions in 1996. Texas implemented an alternative admission plan immediately after banning affirmative action, which permits a short-term assessment of its diversity consequences on freshmen college enrollments at the two flagship universities. Because California's plan has only been implemented this year, enrollment trends for black, Hispanics, and Native American students from 1997 to 1999 portray the scenario in the absence of any deliberate strategy to diversify college campuses.[7] To conclude, I discuss the long-term prospects of percent plans in the context of a highly segregated society, highlighting the criticisms wagered by supporters and critics of the percent plans.

EDUCATIONAL PIPELINES:
TRENDS AND PROSPECTS

National data provide a useful point of departure for appraising educational pipelines in the context of growing population diversity. Currently, two longitudinal data sets permit a national comparison of race and ethnic differences in transitions from high school to college and professional or graduate school. One is the High School and Beyond (HS&B) survey, which interviewed representa-

---

[6] Geiser (1998) showed, moreover, that Asians are likely to be relatively unaffected, and probably stand to benefit from the alternative percent plans considered by the University of California system.

[7] It is noteworthy that very little discussion of preferential treatment has focused on Asian populations even though proportionate to their population size they are overrepresented in selective colleges and universities compared to whites. This circumstance reflects the presumption that Asians deserve their places in competitive colleges and universities because of their educational achievement and board test scores.

tive samples of sophomores and seniors in 1980. Because Hispanic dropout rates are quite high between 10th and 12th grade, I begin with the sophomore cohort so as not to bias downward estimates of transitions from high school to college. The National Education Longitudinal Survey (NELS) surveyed a cohort of 8th graders in 1988 and followed them through the transition to college, and like HS&B, includes oversamples of black, Hispanic, and Asian students. However, available interview data for the NELS cohort do not extend to college graduation and/or graduate training. Therefore, I use the HS&B survey to describe race and ethnic differences in the educational pipeline from high school through college, and to document group representation in selective and nonselective post-secondary institutions, post-graduate, and professional schools.

The tree charts depicted in Figure 1 portray the 1980 sophomores as they progress (or drop) through the educational pipeline. About 8 percent of the sophomore cohort is lost in the transition out of high school. Nationally, over three in five seniors from the 1982 class enrolled in a post-secondary institution. Of these, just over one in three attended a four-year institution; slightly less than one-third attended only two-year institutions like community colleges or technical schools, and 22 percent of seniors who enrolled in college attended both two and four-year institutions. Less than 10 percent of seniors who pursue post-secondary schooling do so in institutions that require less than two years of training.[8] However, enrollment in a post-secondary institution does not guarantee a diploma. Almost half of all seniors who enroll in a college, university, or technical school do not obtain any degree and only about one in three earns a bachelor's degree. Stated differently, only about one-quarter of the 1980 high school sophomore cohort remains in the educational pipeline and goes on to achieve a bachelor's degree or beyond.[9] However, these national averages conceal large disparities along race and ethnic lines.

Figure 2 depicts transitions through the educational pipeline for black, white, Hispanic, and Asian youth. High school graduation rates range from 94 percent for Asians compared to 90, 84, and 80 percent for Whites, Blacks, and Hispanics, respectively. This is the first constriction of the educational pipeline that sorts demographic groups into different educational trajectories. A second constriction occurs in the transition to college, where Hispanics and Blacks are sorted differently from Whites and Asians. Among graduating seniors, 42 percent of Hispanics enroll in post-secondary institutions compared to 48 percent of Blacks, 78 percent of Asians, and 62 percent of Whites.

---

[8] For example, this would include programs for manicurists or trade schools that focus on specific skills.

[9] This calculation pools BA and post-graduate holders and expresses them as a share of the initial 10th grade cohort rather than as a subset of those who sought any form of post-secondary schooling.

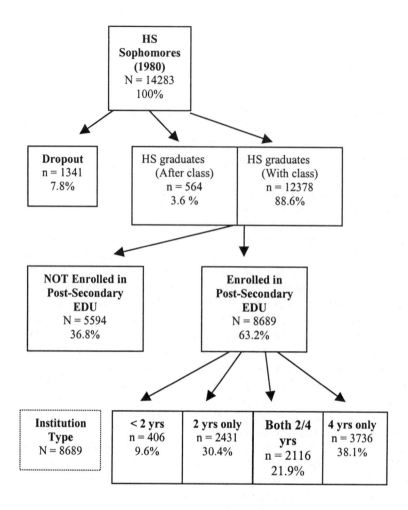

FIGURE 1: The Higher Education Pipeline. Unweighted counts and weighted percents.
SOURCE: High School and Beyond Longitudinal Survey (HS&B) (1980).

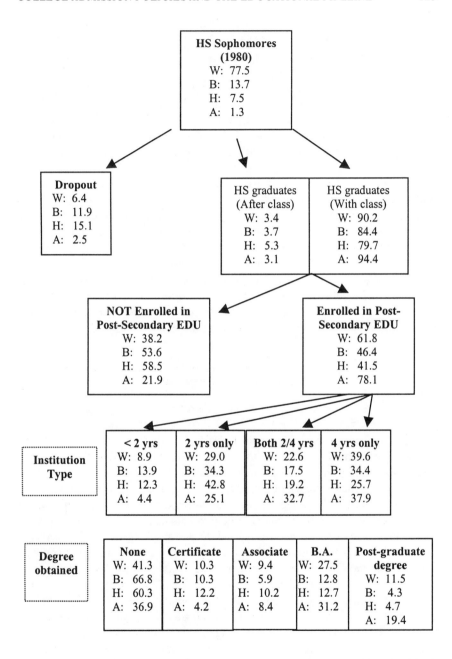

FIGURE 2: The Higher Education Pipeline, by Race. Unweighted counts (n = 14,283) and weighted percents.
SOURCE: High School and Beyond Longitudinal Survey (HS&B) (1980).

Nearly three in four Asians who matriculate in college attend a four-year institution at some point in their post-secondary education, while only 45 percent of Hispanic, 52 percent of black, and 62 percent of white college matriculants do so. Educational inequality along race and ethnic lines is further exacerbated because two-thirds of black post-secondary students do not obtain any degree, compared to 60 percent of Hispanic students, 41 percent of Whites, and only 37 percent of Asians. Consequently, only a small share of the initial cohort of Hispanic and black sophomores both attends and graduates from college—4 and 5 percent, respectively. This is but a trickle of the initial flow into the educational pipeline. It is from this very tiny pool that the medical and professional health sciences draw their candidates. Race and ethnic educational inequality is further accentuated because large numbers of Asian students not only graduate from college, but also pursue postgraduate degrees. Race-sensitive admission policies are about enrollment, but that is only part of the challenge of maintaining diversity in higher education. An equally formidable task is ensuring successful completion of college, and ideally, progression to graduate, medical, and professional schools. This task requires unplugging the pipeline at the elementary and middle school level so that minority students arrive in high school prepared to pursue college preparatory curricula. I return to this theme after illustrating the consequences of eliminating race-sensitive admission policies.

THE RISE AND FALL OF AFFIRMATIVE ACTION: *BAKKE* AND BEYOND

In the 1978 Supreme Court ruling against the University of California, Judge Powell was explicit in noting that race-sensitive admission criteria are permitted to harness the educational benefits that flow from an ethnically diverse student body and to reduce the historic deficit of traditionally disfavored minorities, but *not* for countering the effects of past societal discrimination or to increase the number of educated minorities in underserved communities. However, the extent to which and the ways in which race and ethnic origin figure into college admission decisions is largely unknown and probably highly variable across campuses. Consequently, and despite the longstanding controversy about the merits (and demerits) of considering race and national origin in college admissions, empirical evidence evaluating the costs and benefits of these practices for individuals, institutions, or the society at large is sparse.

Bowen and Bok's landmark study, *The Shape of the River* (1998), represents the first systematic effort to evaluate the advantages and disadvantages of race-sensitive policies from several vantage points based on the long-term experiences of graduates from several of the most selective universities and colleges.[10] Subsequently, Holzer and Newmark (2000) have surveyed empirical studies on the economics of affirmative action and they conclude that the benefits generally outweigh the costs.

The banning of affirmative action in Texas following the 1996 *Hopwood* ruling by the Fifth Circuit Court against the University of Texas Law School, and the passage of Proposition 209 by an overwhelming majority of California voters, not only challenged institutions of higher education to seek alternative strategies to diversify their campuses, but also politicized stakeholders at a time that minorities came to dominate their school-aged populations. Not surprisingly, several other states with large minority populations, notably Florida, Washington, and Georgia, followed suit. Prior to this time, colleges and universities exercised considerable flexibility in devising and implementing admission criteria that conformed to the guidelines of the *Bakke* decision.

The educational value of diversity that Judge Powell underscored in his opinion on the *Bakke* case rests at the core of ongoing litigation to reinstate the use of race-sensitive preferences in some form (*Gratz et al.* v. *Bollinger et al.,* 1999). Selective colleges and universities in states that have banned affirmative action run the risk of becoming dominated by majority white students, particularly those from privileged backgrounds who attend well-endowed secondary schools that offer rigorous college preparatory programs. In response, several states are experimenting with alternative and presumably "color-blind" criteria with potential to achieve the same ends as race-sensitive criteria. For example, because minority students are more likely than Whites to hail from lower socioeconomic origins, one proposed strategy involves targeting applicants based on social class. However, Kane (1998) and Karabel (1998) demonstrated that a class-based strategy is unlikely to succeed in maintaining ethno-racial or geographic diversity because the absolute numbers of nonminority youth in similar circumstances is larger. Therefore, in sheer probabilistic terms, poor Whites are more likely than Blacks, Hispanics, or Native Americans to be admitted to selective institutions. Moreover, because poor Whites generally are not as disadvantaged as poor minorities, their chances of being college-admissible are likely to be greater (Kane, 1998).

The criteria used to achieve diversity in a post-affirmative action period differ appreciably across states. For example, California has adopted a plan to admit the top 4 percent of graduating high school seniors to a university in the UC system. Texas admits the top 10 percent of graduating seniors to a public university of the students' choice. Florida has agreed to preferentially admit the top 20 percent of graduating seniors to a public college or university, but has not yet

---

[10] Several lawsuits initiated to end policies that permit the use of race or national origin in college decisions have prompted additional research to assess the consequences of affirmative action in higher education and more generally, the value of diversity on college campuses (see *Gratz et al.,* v. *Bollinger et al.,* 1999).

specified how the criteria will be implemented among the contending institutions. However, these deceptively simple percentage plans mask a greater complexity based on the diversity among schools and the level of segregation they represent (see Seligno, 2000). Moreover, each state will treat the standardized tests differently, some de-emphasizing the test altogether (e.g., Texas) and some emphasizing particular tests (e.g., California).[11]

California and Texas provide interesting case studies for a comparison of changed college admission policies because both states banned the use of race-sensitive criteria in the same year, yet one state implemented a percent plan shortly after the ban while the other delayed implementation until the current year. Specifically, in 1996 the Texas legislature passed House Bill 588, dubbed the Top 10% Law (or Plan), which guarantees that Texas high school graduates who rank in the top 10 percent of their senior class will be admitted to any state institution of higher learning. This eligibility applies to every public high school in the state with at least 10 seniors, and also to private institutions that implement formal ranking schemes (which not all do). In effect, this policy shifts the foundations of "merit" based on academic performance measures from standardized test scores to achieved grades. California has proposed a similar solution, except that admission is guaranteed only to the top four percent of each high school's graduating class. Furthermore, the California plan only guarantees a slot at a public university, not necessarily the student's top choice or admission to the flagship campuses.

That the Texas plan was implemented partially in 1997 (because the bill was passed while the admission process was already underway), and fully by 1998, permits a preliminary assessment of changes in the ethno-racial composition of the student body under the new plan. California's plan was implemented during the current (2000–2002) academic year; hence, it is too early to evaluate its impact on the diversity of its college campus. Nevertheless, because several years have elapsed since the passage of Proposition 209, it is possible to assess the consequences in the composition of entering classes of having no deliberate strategy to preserve ethno-racial campus diversity. For this comparison, I restrict my focus on the two flagship public universities in both states.[12]

This two-state comparison serves as a quasi-natural experiment that permits a preliminary answer to the following questions: First, how successful is the Texas Top 10 percent plan in maintaining the ethno-racial diversity of the entering classes relative to a regime that permits consideration of race or national origin in college admission decisions? Second, what are the consequences of eliminating race-sensitive admissions in the absence of a substitute plan? My

---

[11] In light of the mounting legal controversy about affirmative action, several states are considering eliminating the SAT. However, this has not been implemented.

[12] How the laws prohibiting consideration of race or national origin in college admissions will affect private universities is yet unclear, but presumably will be raised as a condition of receiving state funds.

tentative answers to these questions are based on recent changes in the ethno-racial composition of the entering cohorts during the 1990s, with a special focus on the period before and after the *Hopwood* decision (Texas) and Proposition 209 (California).

Texas

Texas was the first state to implement a percent plan based on class rankings, which essentially shifts the weight of admissibility from standardized test scores to performance-based measures that are known to be much better predictors of college success.[13] The impact on minority and nonminority populations of the new admission guidelines depends both on demographic and educational trends that shape the student pipelines into higher education and residential segregation patterns that underpin spatially distributed social and economic opportunities.

Two aspects of recent demographic trends in Texas are especially notewor-thy. First, during the last two decades minority population growth (due both to fertility and immigration) has exceeded that of native Whites. By 1996 roughly half of the Texas population under age 25 was Hispanic, black, or Asian (pre-dominantly the former). Murdock and associates (1998, Tables 10–12) estimated that if current demographic trends continue, in 30 years the state's elementary and secondary school-age population will be 70 percent minority, and the col-lege-age population will be 57 percent minority. Second, because the Top 10 percent plan applies uniformly to high schools, the impact on minority and nonminority populations depends heavily on the contours of residential segrega-tion. Calculations from district-level data posted by the Texas Education Agency indicate that nearly 10 percent of all school districts have student bodies that are over 75 percent Hispanic, and an additional 10 percent have student bodies that are 50 to 75 percent Hispanic (Tienda, 2000). The African-American population of Texas is half the size of the Hispanic population, and apparently less segre-gated by school district (although not necessarily less segregated by schools). Only 3 percent of Texas school districts have student bodies that are over 50 percent African American, and an additional 8 percent of districts have student bodies that are over 25 to 50 percent African American. Many of these also have a high concentration of Hispanics.[14]

---

[13] Until 1994, class rank was used in admitting freshmen to the University of Texas at Austin, but because this fact was not publicized, it was not criticized. The controversy surrounding the current use of class rank derives not only from the publicity accorded to the change in admission criteria, but also from claims that the 10% plan is a backdoor affirmative action policy that presuma-bly grants admission to less qualified minority students at the expense of more qualified white stu-dents who attend high-performing schools.

[14] According to the Texas Education Agency, there are approximately 1,573 public and 204 private high schools in Texas as of 1999. The exact number depends on whether alternative cam-puses are included.

How these demographic trends will impact the college-bound population depends on trends in elementary and secondary school enrollment, but most especially high school graduation rates. Hanson and Williams (1999) estimated that the number of graduates from Texas high schools will increase steadily from about 196 thousand in 1999 to about 215 thousand by the year 2010, and level off thereafter. However, these statewide projections obscure pronounced differentials among minority and nonminority populations. Whereas the number of white high school graduates is expected to peak around 2003 and decline thereafter, the number of African-American high school graduates is projected to increase at least through 2009; Asian and Hispanic high school graduates will likely continue to rise rapidly through 2012 and beyond, depending on immigration rates and, for Hispanics, reductions in the high school dropout rate (Hanson & Williams, 1999).

Although these demographic trends indicate a clear growth in the number of minority and nonminority high school graduates who potentially could attend college, the projections reported by Hanson and Williams (1999) also showed a worrisome decline in the minority rate of planned college attendance. Only 36 percent of black high school graduates applied to a four-year institution in 1998. The college-going rate (to four-year institutions) of Hispanic high school graduates is lower still—only 26 percent. Moreover, less than 10 percent of African-American high school graduates and approximately 10 percent of Hispanic high school graduates scored at least 900 on the SAT and graduated in the top 40 percent of their class in 1998. Even lower shares—6 and 7 percent, respectively, of African-American and Hispanic graduates—scored at least 900 on the SAT *and* ranked in the top 20 percent of their high school class. Despite their small sizes, neither of these groups would qualify for automatic admission based on the Top 10 percent plan (Walker, 2000a). Instead, they would have to excel in other areas that are considered by admission officers.[15]

The Texas plan was implemented partially in 1997 because H.B. 588 was passed after the admission process for the 1997 academic year was underway, and fully implemented by 1998. Therefore, its impact on the ethno-racial composition should be evident after 1996, but especially beginning in 1998. In the interest of parsimony, I focus on the two flagship universities with the most competitive admission thresholds.[16] Table 1 presents summary data on matriculants by race and Hispanic origin from 1989 through 1999 for both the University of Texas at Austin and Texas A&M University. At best, the Top 10 percent plan generates mixed

---

[15] This is important because students who are not in the top 10 percent of their graduating class must seek admission based on other criteria, including their class rank, completion of required high school curriculum, SAT or ACT scores, two essays, and evidence of participation in school activities, awards, work experience, service activities, and other indicators of leadership or special circumstances.

[16] UT-Dallas also has selective admission policies and the demand for slots at public universities is likely to spill-over to other campuses, conceivably raising the number of public flagships in the state. However, this speculation will require considerable time to unfold.

results as a strategy to maintain the ethno-racial diversity of the two flagship public college campuses in Texas, but there is reason for optimism overall.

Throughout the decade, the share of white students enrolled at UT Austin declined gradually while the minority share of the total rose. African-American enrollment peaked during the mid-1990s, reaching 6 percent of all freshmen around 1993–1994, while the Hispanic share hovered around 15 to 16 percent through the early 1990s. After 1996, the black and Hispanic shares of the freshmen class fell slightly. By 1999, two years after full implementation, the Top 10 percent plan appears to have restored most of the declines in black and Hispanic freshmen following the *Hopwood* decision. It is noteworthy, however, that the Asian share of all freshmen admits rose steadily throughout the period, even though their relative share of the school-age population is quite small and nowhere near the proportion of Asian freshmen. Correspondingly, the white student share of the 1999 entering class declined to pre-*Hopwood* levels. Native Americans constitute a tiny share of all freshmen and their presence was unaltered by the change in admission criteria. International students slightly increased their share of the freshmen classes, but it is unclear if this represents a real trend or a temporary blip. Whether the "rebound" of black and Hispanic students is attributable to the 10 percent plan or other changes implemented in criteria used by admissions offices remains an open question, but it would seem that changed admission guidelines favored Asians as much as, if not more than, African Americans and Hispanics.

Results for Texas A&M are less encouraging, albeit promising. First, Texas A&M never reached the same level of diversity as the Austin campus. At its peak diversity—right before the *Hopwood* decision—just under one in four freshmen were students of color. This share dropped by almost five percentage points in 1996 and has continued to erode through 1999. Blacks and Hispanics sustained the major losses in the freshmen classes since 1996, while the Asian share climbed slightly. Specifically, Hispanics represented 15 percent of A&M freshmen in 1995, but their share dropped to about 9 percent in 1998 and 1999. Similarly, African Americans constituted close to 5 percent of the A&M entering classes during the mid-1990s, but their share fell to just under 3 percent post-*Hopwood*.

Reasons for the different results on the Austin and A&M campuses are not obvious, but may reflect differing outreach strategies and financial aid packages offered with the new guidelines. The admissions office of UT Austin conducted a rigorous outreach program to advertise the Top 10 percent plan, including distributing a letter signed by then Governor Bush to all graduating seniors throughout the state. Further, university staff made special efforts to visit schools that typically did not send students to the Austin campus, and they established the Longhorn Opportunity Fellowships for economically disadvan-

TABLE 1 Freshmen Enrollment in Texas Flagship Public Universities by Race and Hispanic Origin 1989–1999 (in percent)

UNIVERSITY OF TEXAS AT AUSTIN

Year	White	Black	Hispanic	Asian	Native American	International/ Unknown	Total *(n)*
1989	70.4	5.7	13.0	8.4	0.25	2.2	8,959
1990	67.1	5.5	15.3	9.2	0.36	2.5	7,778
1991	66.1	5.4	15.2	10.2	0.36	2.8	7,551
1992	65.4	5.4	15.6	11.1	0.27	2.2	7,100
1993	64.0	6.0	16.0	11.8	0.40	2.0	7,217
1994	63.7	5.9	15.0	13.4	0.34	1.6	7,371
1995	64.3	5.8	14.7	12.9	0.43	1.9	7,701
1996	63.9	4.8	14.9	13.2	0.51	2.7	7,859
1997	67.0	3.3	13.0	14.2	0.57	2.0	8,258
1998	65.2	3.2	12.6	15.0	0.53	3.6	8,473
1999	62.9	4.2	13.6	15.4	0.44	3.4	8,488

TEXAS A&M UNIVERSITY

Year	White	Black	Hispanic	Asian	Native American	International/ Unknown	Total *(n)*
1989	81.3	4.2	9.9	2.9	0.39	1.4	8,222
1990	80.4	4.2	9.8	3.7	0.41	1.5	7,482
1991	81.3	3.0	10.2	4.2	0.33	1.0	6,087
1992	79.4	4.2	10.7	4.2	0.42	1.1	6,006
1993	78.4	3.7	12.7	3.7	0.28	1.2	6,392
1994	76.3	4.8	13.9	3.5	0.25	1.2	6,047
1995	76.7	4.7	14.7	2.8	0.41	0.7	6,072
1996	80.4	3.6	11.2	2.8	0.38	1.6	6,387
1997	80.5	2.9	9.7	3.6	0.47	2.9	6,233
1998	82.0	2.7	9.1	3.5	0.52	2.1	7,354
1999	83.0	2.7	8.5	3.5	0.49	1.9	6,695

SOURCE: Texas Higher Education Coordinating Board.
NOTES: Enrollment data for Texas A&M University are different from those reported here. The Coordinating Board uses different criteria from that of the university. Accuracy of data subject to verification by the Office of Institutional Studies and Planning, Texas A&M University, College Station, TX.

taged students who qualified for admission on the Top 10 percent criteria.[17] Although the A&M campus is now undertaking similar efforts to recruit students, their lower success in attracting students may reflect differences in the intensity of their outreach efforts and available fellowship support compared to the Austin campuses during the years immediately following *Hopwood*. More time is required to assess these different outcomes. Furthermore, assessing the success of the Top 10 percent plan based only on the ethno-racial composition of entering classes obscures an additional aspect of diversity and broadened opportunity fostered by the new admission criteria, namely the increase in the number of high schools that send students to UT Austin.[18] This aspect of diversity—representation from high and low performing schools—warrants further scrutiny, but it is an important aspect of educational opportunity that also bears on the pipeline to medical and health professions.

Although similar enrollment rates do not guarantee similar graduation rates, there is no *a priori* reason to expect that graduation rates will be dramatically different between the Top 10 percent admits before and after the *Hopwood* decision. Much depends on whether the Top 10 percent students are similar in their readiness to pursue college study to those admitted before admission criteria were changed. Again, early evidence about the performance of the Top 10 admits for the Austin campus is encouraging: these students achieve higher grades than enrolled students who did not rank in the top decile of their senior class. "In fact, Top 10 percent students at every level of the SAT earn grade point averages that exceed those of non-Top 10 percent students having SAT scores that are 200 to 300 points higher" (Faulkner, 2000). This outcome reinforces the well-known fact that high school grades are far better predictors of success in college than test scores. The jury is still out as to whether the new emphasis on performance-based merit criteria will improve the diversity of the graduating classes. Given recent and projected demographic trends, achieving and maintaining the diversity of freshmen classes to the pre-*Hopwood* levels will remain a formidable challenge. However, enrollment of diverse student bodies cannot guarantee narrower gaps in college completion between Hispanics and Blacks relative to Whites and Asians. I return to this theme in the concluding section.

There is another reason for caution in assessing the impact of the changed admission criteria. Because the demand for slots at selective institutions is greater, competition for the fixed number of slots has increased (Reich, 2000). In short, admissions have become tighter. According to President Faulkner, 42 percent of UT Austin freshmen were Top 10 percent graduates before *Hopwood*; currently the share is 47 percent. To accommodate this change, the size of the

---

[17] At a recent presentation (March, 2001) Bruce Walker, Director of Admissions at the Austin campus, reported that the increased availability of scholarships has been largely responsible for the effectiveness of the 10 percent plan in maintaining the diversity of the freshmen classes.

[18] Bruce Walker reports that the 2001 cohort included students from 135 schools that previously had not sent any students to the University of Texas (personal communication, January 25, 2001).

freshman class was increased so that the absolute number of spaces available for non-Top 10 percent graduates remained unchanged (Faulkner, 2000). However, expansion of the largest college campus in the United States—already in excess of 49,000—cannot continue indefinitely. Therefore, accommodating a potentially growing number of Top 10 graduates at the two flagship campuses requires innovative strategies to increase educational capacity, including the possibility that the current promise of admission to the public institution of choice may have to be revised.

The consequences of the *Hopwood* decision also manifest themselves in the minority representation among entering students at Texas medical schools. Before 1996, Hispanics constituted almost 15 percent of the entering class, but only 11 and 12.7 percent of the 1997 and 1998 cohorts, respectively. Similarly, the African-American shares of medical students enrolling in Texas medical schools fell from 5.3 percent before *Hopwood* to 3–4 percent after the repeal of race-sensitive admission policies. That the Texas 10 percent plan does not affect medical and professional schools poses great uncertainty about the future diversity of Texas medical school students. A great deal of this future rests on the success of the Top 10 percent plan in providing an adequate pool of minority college graduates who are admissible to the top medical schools in the state. The jury is out.

California

Like Texas, California's population has grown rapidly during the 1990s, owing both to high rates of natural increase (especially for Hispanics) and immigration. Hispanics and Asians accounted for 60 and 28 percent, respectively, of California's demographic growth between 1990 to 1998, while Blacks, Whites, and Native Americans combined contributed 12 percent of the 3.5 million absolute increase over the decade. Differential fertility, mortality, and migration rates for the major racial and ethnic groups have altered the state's racial and ethnic composition such that the white share of the total has been decreasing gradually while the Hispanic and Asian/Pacific Islander share has grown rapidly. Between 1990 and 1998, the Hispanic population share alone increased from 26 to 30 percent of the total, while the comparable Asian share rose from 9 to 11 percent (California State Department of Finance, 2000). However, black and Native American shares remained constant during the 1990s, at seven and one percent, respectively.

High rates of minority demographic growth in California produced a school-age population that is over half minority. Hispanics currently comprise about 40 percent of California's public school enrollment, and are expected to represent a majority of students by 2006. The California State Department of Finance (2000) projects that the school-age population will grow from its current level of 5.8 million to approximately 6.2 million during the 2007–2008 academic year. Of these, 70 percent are projected to be students of color and for about one in four, English will not be a first language. Recent demographic estimates indicate that the Native American, black, and white pre-college student population will decline between 1999 and 2009, while the Asian and Hispanic groups will increase by 11 and 27 percent, respectively (del Pinal, 1996). On the brighter side, the number of Hispanic high school graduates is projected to increase by 74 percent between 1999 and 2010 (California State Department of Finance, 2000). Whether the improved high school graduation rates of Hispanic students will translate to higher college enrollment rates depends in large measure on the consequences of changed admission guidelines. In the aftermath of Proposition 209, the prospects are not encouraging.

These demographic changes are not well mirrored in the evolving composition of California's flagship universities during the 1990s inasmuch as the Asian share of total enrollment approaches 40 percent at both flagship institutions even though their population share is only one-fourth as large (see Table 2). Moreover, while the Hispanic population share rose sharply, their representation at the Berkeley and UCLA campuses did not grow. Part of this decline is due to the increased numbers of foreign students and those who do not report their race and ethnic origin, but the latter category likely includes many white and Asian students as well.

Thus, by contrast to Texas, the trends in diversity of college freshmen at California's two flagship institutions are discouraging. Although Proposition 209 was passed in 1996, the admission season for the 1997 cohort was essentially completed under guidelines that allow consideration of race and national origin. Therefore, the consequences of the affirmative action ban should manifest themselves after 1997. Although the share of black and Hispanic freshmen enrolled at the two flagship institutions was declining gradually throughout the 1990s, the drop was more dramatic after 1997.

Specifically, the Hispanic share of the Berkeley campus peaked at 19 percent of the 1991 entering class, and remained in the double digits through 1997, the last year that the race-sensitive guidelines were permitted. Between 1998 and 2000, the Hispanic share of the freshman class fell to between 7 and 9 percent. Although the share of Native Americans never exceeded 2 percent of all freshmen, after Proposition 209 went into effect they constituted less than one percent. Concurrently, the Asian share of the entering class, which exceeded one in three of all new matriculants throughout the 1990s and hovered around 40 percent at the time of Proposition 209, rose to nearly 45 percent of Berkeley freshmen after 1998. Interestingly, the white share of college freshmen was not greatly affected by the banning of race-sensitive admission practices, hovering between 29 to 30 percent throughout the period.

Compared to the Berkeley campus, the impact of Proposition 209 at UCLA was less dramatic, yet it is clear that minority representation declined. The His-

TABLE 2 Freshmen Enrollment in California Flagship Public Universities by Race and Hispanic Origin: 1991–2000 (in percent)

UNIVERSITY OF CALIFORNIA AT BERKELEY

Year	White	Black	Hispanic	Asian	Native American	International/ Unknown/ Other	Total (n)
1991	29.0	7.5	18.9	33.5	1.5	9.6	3221
1992	30.0	6.1	13.6	39.5	1.1	9.8	3420
1993	29.3	5.8	16.7	39.1	1.2	7.8	3215
1994	28.9	6.2	14.9	40.5	1.1	8.3	3344
1995	30.0	6.5	15.6	37.2	1.9	8.9	3435
1996	29.4	6.3	14.8	38.6	1.4	9.5	3708
1997	28.5	7.2	13.2	41.1	0.6	9.5	3573
1998	29.2	3.4	7.3	41.9	0.4	17.9	3735
1999	30.7	3.5	9.1	43.8	0.6	12.3	3618
2000	30.1	4.0	9.0	44.6	0.5	11.8	3735

UNIVERSITY OF CALIFORNIA LOS ANGELES

Year	White	Black	Hispanic	Asian	Native American	International/ Unknown/ Other	Total (n)
1991	31.9	5.7	15.9	39.5	1.4	5.5	3983
1992	30.6	7.0	17.8	36.5	1.3	6.9	3460
1993	28.4	7.1	16.4	41.3	0.6	6.2	3391
1994	27.3	6.8	18.0	41.5	1.0	5.3	4129
1995	27.6	7.3	21.6	37.8	1.3	4.4	3701
1996	32.0	6.3	18.3	36.0	0.9	6.6	3821
1997	32.6	5.8	15.0	38.5	1.0	7.0	3810
1998	30.3	3.4	10.5	39.2	0.3	16.3	4200
1999	33.6	3.7	11.8	39.3	0.3	11.3	4131
2000	32.4	3.7	12.5	39.8	0.4	11.2	4203

SOURCE: Statistics for University of California at Berkeley and Los Angeles are from the Office of Student Research, Division of Undergraduate Affairs.

panic share of the freshman class dropped by about one-third, from 18.3 percent in 1996 to between 11 and 12 percent after 1998. Native American representation, which lowered between one and one and a half percent, fell to less than one-half of one percent. Representation of black students in the freshman classes also registered declines, falling from between 6–7 percent annually before

Proposition 209 to less than 4 percent after the legislation went into effect.[19] Thus, it appears that Asian students are the great beneficiaries of the ban on affirmative action, while Blacks and Hispanics are the big losers. In fact, the Asian share of UCLA and Berkeley freshmen is about four times higher than their population shares, while the Hispanic freshman cohort is only half their population share.

These dramatic changes in the composition of college freshmen at California's most selective public institutions will reverberate on the pipeline into medical and professional schools. Karabel (1999, Table 7) reported that before Proposition 209 was passed, the share of black and Hispanic medical students throughout the California system ranged between 16 and 18 percent, and after the legislation went into effect this share declined to 12 percent. Although larger shares were admitted than attended, the drop in admissions is even more precipitous than the decline in the shares enrolled. Karabel (1999, Table 8) shows that in 1993–1994, Blacks and Mexican Americans represented between 21 to 24 percent of students admitted to medical schools in the UC system. In 1996, their combined share dropped to 15 percent, and once the law went into effect the share of black and Hispanic students admitted to California medical schools fell to between 12 and 13 percent. Based on the shrinkage in the size of the minority cohorts entering the UC system medical schools, Karabel estimates that the "social clock" has been set back 25 years; even worse, the representation of black and Mexican-American students in the freshmen classes of Berkeley and UCLA represent a 31-year setback.

California has implemented a percent plan that became effective in the current (2000–2001) academic year. It is unlikely that the Top 4 percent plan will recover any of the ground lost in the diversity of the Berkeley and UCLA campuses because California's percent plan only guarantees a slot in the UC system, not necessarily at the flagship institutions. Moreover, the success of California's Top 4 percent plan depends crucially on the contours of residential segregation. By implementing the percent plan on a school-by-school basis, Geiser (1998) estimated that the eligible pool of black and Hispanic students is approximately 12 percent, which she estimates would produce a 10 percent increase in the pool of underrepresented minorities in the eligibility pool, for a possible yield of 300 to 700 students.[20] Of course, eligibility assures neither application nor enrollment, especially among students whose financial means limit their options for post-secondary schooling. Because these new guidelines have just gone into effect, it is not possible to assess their impact, but the different experiences of

---

[19] That the share of Asian and white students remained fairly steady even as the share of underrepresented minority groups fell partly reflects the growing numbers who refuse to indicate their race or national origin. At both flagship campuses, the share of students who refused to report their race or national origin rose by approximately 9–10 percentage points.

[20] In addition to ethno-racial diversity, California's percent plan will also broaden geographic diversity, as seems to be occurring in Texas.

the Austin and A&M campuses indicate that availability of financial aid probably is an essential complement to maintain campus diversity once a percent plan is implemented. California faces the additional challenge of allocating top 4 percent graduating seniors among public institutions of varying selectivity. This jury has a long wait before reaching a verdict.

Lessons from the Case Studies

Texas and California provide critical vantage points from which to gauge the consequences of changes in admission criteria on minority representation in higher education. Over half of all Hispanics in the United States reside in Texas and California, including an even larger share of the school-age population. When mapped against the rising Hispanic-white gaps in college enrollment and graduation rates, even the seemingly stable enrollment trends at UT Austin are worrisome. In part, this is because the Hispanic population is growing much faster than the rest of the Texas population, and their youthful age structure coupled with high fertility rates portends even larger cohorts of college-age youth well into the future. The erosion of Hispanic representation in California's flagship institutions is even more troubling, and it is unclear whether the Top 4 percent plan will be effective in reversing post-209 trends. If swelling numbers of Hispanic college-age youth are not accompanied by commensurate increases in college attendance and graduation rates, educational inequality will rise dramatically in the near future.

Although only 19.8 percent of all African Americans reside in Texas and California, recent court decisions in Georgia prohibiting consideration of race in college decisions will surely impact the pipeline of African Americans into college and, subsequently, medical and professional schools. Nevertheless, the lower representation of Blacks in both Texas and California flagship institutions signals a reduction in educational opportunity and a regression in time to pre-Civil Rights laws levels. It is discouraging to witness decades of effort to broaden educational opportunity vanish in such a short time. Preventing further erosion in minority representation at selective universities warrants swift and decisive measures to prevent further constriction of the educational pipeline for minority youth.

RECENT DEVELOPMENTS: TIDAL WAVE OR FALSE ALARM?

Whether the Texas and California examples have set a national precedent is unclear because the *Bakke* decision remains the law of the land until the Supreme Court decides to revisit the constitutionality of race-sensitive admission criteria. In recent years, a spate of court decisions and referenda has steadily eroded the use of affirmative action in college admissions in various states. The 1996 *Hopwood* decision remains in litigation and could be the basis on which the Supreme Court reconsiders the *Bakke* decision, but litigation in other states, notably Michigan, may very well provide the grist for the reassessment of race-sensitive admissions. Following the lead of Texas and California, Florida, Washington, and Georgia also have challenged the constitutionality of *Bakke*.

Michigan was the first to follow, when in 1997 the Center for Individual Rights sued the University of Michigan on behalf of two white students denied admission to the University's liberal arts college and, in a separate lawsuit, on behalf of a white woman denied admission to the law school. Rather than cave in, the University of Michigan opted to defend its policies on grounds that clear educational benefits flow from a racially diverse student body (*Gratz* v. *Bollinger et al.*, 1999). In December 1998 and January, 1999, respectively, U.S. district judges certified the lawsuit targeting the university's undergraduate school (Judge Patrick Duggan) and the law school (Judge Bernard A. Friedman) a class action. In June 1999, minorities seeking admission into the university requested permission of the 6th U.S. Circuit Court of Appeals in Cincinnati to intervene in the lawsuits. Two months later, the 6th Circuit Court of Appeals allowed 58 individuals—mostly minority students at Michigan—and four pro-affirmative action groups to join the lawsuits as defendants. Since that time, General Motors, Microsoft, Intel, and 18 other Fortune 500 companies filed briefs supporting the University of Michigan, arguing that eliminating race-sensitive admissions will deprive businesses of well-trained minority candidates. A December 2000 decision upheld the University's admissions policy on the merits of evidence about the educational benefits of a diverse student body. However, the cases are far from over, and the case against the University of Michigan law school resulted in an unfavorable ruling.[21]

On November 3, 1998, voters in the state of Washington passed Initiative 200 (58 to 42 percent) which is modeled after California's Proposition 209. This law prohibits preferential treatment based on race, sex, color, ethnicity, or national origin in public employment, education, and contracting. Although Microsoft, the Association of Washington businesses, and the *Seattle Times* publicly opposed Initiative 200, and although most polls showed that Washington voters believed discrimination against minorities and women exists, the majority of voters were critical of affirmative action policies on grounds that they presumably benefit unqualified minorities and discriminate against white men. Wierzbicki and Hirschman (2000) recorded a slight increase in the white and Asian

---

[21] Typically, the nation's highest court considers cases in which appellate courts have differed on the same issue. In this instance, the 9th U.S. Circuit Court of Appeals in San Francisco sided with the University of Washington, but previously, the 5th U.S. Circuit Court of Appeals ruled unconstitutional the former admissions policy at the University of Texas law school, which had considered minority applicants differently than whites. The suit against the University of Washington law school was brought by the Washington, D.C.-based Center for Individual Rights (the same group that sued UM) on behalf of Katuria Smith.

shares of the freshman class following Initiative 200, while the black and Hispanic shares declined slightly.

Noting significant declines in minority enrollment at the University of Washington, in May 1999, President Richard L. McCormick appointed a broad-based Committee on Diversity charged with developing a 30-year vision for enhancing access to the university and using creative approaches to develop a multicultural learning environment, with its attendant benefits. As a first step, President McCornick announced a $65.6 million scholarship proposal to restore representation of minority students to pre-Initiative 200 levels. However, the jury is still out because the suit against the University of Washington Law School has resulted in a split opinion about the legality of using race as a criterion in making such decisions.

How much the California and Texas decisions currently drive the anti-affirmative action campaigns in other states remains an open question, but it is noteworthy that Ward Connerly, a black businessman and Regent of the University of California vehemently opposed to affirmative action, organized the petition campaign in Florida and obtained 43,000 signatures in July, 1999.[22] To head off Connerly's campaign to put an anti-affirmative action referendum on the ballot, in November of that year, Governor Jeb Bush signed an order, dubbed the "One Florida Plan," eliminating race, ethnicity, and sex as criteria for making admissions decisions. Ironically, this decision has proven extremely divisive along racial lines, especially following criticism that minority votes in Florida were discarded unfairly in the 2000 presidential election. However, the governor's plan includes a measure, called the Talented 20, which guarantees admission to a state university to all seniors who graduate in the top 20 percent of their class.

Despite its seeming generosity, this proposal was bitterly resisted by black leaders who staged a sit-in at his office and a massive protest in March, 2000. In addition to criticism by the U.S. Department of Education, the NAACP is challenging the Talented 20 program on the grounds that the Board of Regents had no authority to make sweeping university admissions decisions required by the One Florida Plan. The case is currently in court, with a decision due in July. The regents have suspended the One Florida Plan until the challenge is settled.

Similar legal challenges and difficulties characterize college admissions in Georgia, which has been sued for allegedly using racial "quotas" to achieve minority representation at its flagship institutions. Ironically, the University of Georgia's history of discrimination against Blacks and 20 years of federally mandated affirmative action are relevant to the development of race-sensitive admission criteria that are currently being challenged in court. The plaintiffs argue that Georgia uses race quotas to enroll about 10 percent minority students in each freshman class. In opposition to the *Bakke* decision, U.S. District Judge

---

[22] Ward Connerly was also instrumental in orchestrating Initiative 200 in the state of Washington.

B. Avant Edenfield ruled that race-conscious admission is unconstitutional. The University of Georgia temporarily dropped its race preference in August, 2000, but President Michael F. Adams has appealed the ruling, invoking *Bakke* v. *Board of Regents*, and noting that race is only one of 12 factors that gives borderline applicants a slight edge. However, legal battles continue as the university faces additional challenges in law school admission and in accommodating the growing Hispanic population's eligibility for affirmative admission.

Obviously, the legal and political climate over the use of affirmative action in college admissions is both highly fluid and politicized. Although many of the legal challenges are directed at law and professional schools, the percent plans are designed to govern admission to undergraduate institutions. The link between minority representation in undergraduate institutions and in post-graduate academic professional and medical schools has not been explicitly considered, although parallel analyses of minority enrollments have been conducted. This issue, which bears directly on the future representation of minorities in health and medical professions, warrants further scrutiny and immediate corrective action to prevent further setbacks in the gains since the first years of the civil rights movement.

CONCLUSIONS

The changing demand for highly educated workers in the burgeoning health professions requires a multi-pronged strategy consisting of early intervention; strong dropout prevention programs; and outreach initiatives between high schools with high minority concentration and selective public and private universities. What is clear from the preliminary evidence presented here is that trends in minority representation in higher education generally, and health and medical professions specifically, will decline precipitously in the absence of compensatory strategies to maintain the ethno-racial diversity of college campuses.

Admission guidelines that identify arbitrary class rank thresholds, such as the 10 percent plan, may serve as temporary solutions until the political fall-out settles, but they are potentially harmful in the long term because they rely on segregation to be minimally effective and because they can be easily undermined by disingenuous redistricting or alteration of ranking systems. The U.S. Commission on Civil Rights condemned the practice of replacing race-sensitive admission policies with statistical "percent" policies guaranteeing admission to public colleges, arguing that these experimental responses are regressive because they exploit segregated schools.

Equally problematic is that percent plans do not deal with the root causes of minority underrepresentation in higher education, which begins early in childhood. With growing educational gaps and strong demographic momentum, both early intervention and prevention programs are required to unplug the minority educational pipelines. My depiction of the national educational pipeline clearly demonstrates the need for deliberate strategies to improve elementary, middle, and high school graduation rates of Blacks and Hispanics, *and* to promote their admission, matriculation, and graduation rates from selective colleges and universities. Failing this, the pool of black and Hispanic students eligible to enter medical school and health professions that require post-secondary schooling will shrink if for no other reason than the momentum of demographic growth. Also needed are vigorous and creative outreach programs that forge academic ties between minority-dominant schools and the top-tier public and private universities, as well as those with two-year colleges. It is surprising, on reflection, that the elite private universities have not united and mobilized a collective response on behalf of the public institutions that have come under attack. Certainly, their admission guidelines will be affected if the Supreme Court, upon reconsidering the merits of race-sensitive admission criteria, decides to reverse the *Bakke* decision.

Objections to race-sensitive admission policies were justified on the grounds that giving preferential advantage to underrepresented groups based on ascribed criteria denies admission to putatively more qualified students (Kane, 1998; Bowen & Bok, 1998). Although Bowen and Bok (1998) demonstrated that the alleged "adverse" impacts are tiny, the movement to eliminate all forms of affirmative action admission policies is gaining momentum as more and more states are challenging the use of race in college decisions. Ironically, similar criticisms are now being wagered about the 10 percent plan, which presumably excludes admissible students from high-performing schools in favor of high-performing students from low-performing schools.

Definitive proof of the impact of the "percent plans" requires comparisons of the performance and qualifications of pools of students admitted under these criteria with those who would have been admitted using the race-sensitive criteria. At the individual level, there are transaction costs associated with changes in admission plans, and mass confusion and misunderstanding in the short run. Students who would have been admitted under the race-sensitive regime may opt to attend college elsewhere under the current guidelines. From a societal standpoint, these costs probably average themselves out over large numbers of people, and based on calculations from Bowen and Bok (1998), are tiny in any event.[23]

In order to maintain and increase diversity in post-baccalaureate programs, it is essential that the key undergraduate feeder institutions reflect the changed population composition in their entering and graduating classes. Broadening the educational pipeline at the lower school levels is crucial to ensure that the shares successfully graduating from institutions that feed the medical schools and

---

[23] That *perceptions* of such costs do not square with empirical evidence is partly responsible for the rising anti-affirmative action sentiment. Specifically, individual perceptions that *they* would have been admitted had a preference regime not been in place gives rise to a great deal of hostility about artificially imposed barriers to "deserving" students.

health professions continues to grow in ways that parallel the national and state contours of diversity. Because the absolute number of applicants to selective institutions is rising and will likely continue to do so as outreach efforts succeed in attracting students from schools that traditionally have not sent students to flagship institutions, admissions will become increasingly competitive. Population projections indicate that demographic pressures will continue well into the 21st century, and as more high schools achieve the excellence they strive for, demands on the higher education system will grow apace. One possible long-term outcome is improved scholastic outcomes for low-performing high schools, particularly if outreach efforts are successful in redirecting curricula toward college preparation. This, in turn, can increase the number of flagship schools in all states where demographic pressures increase the demand for quality post-secondary education and beyond. Until these goals are achieved, however, higher education is well advised to take race into account in order to resolve racism.

REFERENCES

Association of American Medical Colleges (AAMC) (2000). Minority graduates of U.S. medical schools: Trends, 1950–1998. Washington, D.C.

Bowen, WG, & Bok, D (1998). The shape of the river: Long-term consequences of considering race in college and university admissions. Princeton: Princeton University Press.

California State Department of Finance. California public K–12 enrollment projections by ethnicity, 2000 series. Accessed online at http://www.dof.ca.gov/html/Demograp/K12ethtb.htm, on March 5, 2001.

California State Department of Finance (May 2000). Race/ethnic population estimates: Components of change for California counties, April 1990 to July 1998. Sacramento: Department of Finance.

Danziger, S & Gottschalk, P. (1995). America unequal. New York: Russell Sage Foundation.

Del Pinal, J. (1996). "Latino's and California's future: Too few at the schoolhouse door." Paper presented at the Chicano/Latino Policy Project and La Raza Law Journal Fifth Annual Symposium, University of California, Berkley, March.

Faulkner, LR. (2000). "By any measure, 'Top 10 Percent' working for UT." *The Houston Chronicle*. Outlook section; October 29: p. 1.

Geiser, S. (1998). Redefining UC's eligibility pool to include a percentage of students from each high school. Berkeley: UC Office of the President, Student Academic Services.

Gratz et al. v. Bollinger et al. (1999). The compelling need for diversity in higher education. Unpublished manuscript.

Hanson, GR & Williams, A. (1999). The Texas educational pipeline, Office of Student Affairs Research, University of Texas at Austin.

Holzer, H & Newmark, D. (2000). Assessing affirmative action. *Journal of Economic Literature*, 38(September): pp. 483–568.

Kane, T. (1998). Misconceptions in the debate over affirmative action in college admissions. In G. Orfield & E. Miller, (Eds.), Chilling admissions: The affirmative action crisis and the search for alternatives. Cambridge: Harvard Education Publishing Group; pp. 17–32.

Karabel, J. (1998). No alternative: The effects of color blind admissions in California. In G. Orfield & E. Miller, (Eds.), Chilling admissions: The affirmative action crisis and the search for alternatives." Cambridge: Harvard Education Publishing Group; pp. 35–50.

Karabel, J. (1999). The rise and fall of affirmative action at the University of California. University of California, Berkeley, unpublished manuscript.

Levy, F. (1998). The new dollars and dreams: American incomes and economic change. New York: Russell Sage.

Mare, RD. (1995). Changes in educational attainment and school enrollment. In R. Farley (Ed.), State of the union: America in the 1990s. New York: Russell Sage Foundation; pp. 155–213.

Murdock, SH., Pecotte, B. et al. (1998). An assessment of potential needs unmet and opportunities lost as a result of Hopwood. The Hopwood effect: Problems, prospects, and the impact on minorities in higher education. Texas A&M University, College Station, Texas: Unpublished manuscript.

Reich, RB. (2000). How selective colleges heighten inequality. *Chronicle of Higher Education*, Section 2. September 15: pp. B7–B10.

Selingo, J. (2000). What states aren't saying about the "X-percent solution". *Chronicle of Higher Education*. 46(June 2): pp. A31–A34.

Tienda, M. (1999). Immigration, opportunity and social cohesion. In N.J. Smelser & J.C. Alexander (Eds.) Diversity and its discontents: Cultural conflict and common ground in contemporary American society. Princeton, NJ: Princeton University Press; pp. 129–146.

Tienda, M. (2000). Texas college enrollments before and after Hopwood: Assessing the impacts on minorities of changed admission criteria. Research proposal to The Ford Foundation. June.

Tienda, M., Lloyd, K. & Zajacova, A. (2000). Trends in educational achievement of minority students since *Brown* v. *Board of Education*. Paper presented at the NAS Millennium Conference, Achieving High Educational Standards for All, Washington, D.C., September 21–22.

Tienda, M. & Simonelli, S. (2001). Unplugging the pipeline: Hispanics in higher education and affirmative action. *Chronicle of Higher Education* (in press).

Walker, B. (2000a). The Texas plan. Unpublished tabulations presented at the Berkeley Research Symposium, March 31, 2000.

Walker, B. (2000b). Implementation and results of HB 588 at the University of Texas at Austin. Austin, Texas: Unpublished manuscript.

Weirzbicki, S. & Hirschman, C. (2000). The end of affirmative action in Washington state and its impact on the transition from high school to college. Unpublished manuscript, University of Washington, December 11.

Toward Diverse Student Representation and Higher Achievement in Higher Levels American Educational Meritocracy

Michael T. Nettles and Catherine M. Millett
University of Michigan

INTRODUCTION

At the beginning of the 20th century, merit became synonymous with standardized intellectual tests in American education and in key sectors of the workforce. From the First World War when the U.S. Army administered intelligence tests to new recruits, the practice of sorting, selecting, and placing people based upon their test scores was launched. Colleges and universities began the practice using standardized intellectual tests for selecting students a few years later and the practice has grown steadily ever since. Despite the value placed upon other human attributes, tests and assessments are the most powerful levers of opportunity to higher-status education and employment.

Here at the beginning of the 21st century, standardized intellectual tests retain their lofty status as the core indicators of educational merit in America. From elementary and secondary schools up through undergraduate, graduate, and first-professional education, an individual's standardized test scores frequently determine the college or university he or she will attend and the curricula that he or she will experience. The higher one's scores, the higher the quality of schools, curricula, colleges, and professional schools he or she is invited to attend. Higher-quality education in turn leads individuals to higher-status employment and ultimately to a higher quality of life. The process of tracking begins in the early years of school. Moving from the lower to higher status tracks that lead to success is very difficult.

While the central focus of America's meritocracy during the 20th century has been the performance of individual students on standardized intellectual tests, the spotlight and the influence of tests, and more recently assessments, has

143

become much wider in scope. In addition to individual achievement, the measurement of merit today also encompasses the test and assessment performance of population groups (race/ethnic, class, and sex) and educational institutions (schools, colleges, and universities) in addition to individuals. Aggregate test or assessment scores of subpopulation groups are published today with greater frequency and are more often widely disseminated than in the past. Standardized tests and assessments reveal the relative status within the merit hierarchy of race/ethnic groups and their educational institutions. Institutions are ranked, rated, and classified based to a large degree upon the average of their students' scores on various types of tests and assessments.

The consequence is that individual merit and societal expectations are more formally intertwined with race group membership and the predominant race of the schools and colleges and universities. Unless institutions make score adjustments or use special weighting and calibrations on selection criteria, African Americans and Hispanics will be underrepresented in the higher status of American meritocracy. Because of differences in the score performance of students of different race/ethnic groups, there are separate merit scholarship programs for people of various race/ethnic groups. The separation of the National Merit Scholars and the National Achievement Scholars based upon race/ethnicity is one example. Here the Preliminary Scholastic Assessment Test (PSAT) is the instrument used for awarding merit. The history of lower African-American and Hispanic performance and the expectation that students from these two groups will perform relatively low on the test, has caused the National Merit Scholarship Organization to establish racially distinct programs in order to ensure that African Americans and Hispanics are included in relatively representative numbers.

Several leading testing and assessment organizations, colleges, and universities have launched efforts to complement or even supplant traditional indicators of merit with alternative criteria. Criteria such as grades, educational and career aspirations, amount of effort, perseverance, and heritage, are variously considered as being complementary to test scores or to perhaps be possible alternative criteria. But, uniformity and stability are important elements of standardized tests and assessments, which places them in a preeminent role as the most equitable criteria for determining educational merit. Grades earned in school or college, for example, are often only considered to be valuable after weighing the quality of the school/college and curricula in which they were earned. The practice of weighting schools on the basis of their quality serves as a means of establishing uniformity and standardization in grades and other school-based indicators such as class rank, honors, and awards. Because there are no common standards for awarding grades, conditioning is the norm. Tests and assessments administered by independent objective agencies appear to be void of bias because they are administered under similar time and physical conditions and are therefore more credible indicators of merit. There are rarely, if ever, adjustments made in test scores based upon group membership or educational and personal background. Rather, efforts to achieve racial/ethnic diversity are expended either by deciding the amount of weight to assign to test scores relative to complementary criteria, or by policies like the ones that are used by the National Merit Scholarship Program to segment their applicant pools based upon socio-demographic characteristics. Despite the popular anti-testing rhetoric, standardized tests and assessments have become so highly regarded as mediums of meritocracy that they are used to validate grades, curricula, and teaching; to certify the learning and accomplishments of students; to accredit and reward institutions; and to set priorities for public policies.

Reversing the underrepresentation and progress of African Americans and Hispanics in higher levels of American education requires an increase in their participation and performance on test scores and grades. Only then will the members of theses two racial/ethnic groups and their educational institutions achieve higher status in American meritocracy. While all other non-cognitive measures are useful, they are only useful after being conditioned with other criteria. A person's race or heritage, for example, may be used as a criterion for diversifying representation in certain strata of educational institutions such as college enrollments, but even race as a criterion is sometimes only an acceptable criterion after social class is taken into account. Social class appears to be an acceptable means of conditioning race and leads to boosting the opportunities of economically disadvantaged African Americans and Hispanics to attain better educational preparation and quality of life. At the same time, however, using social class as a criterion in conjunction with race reduces the prospect of achieving diversity at higher status colleges and universities. The African Americans and Hispanics who most often possess the backgrounds and credentials to succeed in the most prestigious colleges and universities are not likely to be the most economically disadvantaged.

This paper examines the challenges that African Americans and Hispanics face as they pursue greater representation in the higher levels of America's educational meritocracy. Included in these analyses are the trends in representation of African Americans and Hispanics relative to Whites and Asians, and their performance and the performance of their educational institutions on important indicators of educational merit. Additional criteria are introduced that are likely prospects for increasing the representation and achievement of underrepresented students. These additional criteria are correlates of test and assessment scores and other measures of academic performance. The focus is on the accumulation of human intellectual capital from the early years of preschool through high school and the college years and then the movement from college into first-professional education. The paper concludes with a brief description of four programs that intervene with African-American and Hispanic children during their middle and early high school years to increase the quality of their academic preparation.

Four central questions are addressed in the paper:

• What is the current status of population diversity in the United States and at various levels of education?

• As the primary mediums of meritocracy, how are tests and assessments performing in achieving equality of representation for various under-represented groups?

• What are the correlates of student performance on tests and assessments that are likely to lead to higher performance and consequently to greater access and achievement by underrepresented population groups?

• What actions are needed for expanding merit and eliminating under-representation based upon class and race/ethnicity over the long term and what criteria can be used by colleges and universities to identify additional talent in the short term?

COMPOSITION OF THE U.S. POPULATION AND ENROLLMENTS IN HIGHER EDUCATION

An important symbol in American meritocracy is the academic degree attainment of the adult population. The U.S. population consists of approximately 285,000,000 people, approximately 197,412,000 (69%) of whom are adults 18 years old and older. Figure 1 illustrates the distribution of African Americans, Asian Americans, Hispanics, Native Americans and Whites throughout various age groupings of the entire population from birth through 65 years and above. African Americans and Hispanics comprise a larger share of the school-age population than of the overall adult population, and Whites are represented better at higher age levels than in the younger ages. For example, African Americans and Hispanics constitute 13.9 percent and 18.1 percent, respectively, of children in the category of birth to 5 years, 12 percent and 10.6 percent in the range of 35 to 44, and only 8.1 percent and 5.3 percent in the 65 and above range. On the other hand, Whites are better represented at higher age levels from 62.7 in the earliest ages of 0 to 5 to 72.8 percent in the 35- to 44-year-old age range and 83.9 percent in the age range of 65 and above. Asian Americans retain their representation at around 2.8 percent at each age range (U.S. Census Bureau, 2000a).

Table 1 shows that among adults who are 18 years and older in the United States the educational attainments of African Americans and Hispanics are not commensurate with their representation in the population, whereas Asian Americans far exceed their representation at higher levels of educational attainment.

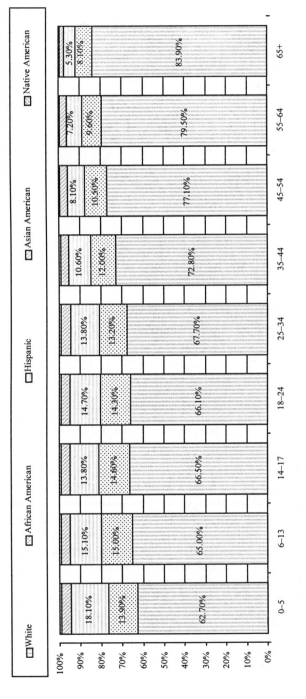

FIGURE 1 U.S. Population by Race and Age in 1999
SOURCE: U.S. Census Bureau, Population Division, Population Estimates Program, 2000.

TABLE 1 Highest Level of Education Attained by Persons Age 18 and Over, by Age, Sex, and Race/Ethnicity (Numbers in Thousands): March 1998

Persons age 18 and over	Total Population	Bachelor's	Master's	Professional	Doctorate
Total Population	197,412	30,087	9,295	2,586	1,869
		15.2%	4.7%	1.3%	0.9%
Race/Ethnicity					
African American	22,552	2,075	662	111	71
	11.4%	6.9%	7.1%	4.3%	3.8%
Hispanic	19,833	1,348	306	132	79
	10.0%	4.5%	3.3%	5.1%	4.2%
Other	8,658	2,001	646	199	156
	4.4%	6.7%	6.9%	7.7%	8.3%
Whites	146,369	24,663	7,681	2,144	1,563
	74.1%	82.0%	82.6%	82.9%	83.6%
Gender					
Males	95,008	14,861	4,656	1,759	1,354
	48.1%	49.4%	50.1%	68.0%	72.4%
Females	102,402	15,228	4,640	827	514
	51.9%	50.6%	49.9%	32.0%	27.5%

\1\Civilian non-institutional population—Data not applicable or not available.
NOTE: Data are based on a sample survey of the noninstitutional population. Although cells with fewer than 75,000 people are subject to relatively wide sampling variation, they are included in the table to permit various types of aggregations. Because of rounding, details may not add to totals.
SOURCE: U.S. Department of Education, National Center for Education Statistics, 2000.

Table 1 shows that while African Americans comprise 11.4 percent of the adult U.S. population, they represent only 6.9 percent of the bachelor's degrees, 7.1 percent of the master's degrees, 4.3 percent of the first-professional degrees, and 3.8 percent of the doctorate degrees in the United States. Hispanics comprise 10 percent of the adult population, but 4.5 percent of the bachelor's, 3.3 percent of the master's, 5.1 percent of the first-professional degrees, and 4.2 percent of the doctorates. Asian and other population groups (primarily non-resident aliens) account for only 4.4 percent of the U.S. adult population, but 6.7 percent of the bachelor's degree holders, 6.9 percent of the master's, 7.7 percent of the first-professionals, and 8.3 percent of the doctorates. Similarly, Whites comprise 74.1 percent of the U.S. adult population, but 82 percent of the bachelor's degree holders, 82.6 percent of the master's, 82.9 percent of the first-professionals, and 83.6 percent of the doctorates (U.S. Department of Education, 2000).

Table 1 also reveals an interesting sex difference in the attainment of merit among adults. Women and men comprise roughly the same share of bachelor's degrees (50.6 percent female, 49.4 percent male) and master's degrees (49.9 percent female and 50.1 percent male), but men hold a rather large advantage in the attainment of first-professional and doctorate degrees. Men constitute 68 and 72.4 percent of the first professional and doctorate degrees, respectively, compared to women who hold 32 and 27.5 percent (U.S. Department of Education, 2000).

Table 2 shows the race/ethnic distribution of the traditional college-age population of 18- to 24-year-olds, first-time full-time freshmen enrollment at four-year colleges and universities, bachelor's degree recipients, and the new medical school entrants in 1997. The gap between representation in the population and among the three indicators of merit for African Americans and Hispanics is similar to the gap observed in Table 1 for the overall adult population.

African Americans represented 14.3 percent of the 18- to 24-year-old population but only 11 percent of the first-time full-time freshmen at four-year colleges and universities, 7.8 percent of bachelor's degree recipients, and 7 percent of new entrants into medical school. Hispanics were 14.3 percent of the 18- to 24-year-olds in the population, 8.3 percent of the first-time full-time freshmen, 6.3 percent of the bachelor's degree recipients, and 6.1 percent of new medical school entrants. Conversely, Asian Americans represented 3.9 percent of the 18- to 24-year-olds in the U.S. population, but 5.9 percent of the first-time

TABLE 2 Population (18–24), First-Time Full-Time Freshmen, Bachelor's Degree Recipients, First-Time Medical School Enrollment, 1997

Population and Degree	Total	Other	African American	Asian American	Hispanic	White
				Race		
U.S. Population Age (18–24)	24,980,036	222,857	3,584,530	973,449	3,561,018	16,638,182
		0.9%	14.3%	3.9%	14.3%	66.6%
First Time, FT FR 4-yr Enroll	1,153,336	33,247	126,360	67,876	95,561	830,292
		2.9%	11.0%	5.9%	8.3%	72.0%
BA Degree	1,188,385	74,822	92,170	67,452	75,012	878,929
		6.3%	7.8%	5.7%	6.3%	74.0%
New Medical School Entrants	16,165	587	1,134	3,131	984	10,329
		3.6%	7.0%	19.4%	6.1%	63.9%

SOURCE: U.S. Census Bureau, Population Division, Population Estimates Program, 2000, 1997 IPEDS Enrollment Data, 1996–1997 IPEDS Completion Data, Association of American Medical Colleges.

full-time freshmen, 5.7 percent of the bachelor's degree recipients, and 19.4 percent of the new entrants into medical school. Similarly Whites made up 66.6 percent of the 18- to 24-year-old population, 72 percent of the first-time full-time freshmen, 74 percent of the bachelor's degree recipients, and 63.9 percent of the new entrants into medical school. It is important to observe that both African Americans and Hispanics are represented among new entrants into medical school at roughly the same rate that they are represented among bachelor's degree recipients. This is due mainly to the lower representation of students who are non-resident aliens among new medical school entrants than among bachelor's degree recipients and not because African Americans and Hispanics enter medical school at the same rate after undergraduate school as Asian Americans and Whites.

In the scheme of American meritocracy, attending college and attaining a bachelor's degree contribute to higher socioeconomic status. But, attending and attaining a degree from relatively prestigious colleges and universities yields advantage in the labor market and in American society (Bowen & Bok, 1998). Table 3 reveals that African Americans and Hispanics are underrepresented among first-time freshmen overall relative to their representation in the 18- to 24-year-old population, but their underrepresentation is most severe among the most prestigious colleges and universities. African Americans are even overrepresented in the least prestigious colleges and universities.

Table 3 shows that African Americans comprise 6.3% and 5.2%, respectively, of students enrolled at the most competitive and highly competitive colleges and universities, but 19% and 15.3%, respectively, of the less competitive and the non-competitive colleges and universities. Hispanics comprise 5.5% in the category of most competitive colleges and universities and 6 percent in the highly competitive category. Asians are overrepresented in the most competitive (13.4%), highly competitive (11.7%), and very competitive categories (7.1%). White students are represented among first-time, full-time freshmen comparable to their representation in the18- to 24-year-old population in the most competitive colleges and universities (69.8%), the highly competitive category (74.2%), and the other four categories.

Among the nation's practicing physicians, Table 4 shows that African Americans comprise just 3.2% and Hispanics 2.4%, which are far below their representation in the U.S. adult population. Even in the fields of internal medicine and obstetrics and gynecology, where African Americans and Hispanics are best represented among all the practice specialties, African Americans comprise just 3.2% and 6.4%, respectively, and Hispanics just 2.3% and 3.3%, respectively. A larger number of Asian Americans (25,441) were practicing physicians than both African Americans and Hispanics overall.

TABLE 3 First-Time Full-Time Freshmen Attending Non-Specialized Four-Year Colleges and Universities (N = 1,395) by Selectivity: 1997

Selectivity	Grand Total*	Total Race Groups	African American	Asian American	Hispanic	White
U.S. Population ages 18–24	24,980,036	24,757,179	3,584,530	973,449	3,561,018	16,638,182
			14.3%	3.9%	14.3%	66.6%
Total First-time Freshmen Enrollment	1,063,710	1,033,677	119,465	65,338	62,970	785,904
			11.2%	6.1%	5.9%	73.9%
Most Competitive (52)	50,932	48,332	3,196	6,814	2,780	35,542
			6.3%	13.4%	5.5%	69.8%
Highly Competitive (90)	120,152	116,656	6,259	14,051	7,196	89,150
			5.2%	11.7%	6.0%	74.2%
Very Competitive (249)	234,596	228,301	13,669	16,593	13,693	184,346
			5.8%	7.1%	5.8%	78.6%
Competitive (583)	413,401	402,298	53,145	20,034	23,055	306,064
			12.9%	4.8%	5.6%	74.0%
Less Competitive (292)	156,342	152,527	29,666	5,869	10,625	106,367
			19.0%	3.8%	6.8%	68.0%
Non-Competitive (129)	88,287	85,563	13,530	1,977	5,621	64,435
			15.3%	2.2%	6.4%	73.0%

NOTE: Grand total for the U.S. population includes Native Americans. Grand totals for freshmen enrollment include Native Americans and non-citizens. Row percents are calculated from the grand totals.

SOURCE: U.S. Census Bureau, Population Division, Population Estimates Program, 2000, IPEDS 1997 Fall Enrollment, Barron's Profiles of American Colleges, 1999.

TABLE 4 Primary Practice Specialty by Race/Ethnicity of U.S. Medical School Graduates

Practice Specialty	African American	Asian American	Hispanic	Native American	All Minorities	All Physicians
Colon & Rectal Surgery	16	29	22	1	68	1,033
Family Practice	2,410	1,979	1,992	278	6,659	64,611
Internal Medicine**	5,031	7,770	3,653	192	16,646	157,450
Medical Genetics	4	7	3	---	14	250
Nuclear Medicine	23	43	42	---	108	1,434
Obstetrics-Gynecology	2,526	1,515	1,303	82	5,426	39,257
Total	20,895	25,441	15,703	1,126	63,165	654,748

Internal Medicine is the most popular primary practice specialty overall as well as the most popular primary practice specialty for African Americans and Hispanics.
SOURCE: AAMC: Minority Graduates of U.S. Medical Schools: Trends, 1950–1998.

TABLE 5 Typical Undergraduate College Criteria for Admission

Test Scores
High School Class Rank
High School Grade Point Averages in College Preparatory Courses
High School Academic Program
Student Essay
Geography
Alumni Relations
Extraordinary Talent

TABLE 6 Typical Medical School Criteria for Admission

Test Scores (MCAT)
College Curriculum/Major
College Grade Point Averages
Pre-Med Courses
(Biology, Physics, English, Chemistry)
Overall Quality (Selectivity) of College Attended
Faculty Recommendations

Representation among new entrants into college, among students attending prestigious colleges and universities, among bachelor's degree recipients, among new entrants into medical school, and among practicing physicians are important markers of merit in American education. The fact that African Americans and Hispanics are severely underrepresented is problematic for achieving representative diversity at upper levels of the educational status hierarchy. Understanding the relative interests and aspirations of African Americans, and their achievement and performance at prior levels of education, is important in addressing their challenges to equality and representation in higher levels of education and in the overall hierarchy of American meritocracy.

PARTICIPATION AND PERFORMANCE OF UNDERREPRESENTED STUDENTS ON EDUCATIONAL TESTS AND ASSESSMENTS

Table 5 presents the criteria for admissions that are commonly used by colleges and universities to select undergraduate students. Table 6 presents the same for medical school admissions. The weight assigned to each criterion depends upon the heterogeneity of the applicant pool at each college, university, or medical school. The more homogeneous the applicant pool on any given criterion, the less weight the criterion has on decisions that the institution makes concerning whom to admit. Some of the criteria that colleges and universities rely on for making undergraduate, graduate, and first-professional degree program admissions decisions are good indicators of what American society accepts as indicators of merit. This is especially so in the case of grades and test scores, which are the two criteria that are used at every level of education as the most important for admissions decisions. The remaining criteria, such as geographical location of the hometown and special talents, are most often used for the purpose of achieving diversity in the student body.

The weight that colleges and universities assign to test scores and grades is more often a reflection of the type of information they need in order to discriminate among applicants within their applicant pool. Even though test scores and grades are typically required in admissions applications at all levels, their weight among the admissions criteria vary from one institution to the next. In fact, it is not surprising for less weight to be assigned to test scores in the most selective colleges than at less selective ones, because the weight is most often dependent upon the variance in the applicant pool rather than the value that colleges and universities believe the test has as a representation of student achievement. In colleges and universities that have large applicant pools and where the test scores of the applicant pool are homogenous, the weight assigned to scores is likely to be low and more weight may be placed on alternative criteria that provide more discrimination among the applicants. Conversely, tests may be the most prominent criteria when the test scores of the applicant pools are heterogeneous and other criteria are homogeneous.

It is difficult to imagine colleges and universities that have large applicant pools relative to the number of available admissions spaces being able to carry out their admissions processes without using a standardized test as a principal medium upon which to make decisions about applicants. As the Chancellor of the University of California system plans to discontinue using the SAT I (aptitude test), he proposes to use the SAT II (achievement test) rather than abandoning the use of standardized tests altogether in the admissions process. Mount Holyoke College and Bates College are two institutions that have made admissions tests optional for students who apply. But the vast majority of colleges and universities require students to submit either ACT or SAT test scores along with transcripts that include grades as a central component of their application for admissions. Grades and test scores may be equally valued in both types of places or even more valued in the place where they have the least weight. And because test scores and grades are the strongest and most visible signs of merit, they are the most important for aspiring students to focus on in achieving high levels of performance.

The trends in the number of students taking admissions tests is another indicator of student aspirations to attend college and post-baccalaureate graduate and professional education. Table 7 presents the trends during the past decade in the number of students of various racial/ethnic groups who took the American College Test (ACT) and the Scholastic Assessment Test (SAT) tests for undergraduate admissions. Table 8 presents the overall trends in students who took the Graduate Record Examination (GRE), the Law School Admissions Test (LSAT), and the Medical College Admissions Test (MCAT). These data reveal steady overall growth in the number of students aspiring to attend college, graduate and first-professional schools and the relatively larger growth in the underrepresented minorities.

Table 7 shows that approximately 113,377 African Americans, 60,878 Asian Americans, and 81,632 Hispanics took the SAT in 1999, representing an increase in participation of 16.9%, 42.9%, and 47.9%, respectively. The 707,851 Whites who took the SAT in 1999 represented a 4.6% increase in white test-taker participation.

Similarly, Table 7 also shows that the 100,282 African Americans, 24,357 Asian Americans, and 46,361 Hispanics took the ACT in 1999—39.8%, 70.3%, and 51.2% more than in 1991, respectively. The 718,498 Whites represented a 22.8% increase over the same time. African-American representation grew by 2.8% from 1991 to 1999 among SAT test-takers and by 10.4% on the ACT, and the representation of Hispanics increased by 30.0% among SAT test-takers and 19.4% among ACT test-takers. African Americans represented 10.3% and 10.5% of SAT and ACT test takers in 1999, respectively, compared with 10.1% and 9.5%, respectively, in 1991. Hispanics represented 7.5% and 4.9%, respectively, of the SAT and ACT test-takers in 1999, compared to 5.7% and 4.1%, respectively, in 1991. The Asian representation among SAT test-takers grew by 25.7%, from 4.4% 1991 to 5.6% in 1999, and by 34.4% on the ACT, from representing 1.9 percent to representing 2.6%.

TABLE 7 SAT I and ACT Test-Takers by Race/Ethnicity and Year

Race	Year						% Change in Participation 1991–1999	% Change in Represen tation 1991–1999
	1991		1995		1999			
	N	%	N	%	N	%		
SAT I								
African American	97,008	10.1	99,252	10.0	113,377	10.3	16.9	2.8
Asian American	42,607	4.4	48,523	4.9	60,878	5.6	42.9	25.7
Hispanic/ Latino	55,211	5.7	67,050	6.8	81,632	7.5	47.9	30.0
Native American	7,828	0.8	8,955	0.9	8,225	0.8	5.1	-7.6
White	676,404	70.2	665,750	67.3	707,851	64.6	4.6	-8.0
Other Citizen	11,422	1.2	19,344	2.0	30,756	2.8	169.3	136.8
Non- Citizen	73,150	7.6	80,258	8.1	92,989	8.5	27.1	11.8
Total	963,630		989,132		1,095,708		13.7	
ACT								
African American	71,722	9.5	87,462	10.1	100,282	10.5	39.8	10.4
Asian American	14,306	1.9	19,622	2.3	24,357	2.6	70.3	34.4
Hispanic/ Latino	30,661	4.1	42,193	4.9	46,361	4.9	51.2	19.4
Native American	9,285	1.2	11,220	1.3	10,612	1.1	14.3	-9.8
White	584,986	77.9	645,915	74.4	718,498	75.5	22.8	-3.0
Other Citizen	21,982	2.9	35,542	4.1	22,870	2.4	4.0	-17.9
Non- Citizen	18,129	2.4	25,772	3.0	28,527	3.0	57.4	24.2
Total	751,071		867,726		951,507		26.7	

SOURCE: Nettles & Millett Analyses of customized data files from ACT Inc., 1999. Nettles & Millett Analyses of customized data files from the College Board and Educational Testing Service, 1999.

TABLE 8 African-American Increase in Graduate and Professional School Test Taking: 1984–1995

Test	1984	1985	1986	1987	1988	1989	1990	1991	1992	1993	1994	1995	Percent Change in Participation 1984–1995
GRE	8,815	9,796	9,928	10,951	12,951	13,862	15,500	17,402	19,905	18,969	18,002	20,064	127.6
LSAT		4,406	4,889	5,079	5,758	6,167	7,109	8,287	9,343	9,577	9,969	9,560	117.0
MCAT	3,546				2,818				4,766			5,624	58.6

SOURCE: Educational Testing Service, Law School Admission Council, Association of American Medical Colleges

TABLE 9 Frequency and Percent of SAT I and ACT Test Takers by Score Ranges and Racial/Ethnic Group, 1999

SAT I	Overall		SAT V + M Score Range less than 1000		1000 to 1090		1100 to 1190		1200 and above	
	N	Mean	N	%	N	%	N	%	N	%
African American	113,377	852	89,560	79.0	12,644	11.2	6,773	6.0	4,400	3.9
Asian American	60,878	1077	22,395	36.8	10,126	16.6	9,511	15.6	18,846	31.0
Hispanic/Latino	81,632	921	53,915	66.0	12,770	15.6	7,977	9.8	6,970	8.5
Native American	8,225	964	4,695	57.1	1,477	18.0	1,037	12.6	1016	12.4

(continued)

	N	Mean	N	%	N	%	N	%	N	%
White	707,851	1054	273,018	38.6	145,925	20.6	124,931	17.6	163,977	23.2
Other Citizen	30,756	1036	13,198	42.9	5,451	17.7	4,641	15.1	7,466	24.3
Non-Citizen	92,989	982	49,693	53.4	14,168	15.2	11,587	12.5	17,541	18.9
All SAT I Test Takers	1,095,708	1017	506,474	46.2	202,561	18.5	166,457	15.2	220,216	20.1

			ACT Score Range							
ACT	Overall		less than 22		22 to 23		24 to 26		27 and above	
	N	Mean	N	%	N	%	N	%	N	%
African American	100,282	17.1	87,880	87.6	6,196	6.2	4,467	4.5	1,739	1.7
Asian American	24,357	22.4	10,994	45.1	3,522	14.5	4,529	18.6	5,312	21.8
Hispanic/Latino	46,361	19.1	33,759	72.8	5,032	10.9	4,830	10.4	2,740	5.9
Native American	10,612	19	7,727	72.8	1,162	10.9	1041	9.8	682	6.4
White	718,498	21.8	361,860	50.4	111,564	15.5	131,704	18.3	113,370	15.8
Other Citizen	22,870	20.6	13,699	59.9	3,053	13.3	3,386	14.8	2,732	11.9
Non-Citizen	28,527	19.3	19,983	70.0	3,033	10.6	3,142	11.0	2,369	8.3
All ACT Test Takers	951,507	21	535,902	56.3	133,562	14.0	153,099	16.1	128,944	13.6

SOURCE: Nettles & Millett Analyses of customized data files from ACT Inc., 1999. Nettles & Millett Analyses of customized data files from the College Board and Educational Testing Service, 1999.

Table 8 presents the trends in participation of African Americans taking the Graduate Record Examination (GRE), Law School Admission Test (LSAT), and the Medical College Admission Test (MCAT). Approximately 20,064 African Americans took the GRE in 1999, representing a 127.6% increase over 1985. The 9,560 African Americans who took the LSAT in 1999 represented a 117% increase in test-taking participation over 1984. The 5,624 African Americans who took the MCAT in 1995 represented a 58.6% increase over 1984.

Table 9 presents student performance in 1999 by race/ethnicity on the SAT and ACT, and the distribution of each group within selected score ranges. The overall combined mean on the SAT was 1,017 in 1999. The mean for African Americans was 852 and for Hispanics 921. The Asian mean was 1,077 and the white mean was 1,054. Approximately 38.6% of Whites and 36.8% of Asians achieved scores below 1,000, compared with 79% of African Americans and 66% of Hispanics. Conversely, 23.2% of Whites and 31% of Asians achieved scores of 1,200 or above, compared with 3.9% of African Americans and 8.5% of Hispanics.

Table 9 presents a similar picture for the ACT. Compared to an overall mean of 21, the mean for African Americans was 17.1, 19.1 for Hispanics, 21.8 for Whites and 22.4 for Asians. Approximately 50.4% of Whites and 45.1% of Asian Americans achieved scores below 22 compared with 87.6% of African Americans and 72.8% of Hispanics. While 21.8% of Asians and 15.8% of Whites achieved ACT scores of 27 or more, only 1.7% of African Americans and 5.9% of Hispanics achieved scores in this range.

Table 10 presents a similar picture on the MCAT in 1998. While the white average was 8.3 in verbal reasoning, 8.4 in the physical sciences, and 8.7 the in biological sciences, and the Asian means were 7.6, 8.9, and 8.8, respectively, the African American means were 6, 6.1, and 6.1, and the Mexican-American averages were 7, 7.1, and 7.4. The comparable scores for Mainland Puerto Ricans were 5.8, 6.3, and 6.4, and for other Hispanics 7.2, 7.6, and 7.8.

The pattern of lower African-American and Hispanic test performance begins in the earliest years of elementary school education. Figures 2 and 3 present the distribution of scores on the National Assessment of Educational Progress (NAEP) for fourth grade reading and mathematics. Over 60% of the African Americans and about 60% of Hispanic fourth graders were below basic in reading, and only 10% and 13%, respectively, were at or above proficient. Nearly 40% of Asians and Whites achieved at or above proficient. Similarly, in mathematics, over 65% of African Americans and nearly 60% of Hispanics were below basic, and around 5% of African Americans and 8% of Hispanics were at or above proficient. In contrast, nearly 30% of Asian Americans and Whites were at or above proficient. The NAEP data, together with the ACT and SAT data presented earlier in the paper, reveal how the gaps between African Americans and Hispanics and Asian Americans and Whites that are observed in elementary school assessments are never eliminated in subsequent tests and assessments.

TABLE 10 MCAT Performance by Race/Ethnicity: April/August 1998

Race	N	Verbal Reasoning	Physical Sciences	Biological Sciences	Writing Sample
Total	57,846*	7.8**	8.2	8.4	O***
African American	5,283	6	6.1	6.1	N
Asian American	12,260	7.6	8.9	8.8	O
American Indian	349	7.4	6.9	7.2	O
Other Hispanic	1,338	7.2	7.6	7.8	O
Mexican American Chicano	1,241	7	7.1	7.4	O
Native Alaskan	8	8.1	7.1	7.8	O
Native Hawaiian	29	6.9	7.6	7.6	O
Puerto Rico-Mainland	477	5.8	6.3	6.4	M
Puerto Rico-Commonwealth	958	4.4	5.3	5.2	K
White	32,967	8.3	8.4	8.7	P

* = Subtotals may not sum to total due to nonresponse of examinees on various demographic data fields.
** = Mean (Standard Deviation).
*** = Median.
SOURCE: Association of American Medical Colleges, 1998.

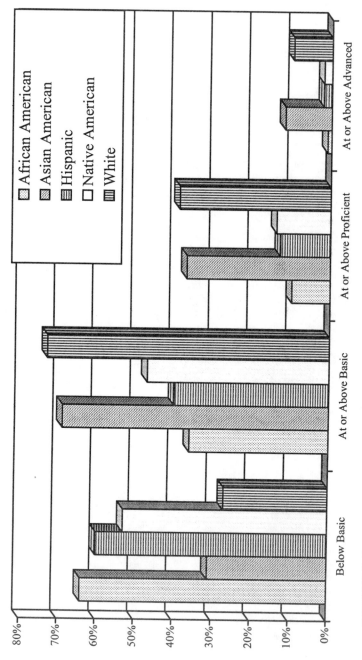

FIGURE 2 Percentage of Students Scoring at Various Levels on the National Assessment of Educational Progress in Reading: 4th Grade

SOURCE: NAEP 1998 Reading Report Card for the Nation and the States

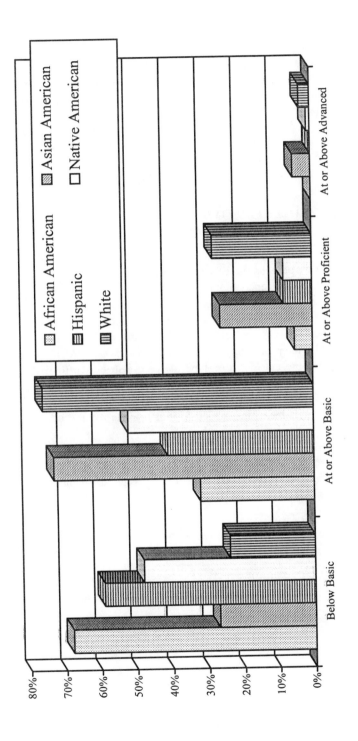

FIGURE 3 Percentage of Students Scoring at Various Levels on the National Assessment of Educational Progress in Mathematics: 4th Grade
SOURCE: NAEP 1996 Mathematics Report Card for the Nation and the States.

The consequence of lower performance of African Americans and Hispanics on these assessments and tests are lower access to high-quality curricula in school, lower access to higher-quality colleges and universities, and lower access to graduate and professional school. It is important to eliminate these performance gaps on standardized tests and assessments in order to achieve racial/ethnic equality in America's educational meritocracy. One place to begin is by examining the correlates of student performance on tests and assessments. These correlates should provide information on educational and other interventions that are needed to improve African-American and Hispanic performance.

FACTORS RELATED TO STUDENT PERFORMANCE ON TESTS AND ASSESSMENTS

Unless one is inclined to believe the "nature versus nurture" orientation of intelligence and merit, perhaps the best initial investment toward narrowing the racial/ethnic gap in performance should be to identify tangible factors that, if altered, could lead to higher performance for African Americans and Hispanics. The scatter plots presented in Figures 4 and 5 show the school-level math scores of African-American and white students in the fourth and eighth grades on NAEP, distributed by the proportion of school population that is African American. Figures 6 and 7 present the same type of score distribution for Hispanics and white students by the proportions of the school population that is Hispanic. The scatter plots use the overall mean of Whites and the means of African Americans as the standards against which to illustrate the mean scores of each racial/ethnic group of students in each school.

The patterns presented in Figures 4 and 5 reveal that the greater the African-American enrollment of a school, the lower the means of both African-Americans and white students in the school are likely to be on the NAEP mathematics assessment.

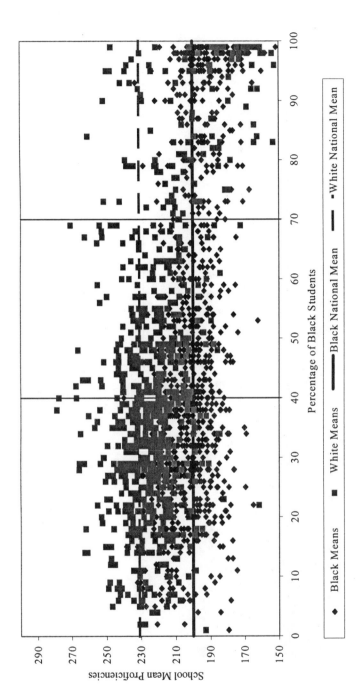

FIGURE 4 Math 1996 Grade 4 Public School State Aggregate A1+A2.
SOURCE: Educational Testing Service 1997 (unpublished raw data)

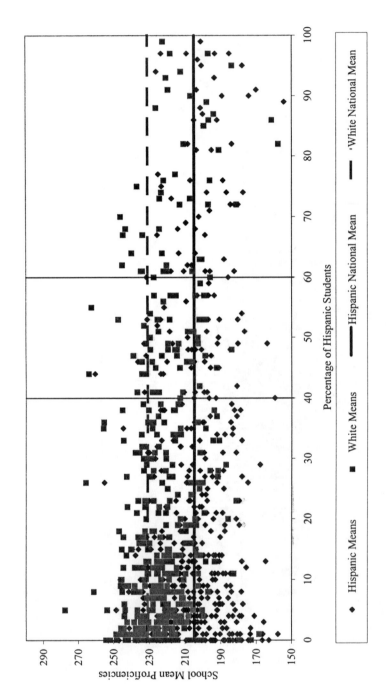

FIGURE 5 Math 1996 Grade 4 Public School State Aggregate S1
SOURCE: Educational Testing Service 1997 (unpublished raw data)

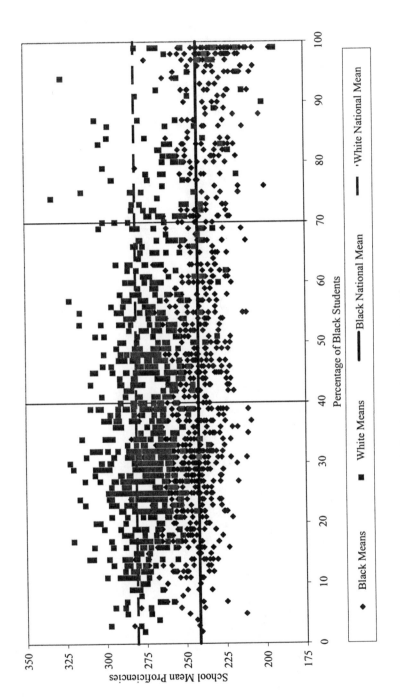

FIGURE 6 Math 1996 Grade 8 Public School State Aggregate A1+A2
SOURCE: Educational Testing Service 1997 (unpublished raw data)

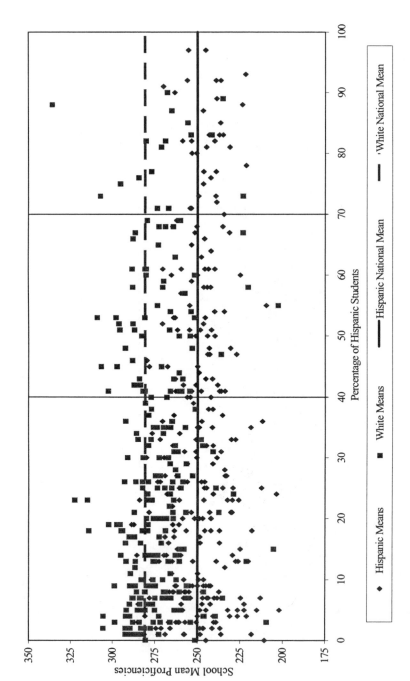

FIGURE 7 Math 1996 Grade 8 Public School State Aggregate S1
SOURCE: Educational Testing Service 1997 (unpublished raw data).

Similarly, Figures 6 and 7 show that the greater the enrollment of Hispanics in a school, the lower the average student performance on the NAEP mathematics assessment. It is a well-established fact that the African Americans and Hispanics in America attend lower-quality schools; therefore, the finding that the perform-ance of their schools on NAEP is lower is not surprising. What is astounding and important is that there are some schools revealed in Figures 4 through 7 that are overwhelmingly African American and Hispanic, and where the mean scores are at or above the white mean. At the same time, there are also some predominantly white schools where the means are around and below the African-American and Hispanic means. In essence, even though the probability of having a low-performing school in mathematics at the fourth and eighth grades is greater if the school is predominantly African American and Hispanic, the data show that there are also many challenges in schools that are all or nearly all white.

Because the schools in the NAEP sample are guaranteed anonymity, the identity of the individual schools cannot be disclosed. But, data regarding such characteristics and qualities as the state where the school is located, whether it is center city, urban, or rural, the size of the school's enrollment, and the percent of students who receive free or reduced-price lunches are available through the NAEP. Much more could be learned about these schools to shed light upon their performance if data about the quality of the teachers, the methods of organizing and teaching the curriculum, and the relationship of the parents with the school were available.

Another way to identify some important factors on which to take action is to identify the correlates of student performance on the college admissions tests. One of the most popular correlates of admissions tests is income. Figures 8 and 9 illustrate the relationship of family income to 1999 ACT and SAT scores, re-spectively. Figure 8 shows that for each racial/ethnic group, family income is proportional to a student's ACT score, and that the relative position of each group remains constant throughout the income distribution. At a family income level of $18,000 and below, Table 11 shows that the average ACT score for Af-rican Americans was 16, for Asian Americans and Whites 20, and for Hispanics 18. At the income range of $50,000 to $60,000, the mean score for African Americans is 18, for Asian Americans 23, for Hispanics 20, and Whites 22. At $100,000 and above, 20 was the average African American score, Asian Ameri-cans 25, Hispanics 22, and Whites 23. Table 12 shows that on the SAT, in the salary range of $10,000 to $20,000 the mean score was 805 for African Ameri-cans, around 856 for Hispanics, 970 for Asian Americans, and 975 for Whites. In the $50,000 to $60,000 range, the mean score was approximately 894 for Af-rican Americans, 1,076 for Asian Americans, 1,040 for Whites and others, and 966 for Hispanics. At $100,000 and above, the African American mean was around 1,000, around 1,070 for Hispanics, around 1,131 for Whites, and 1,217 for Asian Americans.

Income probably serves as a proxy for quality of schools, quality and level of parent education, and overall quality of life. Since efforts to increase the opportunities for underrepresented students to enter higher levels of the meritocracy are not likely to include altering the income distribution of the nation's families, then it is important to identify factors beyond income that might be addressed in improving the scores of African-American and Hispanic students.

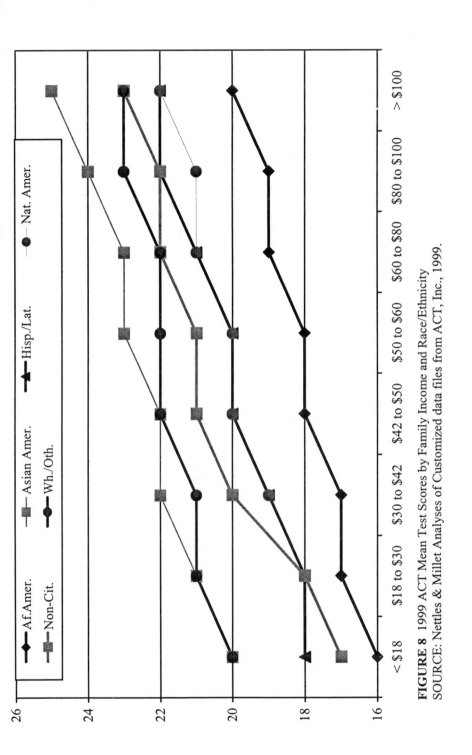

FIGURE 8 1999 ACT Mean Test Scores by Family Income and Race/Ethnicity

SOURCE: Nettles & Millet Analyses of Customized data files from ACT, Inc., 1999.

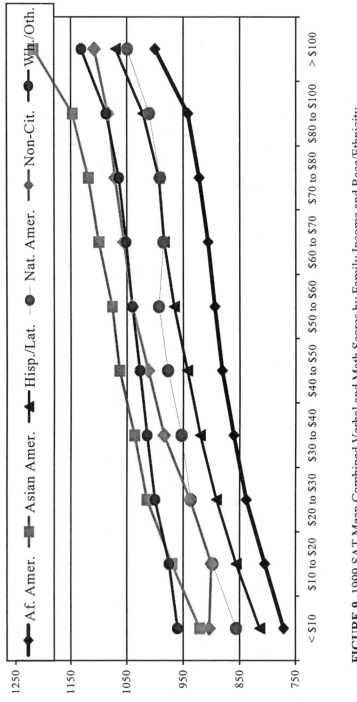

FIGURE 9 1999 SAT Mean Combined Verbal and Math Scores by Family Income and Race/Ethnicity
SOURCE: Nettles & Millet Analyses of Customized data files from the College Board and Educational Testing Service, 1999.

TABLE 11 1999 ACT Mean Test Scores by Family Income (in thousands) and Race/Ethnicity

Race	< $18	$18 to $30	$30 to $42	$42 to $50	$50 to $60	$60 to $80	$80 to $100	> $100
African American	16	17	17	18	18	19	19	20
Asian American	20	21	22	22	23	23	24	25
Hispanic/ Latino	18	18	19	20	20	21	22	22
Native American	17	18	19	20	20	21	21	22
Non-Citizen	17	18	20	21	21	22	22	23
White/Other	20	21	21	22	22	22	23	23

SOURCE: Nettles & Millett Analyses of customized data files from ACT, Inc., 1999

TABLE 12 1999 SAT Mean Combined Verbal and Math Scores by Family Income (in thousands) and Race/Ethnicity

Race	< $10	$10 to $20	$20 to $30	$30 to $40	$40 to $50	$50 to $60	$60 to $70	$70 to $80	$80 to $100	> $100
African American	771	805	838	860	881	894	906	922	942	1000
Asian American	921	970	1014	1036	1063	1076	1100	1118	1147	1217
Hispanic/ Latino	814	856	891	920	943	966	984	993	1021	1070
Native American	856	898	937	953	977	993	985	991	1010	1049
Non-Citizen	904	900	938	984	1012	1040	1055	1071	1084	1108
White/Other	960	975	1000	1014	1027	1040	1051	1064	1087	1131

SOURCE: Nettles & Millett Analyses of customized data files The College Board and Educational Testing Service 1999

Tables 13 and 14 present regression analyses showing the relationship of several student characteristics and attributes of human capital to their composite (English, reading, science, and math) ACT scores and combined (verbal and math) SAT scores. These characteristics and attributes include sex, race, family

TABLE 13 Regression Results for 1999 ACT Composite

Independent Variables	B	SE	t	Sig.	95% Confidence Int Lower	Upper
Intercept	13.27	0.04	339.11		13.19	13.35
English is first language	0.86	0.03	32.33	***	0.81	0.91
Family income $30,000 or less	-0.92	0.02	-60.48	***	-0.95	-0.89
Family income $30,000–60,000	-0.53	0.01	-41.04	***	-0.55	-0.50
Family income $60,000–80,000	-0.26	0.02	-17.23	***	-0.29	-0.23
Intended major: education	-0.97	0.02	-52.26	***	-1.00	-0.93
Intended major: health sciences	-1.01	0.01	-68.16	***	-1.04	-0.98
Intended major: humanities	-0.01	0.02	-0.86	0.39	-0.04	0.02
Intended major: professions	-0.77	0.01	-52.56	***	-0.79	-0.74
Intended major: other	-1.19	0.03	-46.81	***	-1.24	-1.14
Intended major: undecided	-0.69	0.02	-38.59	***	-0.73	-0.66
Male	0.69	0.01	69.94	***	0.67	0.71
African American	-1.93	0.02	-95.40	***	-1.97	-1.89
Asian American	-0.44	0.03	-15.98	***	-0.49	-0.39
Hispanic/Latino	-1.04	0.02	-42.17	***	-1.09	-0.99
Native American	-0.60	0.05	-11.58	***	-0.71	-0.50
Non-citizen	-1.50	0.03	-47.07	***	-1.56	-1.43
Other citizen	-0.47	0.03	-16.06	***	-0.53	-0.42
Course work and achievement	0.15	0.00	569.82	***	0.14	0.15
Number AP courses offered	0.06	0.00	78.22	***	0.06	0.06
Public high school	-0.65	0.02	-43.04	***	-0.68	-0.62
% African-American enrollment in hs	-1.57	0.03	-52.34	***	-1.63	-1.51
% Hispanic enrollment in hs	-2.68	0.03	-78.37	***	-2.74	-2.61

R Squared .51

NOTE: Reference group for family income is $80,000 or more, for intended major is natural science, for race is white, and for public high school is private high school. Coursework and achievement are calculated as: the number of years in a subject area plus 1 if took honors multiplied by average grade in subject area. Scores were summed for six subject areas: math, English, social science, natural science, foreign language, and art/music. Possible scores ranged from 4 to 100.

SOURCE: Nettles & Millett Analyses of customized data files from ACT, Inc., 1999.

TABLE 14 Regression Results for 1999 SAT Combined Verbal and Math

Independent Variables	B	SE	t	Sig.	95% Confidence Int Lower	Upper
Intercept	724.53	1.31	554.97		721.97	727.09
English is first language	13.06	0.78	16.73	***	11.53	14.59
Father has hs diploma or less	-64.21	0.53	-122.25	***	-65.24	-63.18
Father has some college	-45.14	0.49	-91.69	***	-46.10	-44.17
Father has Bachelor's degree	-25.23	0.49	-51.28	***	-26.19	-24.27
Family income $30,000 or less	-35.63	0.57	-62.69	***	-36.74	-34.52
Family income $30,000–60,000	-18.38	0.46	-39.67	***	-19.29	-17.47
Family income $60,000–80,000	-13.99	0.51	-27.30	***	-14.99	-12.98
Intended major: education	-57.23	0.66	-86.94	***	-58.52	-55.94
Intended major: health sciences	-44.36	0.54	-82.23	***	-45.42	-43.30
Intended major: humanities	-14.71	0.51	-28.94	***	-15.70	-13.71
Intended major: professions	-35.03	0.50	-70.12	***	-36.01	-34.05
Intended major: other	-55.67	0.84	-66.35	***	-57.31	-54.02
Intended major: undecided	-25.78	0.74	-34.75	***	-27.24	-24.33
Male	56.04	0.35	161.66	***	55.36	56.72
African American	-67.86	0.68	-99.33	***	-69.20	-66.52
Asian American	7.34	0.72	10.15	***	5.92	8.76
Hispanic/Latino	-33.11	0.74	-44.61	***	-34.57	-31.66
Native American	-22.25	1.95	-11.38	***	-26.08	-18.42
Non-citizen	-41.84	0.90	-46.59	***	-43.60	-40.08
Other citizen	8.19	1.01	8.14	***	6.22	10.16
Course work and achievement	5.48	0.01	615.63	***	5.47	5.50
Number AP courses offered	3.87	0.03	134.62	***	3.81	3.92
Public high school	-29.02	0.50	-58.00	***	-30.00	-28.04
% African-American enrollment in hs	-57.52	1.04	-55.06	***	-59.57	-55.47
% Hispanic enrollment in hs	-87.98	1.04	-84.41	***	-90.02	-85.94

R Squared .52

NOTE: Reference group for family income is $80,000 or more, for intended major is natural science, for race is white, and for public high school is private high school. Coursework and achievement are calculated as: the number of years in a subject area plus 1 if took honors multiplied by average grade in subject area. Scores were summed for six subject areas: math, English, social science, natural science, foreign language, and art/music. Possible scores ranged from 4 to 100.

SOURCE: Nettles & Millett Analyses of customized data files from the College Board and Educational Testing Service, 1999.

income, fathers' education, whether English is the primary language, a measure of the courses taken in high school and their performance in those courses, their intended college major field, attendance at a public or private high school, the availability of Advanced Placement (AP) courses, and the proportion of African-American and Hispanic enrollment. Tables 13 and 14 depict the relationship of these variables to students' scores on the ACT and the SAT, respectively.

Table 13 presents the regression findings for the ACT assessment. The model accounted for 50% of the variance in students' ACT composite score achievement. The strongest predictor overall (based on the t statistic) was the measure of high school courses taken and grades achieved. This measure includes the number of years that a student took courses in the subject areas of math, English, social science, natural science, foreign language, and art/music (students were given an additional point for taking honors courses in a subject), multiplied by the average grade achieved in the subject.

Socioeconomic measures were associated with ACT performance. Students whose first language is English scored .9 points higher than those whose first language is not English. Compared with students whose family incomes were $80,000 or more per year, students with family incomes of $30,000 or less scored, on average, 1 point lower on the ACT. Those with family incomes of $30,000 to $60,000 scored .5 points lower, and those with family incomes of $60,000 to $80,000 scored .3 points lower. Compared to Whites, on average, African-American students scored 1.9 points lower, Asian students scored .4 points lower, Hispanic students scored 1 point lower, Native American students scored .6 points lower, non-citizens scored 1.5 points lower, and other citizens scored .5 points lower. Males scored .7 points higher than females.

High school experiences and characteristics were also significant predictors of ACT performance. For every point they had on the high school curriculum and achievement measure, students scored .15 points higher on the ACT. Students intending to major in a subject other than natural science scored lower, on average, on the ACT. This difference was strongest for students intending to major in other disciplines (they scored 1.2 points lower) and in health sciences (1 point lower). Students achieved .1 point higher on the ACT for each AP course offered at their high school. Students attending public schools achieved .7 points lower on the ACT than students attending private schools. Each 10 percent increment in African-American enrollment at the high school was associated with achieving .16 points lower on the ACT. Each 10 percent increment in Hispanic enrollment at a particular high school was associated with achieving .27 points lower on the ACT.

As shown in Table 14, after controlling for all the other variables in the model, the combination of course work and student grade achievement was the most substantial predictor of students' SAT scores. However, this variable was of somewhat less relative importance as a predictor in the SAT model than the ACT model. This is a reflection of differences in the nature of these tests. The

SAT is intended to measure students' aptitude for college-level work while the ACT is intended to measure students' mastery of high school-level curriculum. Other prominent predictors of SAT scores were fathers' education, sex, and the number of AP courses offered in the school. The model accounted for 52 percent of the variance in students' performance on the SAT.

There was a positive relationship between measures of students' socioeconomic status and SAT performance. Compared with students whose fathers had completed a bachelor's degree and some graduate education, students whose fathers were high school graduates or less scored on average 64 points lower on the SAT. Students whose fathers had some college but were not bachelor's degree recipients achieved, 45 points lower and those whose fathers were bachelor's degree recipients achieved scores 25 points lower. Compared to students whose family incomes were $80,000 or more per year, those with family incomes of $30,000 or less scored, on average, 36 points lower on the SAT; those with family incomes of $30,000 to $60,000 scored 18 points lower; and those with family incomes of $60,000 to $80,000 scored 14 points lower. Compared with Whites, on average, African-American students scored 68 points lower, Asian students scored 7 points more, Hispanic students scored 33 points lower, Native American students scored 22 points lower, non-citizens scored 42 points lower, and other citizens scored 8 points more on the SAT. Students whose first language is English scored 13 points higher than those whose first language is not English. On average, males scored 56 points higher on the SAT than females.

Students' experiences and achievements in high school are also important predictors of SAT performance. For every point they had on the high school course measure, students achieved 5.5 more points on the SAT. Students intending a college major other than natural science scored lower, on average, on the SAT. This difference was strongest for students intending to major in education (they scored 57 points lower) and students intending another major (56 points lower). High school characteristics were also related to students' SAT performance. Students achieved an average of 4 points more on the SAT for each AP course offered at their high school. Students attending public schools achieved 29 points lower on the SAT than students attending private schools. Each 10 percent increment in African-American enrollment at the high school was associated with achieving 6 points less on the SAT. Each 10 percent increment in Hispanic enrollment at the high school was associated with achieving 9 points lower on the SAT.

A statistical method known as bootstrapping was conducted to learn more about the factors that distinguish high-performing test-takers from their lower-performing counterparts who are in the same general socioeconomic status. The bootstrapping technique is described in Appendix A. The analyses presented in this paper are for 1999 test-takers whose family incomes were between $30,000 and $60,000 and whose fathers' education was at least a bachelor's degree. The analyses are also confined to the following four subpopulations of test takers:

African-American females, African-American males, white females and white males. Bootstrapping was used to identify predictor variables that significantly increased or decreased the test score gap between high-performing students (those who achieved a combined math and verbal score at or above 1200 on the SAT) and low-performing students (those who achieved a combined score less than 1200).

The analyses in Tables 15 through 18 reveal that four measures contributed significantly to the test score gap between high- and low-performing students in all four subgroups: taking calculus, taking physics, participation in an academically-oriented extracurricular activity, and taking and achieving high grades in a comprehensive academic curriculum. Only measures that were significant predictors are included in the tables. The tables can be interpreted as follows: measures with a positive coefficient were associated with a significant increase in the test score gap between the high- and low-performing students, while measures with a negative coefficient were associated with a significant decrease in the test score gap.

Holding all other variables in the analyses constant, if high-performing students took calculus and low-performing students did not, the average gap in their test score performance increased by 36.41 points for African-American females, 35.38 points for African-American males, 21.00 points for white females, and 27.96 points for white males. Conversely, if high-performing students did not take calculus and low-performing students did, the average gap in their test performance decreased by 34.74 points for African-American females, 53.80 points for African-American males, and 33.01 points for white males. A similar pattern was associated with taking physics: if high-performing students took physics and low-performing students did not, there was a significant increase in the average test score gap between the two groups for both races and sexes. In general, participation in academically-oriented activities had a beneficial association for low-performing students; the gap between their test scores and those of their higher-performing peers was significantly decreased. Finally, differences in overall course taking and achievement accounted for significant changes in the test score gap between high- and low-performers. For every unit increase in this curriculum measure (values ranged from 1 to 100), that gap increased by approximately 3 points for African-American females and males, and 2 points for white females and males.

Other significant predictors were specific to sub-groups in the analyses. Table 15 reveals that for African-American females, taking honors English, attending a public versus a private high school, and the percentage of white enrollment at the high school were associated with significant differences in the test score gap between high- and low-performing students. Table 16 shows that participating in athletic extracurricular activities, the census region in which

TABLE 15 Bootstrapping Results for African-American Females Taking the 1999 SAT

Predictors of Differences in SAT V+M score	Estimate	SE	SE Median	T	95% Confidence Int Lower	Upper
(Intercept)	260.63	14.26	15.16	17.22	232.13	287.55
Calculus = 1	36.41	11.08	10.62	3.44	14.65	56.50
Physics = 1	55.77	10.34	10.13	5.52	36.04	77.69
Honors English = 1	27.26	11.09	10.68	2.56	5.38	48.61
Academic activity = 3	-33.30	13.40	13.89	-2.39	-59.36	-5.88
High school = 1	-35.41	14.84	16.00	-2.18	-62.28	-4.67
Curriculum measure	2.91	0.26	0.26	11.09	2.44	3.44
% White enrollment	67.12	11.97	11.98	5.59	42.72	89.13

NOTE: Only the significant predictors of differences in 1999 SAT V+M scores are presented.
Calculus = 1 means the >1200 student took calculus and the <1200 student did not.
Physics = 1 means the >1200 student took physics and the <1200 student did not.
Honors English = 1 means the >1200 student took Honors English and the <1200 student did not.
Academic activity = 3 means the >1200 student received an award in an academically oriented extracurricular activity and the <1200 student participated in this type of activity.
High school = 1 means the >1200 student attended a private school and the <1200 student attended a public school.
SOURCE: Nettles & Millett Analyses of customized data files from the College Board and Educational Testing Service, 1999.

students lived, and the percentage of white enrollment made significant contributions to differences in the test scores of high- and low-performing African-American males. Tables 17 and 18 reveal that athletic activity participation, attending a public or private high school, and racial composition of the high school were not significant correlates of increasing or decreasing the test score gap for white female and male students. For these subgroups, significant predictors were restricted to measures of high school course work, extracurricular academic involvement, and grade achievement.

TABLE 16 Bootstrapping Results for African-American Males Taking the 1999 SAT

Predictors of Differences in SAT V+M Scores	Estimate	SE	SE Median	t	95% Confidence Int Lower	Upper
(Intercept)	267.27	15.14	15.83	16.89	238.03	296.73
Calculus = -1	-53.80	16.67	18.60	-2.88	-86.12	-18.56
Calculus = 1	36.41	11.08	10.62	3.44	14.65	56.50
Physics = 1	51.45	10.37	10.36	4.97	31.20	71.64
Academic activity = -3	-63.91	20.20	22.93	-2.79	-104.07	-24.73
Athletic activity = 3	36.20	14.42	15.16	2.39	7.13	64.56
Athletic activity = 4	-44.99	21.24	19.53	-2.32	-85.84	-0.08
Census region	-32.19	15.38	15.95	-2.02	-61.43	-0.87
Curriculum measure	2.70	0.27	0.27	10.14	2.15	3.24
% White enrollment	39.89	12.22	12.42	3.22	16.13	64.38

NOTE: Only the significant predictors of differences in 1999 SAT V+M scores are presented.
Calculus = -1 means the >1200 student did not take calculus and the <1200 student did.
Calculus = 1 means the >1200 student took calculus and the <1200 student did not.
Physics = 1 means the >1200 student took physics and the <1200 student did not.
Academic activity = -3 means the >1200 student participated in an academically oriented activity and the <1200 student received an award in this type of activity.
Athletic activity = 3 means the >1200 student received an athletic award and the <1200 student participated in an athletic activity.
Athletic activity = 4 means the >1200 student received an athletic award and the <1200 student did not participate in an athletic activity.
SOURCE: Nettles & Millett Analyses of customized data files from the College Board and Educational Testing Service, 1999.

TABLE 17 Bootstrapping Results for White Females Taking the 1999 SAT

Predictors of Differences in SAT V+M Score	Estimate	SE	SE Median	*t*	95% Confidence Int Lower	Upper
(Intercept)	214.05	14.24	14.29	14.99	186.69	241.94
Calculus = -1	-35.32	15.14	18.39	-1.91	-63.98	-5.17
Calculus = 1	21.00	9.39	9.60	2.19	2.65	39.07
Physics = 1	29.15	9.69	9.48	3.08	10.60	49.14
Honors English = 1	30.56	9.52	9.79	3.11	11.60	49.17
Academic activity = 4	30.19	15.79	15.29	1.98	0.03	61.34
Curriculum measure	2.07	0.25	0.25	8.41	1.60	2.57

NOTE: Only the significant predictors of differences in 1999 SAT V+M scores are presented. Calculus = -1 means the >1200 student did not take calculus and the <1200 student did. Calculus = 1 means the >1200 student took calculus and the <1200 student did not. Physics = 1 means the >1200 student took physics and the <1200 student did not. Honors English = 1 means the >1200 student took Honors English and the <1200 student did not. Academic activity = 4 means the >1200 student received an award in an academically oriented activity and the <1200 student did not participate in this type of activity.
SOURCE: Nettles & Millett Analyses of customized data files from the College Board and Educational Testing Service, 1999.

TABLE 18 Bootstrapping Results for White Males Taking the 1999 SAT

Predictors of Differences In SAT V+M Score	Estimate	SE	Median	*t*	95% Confidence Int Lower	Upper
(Intercept)	221.55	14.05	14.58	15.16	193.56	248.77
Calculus = -1	-33.01	15.38	18.54	-1.80	-63.88	-1.88
Calculus = 1	35.38	10.29	10.79	3.28	15.21	55.52
Physics = 1	47.10	10.43	10.03	4.68	27.48	67.22
Academic activity = 4	39.91	15.94	15.28	2.60	9.05	72.00
Curriculum measure	1.64	0.24	0.24	6.79	1.17	2.12

NOTE: Only the significant predictors of differences in 1999 SAT V+M scores are presented. Calculus = -1 means the >1200 student did not take calculus and the <1200 student did. Calculus = 1 means the >1200 student took calculus and the <1200 student did not. Physics = 1 means the >1200 student took physics and the <1200 student did not.
SOURCE: Nettles & Millett Analyses of customized data files from the College Board and Educational Testing Service, 1999.

TYPES OF INITIATIVES NEEDED FOR EXPANDING MERIT AND ELIMINATING UNDER-REPRESENTATION

School curricula have the highest probability of possibly supplanting or complementing test scores as indicators of merit. Students who experience the most rigorous curricula in school and earn relatively high grades are promising prospects for success in college and graduate and professional school. Among the best organizations in the nation are A Better Chance, Bank Street College's ILEAD program, the Center for Talented Youth (CTY), and Prep for Prep. Although each one of these programs are unique, the goal of each is to identify students early, provide them with rigorous academic instruction, encourage them to adopt intellectual habits, move them to high-caliber independent and public schools, and guide them into the highest academic tracks in the schools that they attend. In each program—with the exception of the ILEAD—one objective is to identify promising young students at around fifth, sixth, or seventh grade and begin to compensate for the low level of academic preparation they receive in their local public schools. In Prep for Prep, students attend mathematics, history, English, and science classes taught by master teachers throughout the school year on Saturdays from 8 a.m. to 5 p.m. and every Wednesday from 4 p.m. to 6 p.m. The students also devote an intensive three weeks to further instruction during the summers. Standardized tests are used to identify and invite the students to attend and are used throughout the program to measure their progress. The goal of the program is to prepare and then to help students gain admission into independent boarding schools by ninth grade or into the AP and honors tracks of their public high schools.

A Better Chance also identifies students as early as the fifth and sixth grades. Rather than providing instructions and a curriculum of its own, A Better Chance matches students with independent day schools, boarding schools, or a dozen or so outstanding public schools. The Center for Talented Youth at Johns Hopkins University is probably the oldest, most established, and largest of the programs. It has an array of academic-intensive courses for students, mainly during summers, as well as on-line instruction, workshops, and mentoring during the school year. ILEAD works with four Catholic schools in the Bronx, New York, helping to enrich their curriculum and providing professional development for their teachers. Each of these four aims to prepare students for admissions to the nation's most selective colleges and universities. Each one recognizes that success in the competitive admissions process and persistence through completion requires the highest quality of academic preparation and competitive test scores. It is only through academic preparation that the academic and socioeconomic playing field can be leveled for underrepresented African-American and Hispanic youth, and that the colleges and universities at the height of America's meritocracy can become more diverse.

CONCLUSION

Standardized intellectual tests and assessments are important barometers of underrepresented student achievement in America's educational meritocracy. The inter-correlation of individual, group, and institutional test and assessment scores reveals uniformity among these instruments and shows how the nation's social hierarchy is structured. The nation's meritocracy is constituted by all three types of tests and assessments. Underrepresented groups must focus upon all three in order to advance in the nation's educational meritocracy. Regardless of the weight that colleges and universities assign to tests and assessments in the college admissions process, they remain the most challenging and most important focus for African Americans and Hispanics. Unless African Americans and Hispanics are able to close the achievement gap revealed by these assessments, they will not be able to expand their access to the most selective colleges and universities and first-professional schools, and they will remain underrepresented in the highest-status professions.

These tests and assessments can be important in the long term for developing public policies that are aimed toward improving educational outcomes, and in the short-term for extending the benefits of merit to a broader representation of the population.

APPENDIX A

How Bootstrapping Was Implemented for These Data

We used this iterative re-sampling method in order to better understand the inherent difference between high potential students (SAT V+M $\geq$ 1200) and everyone else.

In general, the bootstrap method calls for selecting from the observed sample data a random sample of size n with replacement. Then the bootstrap method calculates the estimated parameter using the same analysis method for each sample drawn. The mean or median of the bootstrap re-sample estimates can be used as the estimated parameter value. Confidence intervals about the parameter value can be produced by taking quantiles (2.5[th] and 97.5[th] for a 95% CI) of the bootstrap re-sample estimates.[1] For example, in a simple case, say you have 20 observations and you want a bootstrap estimate of a confidence interval about the true mean of that parameter. This could happen in a case where you do not know the underlying distribution of the parameter. You re-sample with replacement 20 data points from the original 20 observations. There, of course, will be repeat observations in each bootstrap re-sample. You could then follow the algorithm above to get a confidence for the true mean.

---

[1] Source: Neter et. al, Applied Linear Statistical Models, 1996.

For our data, we would like to investigate differences between high potential students and non-high potential students conditioning on certain uncontrollable factors. The variables that we decided to use were father's level of education, parental income range, race and sex. After splitting the file on these uncontrollable variables, create HiPo (SAT V+M $\geq$ 1200) and ~HiPo (SAT V+M < 1200) data sets for each covariate class (or cell, if you think of these as crosstabs). There would be 4 (number of levels of father's education) x 4 (number of levels of parental income) x 4 (race groups) x 2 (sexes) = 128 total separate bootstraps to do. However, this would take too much time so we decided to do a subset of the combinations of father's education by parental income. However, within each of those subsets, we would do all combinations of race by sex.

1. Randomly select a person from the the HiPo and ~HiPo data sets for a specific covariate class derived after splitting the large data set for uncontrollable variables.
2. Compute the difference between the HiPo and ~HiPo student on SAT V+M and the predictor variables.
3. Repeat (1) – (2) 1,000 times to create bootstrap data set.
4. Regress the differences in the SAT V+M difference, using the 1,000 observations from (3).
5. Store the estimated coefficients.
6. Repeat (1) – (5) 1,000 times.

The result of these 6 steps will be 1,000 estimates for the coefficients and standard errors of the predictors. Take the median of those 1,000 estimates for the coefficient and the standard errors as the final parameter estimate for that coefficient and that standard error. Use the 2.5th and 97.5th quartile of the 1,000 estimates of the coefficients to derive a 95% confidence interval for the parameter estimate. Also, using the 2.5th and 97.5th quartile of the 1,000 estimates of the standard errors will yield a 95% confidence interval for the standard error parameter estimate. If a confidence interval does not include 0, call the variable significant.

Assumptions made:

1. After controlling for the unchangeable variables the students in HiPo are "the same," and the students in ~HiPo are "the same" except for the uncontrollable factors.
2. The HiPo and ~HiPo data sets are representative of the population, after eliminating cases with missing values on any variable.

Results

We used this methodology to derive our estimates for significant factors in predicting differences in SAT scores between high potential and non-high potential students. The predictors that we initially included in the model (after splitting the file on the uncontrollable variables) were took calculus (Y or N); took physics (Y or N); took honors English (Y or N); academic activity status; athletic activity status; census region (4); went to public/private school; high school curriculum measure; student teacher ratio; percentage of white students in school.

REFERENCES

Association of American Medical Colleges (1998). April/August 1997 MCAT Performance by Sex, Racial/Ethnic Group, Age, Language Status, Undergraduate Major and Testing History [On-line]. Available: http://www.aamc.org/students/mcat/scores /examineedata/sum2000.pdf.

Association of American Medical Colleges (1998). [MCAT test takers]. Unpublished raw data.

Association of American Medical Colleges. (2000). Minority Graduates of U.S. Medical Schools: Trends, 1950–1998. Washington, DC: Association of American Medical Colleges.

Barron's profiles of American colleges. (1999). Woodbury, NY: Barron's Educational Series, Inc.

Bowen, W. G., & Bok, D. C. (1998). The shape of the river: Long term consequences of considering race in college and university admissions. Princeton, NJ: Princeton University Press.

Donahue, P.L., Voekl, K.E., Campbell, J. R., and Mazzeo, J. (1999). The NAEP 1998 Reading report card for the Nation and the States. NCES 1999–500. Washington, DC: National Center for Education Statistics.

Educational Testing Service (1997). [1996 NAEP Mathematics results]. Unpublished raw data.

Educational Testing Service, Graduate Examinations Board Programs. [Graduate Records Examination results, 1984–1995]. Unpublished raw data.

Law School Admission Council (2000). [Applicant Counts by Ethnic and Gender Group—1984–85 to Fall 2000]. Unpublished raw data.

Nettles, M. T. & Millett, C. M. (2001). [Customized data files from ACT, Inc., 1999]. Unpublished raw data.

Nettles, M. T. & Millett, C. M. (2001). [Customized data files from the College Board and Educational Testing Service, 1999]. Unpublished raw data.

Neter, J., Wassweman, W., & Kutner, M. H. (1983). Applied linear regression models. Homewood, ILL: R.D. Irwin.

Reese, C. M., Miller, K. E., Mazzeo, J. & Dossey, J. A. (1997). The NAEP 1996 Mathematics report card for the Nation and the States. Washington, DC: National Center for Education Statistics.

U.S. Census Bureau, Population Division, Population Estimates Program (2000). Population Estimates for States by Age, Race, Sex, and Hispanic Origin: July 1, 1999 [On-line]. Available: http://www.census.gov/population/estimates/state/sasrh/sasrh99.txt.

U.S. Census Bureau, Population Division, Population Estimates Program (2000). Population Estimates for States by Age, Race, Sex, and Hispanic Origin: July 1, 1997 [On-line]. Available: http://www.census.gov/population/estimates/state/sasrh/sasrh97.txt.

U.S. Department of Education. National Center for Education Statistics. (2000). Digest of education statistics, 1999. (NCES 2000–031). Washington, DC: U.S Government Printing Office

U.S. Department of Education. National Center for Education Statistics. (1997). Integrated postsecondary education data system. Washington, DC: U.S. Government Printing Office.

Trends in Underrepresented Minority Participation in Health Professions Schools[*]

Kevin Grumbach, Janet Coffman,
Emily Rosenoff, and Claudia Muñoz

University of California, San Francisco
Center for California Health Workforce Studies

INTRODUCTION

African Americans, Latinos, and Native Americans are underrepresented in all the health professions in the United States. In the past decade, educational organizations in the health professions have embarked on initiatives to increase the number of underrepresented minorities (URMs) entering health professions schools. Among the most prominent of these has been the "3000 by 2000" project directed by the Association of American Medical Colleges. URM enrollment in U.S. medical schools increased in the early 1990s, coinciding with the 3000 by 2000 initiative. However, these trends have abruptly reversed in recent years. Many observers have attributed much of this recent decrease to legislative and judicial decisions (e.g., Proposition 209 in California and *Hopwood* v. *Texas*) that have restricted the use of special consideration of race and ethnicity in admissions decisions.

Much less is known about national trends in the past decade in URM enrollment in health professions schools other than allopathic medicine. In addition, prior published analyses of URM trends in allopathic medical schools have not fully scrutinized the interplay between application and admission trends that have resulted in the decline in URM matriculants. To better understand trends in URM student enrollment across professions and to clarify the factors contributing to observed patterns in URM enrollment, we analyzed data for the past decade for a variety of health professions.

[*] Support for this paper was provided by the Bureau of Health Professions, HRSA Grant 5 U76 MB 10003.

METHODS

We contacted associations representing health professions schools to obtain data about each profession for the years 1990–2000. Data were obtained from the following organizations: American Association of Colleges of Nursing, American Association of Colleges of Osteopathic Medicine, American Association of Colleges of Pharmacy, Association of American Medical Colleges, American Dental Education Association, Association of Schools of Public Health, California Postsecondary Education Commission, and the College of Veterinary Medicine at North Carolina State University.

We requested unduplicated national counts of the number of applicants, acceptances, matriculants, and graduates for each year for each type of professional school. To evaluate the possible effects of the Proposition 209 and *Hopwood* v. *Texas* policies, we also requested information separately for California and Texas schools for each of these data elements. Many associations were unable to provide national or state data for some or all of the requested elements; in these instances, we relied on less optimal data such as number of total enrollees rather than number of new matriculants. Additionally, data were not always available for all the years requested. We did not examine retention rates in health professions schools because data on progression of students from matriculation through graduation were not available for most professions.

We defined URMs as African Americans, Latinos, and Native Americans. Some educational organizations use more restrictive definitions of URMs (e.g., include only certain subgroups of Latinos). However, we considered Latinos as a whole to be underrepresented and many organizations have data only for Latinos in the aggregate and not for specific subgroups.

RESULTS

URM trends in matriculants and enrollees over the past decade differ across the health professions (Figure 1). Nursing, public health, and pharmacy have seen a modest but steady rise in the proportion of matriculants and enrollees who are URMs. Other professions, such as allopathic and osteopathic medicine, experienced initial increases followed by decreases in the late 1990s. Dentistry, in contrast, is a profession with a steady decrease in the proportion of URM matriculants over the entire decade. All health professions fall well short of "population parity" measured against the proportion of URMs in the overall U.S. population; according to 2000 U.S. Census data, African Americans, Latinos, and American Indians constitute 25% of the U.S. population.[i]

The number of URMs matriculating is a function of three components: the number of URMs applying, the proportion of URM applicants accepted, and the proportion of the accepted students who matriculate. These dynamics differ for each profession in producing the patterns shown in Figure 1.

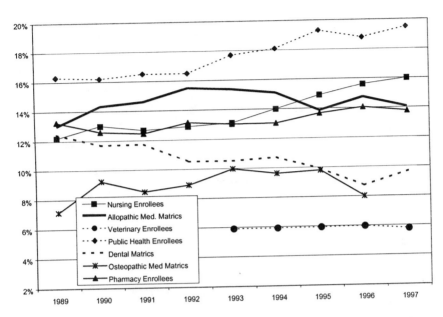

FIGURE 1 URMs as Percent of Matriculants or Total Enrollees—All Professions.

ALLOPATHIC MEDICINE

Data are most complete for medical schools accredited by the Licensing Council for Medical Education (often referred to as allopathic medical schools). The completeness of the data permits a thorough analysis of the dynamics of URM participation in allopathic medical schools. In addition, data from allopathic medical schools are available in detail for years prior to 1990 and we include 1980–1990 data as well as 1990–2000 data in these analyses.

Allopathic medicine experienced a rise and fall in the percent of matriculants who are URMs, reaching a high of 15.5% in 1994 before falling to 13.8% in 2000. Through much of the 1990s, allopathic medicine had a higher proportion of URM students than all health professions other than public health, although nursing has recently surpassed allopathic medicine in its proportion of students who are URMs.

Trends in URM applicants, acceptances, and matriculants track together for allopathic medical schools (Figure A-1). The numbers of both URM applicants and acceptances have dropped off in recent years since peaking in the 1996–1997 period. Because virtually all of URMs (and non-URMs) accepted to

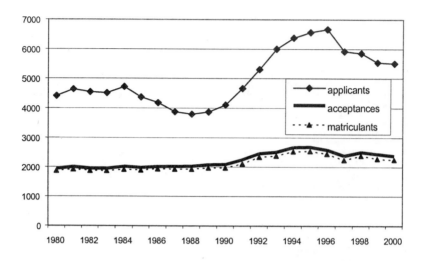

FIGURE A-1 Allopathic Medical School URM Trends.

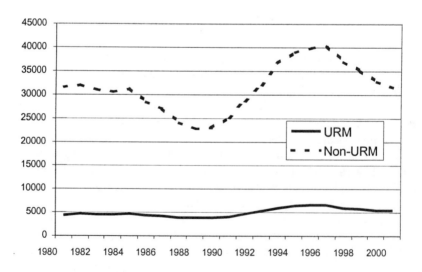

FIGURE A-2 Allopathic Medical School Applicants.

medical school matriculate, the large decrease in URM applicants in the late 1990s has contributed to the decrease in URM matriculants. There were 6,663 URM applicants in 1996, but only 5,511 by 2000 (a 17% decrease). The large decrease in URM applicants parallels the trend for non-URMs, which dropped from 40,304 to 31,581 (a 22% decrease) during the same time period (Figure A-2). Figure A-2 reveals a similar, although less dramatic, trend in the late 1980s for both URM and non-URM applicants, indicating that this cycling is not new to allopathic medicine. However, as Figure A-1 indicates, allopathic medical schools maintained a fairly constant number of URM matriculants in the late 1980s despite the decrease in the number of URM applicants. This contrasts with the case in the late 1990s when the decrease in URM applicants was associated with a commensurate decrease in URM acceptances and matriculants.

Acceptance rates are the key factor explaining the divergence in the applicant and acceptance/matriculant trends for URMs in the 1980s and 1990s. In the late 1980s, acceptance rates for both URM and non-URM applicants increased as the number of applicants fell, producing a fairly stable proportion of URMs in matriculating classes (Figure A-3).

A major shift in acceptance rates for URMs relative to non-URMs then occurred in the early 1990s. As the number of URM and non-URM applicants began to surge in the early 1990s, acceptance rates for non-URMs decreased

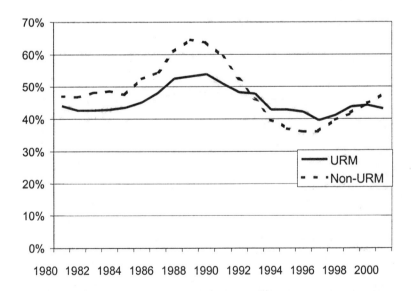

FIGURE A-3 Allopathic Medicine Acceptance Rates.

more than acceptance rates for URMs (Figure A–3). In 1989, 64% of non-URM applicants were accepted by at least one medical school, compared with only 37% in 1994. In contrast, the percent of URM applicants accepted to medical schools declined by a much smaller amount, from 54% in 1989 to 43% in 1994. By the early 1990s, URM applicants were more likely to get into medical school than non-URM applicants for the first time in more than a decade. These changes in acceptance rates largely account for the increasing proportion of URMs in medical school classes in the early 1990s.

This trend began to reverse in 1995. Unlike the case in the early 1980s, the fall in both URM and non-URM applicants in the late 1990s was accompanied by rising fortunes for non-URM—but not URM—applicants in terms of the likelihood of acceptance into medical school (Figure A-3). Acceptance rates for URM applicants stagnated in the late 1990s, while acceptance rates for non-URMs began to increase. By 1999, acceptance rates for URM applicants had once again fallen below those for non-URMS.

As Figure A-4 shows, the net result of these patterns of applicant numbers and acceptance rates is a growth in the proportion of URMs matriculating in allopathic medical schools in the early 1990s, followed by a decrease in the late 1990s. Although the decrease in the number of URM applicants in the late 1990s explains some of the decrease in URM matriculation, it is by no means the whole explanation. In fact, the number of non-URM applicants decreased by an even larger relative amount in the same period. However, unlike URMs, the

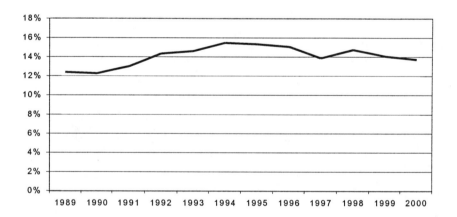

FIGURE A-4 URMs as Percent of Allopathic Medical School Matriculants, United States.

non-URM students applying to medical school in the late 1990s experienced a growing likelihood of acceptance. Clearly, a shift occurred in the late 1990s in the competitiveness of the URM applicant pool and/or in how admissions committees evaluated these applicants relative to non-URMs.

Restrictions on the ability of admissions committees to use race and ethnicity as special considerations in evaluating applicants were felt most heavily in California and Texas in the late 1990s. Were URM acceptance rates in these two states disproportionately affected in the late 1990s?

The trends shown in Figure A-5 suggest that URM acceptance rates did not "recover" in the late 1990s in California and Texas to the same extent that they did in the rest of the United States. While acceptance rates for URMs experienced a modest upturn in the late 1990s in the rest of the United States, URM acceptance rates remained relatively flat in California and Texas—although the differences in late 1990s trends are not terribly dramatic between these states and the rest of the nation.

Medical schools in California and Texas did, however, experience much more substantial decreases than the nation's remaining schools in the proportion of URMs in entering classes in the late 1990s. In Texas, URMs dropped from 21.0% of matriculants to 15.6% in 2000 (Figure A-6). In California, the percent of matriculants who were URMs decreased from a high of 21.9% in 1992 to 15.6% in 2000. These numbers are especially disturbing because of the high proportion of minorities residing in California and Texas. To reach population parity, California would need 40% of matriculants to be URMs, and Texas

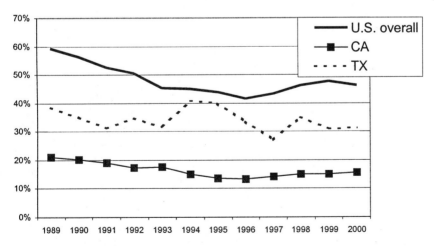

FIGURE A-5 Percent of URM Applicants Accepted to Allopathic Medical Schools: United States vs. CA, TX.

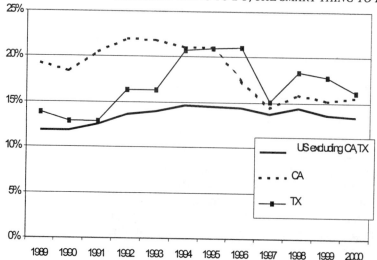

FIGURE A-6 URMs as Percent Allopathic Medicine Matriculants: United States vs. CA, TX.

would need 43%.[ii] In the United States, excluding California and Texas, the percent of matriculants who were URMs decreased much less substantially, from 14.4% in 1996 to 13.4% in 2000. (See Figure A-6) Thus, most of the overall decline in URM matriculation in medical schools in the United States is accounted for by the decreases in California and Texas. In 1995, California and Texas were educating 18.0% of all URMs matriculating in allopathic medical schools in the United States. By 2000, the figure was 15.5% (See Figure A-7).

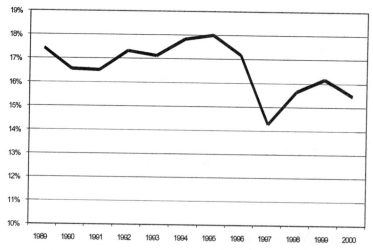

FIGURE A-7 Percent of URM Allopathic Medicine Matriculants Matriculating in CA, TX Schools.

OSTEOPATHIC MEDICINE

Osteopathic medical schools have one of the lowest proportion of URM matriculants among the health professions (See Figure 1). The trend in URM matriculants in osteopathic medical schools in the 1990s follows the same "rise and fall" pattern of allopathic schools, although the proportion of URMs entering osteopathic medical school classes is only about half that of allopathic schools throughout this decade.

One of the most striking health professional school trends in the 1990s was the surge in the total number of applicants to osteopathic medical schools. While the number of applicants to allopathic medical schools approximately doubled in the early 1990s, the number of overall applicants to osteopathic medical schools grew by nearly 350%. It is not known exactly how many osteopathic school applicants also apply to allopathic schools, although presumably many apply to both types of schools (Figure O-1). The number of applicants to osteopathic schools fell off in the late 1990s, but not to the same degree as allopathic applicants. The growth in the number of non-URM applicants outpaced that of URMs. Although the number of URM applicants to osteopathic medical schools doubled between 1990 and 1999, the number of non-URM applicants increased more dramatically, by 168% (Figure O-1).

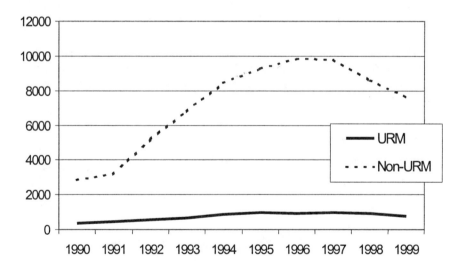

FIGURE O-1 Applicants to Schools of Osteopathy.

Data on the number of students accepted by osteopathic schools were not available. We were able to obtain data on matriculants and could compute "matriculation rates" (that is, the percent of applicants to osteopathic schools who matriculated in an osteopathic school). However, the matriculation rate may have different implications than the acceptance rate, depending on the rate at which accepted applicants actually matriculate. Because almost all accepted students accepted to allopathic medicine programs matriculate, getting accepted into medical school is the key driver of matriculation. It is not clear whether this same pattern holds for osteopathic medical schools. If a more substantial number of accepted students opt not to matriculate in osteopathic medical schools (perhaps because they also applied to allopathic schools and matriculated in an allopathic school), then more caution needs to be exercised in interpreting trends in matriculation rates as indicative of policies affecting admissions decisions or of related factors influencing acceptance rates.

As a result of the increasing number of applicants to osteopathic programs, the matriculation rates fell steeply in the early 1990s. In 1990, the matriculation rate of non-URMs was significantly higher than that of URMs (62.6% compared to 44.9%). This gap between the two groups diminished in the early 1990s and even reversed for a short time. By 1995, the matriculation rate for URMs was 23.5%, compared to 22.1% for non-URMs (Figure O-2). However, as was the case for allopathic medicine, the greater matriculation rates for URMs were a short-lived phenomenon. In 1998 (the last year for which osteopathic data are available), 23.5% of URM and 29.2% of non-URM applicants matriculated at osteopathic medical schools.

The large growth in overall applicants is not the only unique aspect of osteopathic medical school trends. Unlike allopathic medical schools, which have had relatively stable first-year class size for the past decades, osteopathic schools

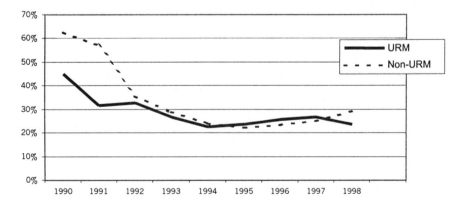

FIGURE O-2 Osteopathic Medical Schools: Percent of Applicants Matriculating.

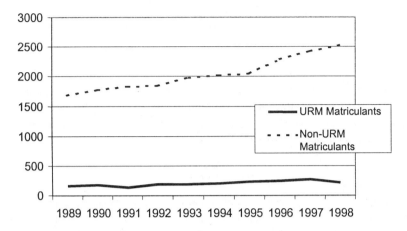

FIGURE O-3 Matriculants to Schools of Osteopathy.

expanded in the 1990s. The overall number of matriculants to osteopathic medical schools increased by almost 50% between 1989 and 1998 (Figure O-3). Non-URM matriculants increased by 50%, from 1,682 to 2,525. URM matriculants increased by 36%, from 162 to 220.

The net result in terms of URMs as a percent of osteopathic matriculants follows many of the same dynamics as observed for allopathic schools. In 1989, URMs represented 8.8% of osteopathic matriculants. This peaked at 10.0% in

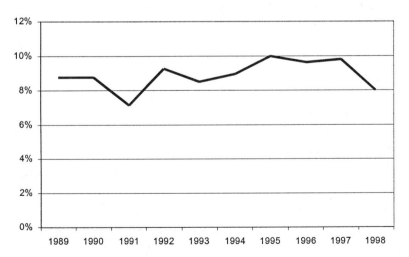

FIGURE O-4 URMs as Percentage Osteopathic Matriculants.

1995, and fell to 8.0% in 1998 (Figure O-4). While the numbers of applicants to both types of schools rose steeply in the early 1990s, matriculation rates decreased by a much greater amount for non-URMs than for URMs. As a result, the proportion of URMs matriculating in both types of medical schools increased in the early 1990s. However, as applicant numbers started to fall off later in the 1990s, acceptance (or matriculation) rates rebounded for non-URMs but not for URMs. In both types of medical schools, URM applicants did not experience the same "bounce" as non-URM applicants from the decreasing overall student demand for medical school slots in the late 1990s.

DENTISTRY

As was the case for osteopathic medicine, data for dentistry are limited to numbers of applicants and matriculants and do not include numbers of students accepted. Dentistry is the only profession among the ones studied that experienced a steady decrease throughout the 1990s in URMs as a proportion of matriculants.

Dental schools experienced a surge in the overall number of applicants in the 1990s, with only a slight fall off in the past few years (Figure D-1). Between 1989 and 1999, the number of non-URM applicants to dental schools increased by 90%, from 4,238 to 8,057. However, the number of URM applicants did not increase proportionally, rising only 26%, from 758 to 953 (Figure D-1).

Unlike the situation for allopathic and osteopathic medicine, dentistry started the 1990s with equivalent matriculation rates for both URM and non-URM applicants. About 7 in 10 applicants in both groups matriculated in 1990. The matriculation rates for URMs and non-URMs followed symmetrical trends throughout the 1990s, with both dropping steadily as a result of the surge in total

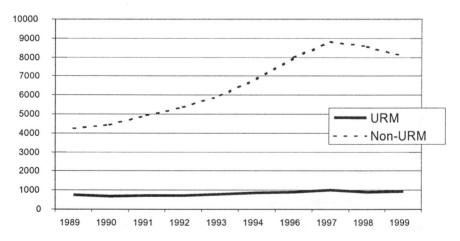

FIGURE D-1 Dental School Applicants.

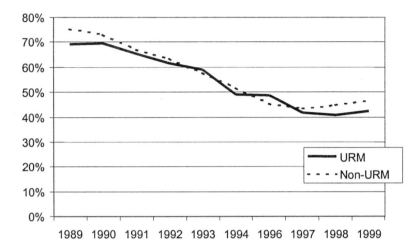

FIGURE D-2 Matriculation Rates for Dental Schools.

number of applicants (Figure D-2). The matriculation rate for URMs went from 69.3% to 42.4%, while the non-URM rate fell from 75.3% to 46.7% between 1989 and 1999. Because the number of non-URM applicants increased by a much larger degree than the number of URM applicants, equivalent matriculation rates among URMs and non-URMs led to fewer URM matriculants and more non-URM matriculants. The number of URM matriculants dropped by 23%—from 525 in 1989 to 404—in 1999. (Figure D-3.) The number of non-

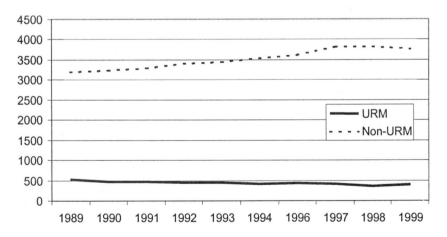

FIGURE D-3 Dental School Matriculants.

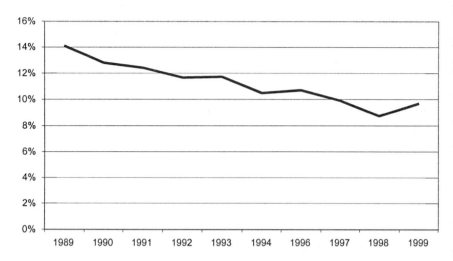

FIGURE D-4 URMs as Percent Dental School Matriculants.

URMs matriculating increased by 18%, from 3,190 to 3,761. URMs as a percent of dental school matriculants fell steadily through the 1990s, from 14.1% in 1989 to 9.7% in 1999 (Figure D-4).

As in the rest of the United States, California and Texas also saw the proportion of URMs matriculating decrease through the 1990s (Figure D–5). In the rest of the United States, (excluding Texas and California), URMs as a percent of total matriculants fell from 15.0% to 10.4% between 1989 and 1999. In

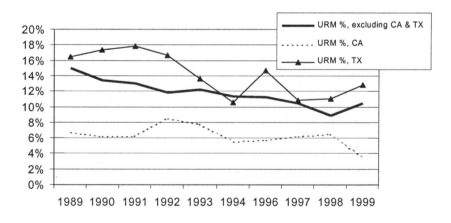

FIGURE D-5 URMs as Percent Matriculants: United States vs. CA and TX .

Texas, the proportion of URMs matriculating fell from 16.5% to 12.9% between 1989 and 1999. California's exceptionally low proportion of URMs fell from 6.7% to 3.6%. California's population consists of 40% URMs,[iii] meaning that the percent of URM dental students in California in 1999 was 10 times below population parity.

Trends in California and Texas may not differ very much from trends in the rest of the United States for dentistry because admissions decisions may not have been the key limiting factor for URM matriculation into dental schools in the 1990s. Unlike the case for allopathic and osteopathic medicine, dentistry began the 1990s with URM applicants already as likely as non-URM applicants to matriculate into dental school. Driving the decrease in URM dental matriculants in the 1990s was the tremendous increase in the popularity of dental careers among non-URM students. Although URM and non-URM applicants had similar (though diminishing) odds of successfully matriculating into dental schools, non-URM students swamped the applicant pool. In 1989, there were about 5.5 non-URM applicants for every 1 URM applicant to dental school. In 1999, there were about 8.5 non-URM applicants for every 1 URM applicant. Thus, for dentistry, the limiting factor for URM matriculation may be attracting sufficient numbers of URM applicants.

PHARMACY

Limited data were available for pharmacy schools, but the available data do indicate that URM enrollment in pharmacy schools has had a modest but steady growth through the 1990s (Figure P-1). The number of URMs enrolled in pharmacy schools (both in B.S. and Pharm.D. programs) increased by 19%, from 3,306 in 1990 to 3,939 in 1999 (Figure P-1). URMs as a percent of total enroll-

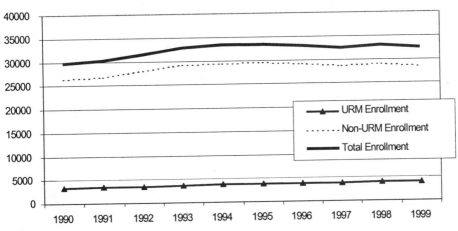

FIGURE P-1 Pharmacy School Total Enrollment.

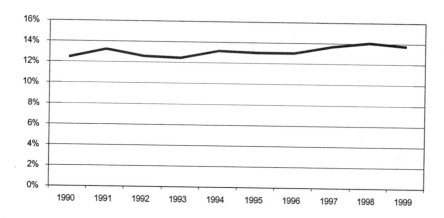

FIGURE P-2 URMs as Percentage of Pharmacy School Total Enrollment.

ment increased from 12.5% in 1990 to 13.8% in 1999 (Figure P-2). Data on unduplicated counts of applicants are not available to analyze applicant trends.

NURSING

Of the health professions analyzed, nursing is the only field that does not require a graduate degree for initial licensure for practice. Nursing has a unique opportunity for URM diversification because of the many educational entry points into the profession. Pre-licensure education is available both at the associate and bachelor degree level. Of all the clinically oriented health professions studied, nursing has exhibited the most sustained increase in the proportion of URM students and now has the highest proportion of URM enrollees of any health profession, other than public health.

Because national annual data on diploma and associate degree nursing programs were not available for all the years studied, we limited our analysis to baccalaureate nursing programs. There has been a steady increase in URM enrollment in baccalaureate nursing programs between 1991 and 1999 (See Figure N-1). URM enrollment increased 48%, from 11,661 to 17,303. This contrasts with a large decrease in non-URM enrollment that began in the mid-1990s.

Because of this decrease in the late 1990s, non-URM enrollment increased a modest 5% between 1991 and 1999, from 89,800 to 93,883. The steady increase in URM enrollment and the minimal increase in non-URM enrollment resulted in a growing percent of URMs in baccalaureate nursing programs (Figure N-2), rising from 12.2% to 16.0%.

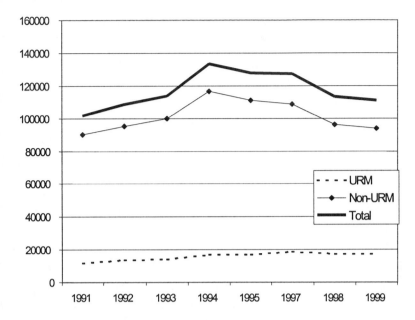

FIGURE N-1 Enrollment in United States Baccalaureate Nursing Programs.

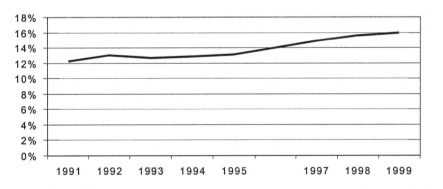

FIGURE N-2 URMs as Percentage of Nursing Enrollment in Baccalaureate Nursing Programs.

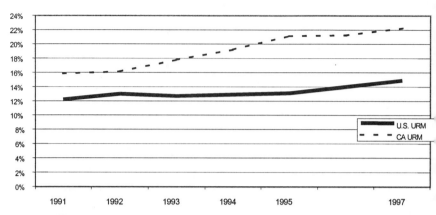

FIGURE N-3 Urms as Percent of Baccalaureate Nursing Enrollment: United States vs. CA.

The recent affirmative action legislation (Proposition 209) does not appear to have affected nursing enrollment in California. Figure N-3 shows that the proportion of URMs enrolled in nursing programs in California (including both associate degree and baccalaureate degree programs) continued to increase even after the 1996 events. URMs as a proportion of enrollees steadily increased from 15.8% in 1991 to 22.2% in 1997. The steady gains in URM enrollment in California enrollment, despite Proposition 209, may be because most basic nursing education in California is done at the community college level rather than at University of California schools or California State University campuses. Seventy-two percent of first-year nursing enrollees in 1998 were enrolled at the associate degree level.[iv] At California community colleges, the admissions process differs from other institutions in that there is not an admissions committee selecting the most "qualified" or well-prepared applicants. Once applicants to a California community college meet minimum criteria, positions are allocated either by waiting lists or by a "lottery system." This admissions process was not affected by Proposition 209.

PUBLIC HEALTH

Public health programs have the highest proportion of URM applicants and enrollees of the health professions. Figure PH-1 shows that through the 1990s, URMs represented 19%–21% of applicants to public health programs. The proportion of URMs in public health programs has been consistently higher than other health professions, and the percentage has been steadily increasing. (Figure PH-2.). URMs represented 15.3% of public health students in 1990 and 19.5% in 1999.

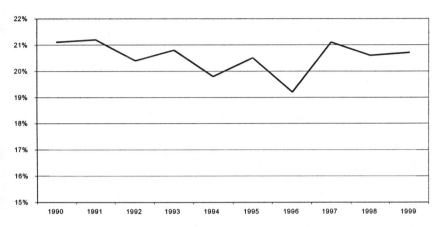

FIGURE PH-1 URMs as Percent of Public Health Applicants.

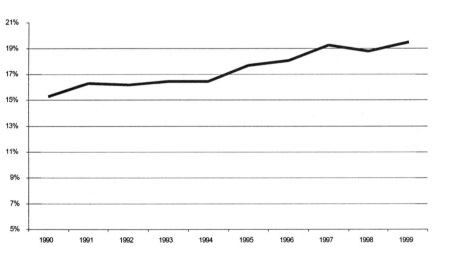

FIGURE PH-2 URMs as Percent of Schools of Public Health Students.

VETERINARY MEDICINE

Veterinary medicine has been called "the health profession serving the most diverse patient population." Veterinary medicine has the lowest proportion of URM applicants, accepted students, and enrollees of the health professions. Figure V-1 shows that in the last five years, approximately 6%–7% of veterinary applicants have been URMs. The application trends have held steady for the last five years. (Data were not available for the early 1990s.) Enrollment trends have also held fairly steady through the last five years, with URMs representing approximately 6% of veterinary students (See Figure V-2).

Veterinary medicine has one of the lowest overall acceptance rates of any health profession. In 1995, the acceptance rate for non-URMs was 35%, while the acceptance rate for URMs was 25% (See Figure V-3). Acceptance rates converged in the 1995–1997 period. However, as was the case for allopathic and osteopathic medicine, acceptance rates for non-URMs, but not for URMs, started to increase again in the late 1990s. This suggest that admissions decisions may have become less favorable towards URMs in recent years.

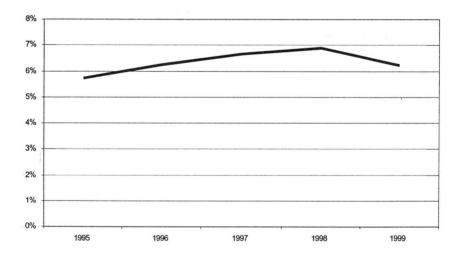

FIGURE V-1 URMs as Percent of Veterinary School Applicants.

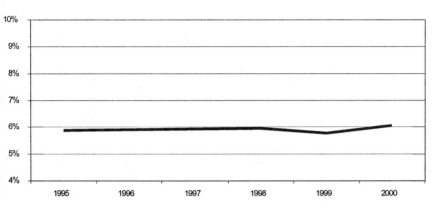

FIGURE V-2 URMs as Percent of Enrolled Veterinary Students.

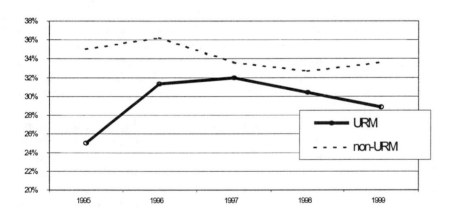

FIGURE V-3 Veterinary School Acceptance Rates.

CONCLUSIONS

Disparities in the racial and ethnic composition of the student body of health professions schools continue to exist for all the health professions studied. However, URM matriculation and enrollment does not follow a single trend for all the health professions. While some professions have made improvements and are moving closer to racial and ethnic parity with the U.S. population, others seem to be losing ground. Some professions have been more successful than others in attracting URM applicants during cycles of rising and lowering popularity of the profession among students overall.

Although trends in the number of applicants is an important influence of trends in URM matriculation and enrollment in health professions schools, admissions decisions and other factors affecting the likelihood of an applicant being accepted remain a key determinant of matriculation and enrollment trends. In allopathic medicine, osteopathic medicine, dentistry, and veterinary medicine, there is an emerging gap in acceptance and matriculation rates for URM applicants compared with non-URMs, with URM rates falling behind.

There is circumstantial evidence that recent legislative and judicial decisions limiting the consideration of race and ethnicity in health professions schools' admissions decisions may be contributing to diverging trends for URM and non-URM acceptance rates, at least for allopathic medicine. Unlike the case for schools in the rest of the nation, acceptance rates for URM applicants to California and Texas schools have not started to rise in response to a decreasing number of applicants. A decreasing proportion of URM medical students in the United States is enrolling in schools in California and Texas. For other health professions schools, trends in California and Texas are more consistent with trends in the rest of the nation. This may be because these schools and their admissions committees are under less public scrutiny than those in medicine or are less affected by recent changes in public policy. In addition, in professions such as dentistry, the small pool of URM applicants may be the overwhelming factor limiting URM admissions.

Trends in URM matriculation in public health, nursing, and pharmacy are encouraging. Although large disparities remain, the trends in these professions suggest that progress is possible. Continued progress will require ongoing commitment to racial and ethnic diversity in health professions schools. Moreover, all health professions schools stand to benefit from policies that promote greater educational achievement for URMs at all levels of the educational pipeline, from primary grades through college. Sustained growth in URM enrollment in health professions schools will require a more academically prepared pool of URM students who are interested in careers in the health professions.

Ongoing monitoring of trends in URM participation in health professions schools would benefit from more systematic and standardized reporting of data. Although some professions have excellent, comprehensive databases on unduplicated applicants, acceptances, and matriculants, data are very limited in many professions. For most of the professions, systematically collected data on attrition after matriculation are absent. Improved analysis of the dynamics of applicant numbers, acceptance rates, matriculation rates, and attrition rates would allow for more informed policymaking to tailor interventions to the unique dynamics of each profession.

ACKNOWLEDGMENTS

The authors thank the following organizations and individuals for supplying the data for the analyses in this paper: David Bristol, College of Veterinary Medicine at North Carolina State University; Lois Colburn and Kuhua Zhang, Association of American Medical Colleges (AAMC); Karen Helsing, Association of Schools of Public Health (ASPH); Susan Meyer, American Association of Colleges of Pharmacy (AACP); Charles Ratliff and Leslie Taylor, California Postsecondary Education Commission (CPEC); Janis Stennett, American Association of Colleges of Nursing (AACN); Lorrie Van Akkeren, American Association of Colleges of Osteopathic Medicine (AACOM); and Richard Weaver, American Dental Education Association (ADEA).

---

[i] U.S. Census Bureau, Census 2000 Brief, *Overview of Race and Hispanic Origin 2000*, issued March 2001 http://www.census.gov/population/www/cen2000/briefs.html. The U.S. Census separates race from "Hispanic or Latino" origin. For our purposes we combined Hispanic or Latino origin (12.5%) with Black or African American (12.3%) and American Indian or Alaska Native (.9%). Because of this, the statistic may be slightly inflated because of Blacks or African Americans and American Indians who are of Hispanic or Latino origin.

[ii] U.S. Census estimates for July 1999. http://www.census.gov/population/estimates/state/srh/srh99.txt. For this comparison we considered Blacks, American Indian/Alaska Natives and those of Hispanic origin to be URMs.

[iii] U.S. Census estimates for July 1999. http://www.census.gov/population/estimates/state/srh/srh99.txt. For this comparison we considered Blacks, American Indian/Alaska Natives and those of Hispanic origin to be URMs.

[iv] California Board of Registered Nursing. (2000). *Annual School Report, 1998–1999*. Sacramento, CA.

Inequality in Teaching and Schooling: How Opportunity Is Rationed to Students of Color in America

Linda Darling-Hammond
Stanford University School of Education

Despite the rhetoric of American equality, the school experiences of African-American and other "minority" students in the United States continue to be substantially separate and unequal. Few Americans realize that the U.S. educational system is one of the most unequal in the industrialized world, and that students routinely receive dramatically different learning opportunities based on their social status. In contrast to European and Asian nations that fund schools centrally and equally, the wealthiest 10% of school districts in the United States spend nearly 10 times more than the poorest 10%, and spending ratios of 3 to 1 are common within states. Poor and minority students are concentrated in the least well-funded schools, most of which are located in central cities or rural areas and funded at levels substantially below those of neighboring suburban districts. Recent analyses of data prepared for school finance cases in Alabama, New Jersey, New York, Louisiana, and Texas have found that on every tangible measure—from qualified teachers to curriculum offerings—schools serving greater numbers of students of color had significantly fewer resources than schools serving mostly white students.

Not only do funding systems allocate fewer resources to poor urban districts than to their suburban neighbors, but studies consistently show that, *within* these districts, schools with high concentrations of low-income and "minority" students receive fewer instructional resources than others in the same district. And tracking systems exacerbate these inequalities by segregating many low-income and minority students within schools (Kozol, 1991; Taylor & Piche, 1991). In combination, policies associated with school funding, resource allocations, and tracking leave minority students with fewer and lower-quality books, curriculum materials, laboratories, and computers; significantly larger class sizes; less qualified and experienced teachers; and less access to high-quality curriculum.

The end results of these educational inequalities are increasingly tragic. More than ever before in our nation's history, education is not only the ticket to economic success, but also to basic survival. Whereas a high school dropout had two chances out of three of getting a job 20 years ago, today he or she has less than one chance out of three, and the job he or she can get pays less than half of what would have been earned 20 years earlier (WT Grant Foundation, 1988). The effects of dropping out are much worse for young people of color than for whites. In 1993, a recent school dropout who was black had only a one in four chance of being employed, whereas the odds for his or her white counterpart were about 50% (NCES, 1995, p. 88). Even recent graduates from high school struggle to find jobs. Among African-American high school graduates not enrolled in college, only 42% were employed in 1993, as compared with 72% of white graduates. Those who do not succeed in school are becoming part of a growing underclass, cut off from productive engagement in society. In addition, working class young people and adults who were prepared for the disappearing jobs of the past teeter on the brink of downward social mobility.

Because the economy can no longer absorb many unskilled workers at decent wages, lack of education is increasingly linked to crime and welfare dependency. Women who have not finished high school are much more likely than others to be on welfare, while men are much more likely to be in prison. National investments in the last decade have tipped heavily toward incarceration rather than education. Nationwide, during the 1980s, federal, state, and local expenditures for corrections grew by over 900%, and for prosecution and legal services by more than 1000% (Miller, 1997), while prison populations more than doubled (U.S. Department of Commerce, 1996, p. 219). During the same decade, per pupil expenditures for schools grew by only about 26% in real dollar terms, and much less in cities (NCES, 1994). The situation is worse in some parts of the country. While schools in California have experienced continuous cutbacks over the last decade, the prison population there has increased by more than 300%.

In 1993, there were more African-American citizens on probation, in jail, in prison, or on parole (1,985,000) than there were in college (1,412,000) (U.S. Department of Commerce, table numbers 281 and 354, pp. 181 and 221). Increased incarceration, and its disproportionate effects upon the African-American community, are a function of new criminal justice policies and ongoing police discrimination (Miller, 1997) as well as lack of access to education. More than half the adult prison population has literacy skills below those required by the labor market (Barton & Coley, 1996), and nearly 40% of adjudicated juvenile delinquents have treatable learning disabilities that went undiagnosed in the schools (Gemignani, 1994).

Meanwhile, schools have changed slowly. Most are still organized to prepare only about 20% of their students for "thinking work"—those students who are tracked very early into gifted and talented, "advanced," or honors courses. These opportunities are least available to African-American, Latino, and Native American students. As a consequence of structural inequalities in access to knowledge and resources, students from racial and ethnic "minority" groups in the United States face persistent and profound barriers to educational opportunity. As I describe below, schools that serve large numbers of students of color are least likely to offer the kind of curriculum and teaching needed to meet the new standards being enacted across the states and to help students attain the skills needed in a knowledge work economy. In most states, schools serving minority and low-income students lack the courses, materials, equipment, and qualified teachers that would give students access to the education they will need to participate in today's and tomorrow's world.

CLOSING THE GAP: CHANGES IN EDUCATIONAL ACHIEVEMENT

While the demands for knowledge and skill are growing, the gap in educational opportunity between majority and minority students has been widening. Although overall educational attainment for black Americans increased steadily between 1960 and 1990, this trend is reversing in some states that have imposed graduation exams without improving opportunities to learn. By 1995, 74% of black Americans had completed four or more years of high school—up from only 20% in 1960. However, dropout rates have been increasing for black male students since 1994. Recent evidence from individual states like Texas, Florida, and Georgia where exit exams have been instituted indicates that dropout and pushout rates have increased substantially for African-American and Hispanic students during the 1990s (Haney, 1999).

On national assessments in reading, writing, mathematics, and science, minority students' performance lags behind that of white students, and the gap has widened in most areas during the 1990s. The situation in many urban school systems deteriorated throughout the 1980s and 1990s as drops in per pupil expenditures have accompanied tax cuts while immigration and enrollments have grown. Urban schools serve increased numbers of students who do not speak English as their native language and growing proportions requiring special educational services. These students are increasingly served by growing numbers of unqualified teachers who have been hired since the late 1980s.

In addition, many urban systems have focused their curricula more on rote learning of "basic" skills than on problem solving, thoughtful examination of serious texts and ideas, or assignments requiring frequent and extended writing (Cooper & Sherk, 1989; Darling-Hammond, 1997). As new tests in many states (and the National Assessment of Educational Progress, 1994) focus more on higher-order skills, problem solving, analytic and writing ability, they diverge from the lower-level skills taught in many texts and tested by widely used multiple choice examinations. Students whose education is guided mostly by workbooks compatible with basic skills tests find themselves at a growing disadvantage when they confront the more challenging expectations of new standards and the assessments that accompany them.

INEQUALITY AND ACHIEVEMENT

The concentration of minority students in high-minority schools facilitates inequality. Nearly two-thirds of "minority" students attend predominantly minority schools, and one-third of black students attend intensely segregated schools (90% or more minority enrollment), most of which are in central cities (Schofield, 1991, p. 336). By 1993, 55% of all students in central city schools were black or Hispanic (National Center for Educational Statistics, NCES, 1995, p. 121). As Taylor and Piche (1991) noted:

> Inequitable systems of school finance inflict disproportionate harm on minority and economically disadvantaged students. On an *inter*-state basis, such students are concentrated in states, primarily in the South, that have the lowest capacities to finance public education. On an *intra*-state basis, many of the states with the widest disparities in educational expenditures are large industrial states. In these states, many minorities and economically disadvantaged students are located in property-poor urban districts which fare the worst in educational expenditures. In addition, in several states economically disadvantaged students, white and black, are concentrated in rural districts which suffer from fiscal inequity (pp. xi–xii).

Not only do funding systems and tax policies leave most urban districts with fewer resources than their suburban neighbors, but schools with high concentrations of "minority" students receive fewer resources than other schools within these districts. And tracking systems exacerbate these inequalities by segregating many "minority" students within schools, allocating still fewer educational opportunities to them at the classroom level. In their review of resource allocation studies, MacPhail-Wilcox and King (1986) summarized the resulting situation as follows:

> School expenditure levels correlate positively with student socioeconomic status and negatively with educational need when school size and grade level are controlled statistically . . . Teachers with higher salaries are concentrated in high-income and low-minority schools. Furthermore, pupil-teacher ratios are higher in schools with larger minority and low-income student populations . . . Educational units with higher proportions of low-income and minority students are allocated fewer fiscal and educational resources than are more affluent educational units, despite the probability that these students have substantially greater need for both (p. 425).

These inequalities are increasingly the subject of legal action. The State of New York provides a recent example. Studies have found that by virtually any resource measure—state and local dollars per pupil, student-teacher ratios and student-staff ratios, class sizes, teacher experience, and teacher qualifications— districts with greater proportions of poor and minority students receive fewer resources than others (Berne, 1995). In January 2001, the New York State Supreme Court declared the funding system unconstitutional because it denies students in high-need, low-spending districts like New York City the opportunities to learn needed to meet the state's standards, including well-qualified teachers and curriculum supports (*Campaign for Fiscal Equity* v. *State of New York*). A similar suit is now pending in the Superior Court of California (*Williams* v. *State of California*).

A critical problem is that shortages of funds make it difficult for urban and poor rural schools to compete in the marketplace for qualified teachers. When districts do not find qualified teachers, they assign the least able individuals to the students with the least political clout. In 1990, for example, the Los Angeles City School District was sued by students in predominantly minority schools because their schools were not only overcrowded and less well funded than other schools, they were also disproportionately staffed by inexperienced and unprepared teachers hired on emergency credentials (*Rodriguez et al.* v. *Los Angeles Unified School District*, Superior Court of the County of Los Angeles #C611358. Consent decree filed August 12, 1992). In 1999, students in California's predominantly minority schools were 10 times more likely to have uncertified teachers than those in predominantly white schools (Shields et al., 1999).

A growing body of research suggests that inequitable distributions of qualified teachers are a major cause of the achievement gap. Recent studies have found that differential teacher effectiveness is an extremely strong determinant of differences in student learning, far outweighing the effects of differences in class size and heterogenity. Students who are assigned to several ineffective teachers in a row have significantly lower achievement gains—creating differences of as much as 50 percentile points over three years—than those who are assigned to several highly effective teachers in a row (Sanders & Rivers, 1996). These studies also find evidence of bias in assignment of students to teachers of different effectiveness levels, including indications that African American students are nearly twice as likely to be assigned to the most ineffective teachers and about half as likely to be assigned to the most effective teachers.

Analyzing a data set covering 900 Texas school districts, Ronald Ferguson (1991) found that the single most important measurable cause of increased student learning was teacher expertise, measured by teacher performance on a state certification exam, along with teacher experience and master's degrees. Together these variables accounted for about 40% of the measured variance in student test scores. Holding socioeconomic status (SES) constant, the wide variation in teachers' qualifications in Texas accounted for almost all of the variation in black and white students' test scores. That is, after controlling for SES, black students' achievement would have nearly equaled that of whites if they had been assigned equally qualified teachers.

Ferguson also found that class size, at the critical point of a teacher/student ratio of 1:18, was a statistically significant determinant of student outcomes (Ferguson, 1991), as was small school size. Other data also indicate that black students are more likely to attend large schools than white students (Paterson Institute, 1996), with much larger than average class sizes (NCES, 1997a, p. A-119), and confirm that smaller schools and classes make a difference for student achievement (for a review, see Darling-Hammond, 1997).

Ferguson repeated this analysis in Alabama, and still found sizable influences of teacher expertise and smaller class sizes on student achievement gains in reading and mathematics (Ferguson & Ladd, 1996). They found that 31% of the predicted difference in mathematics achievement between districts in the top and bottom quartiles was explained by teacher qualifications and class sizes, while 29.5% was explained by poverty, race, and parent education.

These findings are confirmed elsewhere. For example, in North Carolina, Strauss and Sawyer (1986) found a strong influence on average school district test performance of teachers' average scores on the National Teacher Examinations (NTE) measuring subject matter and teaching knowledge. After taking

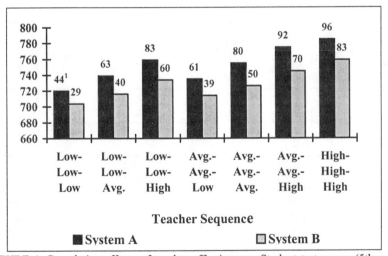

FIGURE 1 Cumulative effects of teacher effectiveness. Student test scores (5th grade math) by effectiveness level of teachers over a three-year period, for two metropolitan school systems.
SOURCE: W. L. Sanders and J. C. Rivers. *Cumulative and Residual Effects of Teachers on Future Student Academic Achievement.* Knoxville: University of Tennessee, 1996.

account of community wealth and other resources, teachers' test scores had a strikingly large effect on students' success on the state competency examinations: a 1% increase in teacher quality (as measured by NTE scores) was associated with a 3% to 5% decline in the percentage of students failing the exam. The authors' conclusion is similar to Ferguson's:

> Of the inputs which are potentially policy-controllable (teacher quality, teacher numbers via the pupil-teacher ratio and capital stock) our analysis indicates quite clearly that improving the quality of teachers in the classroom will do more for students who are most educationally at risk, those prone to fail, than reducing the class size or improving the capital stock by any reasonable margin which would be available to policy makers (p. 47).

These findings are reinforced by a recent review of 60 production function studies, which found that teacher education, ability, and experience—along with small schools and lower teacher-pupil ratios—are associated with significant increases in student achievement (Greenwald, Hedges, & Laine, 1996). In this study's estimate of the achievement gains associated with expenditure increments, spending on teacher education swamped other variables as the most productive investment for schools.

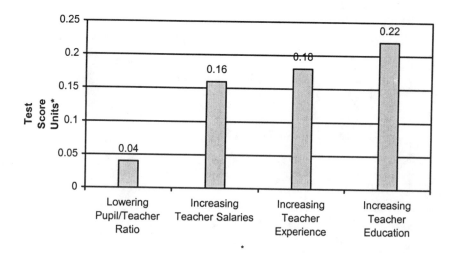

FIGURE 2 Effects of educational investments: size of increase in student achievement for every $500 spent on: Achievement gains were calculated as standard deviation units on a range of achievement tests in the 60 studies reviewed.

WHAT MATTERS IN TEACHING?

Unfortunately, policymakers have nearly always been willing to fill teaching vacancies by lowering standards so that people who have had little or no preparation for teaching can be hired, especially if their clients are minority and low-income students. Although this practice is often excused by the presumption that virtually anyone can figure out how to teach, research consistently shows that fully prepared and certified teachers—those with both subject matter knowledge and knowledge of teaching and learning—are more highly rated and more successful with students than teachers without full preparation (Druva & Anderson, 1983; Greenberg, 1983; Evertson, Hawley, & Zlotnik, 1985; Ashton & Crocker, 1986, 1987; Darling-Hammond, 1992). As Evertson and colleagues (1985) concluded:

> (T)he available research suggests that among students who become teachers, those enrolled in formal preservice preparation programs are more likely to be effective than those who do not have such training. Moreover, almost all well planned and executed efforts within teacher preparation programs to teach students specific knowledge or skills seem to succeed, at least in the short run (p. 8).

A number of studies have found that teachers who enter the teaching profession without full preparation are less able to plan and redirect instruction to meet students' needs (and less aware of the need to do so), less skilled in implementing instruction, less able to anticipate students' knowledge and potential difficulties, and less likely to see it as their job to do so, often blaming students if their teaching is not successful (Bledsoe, Cox, & Burnham, 1967; Copley, 1974; Gomez & Grobe, 1990; Grossman, 1989; 1990; Bents & Bents, 1990; Rottenberg & Berliner, 1990;). Most important, their students learn at lower levels (See figure 3).

Teacher expertise and curriculum quality are interrelated, because expert teachers are a prerequisite for the successful implementation of challenging curriculum. Teachers who are well-prepared are better able to use teaching strategies that respond to students' needs and learning styles and that encourage higher-order learning (Peikes, 1967–1968; Skipper & Quantz, 1987; Hansen, 1988). Since the novel tasks required for problem solving are more difficult to manage than the routine tasks associated with rote learning, lack of knowledge about how to manage an active, inquiry-oriented classroom can lead teachers to turn to passive tactics that "dumb down" the curriculum, busying students with workbooks rather than complex tasks that require more skill to orchestrate (Carter & Doyle, 1987; Doyle, 1986; Cooper & Sherk, 1989). Teacher education is also related to the use of teaching strategies that encourage higher-order learning and the use of strategies responsive to students' needs and learning styles. Thus, policies that resolve shortages in poor districts by hiring unprepared teachers serve only to exacerbate the inequalities low-income and minority children experience.

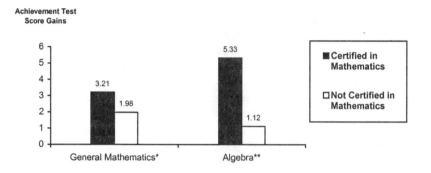

Achievement Test
Score Gains

FIGURE 3 Effects on student achievement of teacher certification in mathematics. ANOVA results: * p < .01 ** p < .001
SOURCE: P. Hawk, C. Coble, and M. Swanson. Certification: It Does Matter. *Journal of Teacher Education*, 36 (3) May–June 1985; pp. 13–15.

Access to Good Teaching

In "Closing the Divide," Robert Dreeben (1987) described the results of his study of reading instruction and outcomes for 300 black and white first graders across seven schools in the Chicago area. He found that differences in reading outcomes among students were almost entirely explained not by socioeconomic status or race, but by the quality of instruction the students received:

> Our evidence shows that the level of learning responds strongly to the quality of instruction: having and using enough time, covering a substantial amount of rich curricular material, and matching instruction appropriately to the ability levels of groups . . . When black and white children of comparable ability experience the same instruction, they do about equally well, and this is true when the instruction is excellent in quality and when it is inadequate (p. 34).

However, the study also found that the quality of instruction received by African-American students was, on average, much lower than that received by white students, thus creating a racial gap in aggregate achievement at the end of first grade. In fact, the highest ability group in Dreeben's sample was in a school in a low-income, African-American neighborhood. These students, though, learned less during first grade than their lower-aptitude white counterparts because their teacher was unable to provide the quality instruction this talented group deserved.

The National Assessment of Educational Progress (NAEP) has documented that the qualifications and training of students' teachers are among the correlates of reading achievement. Students of teachers who are fully certified, who have master's degrees, and who have had professional coursework in literature-based instruction do better on reading assessments. Furthermore, teachers who have had more professional coursework are more likely to use an approach that integrates literature and writing, which is associated with stronger achievement. For example, teachers with more staff development hours in reading are much more likely to use a wide variety of books, newspapers, and materials from other subject areas and to engage students in regular writing, all of which are associated with higher reading achievement. They are also less likely to use reading kits, basal readers, and workbooks which are associated with lower levels of reading achievement (NAEP, 1994).

Curricular differences like these are widespread, and they explain much of the disparity between the achievement of white and minority students and between those of higher- and lower-income levels (Oakes, 1985; Lee & Bryk, 1988). When students of similar backgrounds and initial achievement levels are exposed to more and less challenging curriculum material, those given the richer curriculum opportunities outperform those placed in less challenging classes (Alexander & McDill, 1976; Oakes, 1985; Gamoran & Behrends, 1987).

Most studies have estimated effects statistically based on natural occurrences of different tracking policies. However, one study that randomly assigned 7th grade "at-risk" students to remedial, average, and honors mathematics classes found that at the end of the year, the at-risk students who took the honors class offering a pre-algebra curriculum outperformed all other students of similar backgrounds (Peterson, 1989).

Another study of African-American high school youth randomly placed in public housing in the Chicago suburbs rather than in the city, found similar results. Compared to their comparable city-placed peers who were of equivalent income and initial academic attainment, the students who were enabled to attend largely white and better-funded suburban schools had better educational outcomes across many dimensions. They were substantially more likely to have the opportunity to take challenging courses, receive additional academic help, graduate on time, attend college, and secure good jobs (Kaufman & Rosenbaum, 1992).

These examples are drawn from carefully controlled studies that confirm what many other studies have suggested. Much of the difference in school achievement found between African-American students and others is due to the effects of substantially different school opportunities, and in particular, greatly disparate access to high-quality teachers and teaching (Barr & Dreeben, 1983; College Board, 1985; Dreeben & Gamoran, 1986; Dreeben & Barr, 1987; Oakes, 1990; Darling-Hammond & Snyder, 1992).

The Unequal Distribution Of Teachers

Minority and low-income students in urban settings are most likely to find themselves in classrooms staffed by inadequately prepared, inexperienced, and ill-qualified teachers because funding inequities, distributions of local power, labor market conditions, and dysfunctional hiring practices conspire to produce teacher shortages of which they bear the brunt. By every measure of qualifications, unqualified and underprepared teachers continue to be found disproportionately in schools serving greater numbers of low-income or minority students (NCES, 1997a). In 1994, just over 20% of newly hired public school teachers were hired without having met regular certification requirements (NCTAF, 1997). The vast majority of these teachers were assigned to the most disadvantaged schools in central city and poor rural school districts.

Districts with the greatest concentrations of poor children, minority children, and children of immigrants are also those where incoming teachers are least likely to have learned about up-to-date teaching methods or about how children grow, learn, and develop—and what to do if they are having difficulties. In addition, when faced with shortages, districts often hire substitutes, assign teachers outside their fields of qualification, expand class sizes, or cancel course offerings. These strategies are used most frequently in schools serving large numbers of minority students (NCES, 1997a; NCTAF, 1997). No matter what strategies are adopted, the quality of instruction suffers.

This situation is partly a function of real shortages, but it is also due to urban district hiring practices that are often cumbersome, poorly managed, insensitive to teacher qualifications, and delayed by seniority transfer rules and a variety of other self-inflicted procedures (National Commission on Teaching and America's Future, 1996). Furthermore, since many of the more expert, experienced teachers transfer to more desirable schools and districts when they are able, new teachers and those without training are typically given assignments in the most disadvantaged schools that offer the fewest supports (Wise, Darling-Hammond, & Berry, 1987; Murnane et al., 1991). Because they confront challenging assignments without mentoring or other help, attrition rates for new teachers, especially in cities, average 30% or more over the first five years of teaching (Grissmer & Kirby, 1987; Wise, Darling-Hammond, & Berry, 1987; NCES, 1997b).

This adds additional problems of staff instability to the already difficult circumstances in which central city youth attend school. Where these practices persist, many children in central city schools are taught by a parade of short-term substitute teachers, inexperienced teachers without support, and under-qualified teachers who are not really familiar with either their subject matter or effective methods. The California Commission on the Teaching Profession (1985) concluded that disproportionate numbers of minority and poor students are taught throughout their entire school careers by the least qualified teachers. This sets up the school failure that society predicts for them.

Oakes' (1990) nationwide study of the distribution of mathematics and science opportunities confirmed these pervasive patterns. Based on teacher experience, certification status, preparation in the discipline, degrees, self-confidence, and teacher and principal perceptions of competence, it is clear that low-income and minority students have less contact with the best-qualified science and mathematics teachers. Students in high-minority schools have only a 50% chance of being taught by a math or science teacher who is certified at all, and an even lower chance of being taught by teachers who are fully qualified for their teaching assignment by virtue of the subject area(s) they are prepared to teach. Oakes concluded:

> Our evidence lends considerable support to the argument that low-income, minority, and inner-city students have fewer opportunities . . . They have considerably less access to science and mathematics knowledge at school, fewer material resources, less-engaging learning activities in their classrooms, and less-qualified teachers . . . (p. x–xi).

Access to High-Quality Curriculum

In addition to being taught by teachers less qualified than those of their white and suburban counterparts, urban and minority students face dramatic differences in courses, curriculum materials, and equipment. Unequal access to high-level courses and challenging curriculum explains much of the difference in achievement between minority students and white students. For example, analyses of data from the High School and Beyond surveys demonstrate dramatic differences among students of various racial and ethnic groups in course taking in such areas as mathematics, science, and foreign languages (Pelavin & Kane, 1990). These data also demonstrate that for students of all racial and ethnic groups, course taking is strongly related to achievement. For students with similar course taking records, achievement test score differences by race or ethnicity narrow substantially (Jones, 1984; College Board, 1985, p. 38; Moore & Smith, 1985; Jones et al., 1986).

One source of inequality is the fact that high-minority schools are much less likely to offer advanced and college preparatory courses in mathematics and science than are schools that serve affluent and largely white populations of students (Matthews, 1984; Oakes, 1990). Schools serving predominantly minority and poor populations offer fewer advanced courses and more remedial courses in academic subjects, and they have smaller academic tracks and larger vocational programs (NCES, 1985; Rock et al., 1985). The size and rigor of college preparatory programs within schools vary with the race and socioeconomic status of school populations (California State Department of Education, 1984). As plaintiffs noted in the New Jersey school finance case, wealthy and predominantly white Montclair offers foreign languages at the preschool level, while poor and predominantly black Paterson does not offer any until high school—

and then, relatively few. And while 20% of 11th and 12th graders in wealthy Moorestown participate in Advanced Placement courses, none are even offered in any school in poor and predominantly black Camden and East Orange (ETS, 1991, p. 9).

When high-minority, low-income schools offer any advanced or college preparatory courses, they offer them to only a very tiny fraction of students. Thus, at the high school level, African American, Hispanics, and Native Americans have traditionally been underrepresented in academic programs and overrepresented in general education or vocational education programs, where they receive fewer courses in areas such as English, mathematics, and science (College Board, 1985). Even among the college-bound, non-Asian minority students take fewer and less demanding mathematics, science, and foreign language courses (Pelavin & Kane, 1990).

The unavailability of teachers who could teach these upper-level courses, or who can successfully teach heterogeneous groups of students, reinforces these inequalities in access to high-quality curricula. Tracking persists in the face of growing evidence that it does not substantially benefit high achievers and tends to put low achievers at a serious disadvantage (Kulik & Kulik, 1982;Oakes, 1985; 1986; Slavin, 1990; Hoffer, 1992), in part because good teaching is a scarce resource, and thus must be allocated. Scarce resources tend to get allocated to the students whose parents, advocates, or representatives have the most political clout. This results, not entirely but disproportionately, in the most highly qualified teachers teaching the most enriched curricula to the most advantaged students. Evidence suggests that teachers themselves are tracked, with those judged to be the most competent, experienced, or with the highest status assigned to the top tracks (Rosenbaum, 1976; Finley, 1984; Davis, 1986; Oakes, 1986; Talbert, 1990; NCTAF, 1996).

Tracking in U. S. schools is much more extensive at much earlier grade levels than in most other countries. Starting in elementary schools with the designation of instructional groups and programs based on test scores and recommendations, it becomes highly formalized by junior high school. The result of this practice is that challenging curricula are rationed to a very small proportion of students, and far fewer of our students ever encounter the types of curricula that students in other countries typically experience (McKnight et al., 1987; Usiskin, 1987; Useem, 1990; Wheelock, 1992).

Although test scores and prior educational opportunities partially explain these differential placements, race and socioeconomic status play a distinct role. Even after test scores are controlled, race and socioeconomic status determine assignments to high school honors courses (Gamoran, 1992), as well as vocational and academic programs and more or less challenging courses within them (Useem, 1990; Oakes, 1992). This is true in part because of prior placements of students in upper tracks in earlier grades, in part due to counselors' views that they should advise students in ways that are "realistic" about their futures, and in part because of the greater effectiveness of parent interventions in tracking decisions for higher-SES students (Moore & Davenport, 1988).

From "gifted and talented" programs at the elementary level through advanced courses in secondary schools, teachers who are generally the most skilled offer rich, challenging curricula to select groups of students, based on the theory that only a few students can benefit from such curricula. Yet the distinguishing feature of such programs, particularly at the elementary level, is not their difficulty, but their quality. Students in these programs are given opportunities to integrate ideas across fields of study. They have opportunities to think, write, create, and develop projects. They are challenged to explore. Though virtually all students would benefit from being similarly challenged, the opportunity for this sort of schooling remains acutely restricted.

Meanwhile, students placed in lower tracks are exposed to a limited, rote-oriented curriculum and ultimately achieve less than students of similar aptitude who are placed in academic programs or untracked classes (Gamoran & Mare, 1989; Oakes, 1985, 1990; Gamoran, 1990). Teacher interaction with students in lower track classes is less motivating, less supportive, and less demanding of higher-order reasoning and responses (Good & Brophy, 1987). These interactions are also less academically oriented, and more likely to focus on behavioral criticisms, especially for minority students (Oakes, 1985; Eckstrom & Villegas, 1991). Presentations are less clear and less focused on higher-order cognitive goals (Oakes, 1985).

In addition, many studies have found that students placed in the lowest tracks or in remedial programs—disproportionately low-income and minority students—are most apt to experience instruction geared only to multiple-choice tests, working at a low cognitive level on test-oriented tasks that are profoundly disconnected from the skills they need to learn. Rarely are they given the opportunity to talk about what they know, to read real books, to write, or to construct and solve problems in mathematics, science, or other subjects (Oakes, 1985; Davis, 1986; Trimble & Sinclair, 1986; Cooper & Sherk, 1989).

POLICY FOR EQUALITY: TOWARD EQUALIZATION OF EDUCATIONAL OPPORTUNITY

The common presumption about educational inequality is that it resides primarily in those students who come to school with inadequate capacities to benefit from what education the school has to offer. The fact that U. S. schools are structured such that students routinely receive dramatically unequal learning opportunities based on their race and social status is simply not widely recognized. If the academic outcomes for minority and low-income children are to change, reforms must alter the caliber and quantity of learning opportunities they encounter. These efforts must include equalization of financial resources, changes in curriculum and testing policies, and improvements in the supply of highly qualified teachers to all students.

Resource Equalization

Progress in equalizing resources to students will require attention to inequalities at all levels—between states, among districts, among schools within districts, and among students differentially placed in classrooms, courses, and tracks that offer substantially disparate opportunities to learn. As a consequence of systematic inequalities at each of these levels, minority and low-income students are frequently "at risk" not from their homes or family factors but from the major shortcomings of the schools they attend.

Special programs such as compensatory or bilingual education will never be effective at remedying underachievement as long as these services are layered on a system that so poorly educates minority and low-income children to begin with. The presumption that "the schools are fine, it's the children who need help" is flawed. The schools serving large concentrations of low-income and minority students are generally not fine, and many of their problems originate with district and state policies and practices that fund them inadequately, send them incompetent staff, require inordinate attention to arcane administrative requirements that fragment educational programs and drain resources from classrooms, and preclude the adoption of more promising curriculum and teaching strategies.

Current initiatives to create special labels and programs for "at-risk" children and youth—including mass summer school programs and mandatory Saturday classes for the hundreds of thousands of students who are threatened with grade retention under new promotion rules—are unlikely to succeed if they do not attend to the structural conditions of schools that place children at risk. In the pursuit of equity, our goal should be to develop strategies that improve the core practices of schooling rather than layering additional programs and regulations on foundations that are already faulty. The pressures to respond to special circumstances with special categorical programs are great, and the tradition of succumbing to those pressures in an add-on fashion is well established, in education as in other areas of national life. But special programs, with all their accoutrements of new rules and procedures, separate budgets, and fragmented, pull-out programs will be counterproductive as long as the status quo remains unchanged in more significant ways.

As the 1992 interim report of an independent commission on Chapter 1 observed: "Given the inequitable distribution of state and local resources, the current notion that Chapter 1 provides supplemental aid to disadvantaged children added to a level playing field is a fiction" (Commission on Chapter 1, 1992, p. 4). The Commission proposed that each state be held accountable for assuring comparability in "vital services" among all its districts as well as in all schools within each district. Among these vital services, perhaps the most important is highly qualified teachers, not just for specific Chapter 1 services but for all classrooms.

Ferguson's (1991) recommendation that equalization focus on district capacity to hire high-quality teachers is an important one. In addition to the weight of evidence indicating the central importance of qualified teachers to student learning, there is real-world experience with the positive effects on teacher quality and distribution of such policies. When Connecticut raised and equalized beginning teacher salaries under its 1986 Education Enhancement Act, shortages of teachers (including those that had plagued urban areas) evaporated. By 1989, most teaching fields showed surpluses. The state raised standards for teacher education and licensing, initiated scholarships and forgivable loans to recruit high-need teachers into the profession (including teachers in shortage fields, those who would teach in high-need locations, and minority teachers), created a mentoring and assessment program for all beginning teachers, and invested money in high-quality professional development, with special aid to low-achieving districts. The state also developed a low-stakes, performance-oriented assessment program focused on higher-order thinking and performance skills, which is used to provide information to schools and districts, but not to punish children or teachers. By 1998, Connecticut had surpassed all other states in 4th grade reading and mathematics achievement on the NAEP and scored at the top in 8th grade mathematics, science, and writing. Although Connecticut still has an achievement gap it is working to close, black students in Connecticut score significantly higher than their counterparts elsewhere in the county (Baron, 1999; Wilson, Darling-Hammond, & Berry, 2000).

The new wave of school finance lawsuits that are challenging both within state and within district resource allocation disparities are also promising. These suits are increasingly able to demonstrate how access to concrete learning opportunities is impaired by differential access to money, and how these learning opportunities translate into academic achievement for students. As standards are used to articulate clearer conceptions of what students need to learn to function in today's society and what schools need to do to support these levels of learning, lawsuits like ones recently won in Alabama and New York may be linked to definitions of the quality of education that is "adequate" to meet the state's expectations for student achievement. Such cases are requiring remedies that link levels of funding to minimum standards of learning and teaching. As suits brought on the adequacy theory establish that learning experiences depend on resources and influence outcomes, they establish a principle of "opportunity to learn" that could allow states to define a curriculum entitlement that becomes the basis for both funding and review of school practices.

Opportunity to Learn Standards

The idea of opportunity to learn standards was first articulated by the National Council on Education Standards and Testing (NCEST), which argued for student performance standards but acknowledged they would result in greater inequality if not accompanied by policies ensuring access to resources, including appropriate instructional materials and well-prepared teachers (NCEST, 1992, E12–E13). The Commission's Assessment Task Force proposed that states collect evidence on the extent to which schools and districts provide opportunity to learn the curricula implied by standards as a prerequisite to using tests for school graduation or other decisions (NCEST, 1992, F17–F18).

Opportunity-to-learn standards would establish, for example, that if a state's curriculum frameworks and assessments outlined standards for science learning that require laboratory work and computers, specific coursework, and particular knowledge for teaching, resources must be allocated and policies must be fashioned to provide for these entitlements. Such a strategy would leverage both school improvement and school equity reform, providing a basis for state legislation or litigation where opportunities to learn were not adequately funded.

Opportunity-to-learn standards would define a floor of core resources, coupled with incentives for schools to work toward professional standards of practice that support high-quality learning opportunities. Such standards would provide a basis for:

• state legislation and, if necessary, litigation that supports greater equity in funding and in the distribution of qualified teachers;

• information about the nature of the teaching and learning opportunities made available to students in different districts and schools across the state;

• incentives for states and school districts to create policies that ensure adequate and equitable resources, curriculum opportunities, and teaching to all schools;

• a school review process that helps schools and districts engage in self-assessments and external reviews of practice in light of standards; and

• identification of schools that need additional support or intervention to achieve adequate opportunities to learn for their students.

Curriculum and Assessment Reform

As noted above, the curriculum offered to many students—and to most African American students—in U. S. schools is geared primarily toward lower-order "rote" skills—memorizing pieces of information and conducting simple operations based on formulas or rules—that are not sufficient for the demands of modern life or for the new standards being proposed and enacted by states and national associations. These new standards will require students to be able to engage in independent analysis and problem solving, extensive research and writing, use of new technologies, and various strategies for accessing and using resources in new situations. Major changes in curriculum and resources will be needed to ensure that these kinds of activities are commonplace in the classrooms of minority students and others.

These efforts to create a "thinking curriculum" for all students are important to individual futures and our national welfare. They are unlikely to pay off, however, unless other critical changes are made in curriculum, in the ways students are tracked for instruction, and the ways teachers are prepared and supported. Although mounting evidence indicates that low-tracked students are disadvantaged by current practice and that high-ability students do not benefit more from homogeneous classrooms (Slavin, 1990), the long-established American tracking system will be difficult to reform until there is an adequate supply of well-trained teachers—teachers who are both prepared to teach the more advanced curriculum that U.S. schools now fail to offer most students and to assume the challenging task of teaching many kinds of students with diverse needs, interests, aptitudes, and learning styles in integrated classroom settings.

Other important changes concern the types and uses of achievement tests in U. S. schools. As a 1990 study of the implementation of California's new mathematics curriculum framework points out, when a curriculum reform aimed at problem solving and higher-order thinking skills encounters an already mandated rote-oriented basic skills testing program, the tests win out (Cohen et al., 1990; Darling-Hammond, 1990b). As one teacher put it:

> Teaching for understanding is what we are supposed to be doing . . . (but) the bottom line here is that all they really want to know is how are these kids doing on the tests? . . . They want me to teach in a way that they can't test, except that I'm held accountable to the test. It's a Catch 22 . . . (Wilson, 1990, p. 318).

Students in schools that organize most of their efforts around the kinds of low-level learning represented by commercially developed multiple-choice tests will be profoundly disadvantaged when they encounter more rigorous evaluations that require greater analysis, writing, and production of elaborated answers. Initiatives in some states (e.g., Connecticut, Kentucky) and cities (e.g., New York, San Diego) to develop more performance-oriented assessments that develop higher-order skills may begin to address this problem.

An equally important issue is how tests are used. If new assessments are used, like current tests are, primarily for sorting, screening, and tracking, the quality of education for minority students is unlikely to improve. Qualitatively better education will come only from developing and using assessment not for punishment but as a tool for identifying student strengths and needs as a basis for adapting instruction more successfully (Glaser, 1981, 1990). Robert Glaser (1990) argued that schools must shift from an approach "characterized by minimal variation in the conditions for learning" in which "a narrow range of instructional options and a limited number of paths to success are available," (p.16) to one in which "conceptions of learning and modes of teaching are adjusted to individuals—their backgrounds, talents, interests, and the nature of their past performances and experiences" (p. 17).

The outcomes of the current wave of curriculum and assessment reforms will depend in large measure on the extent to which developers and users of new standards and tests use them to improve teaching and learning rather than merely reinforcing our tendencies to sort and select those who will get high-quality education from those who will not. They will also need to pursue broader reforms to improve and equalize access to educational resources and support the professional development of teachers, so that new standards and tests are used to inform more skillful and adaptive teaching that enables more successful learning for all students.

Investments in Quality Teaching

A key corollary to this analysis is that improved opportunities for minority students will rest, in large part, on policies that professionalize teaching by increasing the knowledge base for teaching and ensuring mastery of this knowledge by all teachers permitted to practice. This means providing *all* teachers with a stronger understanding of how children learn and develop, how a variety of curricular and instructional strategies can address their needs, and how changes in school and classroom practices can support their growth and achievement.

There are two reasons for this approach. First, the professionalization of an occupation raises the floor below which no entrants will be admitted to practice. It eliminates practices that allow untrained entrants to practice disproportionately on underserved and poorly protected clients. Second, professionalization increases the overall knowledge base for the occupation, thus improving the quality of services for all clients, especially those most in need of high-quality teaching (Wise & Darling-Hammond, 1987; Darling-Hammond, 1990a).

The students who have, in general, the poorest opportunities to learn—those attending the inner-city schools that are compelled by the current incentive structure to hire disproportionate numbers of substitute teachers, uncertified teachers, and inexperienced teachers and that lack resources for mitigating the uneven distribution of good teaching—are the students who will benefit most from measures that raise the standards of practice for all teachers. They will also benefit from targeted policies that provide quality preparation programs and financial aid for highly qualified prospective teachers who will teach in central cities and poor rural areas. Providing equity in the distribution of teacher quality requires changing policies and long-standing incentive structures in education so that shortages of trained teachers are overcome, and that schools serving low-income and minority students are not disadvantaged by lower salaries and poorer working conditions in the bidding war for good teachers.

Building and sustaining a well-prepared teaching force will require local, state, and federal initiatives. To recruit an adequate supply of teachers, states and localities will need to upgrade teachers' salaries to levels competitive with those of college graduates in other occupations, who currently earn 20% to 50% more, depending on the field. States should also strengthen teacher education and certification. In almost all states, teacher education is more poorly funded than other university departments (Ebmeier, Twombly, & Teeter, 1990). It has long been used as a revenue producer for programs that train engineers, accountants, lawyers, and doctors. Rather than bemoaning the quality of teacher training, policy makers should invest in its improvement, require schools of education to become accredited, and insist that teachers pass performance examinations for licensing that demonstrate they can teach well. Shortages should be met by enhanced incentives rather than by lowering standards, especially for those who teach children in central cities and poor rural schools.

The federal government can play a leadership role in providing an adequate supply of well-qualified teachers just as it has in providing an adequate supply of qualified physicians. When shortages of physicians were a major problem more than 30 years ago, Congress passed the 1963 Health Professions Education Assistance Act to support and improve the caliber of medical training, to create and strengthen teaching hospitals, to provide scholarships and loans to medical students, and to create incentives for physicians to train in shortage specialties and to locate in underserved areas. Similarly, federal initiatives in education should seek to:

1. *Recruit new teachers*, especially in shortage fields and in shortage locations, through scholarships and forgivable loans for high-quality teacher education.
2. *Strengthen and improve teachers' preparation* through improvement incentive grants to schools of education and supports for licensing reform.
3. *Improve teacher retention and effectiveness* by improving clinical training and support during the beginning teaching stage when 30% leave. This would include funding mentoring programs for new teachers in which they receive structured coaching from expert veterans.

If the interaction between teachers and students is the most important aspect of effective schooling, then reducing inequality in learning has to rely on policies that provide equal access to competent, well-supported teachers. The public education system ought to be able to guarantee that every child who is forced by law to go to school is taught by someone who is knowledgeable, competent, and caring. That is real accountability. As Carl Grant (1989) put it:

Teachers who perform high-quality work in urban schools know that, despite reform efforts and endless debates, it is meaningful curricula and dedicated and knowledgeable teachers that make the difference in the education of urban students (p. 770).

When it comes to equalizing opportunities for students to learn, that is the bottom line.

REFERENCES

Alexander, K.L., & McDill, E.L. (1976). Selection and allocation within schools: Some causes and consequences of curriculum placement. American Sociological Review, 41, pp. 963–980.

Ashton, P., & Crocker, L. (1986). Does teacher certification make a difference? Florida Journal of Teacher Education, 38(3), pp. 73–83.

Ashton, P., & Crocker, L. (1987, May–June). Systematic study of planned variations: The essential focus of teacher education reform. Journal of Teacher Education, 38, pp. 2–8.

Baron, J. B. (1999). Exploring high and improving reading achievement in Connecticut. Washington, DC: National Educational Goals Panel.

Barr, R., & Dreeben, R. (1983). How schools work. Chicago: University of Chicago Press.

Barton, Paul E. & Coley, R. J. (1996). Captive students: Education and training in America's prisons. Princeton, N.J.: Educational Testing Service.

Bents, M., & Bents, R.B. (1990). Perceptions of good teaching among novice, advanced beginner and expert teachers. Paper presented at the Annual Meeting of the American Educational Research Association, Boston.

Berne, R. (1995). Educational input and outcome inequities in New York State. In R. Berne and L.O. Picus (eds.), Outcome Equity in Education, pp. 191–223. Thousand Oaks, CA.: Corwin Press.

Bledsoe, J.C., Cox, J.V., & Burnham, R. (1967). Comparison between selected characteristics and performance of provisionally and professionally certified beginning teachers in Georgia. Washington, D.C.: U.S. Department of Health, Education, and Welfare.

California Commission on the Teaching Profession (1985). Who will teach our children? Sacramento: California Commission on the Teaching Profession.

California State Department of Education (1984). California high school curriculum study: Path through high school. Sacramento: California State Department of Education.

Carter, K., & Doyle, W. (1987). Teachers' knowledge structures and comprehension processes. In J. Calderhead (Ed.), Exploring Teacher Thinking, pp. 147–160. London: Cassell.

Cohen, D., et al. (1990). Case Studies of Curriculum Implementation, Educational Evaluation and Policy Analysis, 12(3).

College Board (1985). Equality and excellence: The educational status of black Americans. New York: College Entrance Examination Board.

Commission on Chapter 1 (1992). High performance schools: No exceptions, no excuses. Washington, D.C.: Author.

Cooper, E. & Sherk, J. (1989). Addressing urban school reform: Issues and alliances. Journal of Negro Education, 58(3), pp.315–331.

Copley, P.O. (1974). A study of the effect of professional education courses on beginning teachers. Springfield, MO: Southwest Missouri State University. ERIC Document No. ED 098-147.

Darling-Hammond, L. (1990a). Teacher quality and equality. In J. Goodlad, & P. Keating (Eds.), Access to Knowledge: An Agenda for Our Nation's Schools, pp. 237–258. NY: College Entrance Examination Board.

Darling-Hammond, L. (1990b). Instructional policy into practice: "The power of the bottom over the top." Educational Evaluation and Policy Analysis, 12(3), pp. 233–242.

Darling-Hammond, L. (1992). Teaching and knowledge: Policy issues posed by alternate certification for teachers. Peabody Journal of Education, 67(3), pp. 123–154.

Darling-Hammond, L. (1997). The right to learn: A blueprint for creating schools that work. San Francisco: Jossey-Bass.

Darling-Hammond, L. & Snyder, J. (1992). Traditions of curriculum inquiry: The scientific tradition. In P.W. Jackson (Ed.), Handbook of Research on Curriculum. New York: Macmillan.

Davis, D.G. (1986). A pilot study to assess equity in selected curricular offerings across three diverse schools in a large urban school district. Paper presented at the Annual Meeting of the American Educational Research Association, San Francisco.

Doyle, W. (1986). Content representation in teachers' definitions of academic work. Journal of Curriculum Studies, 18, pp. 365–379.

Dreeben, R. (1987, Winter). Closing the divide: What teachers and administrators can do to help black students reach their reading potential, American Educator, 11(4), pp. 28–35.

Dreeben, R. & Barr, R. (1987). Class composition and the design of instruction. Paper presented at the Annual Meeting of the American Education Research Association, Washington, D.C.

Dreeben, R. & Gamoran, A. (1986). Race, instruction, and learning. American Sociological Review, 51(5), pp. 660–669.

Druva, C.A., & Anderson, R.D. (1983). Science teacher characteristics by teacher behavior and by student outcome: A meta-analysis of research. Journal of Research in Science Teaching, 20(5), pp. 467–479.

Ebmeier, H., Twombly, S., & Teeter, D. (1990). The comparability and adequacy of financial support for schools of education. Journal of Teacher Education, 42 (3): pp. 226–235.

Eckstrom, R., & Villegas, A.M. (1991). Ability grouping in middle grade mathematics: Process and consequences. Research in Middle Level Education, 15(1), pp. 1–20.

Educational Testing Service (1991). The state of inequality. Princeton, NJ: ETS.

Evertson, C., Hawley, W., & Zlotnick, M. (1985). Making a difference in educational quality through teacher education. Journal of Teacher Education, 36(3), pp. 2–12.

Ferguson, R.F. (1991, Summer). Paying for public education: New evidence on how and why money matters. Harvard Journal on Legislation 28(2), pp. 465–498.

Ferguson, R.F. & Ladd, H.F. How and why money matters: An analysis of Alabama schools.

Finley, M.K. (1984). Teachers and tracking in a comprehensive high school. Sociology of Education, 57, pp. 233–243.

Gamoran, A. (1990). The consequences of track-related instructional differences for student achievement. Paper presented at the Annual Meeting of the American Educational Research Association, Boston.

Gamoran, A. (1992). Access to excellence: Assignment to honors English classes in the transition from middle to high school. Educational Evaluation and Policy Analysis, 14(3), pp. 185–204.

Gamoran, A., & Berends, M. (1987). The effects of stratification in secondary schools: Synthesis of survey and ethnographic research. Review of Educational Research, 57, pp. 415–436.

Gamoran, A., & Mare, R. (1989). Secondary school tracking and eduational inequality: Compensation, reinforcement or neutrality? American Journal of Sociology, 94, pp. 1146–1183.

Gemignani, Robert J. (1994, October). Juvenile correctional education: A time for change. Update on research. Juvenile Justice Bulletin. Washington, DC: U.S. Department of Justice, Office of Juvenile Justice and Delinquency Prevention.

230 THE RIGHT THING TO DO, THE SMART THING TO DO

Glaser, R. (1981). The future of testing: A research agenda for cognitive psychology and psychometrics. American Psychologist, 39(9), pp. 923–936.

Glaser, R. (1990). Testing and assessment: O tempora! O mores! Pittsburgh, PA: University of Pittsburgh, Learning Research and Development Center.

Gomez, D.L., & Grobe, R.P. (1990). Three years of alternative certification in Dallas: Where are we? Paper presented at the Annual Meeting of the American Educational Research Association, Boston.

Good, T.L., & Brophy, J. (1987). Looking in Classrooms. New York: Harper and Row.

Grant, C.A. (1989, June). Urban teachers: Their new colleagues and curriculum. Phi Delta Kappan, 70(10), pp. 764–770.

Greenberg, J.D. (1983). The case for teacher education: Open and shut. Journal of Teacher Education, 34(4), pp. 2–5.

Greenwald, R., Hedges, L.V., and Laine, R.D. (1996). The effect of school resources on student achievement, Review of Educational Research, 66: pp. 361–396.

Grissmer, D.W. & Kirby, S.N. (1987). Teacher attrition: The uphill climb to staff the nation's schools. Santa Monica: Rand Corporation.

Grossman, P. L. (1989). Learning to teach without teacher education. Teachers College Record, 91(2), pp. 191–208.

Grossman, P.L. (1990). The making of a teacher: Teacher knowledge and teacher education. New York: Teachers College Press.

Haney, W. (1999). Supplementary report on Texas Assessment of Academic Skills Exit Test (TAAS–X). Boston: Center for the Study of Testing, Evaluation, and Educational Policy.

Hansen, J.B. (1988). The relationship of skills and classroom climate of trained and untrained teachers of gifted students. Unpublished doctoral dissertation, Purdue University.

Hawk, P., Coble, C.R., & Swanson, M. (1985). Certification: It does matter, Journal of Teacher Education, 36(3): pp. 23–15.

Hoffer, T.B. (1992). Middle school ability grouping and student achievement in science and mathematics. Educational Evaluation and Policy Analysis, 14(3), pp. 205–227.

Jones, L.V. (1984). White-black achievement differences: The narrowing gap. American Psychologist, 39, pp. 1207–1213.

Jones, L.V., Burton, N.W., & Davenport, E.C. (1984). Monitoring the achievement of black students. Journal for Research in Mathematics Education, 15, pp. 154–164.

Kaufman, J.E., & Rosenbaum, J.E. (1992). Education and employment of low-income black youth in white suburbs. Educational Evaluation and Policy Analysis, 14(3), pp. 229–240.

Kozol, J. (1991). Savage inequalities. New York: Crown.

Kulik, C.C., & Kulik, J.A. (1982). Effects of ability grouping on secondary school students: A meta-analysis of evaluation findings. American Education Research Journal, 19, pp. 415–428.

Lee, V., & Bryk, A. (1988). Curriculum tracking as mediating the social distribution of high school achievement. Sociology of Education, 61, pp. 78–94.

MacPhail-Wilcox, B. & King, R.A. (1986). Resource allocation studies: Implications for school improvement and school finance research. Journal of Education Finance, 11, pp. 416–432.

Matthews, W. (1984). Influences on the learning and participation of minorities in mathematics. Journal for Research in Mathematics Education, 15, pp. 84–95.

McKnight, C.C., Crosswhite, J.A., Dossey, J.A., Kifer, E., Swafford, S.O., Travers, K.J., & Cooney, T.J. (1987). The underachieving curriculum: Assessing U.S. school mathematics from an international perspective. Champaign, IL: Stipes Publishing.

Miller, J.G. (1997, June). African American males in the criminal justice system. Phi Delta Kappan, pp. K1–K12.

Moore, D., & Davenport, S. (1988). The new improved sorting machine. Madison, WI: National Center on Effective Secondary Schools.

Moore, E.G. & Smith, A.W. (1985). Mathematics aptitude: Effects of coursework, household language, and ethnic differences. Urban Education, 20, pp. 273–294.

Murnane, R.J. & Phillips, B.R. (1981, Fall). Learning by doing, vintage, and selection: Three pieces of the puzzle relating teaching experience and teaching performance. Economics of Education Review, 1(4), pp. 453–465.

Murnane, R.J., Singer, J.D., Willett, J.B., Kemple, J.J., & Olsen, R.J. (1991). Who will teach? Policies that matter. Cambridge, MA: Harvard University Press.

National Assessment of Educational Progress (1994). NAEP Trial State Assessment. Washington, D.C.: U.S. Department of Education.

National Center for Education Statistics (1985). The condition of education, 1985. Washington, D.C.: U.S. Department of Education.

National Center for Education Statistics (NCES) (1994). Digest of education statistics, 1994. Washington, D.C.: U.S. Department of Education.

National Center for Education Statistics (1995). The condition of education, 1995. Washington, D.C: U.S. Department of Education.

National Center for Education Statistics (NCES) (1996). Schools and staffing in the United States: A statistical profile, 1993–94. Washington, D.C.: U.S. Department of Education.

National Center for Education Statistics (NCES) (1997a). America's teachers: Profile of a profession, 1993–94. Washington, D.C.: U.S. Department of Education.

National Center for Education Statistics (NCES) (1997b). Characteristics of stayers, movers, and leavers: Results from the Teacher Followup Survey, 1994–95. Washington, D.C.: U.S. Department of Education.

National Commission on Teaching and America's Future (NCTAF) (1996). What matters most: Teaching for America's future. New York: Author.

National Commission on Teaching and America's Future (NCTAF) (1997). Unpublished tabulations from the 1993–94 Schools and Staffing Surveys.

National Council on Education Standards and Testing (NCEST). (1992). Raising standards for American education. Washington, D.C.: U.S. Government Printing Office.

Oakes, J. (1985). Keeping track. New Haven: Yale University Press.

Oakes, J. (1990). Multiplying inequalities: The effects of race, social class, and tracking on opportunities to learn mathematics and science. Santa Monica: The RAND Corporation.

Oakes, J. (1992, May). Can tracking research inform practice? Technical, normative, and political considerations. Educational Researcher, 21(4), pp. 12–21.

Oakes, J. (June 1986). "Tracking in secondary schools: A contextual perspective." Educational Psychologist, 22:pp. 129–154.

Paterson Institute (1996). African American data book. Arlington, VA: Paterson Institute.

Peikes, V.A. (1967–1968). Junior high schools science teacher preparation, teaching behavior, and student achievement. Journal of Research in Science Teaching, 6(4): pp. 121–126.

Pelavin, S.H. & Kane, M. (1990). Changing the odds: Factors increasing access to college. New York: College Entrance Examination Board.

Peterson, P. (1989). Remediation is no remedy. Educational Leadership, 46(60); pp. 24–25.

Rock, D.A., Hilton, T.L., Pollack, J., Ekstrom, R.B., & Goertz, M.E. (1985). A study of excellence in high school education: Educational policies, school quality, and student outcomes. Washington, D.C.: National Center for Education Statistics.

Rosenbaum, J. (1976). Making inequality: The hidden curriculum of high school tracking. New York: Wiley.

Rottenberg, C.J. & Berliner, D.C. (1990). Expert and novice teachers' conceptions of common classroom activities. Paper presented at the annual meeting of the American Educational Research Association.

Sanders, W. L. & Rivers, J. C. Cumulative and Residual Effects of Teachers on Future Student Academic Achievement. Knoxville: University of Tennessee, 1996.

Schofield, J.W. (1991). School desegregation and intergroup relations. In G. Grant (Ed.), Review of Research in Education, 17, pp. 335–409. Washington, DC: American Educational Research Association.

Shields, P. M., Esch, C., Humphrey, D. C., Young, V. M., Gaston, M., & Hunt, H. (1999). The status of the teaching profession: Research findings and policy recommendations. A report to the Teaching and California's Future Task Force. Santa Cruz, CA: The Center for the Future of Teaching and Learning.

Skipper, C.E. and Quantz, R. 1987). Changes in educational attudies of education and arts and science students during four years of college. Journal of Teacher Education, May–June: pp. 39–44.

Slavin, R.E. (1990). Achievement effects of ability grouping in secondary schools: A best evidence synthesis. Review of Educational Research, 60(3), pp. 471–500.

Strauss, R.P. & Sawyer, E.A. (1986). Some new evidence on teacher and student competencies. Economics of Education Review, 5(1): pp. 41–48.

Strickland, D. (1985). Early childhood development and reading instruction. In C. Brooks (Ed.), Tapping potential: English and language arts for the black learner. National Council of Teachers of English.

Sutton, R.E. (1991). Equity and computers in the schools: A decade of research. Review of Educational Research, 61(4), pp. 475–503.

Talbert, J.E. (1990). Teacher tracking: Exacerbating inequalities in the high school. Stanford, CA: Center for Research on the Context of Secondary Teaching, Stanford University.

Taylor, W.L., & Piche, D.M. (1991). A report on shortchanging children: The impact of fiscal inequity on the education of students at risk. Prepared for the Committee on Education and Labor, U.S. House of Representatives. Washington, DC: U.S. Government Printing Office.

Trimble, K., & Sinclair, R.L. (1986). Ability grouping and differing conditions for learning: An analysis of content and instruction in ability-grouped classes. Paper presented at the annual meeting of the American Educational Research Association, San Francisco.

U.S. Department of Commerce (1996). Statistical abstract of the United States: 1996.,116th edition. Washington, DC: Bureau of the Census.

Useem, E.L. (1990, Fall). You're good, but you're not good enough: Tracking students out of advanced mathematics. American Educator, 14(3), pp. 24–27, 43–46.

Usiskin, Z. (1987). Why elementary algebra can, should, and must be an eighth grade course for average students. Mathematics Teacher, 80, pp. 428–438.

Wheelock, A. (1992). Crossing the tracks. New York: The New Press.

William T. Grant Foundation, Commission on Work, Family and Citizenship (1988). The forgotten half: Non-college youth in America. Washington, D.C.: Author.

Wilson, S. (1990). A conflict of interests: Constraints that affect teaching and change. Educational Evaluation and Policy Analysis, 12(3), pp. 309–326.

Wilson, S.M., Darling-Hammond, L, & Berry, B. (2000). Teaching policy: Connecticut's long term efforts to improve teaching and learning. Seattle: Center for the Study of Teaching and Policy, University of Washington.

Winkler, J.D., Shavelson, R.J., Stasz, C., Robyn, A., & Feibel, W. (1984). How effective teachers use microcomputers for instruction. Santa Monica, CA: The RAND Corporation.

Wise, A.E., & Darling-Hammond, L. (1987). Licensing teachers: Design for a teaching profession. Santa Monica, CA: RAND Corporation.

Wise, A.E., Darling-Hammond, L., & Berry, B. (1987). Effective teacher selection: From recruitment to retention. Santa Monica, CA: The RAND Corporation.

Lost Opportunities: The Difficult Journey to Higher Education for Underrepresented Minority Students

Patricia Gándara
University of California, Davis

As a group, African-American, Latino, and Native American students do not fare well in American schools. Beginning with their very first encounters with the U.S. education system, these students appear to underperform academically when compared with their white and Asian peers. Numerous explanations are provided for this phenomenon, and some inroads have been made in recent years in closing the achievement gaps. However, disparities among groups remain large, and in some cases, appear to be growing. By the time that students complete their K–12 schooling and go on to higher education, outcomes for the various ethnic groups are significantly different. White students are *twice as likely* as black students to earn a college degree, and Asians are *more than five times* as likely as Hispanics to reach this level of education. Of course, these enormous discrepancies in education result in very different life chances.

At the beginning of the 21st century, Latinos are emerging as the nation's largest minority group, and California is the state with the largest Latino popu-

TABLE 1 Percent of 25–29 Year Olds with BA degrees, by Ethnicity, 2000

Ethnic Group	Percent with BA
Asian	53.9
White	34.0
Black	17.8
Latino	9.7

SOURCE: U.S. Census Bureau data, 2000.

lation. Unfortunately, Latinos are also the least educated of all ethnic groups. Recent years have also seen the increasing dispersion of Latinos, and other immigrants, across the country, such that the population diversity that characterizes California—a state in which there is no ethnic majority—is soon to be replicated across the nation. Thus, as the harbinger of the nation's future, California's experiences are worth noting. As the American humorist, Richard Armour, noted,

> "So leap with joy, be blithe and gay
> Or weep my friends with sorrow
> What California is today,
> The rest will be tomorrow."

For this reason, this paper will occasionally return to California as an indicator of future trends for the nation. Certainly one disturbing trend that can be seen in California is the large gap in educational achievement and attainment by ethnicity that exists in the state, and the consequences this has for the economic welfare of California's citizens. For example, while Latinos represent 28% of the labor force in the state, they earn only 19% of the wage income. The single biggest reason for this discrepancy is the education gap between Latinos and all other workers. Similar to national data, 33% of white wage earners have at least a bachelor's degree, but only 8% of Latinos are similarly well educated (López et al., 1999). As Latinos form a larger share of the population—by 2020 they are projected to exceed 50%—their level of education will surely affect the structure of the state's economy. The impact on the nation will undoubtedly follow.

WHAT DOES THE EDUCATIONAL PIPELINE LOOK LIKE FOR THESE DIFFERENT GROUPS AND WHERE ARE THE POINTS OF LEAKAGE?

Why do some children do so much more poorly in school than others? Where are the points along the way where these students are lost? Below, I trace the pathways of underrepresented students through school in order to identify the significant points of leakage from the pipeline, and the areas in which there exist often untapped opportunities to change this scenario.

Access to Preschool

Attending center-based preschool is linked to higher emerging literacy scores for both disadvantaged and advantaged children (National Center for Education Statistics, 1995). However, the opportunity to "catch up" to the skills of more advantaged peers is particularly critical for black and Hispanic children who are more than four times as likely as non-Hispanic whites to be raised in

TABLE 2 3- to 5- Year-Olds in Center-Based Preschool and Kindergarten in the United States by Ethnicity, 1999

Ethnicity	Preschool Age 3	Preschool Age 4	Kinder Age 4	Total Age 4*	Preschool Age 5	Kinder Age 5	Total Age 5*
White	46.0	66.2	1.8	69.3	23.1	54.7	92.9
Black	59.2	79.4	1.3	81.4	20.2	55.2	98.5
Hispanic	25.0	56.8	5.8	63.6	13.4	66.2	88.6
Other	56.3	65.0	4.5	70.0	23.4	61.1	97.8

SOURCE: U.S. Department of Education, NCES, Digest of Education Statistics, 2000.

poverty (U.S. Department of Education, 1995), and there are large differences in preschool attendance by ethnicity. Nationally, black children are more likely to attend preschool than any other group; but Hispanics are the least likely to attend (U.S. Dept of Education, 2000). These differences in participation reflect both cultural and socioeconomic realities (Fuller et al., 1994). The pattern of differences in preschool attendance, however, demonstrates the ways in which some children may be placed at higher risk for school failure than others. Table 2 shows the rates of preschool and kindergarten attendance for 4- and 5-year-old children by ethnicity.

Black children attend center-based preschool programs at the highest rate of all children and Hispanic children are much less likely to be in a program than all others. Hispanic children, however, are much more likely to go to kindergarten at an early age than other groups. A relatively common pattern for Hispanics appears to be early enrollment in kindergarten without attending preschool, as Hispanic children are much more likely than others to be found in kindergarten at ages four and five. Early enrollment in kindergarten is also associated with higher risk for less positive educational outcomes, especially when kindergarten has not been preceded by preschool attendance (NCES, 1995).

National data can obscure as much as they reveal because population characteristics differ widely across the states. For example, the Hispanic population in the United States is comprised of high-income, well-educated Cuban-American families in the Southeast, and low-income, poorly educated Mexican Americans in the Southwest, as well as more moderately educated, middle-income *Hispanos* who have lived in New Mexico since the founding of the nation. This wide variation in Hispanic groups obscures the particular challenges that exist for some segments of this population. California has the largest Hispanic population of any state, and being largely Mexican origin, it is also among the poorest and least well educated. Figure 1 shows the preschool attendance rates of entering kindergartners in that state by ethnicity, and here it is apparent that all non-white groups attend preschool in much lower proportions than white students, but this is particularly true for Hispanics (Latinos).

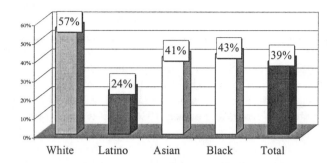

FIGURE 1 Children in Kindergarten Who Attended Preschool the Year Before, by Ethnic Group (1997).
SOURCE: California Research Bureau of the California State Library using the 1997 October Current Population Survey. Estimates for this graph on Asians and Blacks are based on a small sample size and thus many may be unreliable.

A recent study of the characteristics of entering kindergartners shows that black and Hispanic children are much more likely than white or Asian children to have multiple risk factors for school failure (NCES, 1995). This study considered five factors known to be associated with depressed schooling outcomes: poverty, single parent household, mother with less than high school education, primary language other than English, and mother unmarried at time of child's birth. Whereas only 6% of Whites and 17% of Asians had two or more of these risk factors, 27% of Blacks and fully one-third (33%) of Hispanics had two or more risk factors. Conversely, 71% of white kindergartners and 39% of Asians had no risk factors, while only 28% of both black and Hispanic children were without risk factors. In sum, black and Hispanic children are much more likely to enter kindergarten with multiple risk factors related to poor school outcomes, while Hispanics are much more likely to begin kindergarten early—a potential risk factor—but only Blacks appear to offset the risks by attending preschool in high proportions.

While the social class of children does not appear to be highly related to whether they attend preschool for all but white children (U.S. Department of Education, 2000), *the kind* of preschool experience they have is related to their family's socioeconomic status. Middle-class children may attend a wide variety of private preschools as well as publicly supported programs in the community. More high-quality preschool options exist for those individuals who can afford to pay for them. Moreover, for those middle-class children who stay at home, many will receive enriched educational opportunities from well-educated parents and care givers, in more informal contexts. Considerable research evidence exists showing positive effects on cognitive functioning, health status, and socioemotional adjustment of children who attend high-quality preschool programs (Zigler

& Styfco, 1993; Karoly et al., 1998). However, for low-income children, the opportunity to attend high-quality preschool programs is much more limited. Head Start is the primary federally sponsored program for low-income preschoolers, but its quality is uneven (Zigler & Styfco, 1993), and it is only able to serve about half of all eligible children (Children's Defense Fund, 2000).

A substantial body of research has demonstrated that very early intervention can prevent negative outcomes for at-risk students (Haskins, 1989; Karoly et al. 1998; Schweinhart, Weikart, & Learner, 1986). Karoly et al. (1998) reviewed nine preschool programs that served low-income children and that had been carefully evaluated. They concluded that high-quality preschool intervention can have a significant impact on long-term outcomes for participants. Included in the study was the now-famous Perry Preschool Program (Schweinhart et al., 1986). While cognitive effects as measured by IQ tests were not sustained over time for the Perry preschoolers, program participants had higher rates of high school completion and employment and lower rates of delinquency and teen pregnancy than the control group, which had not been exposed to any preschool intervention.

Campbell and Ramey (1995) reported on a carefully designed study of the effects of high-quality preschool intervention on at-risk youngsters. The Carolina Abecedarian Project involved four groups of students: a preschool and early elementary intervention group, a preschool-only group, an early elementary intervention group only, and a control group. Altogether, 111 children and their families, of which 98% were African American, were involved in the experiment. All of the children were considered at risk for poor developmental outcomes and the intervention involved parent training as well as extensive educational enrichment for the treatment children. On the basis of a longitudinal study of the children—seven to ten years after intervention had ceased—the researchers concluded that early intervention in infancy resulted in better academic outcomes, including maintenance of IQ advantages and higher academic achievement, than the control group or the early elementary group. The research supports the idea of intervening early and intensively in the lives of low-income and minority youth and suggests that when intervention occurs early and extends over a lengthy period, intellectual gains may be sustained over time.

Head Start is the primary program supported by the federal government to intervene in the lives of low-income and minority children. However, Zigler et al. noted that because Head Start is a funding source and not a specific intervention, there is large variation in the way it is implemented. Nonetheless, a recent study of the effects of selected Head Start programs for children from different racial and ethnic backgrounds found that cognitive gains may be substantial and persistent for Mexican-American children. When compared to stay-at-home siblings, some programs were able to narrow the test score gap with white children by at least one-quarter and to close the gap in the probability of having to repeat a grade by about two-thirds. African-American students also made significant test score gains as a result of completing a Head Start program; however, unlike white students, for whom the test scores gains were sustained, black students' gains were quickly lost (Currie & Thomas, 1996). The researchers argued that this is probably related to the poor schooling that so many African-American students receive subsequent to preschool (Currie and Thomas, 1995).

In sum, the evidence suggests that early intensive enrichment can have long-term effects on cognitive functioning. This finding also lends support to the notion that early intervention could have a positive impact on higher-level functioning for children who are not at serious risk. However, low-income, minority children are less likely to have access to high-quality preschool experiences that could result in better educational outcomes for them. Thus, differences in both rates of preschool attendance, as well as the quality of that experience, represent initial lost opportunities to affect the academic fate of many low-income and minority youngsters.

Kindergarten

While some research has suggested that children from different ethnic groups begin school with similar skills and that differentiation occurs as a by-product of schooling (Entwisle & Alexander, 1992), recent national data on kindergartners suggest otherwise. The achievement gaps among groups are noticeable at the earliest stages of formal academic assessment. Table 3 shows the percentages of kindergartners in different ethnic groups who score in the lowest or in the highest quartile on reading and math readiness. The lower performance of Hispanic children vis-à-vis African-American children, in spite of the fact that they outperform Blacks on tests of academic achievement in elementary school, is probably related to the large numbers of Hispanic kindergartners who are tested in English, but who do not speak the language when they enter school.

TABLE 3 Percent of Kindergartners in Lowest and Highest Quartile of Reading Skills, by Ethnicity, Fall 1998

Group	Percent Lowest Quartile/ Reading	Percent Highest Quartile/ Reading	Percent Lowest Quartile/ Math	Percent Highest Quartile/ Math
Black	34	15	39	10
Latino	42	15	40	14
Native American	57	9	50	9
Asian	13	39	13	38
White	18	30	18	32

SOURCE: America's Kindergartners, U.S. Dept of Education, NCES, 2000.

The very large discrepancies in academic performance among the ethnic groups at the very beginning of schooling suggests that where preschool was provided, it was not of high enough quality or long enough duration to equalize home advantages. Moreover, these early differences presage a pattern of lower achievement for those students who begin school behind. If children leave kindergarten with significantly lower reading readiness skills than their peers, they can be expected to be placed in lower reading groups in first grade, and this fact augurs poorly for their later academic outcomes. Barr and Dreeben (1983) have shown how, in spite of the best intentions of teachers, the boundaries between reading groups formed early in the first grade often become impermeable barriers to upward advancement in reading groups thereafter. Students have a strong tendency to stay in the groups into which they are initially placed. Those students who come to school with readiness to read—usually those from more advantaged homes that have encouraged early literacy—tend to maintain their advantage over time. This is largely because low-level reading groups cover significantly less material than high-level reading groups, increasing the gaps in exposure to curriculum content among different reading groups over time. In this way, teachers' early judgments at the beginning of schooling, based in part on preschool experiences, can set the stage for underachievement thereafter. What might be an opportunity to equalize children's life chances is turned into a vehicle for solidifying the status with which they entered school.

Many states have policies that delay the entry of children into kindergarten until they can pass a screening test of school readiness skills (Meisels, 1986). This policy has been a response to the studies that show that younger children, as well as children who have not met certain developmental milestones, tend to do more poorly in kindergarten than older, more developmentally advanced children (Shepard & Smith, 1989). Such a policy makes sense if the objective is to equalize students' skills at the beginning of kindergarten. However, if kindergarten is viewed as an opportunity to strengthen students' skills in order to get them ready for first grade, then such a policy defeats that goal. Delaying the kindergarten entry of low-income children and those from backgrounds that may not be able to provide the skills and knowledge valued by school only sets these children farther behind their peers. Failure to provide high-quality, intensive preschool and kindergarten experiences for low-income minority children constitutes a significant lost opportunity to capture more of these children in the academic pipeline.

Elementary School

Researchers studying the academic achievement of children in federally funded programs for low-income, low-performing students (Chapter 1) found that achievement gaps between white students and Latino and African-American students in Chapter 1 schools remain relatively constant across the six elementary grades (Stringfield et al., 1997). This study, known as the *Special Strategies Study*, found that African-American students trailed white students on CTBS/4 reading by .71 to .82 standards deviations, while Latino students lagged about one-half standard deviation behind white students. Likewise, the 1998 National Assessment of Educational Progress (NAEP) showed similar discrepancies. While 39% of white students in the fourth grade scored at or above proficient, only 10% of African Americans and 13% of Latinos reached this level (Donahue et al., 1999). Similarly, African-American students remained more than three-quarters of a standard deviation behind white students through elementary school on the mathematics portion of the CTBS/4, while the gap between Latino and white students ranged between one-third and two-thirds of a standard deviation.

The *Special Strategies Study* attempted to assess the effectiveness of several school-wide intervention programs in K–6, including *Success for All*, the *School Development Program* (Comer, 1988), *Padeia, Chapter 1* school-wide projects, and *Chapter 1* extended-year projects. Data were aggregated to ascertain if they yielded significant improvement in academic achievement of program partici-pants. All students served by these programs, as well as the control group stu-dents, were in schools serving low-income (minority) students. Data for students from the national study of Title 1, *Prospects* (Puma et al., 1997) were used as controls. Stringfield et al. found African-American students in the *Special Strategies* schools learned at a faster rate than their controls, and that their achievement levels surpassed the controls' over the four-year period of the study. More importantly, the high-achieving African-American math students not only grew at a faster rate, but they also surpassed the achievement levels of all initially high-achieving math students in the control group (Borman et al., 2000). Thus, without disaggregating data to determine the independent effects of particular programs or implementations, the *Special Strategies* study did confirm that school-wide reform efforts directed toward strengthening the curriculum (among other things) can have an impact on raising the achievement of high-achieving African Americans to even higher levels.

One troubling finding from the study, however, was the extent to which low-income students continued to disengage from school throughout the ele-mentary years. Researchers defined disengagement as the downward trajectory of grades for students who initially were high performers. They noted that "the process of disengagement begins at first grade and continues through the sixth grade for high achieving students of low SES levels [and] . . . . African Ameri-can students who began third grade at or above the 50th percentile disengage at a significantly faster rate than comparable white students" (Borman et al., 2000, p. 79). It would appear, then, that some of the potentially most academically tal-ented minority students are at greatest risk for academic failure.

Many other school reform strategies geared toward increasing the achieve-ment of low-income and minority children in grades K–8 are underway across the nation. Unfortunately, very few rigorously evaluate their activities and so it is difficult in most cases to know what is working, and why. One exception is the work of Cook, Hunt, and Murphy (1998). This was a very careful longitudinal study of 10 elementary schools in Chicago that had implemented the Comer program—a school-wide reform effort that focuses on bringing the community into meaningful contact with the schools in an effort to change fundamentally the schools' climate—the attitudes and aspirations that school personnel have for their students (Comer, 1988). The investigators compared the reforming schools with 9 others in the district that had similar demographic characteristics, and statistically controlled for the differences that remained. They found that where the program was carefully implemented and also had a strong focus on strengthening the rigor of the curriculum to which students were exposed, there were small, but significant and positive differences in both behavioral indicators (decreased behavioral problems) and academic achievement. While the differences were not earth-shattering in size, the findings were nonetheless very important. Detecting differences in *anything* in whole school efforts, with all the messy variation that exists across classrooms, teachers, and students, can be viewed as an indicator of probable larger effects, if only our instruments were more sensitive and our samples more stable.

Project GRAD, a Ford Foundation-sponsored program that began in Houston, Texas, is another such beacon of hope in the evaluation literature. Project GRAD is a large-scale effort now being implemented in several sites around the country. Its goal is to provide every student with a greater opportunity to learn. It involves research-based instructional reforms and addresses many of the shortcomings of low-income, inner-city schools. Although it is relatively new, it appears to be already creating important changes in school climate and some student achievement indicators. A recent evaluation of the Houston site reveals that referrals to the principal's office across the feeder elementary schools declined by 74% since the inception of the program in 1994–95. Student achievement is also on the upswing. Across all cohorts of students in the original feeder elementary school cluster, as well as in the 10th grade of the high school, Project GRAD students are outperforming their comparison schools in math, and in some cases in reading on the Texas Assessment of Academic Skills (TAAS) test (Opuni, 1998). Such programs appear to demonstrate that the achievement of underrepresented students can be enhanced on a large scale, with structured, sustained efforts. Unfortunately, most schools are untouched by truly systemic reform, and most children must rely on the traditional means that have largely failed them, for gaining access to a high standards curricula. A primary gateway is through the gifted and talented programs.

Considering their overall achievement patterns, it is not surprising that African-American, Latino, and Native American students are underrepresented in programs for the gifted and talented throughout the nation, and white and Asian students are overrepresented. Table 4 shows the percentage of each ethnic group participating in these classes in K–12 in the 1997 school year.

TABLE 4 Percent Participation in Gifted and Talented Classes by Ethnic Group and Percent K–12 Population, 1997

Ethnic Group	Percent of Gifted	Percent K–12 Population
White	76.61	64.0
Black	6.63	17.0
Hispanic	8.56	14.3
Asian	6.63	3.1
Native American	.90	1.1

SOURCE: U.S. Department of Education, Office for Civil Rights, 1999.

Access to gifted and talented programs in elementary school is important because it predicts placement in high-level math courses in middle school, which determines the level of mathematics a student will be able to complete in high school. Based on analyses of High School and Beyond data, Adelman (1999) concluded that the rigor of the curriculum to which students are exposed is more predictive of long-term academic outcomes than even the powerful variable of family socioeconomic status. Adelman argued that the greatest amount of the variance in long-term academic outcomes among ethnic groups can be attributed to the differences in the groups' exposure to high-level curricula— most particularly to advanced mathematics, which black and Latino students are least likely to take. Given the important gateway role that classes for the gifted play, many educators have long rued the underrepresentation of minority students in the programs (Figueroa & Ruiz, 1999). The failure to identify and place more minority students in these programs represents another lost opportunity to increase the achievement trajectory of these students.

Middle School

While grouping practices in elementary schools determine to a large extent the breadth and depth of curriculum to which students will be exposed, curriculum tracking begins in earnest in the middle schools. Students who are assigned to pre-algebra in the 7th grade and algebra in the 8th grade are on track for a college preparatory curriculum (Adelman, 1999). Those who are held back in more basic mathematics courses will have difficulty catching up and may not be able to complete the college preparatory science prerequisites either. Using 8th grade data from the NELS database, Rumberger and Gándara (2000) asked if students from different ethnic groups who were in gifted programs had an equal chance of being assigned to algebra in the 8th grade. Table 5 displays the percentages of students from each major ethnic group who were in gifted and talented programs in the 8th grade and who were also assigned to algebra. All data are based on student self-report.

TABLE 5 Percent of Students in Gifted and not in Gifted Programs Who Are Assigned to Algebra in Grade 8 (NELS 88 Database)

Ethnicity	Percent Gifted in Algebra	Percent Non-Gifted in Algebra
White	73	28
Hispanic	52	26
Black	60	27
Asian	83	35

Evidently, being in a gifted and talented program is highly associated with being assigned to algebra in the 8th grade, suggesting that students who have been identified as gifted are generally perceived as being more academically able, at least in mathematics. Students in gifted and talented programs were two to three times more likely to be assigned to algebra than students who were not in the program. For students not in a gifted program, differences among ethnic groups in the percentage of students assigned to algebra were relatively small. However, there are considerable discrepancies by ethnicity in assignment to algebra for students who are in a gifted and talented program. Asian and white students are much more likely to be assigned to algebra than are African-American and His-panic students. Hispanic students have the least likelihood of being in algebra, whether they are in the program or not. To determine why this is so, we examined grades and achievement test scores for each of the groups to determine if stu-dents' grades or test scores were responsible for the discrepancies in algebra placement. Table 6 displays the percentages of students falling into each test score quartile and at each of four levels of grade point average by ethnicity.

Grades and test scores probably explain a fair amount of the variance in as-signment to algebra in the 8th grade by ethnicity. For white students, 82.4% had overall grades of 3.0 or higher, and for Asians, 90.4% had 3.0 or higher, while 20 to 30% fewer black and Hispanic students had grades this high. Overall, grades correlate highly with assignment to upper-track classes. However, the

TABLE 6 Percent of Students with Specified Grades and Test Scores by Eth-nicity for 8th Grade Gifted and Talented Students (NELS 88 Database)

Ethnicity	Test Score 1st Quartile (Low)	Test Score 2nd Quartile	Test Score 3rd Quartile	Test Score 4th Quar-tile (High)	Grades Less than 2.0	Grades 2.0–2.99	Grades 3.0–3.49	Grades 3.5+
White	18.1	25.8	30.3	23.0	2.2	15.3	20.0	62.4
Hispanic	29.7	22.6	22.9	20.9	6.9	24.8	28.3	40.1
Black	39.6	19.1	13.7	18.9	17.7	30.4	22.6	29.3
Asian	11.4	7.7	17.0	37.9	2.2	7.5	21.7	68.7

fact that Hispanic students were *less likely* than African Americans to be assigned to algebra is not explained by grades or test scores, inasmuch as both were higher for Hispanics than for African-American students. This may be related to findings that teachers are somewhat less likely to identify Hispanic students for gifted classes and that even training in identification procedures does not appear to reduce this problem substantially (Burstein & Cabello, 1989). The discrepancies in grades among different ethnic groups does raise another fundamental concern: are students from different ethnic groups being selected into gifted and talented programs on the basis of very different criteria? And, if this is the case, does the curriculum to which they are exposed in the program meet their needs equally? Put another way, does the experience of being in a gifted program contribute significantly to closing the high achievement gap between groups? The answer to this question is largely unknown. The labeling effect of being identified as gifted may be a factor in some African-American and Latino students being assigned to algebra (given their overall lower grades and test scores). However, it is difficult to know to what extent the benefits of the program extend beyond the label for these underrepresented students.

Quality of Teachers

Not only are schools in more affluent areas better organized to provide more rigorous curricula, they also tend to have better prepared teachers (Haycock, 1998; Ferguson, 1998; Betts et al., 2000). However, Haycock (1998) reviewed data showing that children of color, regardless of their socioeconomic level, are more likely to be taught by teachers with lower test scores and less academic preparation than are white children. And the quality of the teacher, measured by certification, quality of institution from which the teacher received his or her degree, and test scores, has been shown in a number of studies to have a significant impact on student performance. Ferguson (1998) reviewed data from Texas in the 1980s and found that teachers with higher scores on the Texas teachers' test were more likely to produce significant gains in student achievement than their lower scoring counterparts. Goldhaber and Brewer (1996), in an analysis of NELS 88 data, showed a positive relationship between teachers' degrees in technical areas (math and science) and students' achievement. Teachers' expectations of children's abilities can also affect their school performance.

Teachers can be very effective in sending non-verbal messages to students about the amount of confidence they have in their abilities. For example, teachers not only call on favorite students more often, but research has shown that they wait longer for an answer from a student they believe knows the answer than from one in whom the teacher has little confidence. With the latter, the teacher is more likely to provide the correct answer, or move quickly on to another student (Brophy & Good, 1974). Students have also been shown to be very sensitive to these subtle teacher behaviors, to "read" their teachers' attitudes quite accurately (Weinstein, 1989), and, arguably, to internalize these attitudes in ways that can reduce achievement (Rist, 1970).

Teachers' assessments of student potential begin at a very early age. Alexander, Entwisle, & Thompson (1987) showed that social distance, which is the difference in social and economic status, between first graders and their teachers resulted in lower expectations and lower assessments of maturity and behavior for low-income students. Moreover, these early assessments resulted in lower academic achievement in subsequent years (Entwisle et al., 1997). Because teachers are more likely to assess middle-class and non-minority students as having higher ability than their low-income and minority peers (Baron et al., 1985), inequalities in schooling expectations, access to demanding curricula, and other schooling opportunities are established early in children's school careers. Unfortunately, it also appears that if students do not leave middle school with a strong academic foundation, it is very unlikely that high schools will be able to change their academic trajectory (Gándara & Bial, 2001). For this reason, the federal government's newest foray into providing comprehensive services for low-income and minority students—GEAR UP (Gaining Early Awareness and Readiness for Undergraduate Programs)—is designed to begin no later than 7th grade, and to follow students through to high school graduation. Because the program is new, evaluation data are not yet available, but the program design is research-based and theoretically grounded. GEAR UP may represent a real opportunity for some low-income and minority students.

High School

Although considerable dropping out occurs in middle school, especially for Hispanics (Rumberger, 2000), most state and federal agencies do not collect data on dropout until high school. Drop-out rates for underrepresented students are much higher than for white and Asian students, and this is especially true for Latinos. In 1998, the dropout rates among persons 16 to 24 years old were 7.7% (white, non-Hispanics), 13.8% (black, non-Hispanics), and 29.5% (Hispanics) (U.S. Department of Education, National Center for Education Statistics, 2000, Table 108). The high dropout rate among Hispanics has been a particular concern for the federal government, which recently issued a report on this problem (Secada et al., 1998).[1] The Native American dropout rate appears to be about 30% as well, with accurate counts for this population being difficult to obtain (Swisher & Hoisch, 1992). While the Department of Education does not report dropout rates

---

[1] Although dropout rates for Hispanics are indeed high, two-thirds of all young Hispanics are foreign-born and more than 40% of foreign-born Hispanics never attended school in the United States (McMillen et al., 1997, Table 16). In 1995, the last time these figures were computed, the dropout rate among U.S.-born Hispanics was 18%, compared to 12% for U.S.-born black, non-Hispanics, and 9% for white, non-Hispanics.

for Asians, Census Bureau data suggest that the high school completion rate for Asians is identical to that of white students (Hune and Chan, 1997).

Social and academic integration into school are two factors that have been consistently associated with persistence in both high school and college. Students who are active in extracurricular activities and who have meaningful relationships with other students and faculty are less likely to drop out of school than students who do not participate in such activities or have such relationships (Mahoney & Cairns, 1997). This is probably one reason why high residential mobility among many low-income and minority students has such negative effects on school persistence—because it is difficult for many students to reestablish relationships and group affiliations in each new school to which they are assigned. Adolescents, in particular, are notoriously peer-oriented, and it can be difficult for a new student to enter into already-established friendship groups. Fine (1991), however, has questioned to what extent low-income and underrepresented minority students actually *choose* to drop out of school and to what extent this is a choice made for them—either by a system that is anxious to be rid of them, or by school personnel who are indifferent to their needs so that some students find little point, and few, if any rewards, in staying.

There is both a push and pull effect in the phenomenon of exiting school before graduation. Schools push some students out. Pull factors also contribute to disengagement from school. One significant pull factor is primary friendships outside of school, particularly when these friends are school dropouts; students with significant friendships with peers who have left school are more likely to leave school themselves (Epstein & Karweit, 1983; Rumberger, 1981). Another pull factor is employment that intrudes on both time to study and time to attend classes. Students who are employed more than 20 hours per week are at high risk for having lower grades and less engagement with school, which in turn increase their risk of dropping out of school (Steinberg, 1996). Interventions with students who experience residential mobility, as well as those students of color who often feel marginalized by schools because of their cultural and linguistic differences could increase schools' holding power and these students' chances of completing higher education. However, it is rare to find schools that attend to these issues, which certainly constitute another important lost opportunity to prevent further leakage from the academic pipeline.

Gender Differences

Recent data show that in almost all schooling domains, females outperform males, and this is especially true for minority students. Males are routinely identified at higher rates for all kinds of learning disabilities, while females are somewhat more likely to be represented in programs for the gifted and talented.

TABLE 7 Grade Point Averages for U.S. College-Bound Students by Ethnicity and Gender, 1998

Ethnicity	Male	Female
White	3.21	3.37
Asian	3.29	3.42
Mexican American	3.12	3.22
Native American	3.01	3.16
Black	2.75	2.95

SOURCE: The College Board, 1998.

This is especially true for African-American and Hispanic females (Mortensen, 1999; U.S. Department of Education, Office for Civil Rights, 1999). The greater vulnerability of minority males to various kinds of disabilities is reflected also in the grades they receive in school. For example, 1992 data from the National Educational Longitudinal Study (NELS 88) show that while 22.5% of females completed high school with a 3.5 GPA or better, only 15.3% of males performed as well (Owings, 1995). Moreover, this discrepancy in GPA holds true for all ethnic groups, but is especially pronounced for African Americans. It is difficult to find large sample data on GPAs by ethnicity and gender, but the College Board does collect these figures for college-bound students. Table 7 shows the GPA discrepancies among ethnic groups by gender for 1998. Because the College Board also disaggregates Hispanic subgroups, it is possible to look at one group more prone to underachievement—Mexican Americans.

It should not be assumed that all students who complete high school have even vaguely similar experiences in school or are exposed to even remotely similar curricula. The grades and test scores of students by ethnic group provide some indication of the extent to which these students' academic experiences vary. Table 8 shows the relative SAT scores for six different ethnic groups and the percentage of students within each group who scored at or above the median score on the test.

The discrepancies in SAT scores among different ethnic groups exist even when controlling for family income. For example, high-income black students perform about as well on the SAT as low-income white students, and Latinos fare only slightly better. This suggests at least two things: race alone matters as a variable in academic achievement, and the education that students of different racial/ethnic backgrounds receive is not equalized by income. These data also indicate something more. Standard social science methods for determining socioeconomic status fall short of fully describing the social and cultural capital that different groups possess. Because underrepresented minorities attend and

TABLE 8 SAT Scores for Six Ethnic Groups: National SAT Sample, 1999.

	Verbal	Math	Percent Scoring 500+ Verbal	Percent Scoring 500+ Math
White (705,019)	527	528	61%	61%
Asian American (85,128)	497	552	50%	66%
Mexican American (42,750)	452	456	32%	33%
Native American (8,118)	484	481	45%	43%
Puerto Rican (13,897)	455	448	33%	30%
African American (116,144)	433	421	25%	21%

SOURCE: The College Board, 1999 SAT administration data.

graduate from schools that provide a less enriched education than those attended by Whites and Asians, all diplomas and degrees are not equal. Moreover, in many minority families, it may take several wage earners to produce the income that one working member of a white or Asian family can provide. Finally, many minority families that are categorized as middle class may have held this status no more than one generation—scant time to establish the patterns and routines that promote high educational achievement in youth (Miller, 1995).

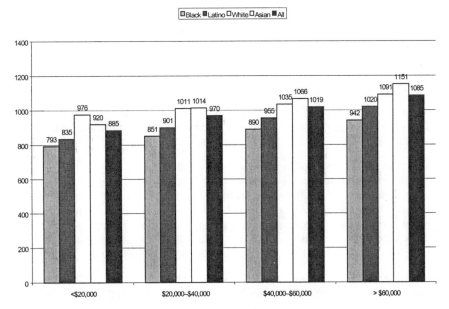

FIGURE 2 Mean SAT Scores by Income and Ethnicity

The particular high school that a student attends can also have a significant impact on his or her academic achievement. Schools in more affluent neighborhoods have been shown to provide more rigorous college preparatory and honors courses than schools in lower-income communities that largely serve populations of underrepresented students. For example, in a recent study of California schools, Betts et al., (2000) found that the lowest-income schools offered only 52% of classes that met college preparatory requirements, while this figure rose to 63% in the highest-income schools. Similar patterns held up when the analysis was done by percent non-white in the school. Likewise, Betts et al. found that "the median high-SES school has over 50% more AP courses than the median low-SES school" (p. 72). Unlike many other states, the University of California awards additional grade points for AP and honors courses. Thus, students who take these classes have a significant advantage over those who do not when calculating grade point averages. Of course, if the particular school does not offer these courses, students are at a significant disadvantage. As important as grade point average, however, is the effect that taking these courses has on students' test scores. Students who take rigorous AP and honors classes are more likely to score high on college entrance exams, thereby increasing their chances of gaining entry to more selective colleges (Adelman, 1999).

Segregation of Minority Students Within and Between Schools

Racial and ethnic segregation continue to have an impact on school performance for underrepresented students. Inequalities in educational opportunity between segregated white schools and segregated schools with students of color have been well documented (Orfield, 1996) and served as the catalyst for a decades-long experiment with desegregation and busing. That experiment has largely come to an end. Today, both black and Latino students attend increasingly segregated schools. Latino segregation has been increasing since data were first collected in the 1960s. In 1997, 35.4% of Latino students were attending schools that were 90% to 100% minority (Orfield & Yun, 1999). And as Orfield (1996) pointed out:

> Low-income and minority students are concentrated in schools within metropolitan areas that tend to offer different and inferior courses and levels of competition, creating a situation where the most disadvantaged students receive the least effective preparation for college. A fundamental reason is that schools do not provide a fixed high school curriculum taught at a common depth and pace. Th actual working curriculum of a high school is the result of the ability of teachers, the quality of counseling, and enrollment patterns of students. (p. 67)

Not surprisingly, Borman et al. (2000) also found that high-achieving black students tended to come from more desegregated schools than their lower-performing black peers.

Of course, even within nominally desegregated schools, the organization of schooling often operates to re-segregate students by ability track within the school. Thus, minority students are much more likely to be found in the vocational and general education tracks that provide weaker curricula and fail to prepare students for the option of going to college than are white or Asian students (Oakes, 1985).

Failure to acknowledge and compensate for very large gaps in family and community resources among groups places many underrepresented minority students at a serious disadvantage in any academic competition. Greater resources and more time to acquire the skills and abilities that many more advantaged children bring from home must be provided if there is to be any hope of narrowing the performance gaps among groups. College access programs now proliferate in schools across the nation. The goal of these programs is to prepare students who would otherwise not go on to college with the prerequisites to attend college. These programs include access to college preparatory curricula, counseling, tutoring, mentoring, college field trips, and sometimes parent involvement activities. As with the school reform projects, few good evaluations of these programs exist; however, those that have been conducted provide us some insights into what can and cannot be accomplished over the high school years. The best of these programs appear to significantly increase the college-going rates of participants, and to ratchet up students' aspirations. Students who might otherwise have only attended a two-year college will more often attend a four-year college, and those who were not headed for college at all are more likely to enroll in a local community college. These changes in students' college-going behavior may set them on an entirely different life trajectory than they had once aspired to. However, the challenge of significantly changing most students' academic profiles (grades and test scores) appears to be more than a single program can usually deliver. To change this would require the more long-term and intensive efforts of systemic school reform (Gándara & Bial, 2001). Nonetheless, such programs appear to lift some participants over the final hurdles to college and to help ensure that well-prepared students from low-income and minority backgrounds actually get there—an outcome that is far from certain even for the best prepared students from disadvantaged backgrounds.

The Special Challenges for Limited English-Proficient Students

Most students with limited English proficiency also come from low-income homes and confront the same challenges as other underrepresented students. However, these impediments are typically accompanied by additional barriers. A recent study in California—the state with the highest number and proportion of limited English-proficient students—showed that these students were the most likely to have a teacher without adequate training as measured by possessing appropriate, or any, teaching credentials (Shields et al., 1999). The underpreparation of teachers to serve limited English-proficient students has been a longstanding problem in the United States as controversies over best methods of instruction have unnecessarily impeded real attention in preparing teachers to meet the needs of these children (August & Hakuta, 1997; Gándara & Maxwell-Jolly, 2000).

In addition to underprepared teachers, most limited English-proficient students face classrooms that either do not take their language needs into account, or are structured to provide an impoverished curriculum that often does not prepare them to succeed academically or meet the requirements for high school graduation or college admission (August & Hakuta, 1997; Olsen 1999; Ruiz-de-Velasco & Fix, 2000). The Prospects Study (Puma et al. 1997), a federally mandated study of student achievement, found that limited English-proficient students scored consistently lower than all other children on achievement tests, even when compared to students at similar high-poverty levels. And even highly competent limited English-proficient students, who may have mastered the grade-level curriculum in their primary language, can find themselves unable to pass English tests and gain access to the classes they need to graduate from high school or attend college (Minicucci & Olsen, 1992). Disenfranchised and discouraged, they frequently drop out of school altogether (Steinberg et al., 1997). By failing to provide classes tailored to the needs of the more than seven million limited English children in the United States, a critical asset is lost. Research has shown that many of these students—immigrants and children of immigrants—are among the most ambitious and high-aspiring students in our schools (Suárez-Orozco & Suárez-Orozco, 1996; Rumbaut & Cornelius, 1995).

Higher Education

Gaining access to college is important, but it is only part of the story. *Where* students go to college is almost as important as going at all. There is considerable difference among ethnic groups in the types of postsecondary institutions that students attend. Lower-income, African-American, and especially Latino students, are much more likely to go to two-year colleges than are white and Asian students, and they are much *less* likely to actually complete their degrees (Rendon & Garza, 1996; Grubb, 1991). Moreover, while a little more than one-third of all college students attend two-year institutions, more than half of all Latino and Native American students who attend college are found in these institutions.

One primary mission of the community colleges is to provide low-cost, easy, and local access to postsecondary education for students who might not otherwise be able to attend because of limited resources or inadequate preparation for a four-year university. But these colleges can also function to divert students off the path to an undergraduate degree (Rendón & Garza, 1996). Burton Clark (1980) first identified the "cooling out" function of two-year institutions, citing the multiple ways in which they can dampen, rather than encourage, aspirations of low-income youth through organizational, cultural, and curricular

TABLE 9 Percentage of Students Enrolled in Two-Year Colleges, by Ethnicity, 1996

Group	Percent enrolled
White	36.8
Asian	39.4
Black	41.5
Latino	56.0
Native American	51.0
All	38.7

SOURCE: Almanac of Higher Education, 1998–99, Chronicle of Higher Education, 1999.

features that may fail to meet the needs and expectations of students. It would be unfair, however, to lay the problem of uncompleted college education solely at the feet of the community colleges. These colleges serve multiple functions and, therefore, their success rests on many different kinds of outcomes. Many students who enter community colleges do not have the intention of completing a four-year degree in the near term, or ever. Many who do articulate such a goal, however, may be less well prepared and less focused in their objectives than students who go immediately to four-year colleges. Thus, there is a clear interaction between the goals and preparation of the students and the effectiveness of the institutions in ensuring the completion of an undergraduate degree.

Given the multiple barriers that minority students face through the educational pipeline, it is not surprising that African-American, Latino, and Native American students are significantly underrepresented among the pool of students receiving bachelor's degrees from American universities and colleges (Table 1). The failure to attend to the significant loss of potential college graduates from this sector of the higher education system is a lost opportunity of major dimensions.

Underrepresented students are even less likely to be enrolled in biological/life sciences or health professions (nursing and other non-physician) undergraduate programs than the typical white or Asian student.

TABLE 10 Bachelor's Degrees Conferred, by Ethnicity (U.S. Citizens), 1997

Group	Percent of U.S. Population	Percent of All B.A.s Conferred
White	72.0	76.9
Asian	3.5	5.8
Black	12.0	8.1
Latino	11.0	5.3
Native American	.7	.6

SOURCE: American Council on Education, 2000

254

THE RIGHT THING TO DO, THE SMART THING TO DO

TABLE 11 Percent of Students in Biological and Health Professions Undergraduate Programs by Ethnicity, 1997

Group	Percent of Population	Biological/ Life Sciences	Health Professions
White	72.0	72.5	81.3
Asian	3.5	13.6	5.2
Latino	11.5	4.4	3.6
Black	12.0	6.5	7.7
Native American	.7	.4	.6

SOURCE: American Council on Education, 2000.

FUTURE PROJECTIONS

Vernez and Krop (1999) have projected the educational scenario for American minorities for the year 2015, based on 1990 census data. In these projections, Hispanics take on an even larger role in the nation's future well-being. They calculate that Hispanics will double in number over this period of time and that Hispanics will make up 13.6% of the United States adult population. Blacks, too, will actually increase their population share slightly from about 10.5 to 11.6% of the adult population. Asians should also double their population from 2.7% in 1990 to 5.8% of the population in 2015. In turn, the share of the non-Hispanic white population is projected to decline from almost 80% of the population to just 70%. The youth population (0–24) is faster growing than adults. While the percentage of the total youth population is just slightly higher for all ethnic groups except Whites (for whom there is a precipitous drop in population share from about 70% in 1990 to less than 58% in 2015) in 2015 compared to 1990, it is among the Hispanic population that the greatest growth is noted. While only about 12% of the youth population was Hispanic in 1990, by 2015 nearly 21% will be.

All groups are projected to increase their educational attainment. However, the disparities in attainment are projected to increase among groups, and particularly between Hispanics and all others. Whereas in 1990 Mexican-origin adults in the United States were *three* times more likely than white adults to have fewer than 12 years of education, they will be *four* times more likely to have this low level of education in 2015. A majority of the children in the United States who will be raised by parents without a high school education in 2015 are projected to be Hispanics and their numbers are projected to double from 1990 levels. Thirty percent of all Hispanic children will be raised in families without a high school education. All told, 85% of children from families with parents who have fewer than 12 years of education will be underrepresented minorities. The anticipated changes in demography will occur even more quickly in the high immigrant-receiving states like California, because immigration is viewed as a major driver of these changes. Projected changes in the ethnic composition of the United States and the concurrent shift in educational preparation of parents raise serious questions for the nation. A country that is increasingly Hispanic—with a Hispanic population that is seriously undereducated—represents a challenge of enormous proportions, and one that we have not met well to date. Vernez et al. (1999) also looked at the potential costs and benefits of closing the education gap between white and Asian students and underrepresented minorities. Their calculations show that under any scenario—closing the high school graduation, college going, or college completion gap between these groups—the public benefits, including decreased social welfare costs and increased taxes, outweigh the costs to provide the education. It behooves us all to seize upon the multiple lost opportunities in the academic pipeline to capture these students before they are lost, and to make every effort to defy the educational projections for the year 2015.

REFERENCES

Adelman, C. (1999). Answers in the tool box. Academic intensity, attendance patterns, and bachelor's degree attainment. Washington D.C.: U.S. Department of Education, Office of Educational Research and Improvement.

Alexander, K., Entwisle, D., & Thompson, M. (1987). School performance, status relations, and the structure of sentiment: Bringing the teacher back in. American Sociological Review, 52, pp. 665–682.

August, D., & Hakuta, K. (1997). Improving schooling for language minority children. A research agenda. Washington, D.C.: National Research Council. Institute of Medicine.

Baron, R., Tom, D., & Cooper, H. (1985). Social class, race, and teacher expectations. In J. Duser (Ed.), Teacher expectations. Hillsdale, NJ: Erlbaum.

Barr, R., & Dreeben, R. (1983). How schools work. Chicago: University of Chicago Press.

Betts, J., Rueben, K., & Dannenberg, A. (2000). Equal resources, equal outcomes? The distribution of school resources and student achievement in California. San Francisco: The Public Policy Institute of California.

Borman, G., Stringfield, S., & Rachuba, L. (2000). Advancing minority high achievement: National trends and promising programs and practices. New York: The College Board.

Brooks-Gunn, J., Denner, J., & Klebanov, P. (1995). Families and neighborhoods as contexts for education. In E. Flaxman & A. Passow, (Eds) Changing populations, changing schools: Ninety-fourth yearbook for the National Society for the Study of Education, Part II. Chicago: National Society for the Study of Education.

Brophy, G., & Good, T. (1974). Teacher-Student relationships: Causes and consequences. New York: Holt, Rinehart & Winston.

Burstein, N., & Cabello, B. (1989). Preparing teachers to work with culturally diverse students: Another educational model. Journal of Teacher Education, 40, pp. 9–16.

Campbell, F., & Ramey, C. (1995). Cognitive and school outcomes for high risk African American students at middle adolescence: Positive effects of early intervention. American Educational Research Journal, 32, pp. 743–772.

Children's Defense Fund (2000). Fact sheet on Head Start. www. Childrensdefense.org.

Chronicle of Higher Education (1998). Almanac of Higher Education, 1998–99. Washington D.C.: Chronicle of Higher Education.

Clark, B. (1980). The "cooling out function" revisited. New Directions for Community Colleges, 8, pp. 15–31.

College Board (The) (1998). Unpublished SAT administration data, 1998.

College Board (1999). Unpublished SAT administration data, 1999.

Comer, J. (1988). Educating poor minority children, Scientific American, 259, pp. 42–48.

Cook, T., Hunt, H.D., & Murphy, R. (1998). Comer's School Development Program in Chicago: A theory-based evaluation. Chicago: Institute for Policy Research, Northwestern University. WP–98–24.

Currie, J., & Thomas, D. (1995). Does Head Start make a difference? The American Economic Review, 85, pp. 361–364.

Currie, J., & Thomas, D. (1996). Does Head Start help Hispanic children? Santa Monica, CA: RAND, DRU–1528–RC.

Darling, N., & Steinberg, L. (1997). Community influences on adolescent achievement and deviance. In J. Brooks-Gunn, G. Duncan, & Aber, L. (Eds.), Neighborhood poverty. Volume II. Policy implications in studying neighborhoods. New York: Russell Sage Foundation.

del Pinal, J., & Singer, A. (1997). Generations of diversity: Latinos in the United States. Washington, D.C.: Population Reference Bureau.

Donahue, P., Voelkl, K., Campbell, J., & Mazzeo, J. (1999). NAEP 1998 reading report card for the nation and the states. Washington, D.C.: U.S. Department of Education, Office of Educational Research and Improvement.

Entwisle, D., and Alexander, K. (1992). Summer setback: Race, poverty, school composition, and mathematics achievement in the first two years of school. American Sociological Review, 57, pp. 72–84.

Entwisle, D., Alexander, K., & Olson, L.S. (1997). Children, schools, & inequality. Boulder, CO: Westview Press.

Epstein, J., & Karweit, N. (eds.) (1983). Friends in school: Patterns of selection and influence in secondary schools. New York: Academic Press.

Ferguson, R. (1998). Can schools narrow the black-white test score gap? In C. Jencks & M. Phillips (Eds.), The black-white test score gap. Washington, D.C.: The Brookings Institution.

Figueroa, R., & Ruiz, N. (1999). Minority underrepresentation in gifted programs: Old problems, new perspectives. In A. Tashakkori & S. Ochoa (Eds.), Readings on equal education. Vol. 16. Educating Hispanics in the U.S.: Politics, policies, and outcomes. New York: AMS Press Inc. Pp. 119–141.

Fine, M. (1991). Framing dropouts: Notes on the politics of an urban public high school. Albany: State University of New York Press.

Fuller, B., Eggers-Pierola, C., Holloway, S. D., Liang, X., & Rambaud, M. (1994). Rich culture, poor markets: Why do Latino parents choose to forego preschooling? Washington, DC: American Educational Research Association and National Science Foundation (ED 371 855).

Gándara, P., & Bial, D. (2001). Paving the way to postsecondary education: K–12 intervention programs for underrepresented youth. Washington, D.C.: National Postsecondary Education Cooperative, National Center for Education Statistics.

Gándara, P., & Maxwell-Jolly, J. (2000). Preparing teachers for diversity. A dilemma of quantity and quality. Santa Cruz, CA: The Center for the Future of Teaching and Learning.

Goldhaber, D., & Brewer, D. (1996). Evaluating the effect of teacher degree level on educational performance. Rockford, MD: Westat.

Grubb, N. (1991). The decline of community college transfer rates: Evidence from national longitudinal surveys, Journal of Higher Education, 62, pp. 194–222.

Haskins, R. (1989). Beyond metaphor: The efficacy of early childhood education. American Psychologist, 44, pp. 274–282.

Haycock, K. (1998, summer). Good teaching matters. How well-qualified teachers can close the gap. Thinking K–16, 3, pp. 1–14.

Hune, S., and Chan, K. (1997). Special focus: Asian Pacific American demographic and educational trends. In D. Carter and R. Wilson, Minorities in Higher Education. 15th Annual Report. Washington, DC: American Council on Education. Pp. 39–67.

Karoly, L., Greenwood, P., Everingham, S., Hoube, J., Kilburn, R., Rydell, C.P., Sanders, M. & Chiesa, J. (1998). Investing in our children: What we know and don't know about the costs and benefits of early childhood interventions. Santa Monica, CA: RAND.

López, E., Ramírez, E., & Rochin, R. (1999). Latinos and economic development in California. Sacramento: California Research Bureau.

Mahoney, J., & Cairns, R. (1997). Do extracurricular activities protect against early school drop out? Developmental Psychology, 33, pp. 241–253.

McKey, R., Condelli, L., Ganson, H., Barrett, B., McConkey, C., & Plantz, M. (1985). The impact of Head Start on children, families, and communities. Washington, D.C.: U.S. Government Printing Office.

Meisels, S. (1987). Uses and abuses of developmental screening and school readiness testing. Young Children, January, pp. 4–8.

Miller, S. (1995). An American imperative. New Haven: Yale University Press.

Minicucci, C., & Olsen, L. (1992). An exploratory study of secondary LEP programs. Vol V of meeting the challenge of language diversity: An evaluation of programs for pupils with limited proficiency in English. Berkeley, CA: BW Associates.

Mortenson, T. (1999). Where are the boys? The growing gender gap in higher education. The College Board Review, 188, pp. 8–17.

National Center for Education Statistics (NCES) (1995). Approaching kindergarten: A look at preschoolers in the United States. NCES 95–280. Washington, DC: NCES.

Oakes, J. (1985), Keeping track: How schools structure inequality. New Haven: Yale University Press.

Olsen, L., Jaramillo, A., McCall-Pérez, Z., White, J., & Minicucci, C. (1999). Igniting change for immigrant students. Oakland: California Tomorrow.

Opuni, K. (1998). Project GRAD. Graduation Really Achieves Dreams, 1997–98 Program evaluation report. Houston: Project GRAD.

Orfield, G. (1996). The growth of segregation. In G. Orfield & S. Eaton (Eds.) Dismantling desegregation. The quiet reversal of Brown v. Board of Education. New York: The New Press.

Orfield, G. & Yun, J. (1999). Resegregation in American schools. Cambridge: Harvard Civil Rights Project.

Owings, J. (1995). Making the cut: Who meets highly selective college entrance criteria? Washington, DC: National Center for Education Statistics. Publication No. 95732.

Puma, M. Karweit, N., Price, C., Ricciuti, A., Thompson, W., & Vaden-Kiernan, M. (1997). Prospects: Final report on student outcomes. Washington, D.C.: U.S. Department of Education, Office of the Under Secretary.

Rendón L. & Garza, H. (1996). Closing the gap between two- and four-year institutions. In L. Rendón & R. Hope (Eds.), Educating a new majority: Transforming America's educational system for diversity. San Francisco: Jossey-Bass. Pp. 289–308.

Rist, R. (1970). Social class and teacher expectations: The self-fulfilling prophecy in ghetto education. Harvard Educational Review, 40, pp. 411–251.

Ruiz-de-Velasco, J., & Fix, M. (2000). Overlooked and underserved: Immigrant students in U.S. secondary schools. Washington, DC: The Urban Institute.

Rumbaut, R., & Cornelius, W. (1995). California's immigrant children: Theory, research, and implications for educational policy. San Diego: Center for U.S.-Mexican Studies, University of California, San Diego.

Rumberger, R. (1991). Chicano drop outs. In R. Valencia (Ed.) Chicano school failure and success: Research and policy agendas for the 1990s. London and New York: Falmer Press.

Rumberger, R. (2000). Why students drop out of school and what can be done. Paper presented at the conference, Dropouts in America: How Severe Is the Problem? What Do We Know About Intervention and Prevention? Harvard University, January 13, 2001.

Rumberger, R., & Gándara, P. (2000). GATE education and access to higher level curricula: An exploration of NELS 88. University of California, Santa Barbara.

Rumberger, R., & Larson, K. (1998). Student mobility and increased risk of high school dropout. American Journal of Education, 107, pp. 1–35.

Secada, W., Chavez-Chavez, R., Gracia, E., Muñoz, C., Oakes, J. Santiago-Santiago, I., & Slavin, R. (1998). No more excuses: The final report of the Hispanic drop out project. Washington, DC: U.S. Department of Education.

Schweinhart, L., Weikart, D., & Learner, M. (1986). Consequences of three preschool curriculum models through age 15. Early Childhood Research Quarterly, 1, pp. 15–45.

Shephard, L., & Smith, M.L. (1989). Flunking grades: Research and policies on retention. London: Falmer Press.

Shields, P., Esch, C., Humphrey, D., Young, V., Gaston, M., & Hunt, H. (1999). The status of the teaching profession: Research findings and policy recommendations. A report to the teaching and California's future task force. Santa Cruz, CA: The Center for the Future of Teaching and Learning.

Steinberg, L., Blinde, P., & Chan, K. (1984). Dropping out among language minority youth. Review of Educational Research, 54, pp. 113–132.

Steinberg, L. (1996). Beyond the classroom: Why school reform has failed and what parents need to do. New York: Simon & Shuster.

Stringfield, S., Millsap, R., Herman, N., Yoder, N., Brigham, P, Nesselrodt, E., Schaffer, N., Karweit, N, Levin, M., & Stevens, R. (1997). Urban and suburban/rural special strategies for educating disadvantaged children. Final report. Washington, D.C.: U.S. Department of Education.

Suárez-Orozco, M., & Suárez-Orozco, C. (1996). Trans-formations: Migration, family life, and achievement motivation among Latino adolescents. Stanford: Stanford University Press.

Swisher, K., & Hoisch, M. (1992). Dropping out among American Indians and Alaska natives: A review of studies. Journal of American Indian Education, 31, pp. 3–23.

United States Department of Education, (1995) Digest of Education Statistics. Washington DC: U.S. Dept of Education, National Center for Education Statistics.

United States Department of Education (1999). The condition of education 1998. Washington, D.C.: National Center for Education Statistics.

United States Department of Education (2000). The condition of education 1999. Washington, D.C.: National Center for Education Statistics.

United States Department of Education, Office for Civil Rights (1999). 1997 elementary and secondary school civil rights compliance report. National and state projections. Washington DC: Department of Education.

Vernez, G., & Krop, R. (1998). Projected social context for education of children: 1990–2015. New York: The College Board.

Vernez, G., Krop, R., & Rydell, C. P. (1999). Closing the education gap. Santa Monica, CA: RAND Corporation.

Weinstein, R. (1989). Perceptions of classroom processes and student motivation: Children's views of self-fulfilling prophecies. In R. Ames & C. Ames (Eds.), Research on motivation in education: Goals and cognitions. Vol. 3. New York: Academic Press. Pp. 187–221.

West, J., Denton, K., Germino-Hausken, E. (2000). America's kindergartners. Washington D.C.: National Center for Education Statistics.

Zigler, E., & Styfco (1993). Head Start and beyond. New Haven: Yale University Press.

Systemic Reform and Minority Student High Achievement

Philip Uri Treisman and Stephanie A. Surles[1]
University of Texas, Austin

INTRODUCTION

The underrepresentation of African-American and Latino[2] students among the ranks of high achievers on standardized tests, among the honors graduates of most American colleges and universities, and among the practitioners of mathematics- and science-based professions, has been exhaustively documented (Borman, Stringfield, & Rachuba, 2000). This underrepresentation is not limited to the poor, nor is it limited to those with little family history of higher education. The problem is endemic and widespread, and close inspection of the data belies simple explanations.

The dimensions of the underrepresentation problem have been well examined in *Reaching the Top*, a 1999 report of the College Board's National Task Force on Minority High Achievement. According to the task force report, student performance differentials by race and ethnicity appear as early as elementary school and persist through college (College Entrance Examination Board, 1999). The report states that in 1995, African Americans, Latinos, and Native Americans accounted for only 13 percent of the bachelor's degrees, 11 percent of the professional degrees, and 6 percent of the doctoral degrees awarded by U.S. colleges and universities. To put these statistics into perspective, these

---

[1] The authors wish to thank Catherine Clark and Janis Guerrero for their targeted and thoughtful comments on this paper. We also thank Rachel Jenkins for her keen editorial eye and Brenda Nelson for her timely review.
[2] The terminology used to refer to different ethnic and racial groups varies throughout this paper. We have used the language of the studies we are citing to minimize confusion between categories.

groups constituted 30 percent of the under-18 population at that time (College Entrance Examination Board, 1999).

The underrepresentation of minority students is especially severe in mathematics- and science-based majors. This underrepresentation is not due to lack of interest on the part of students. In fact, most high school students heading for college select roughly the same intended majors, regardless of their ethnic background. For example, in a national survey, 21.5 percent of black students, 21.5 percent of Hispanic students and 20.9 percent of white students selected science or engineering as their intended majors in 1998. This data includes majors in the natural sciences, engineering, and mathematics and computer sciences (National Science Board, 2000).

The task force also documented very low percentages of high performers among minority students on various tests, including the SAT I and the National Assessment of Educational Progress assessments in reading, mathematics, and science. Critics of standardized testing often attribute these low percentages of minority students among high achievers—and the low average scores of certain minority groups—to cultural and economic biases or other deficiencies of the tests.[3] Although it is well documented that family income levels are positively correlated with student achievement levels, low minority academic performance is not restricted to the children of low-income families. In 1998, the mean SAT I scores of white and Asian students in low-income families, defined as families earning less than $20,000, were *higher* than the mean SAT I scores of African-American students in high-income families, defined as families earning more than $60,000 (Gandara & Maxwell-Jolly, 1999). Thus, variation in family income is only one of several factors that affect test scores, and the contribution of these factors to minority test scores appears to be less than is often presumed.

The predictive value of test scores is another issue that is more complex than generally thought. One would expect that given the impoverished primary and secondary schools many minority students attend, these students would so flourish academically once they reach the fertile soil of higher education that their performance in college would be better than their SAT I scores would predict. Instead, the SAT I scores of minority students overpredict performance at traditionally white colleges and universities (Bowen & Bok, 1998; College Entrance Examination Board, 1999). In other words, within the same range of SAT I scores, the average college grades of minority students are lower than the average college grades of white students.

The overall evidence on the correlates and predictive value of test scores suggests a pernicious problem—namely, that the forces impeding the academic achievement of minority students persist and take new forms at each level of

---

[3] See, for example, the work of FairTest: The National Center for Fair & Open Testing, at www.fairtest.org.

schooling. These counterforces to minority academic advancement remain poorly understood and must become a major focus of American educational research.

Because this country's population is undergoing a demographic shift, and because this shift is even more dramatic in the school-aged population, the difference in performance among students of different ethnic and racial groups is growing in social consequence. If the inequity in educational opportunity that exists today is not addressed, particularly the opportunity that nurtures high levels of achievement, then this inequity will become an increasingly powerful source of division and inequality.

Furthermore, given recent limitations driven by state policy and court rulings on the use of race and ethnicity as factors in undergraduate and graduate school admissions, without a dramatic narrowing of the achievement gap among racial and ethnic groups, the nation's professional and political leadership could grow less and less demographically representative of the population it serves. In both California and Texas, for example, the law schools of the states' flagship public research universities have graduated individuals who constitute a large percentage of each state's minority legislators.[4] The question then arises: will professional and political leadership in a pluralistic democracy retain its authority if it does not truly reflect the diversity of the population it serves?

MODERN SYSTEMIC REFORM
AND HIGH-STAKES TESTING

Our purpose in this paper is to explore the extent to which the current American educational reform movement is achieving the important goal of substantially improving overall student achievement, and especially high achievement, while at the same time reducing achievement gaps among racial and ethnic groups. The fundamental presumption of modern educational reform is that all children should have equal access to high-quality contemporary curricula, and that all students (or in practical terms, nearly all) should be expected to master the content of these challenging curricula and related complex problem-solving skills. Modern reform ideas, as articulated by scholars and policy analysts representing a broad cross-section of political thought, justify this presumption both in economic terms, as necessary for our international economic competitiveness, and in terms of basic justice, as a natural extension of the American equity creed.

Modern systemic reform frameworks typically consist of four interconnected mechanisms designed to increase educational system coherence in the

---

[4] California is effected by Proposition 209, which went into effect on August 28, 1997. It is now Section 31 of Article I of the California State Constitution. Texas, Louisiana, and Mississippi are affected by the decision of the U.S. Court of Appeals for the Fifth Circuit in *Hopwood* v. *Texas*, 78 F.3d 932 (5th Cir. 1996).

belief that such coherence will lead to greater student achievement. The first mechanism consists of three subsystems: a curriculum guidance system driven by state curriculum documents that define what children should know and be able to do, an assessment system that measures student progress in learning content delineated in the curriculum documents, and an accountability system in which schools are rewarded or sanctioned based on their students' performance. The curriculum documents that drive the system should ideally be developed through a participatory process that balances the judgments of scholars and professional educators with those of the business leaders and members of the public at large. This tripartite first mechanism is most commonly thought to be synonymous with systemic reform, but most policy analysts believe that it alone is not enough to make lasting or significant change. The following three additional mechanisms are also essential to the success of systemic reform efforts.

The second mechanism of modern systemic reform is the alignment of state policies concerning textbook adoption; administrator certification; and teacher preparation, licensure, and continuing education, as well as the panoply of related issues that shape who teaches and what gets taught. In systemic reform, each of these domains is organized or reorganized to align with the state's adopted curriculum. This alignment ensures, at least in principle, that all major efforts and expenditures are focused on the same end.

The third mechanism is a restructured educational governance system that in exchange for greater state-level authority over curriculum, grants local schools and school districts greater autonomy in local school management—that is, more flexibility in rules for hiring, in making expenditures, and so on. In essence, then, modern systemic reform gives up certain forms of state control in exchange for the state's greater authority over curriculum. This exchange of power is necessary in a reform agenda focused on the substance of what children learn. In the words of Marshall Smith, one of the architects of standards-based reform, "this model of content-driven systemic reform would . . . marry the vision and guidance provided by coherent, integrated, centralized education policies common in many nations with the high degree of local responsibility and control demanded by U.S. tradition" (O'Day & Smith, 1993).

The fourth mechanism, which has received relatively little attention in current reform efforts, is a strategy for ensuring the availability of resources necessary to bring about desired changes in learning. Smith argued that without adequate resources available to schools that serve poor and minority students, higher standards would lead to an increase in the achievement gap and greater levels of failure for minority and poor children. Adequate resources, including qualified teachers, adequate facilities, and proper instructional materials, constitute what is often called "opportunity to learn" (Rothstein, 2001). Certainly, the determination of what constitutes an adequate level of resources is at the center of one of the liveliest debates in American education policy and politics (Guthrie & Rothstein, 2001).

The humbling challenge facing proponents of systemic reform, or of any other broad reform strategy, is the essential localism of American education. Although the modern American education system and its ideas of positive governmental responsibility for education is largely a post-Civil War construction, the tradition of local governance is deeply grounded in American history and culture. Its roots can be traced to the sentiments of the country's founders, who came to America seeking relief from religious persecution by European governments (Tyack, 1974; Ravitch, 1995). This venerable tradition of local control now finds support both among conservatives, who oppose on principle expanded roles of the federal government, and among liberals, who fear that a national system based on high standards might reinforce existing social stratification and devalue minority cultures. Conservative and liberal critics alike fear that a national curriculum would, of necessity, be a product of compromises that could lead to a sterile and narrow curriculum and to impoverished, test-driven pedagogy. The deeply held belief that those closest to children should determine the content of their education has produced a national educational enterprise with an almost immunological ability to resist centralized reform initiatives.

American education today consists of 50 state systems, each composed of multiple school districts[5] governed by locally elected school board members who do not report in any substantive way to a state board of education. Further, these school districts are managed by superintendents who do not report formally to the state superintendent. Thus, movements to modernize or reform schools must gain the support of the citizenry if they are to affect local education practice. In some sense, then, the effectiveness of national reform strategies can be assessed by the robustness of their strategies for inculcating coherence in a system designed to resist such coherence.

HISTORICAL ANTECEDENTS OF SYSTEMIC REFORM STRATEGIES

Neither high-stakes testing nor standards setting—components of the modern systemic reform movement—is new. With roots that go back at least two millennia to the civil service examination system of the Han Dynasty (206 B.C.–220 A.D.), high-stakes testing has a long and venerable history as a driver of educational systems and as a controller of who, by virtue of their education, can have access to power. The issues of testing and equity are not new, either. By the 13th century, China had created a broad-based system of public schools explicitly designed to prepare the talented but indigent for the high-stakes civil service examinations.

During the Ming Dynasty (1368 A.D.–1644 A.D.), China's civil service examination system evolved in ways that today might be called standards-based.

---

[5] With the exception of Hawaii, which has only one statewide school district.

Examination content was exclusively drawn from the Nine Classics of Confucianism and an established form emerged for the questions and the required answers.[6] The Chinese civil service examination system, which was abolished at the beginning of the 20th century, strongly influenced the British civil service examination system, as well as those of other former European colonial empires.

The notion of standards setting also has very early roots in American education, as evidenced by Webster's "Blue-backed" speller (1782), which taught American children how to read, spell, and pronounce words (Ravitch, 1995). Testing also has a long history in America, with roots going back to the 1890s. That decade marked the beginning of standardized testing to measure learning outcomes by school and the development of intelligence tests to measure students' mental ability. By the 1920s, both forms of testing were powerful forces in big city school systems and were the basis for ability differentiated learning groups, or curricular "tracking"—a practice that remains commonplace in U.S. education and that remains a major concern for advocates of educational equity.

In 1900, the College Entrance Examination Board (CEEB) created the first coherent American system of high-stakes testing designed to directly influence school curriculum, albeit in a small and specialized collection of high schools (Valentine, 1987). At that time, independent colleges and universities paid little attention to students' prior academic achievement in their admissions decisions. Instead, they focused on ability to pay, religion, and social status. In many cases, wealthy families enrolled their children in college at birth. Before 1900, each selective Ivy League college used its own admissions test. Tests were sufficiently different from one another to create formidable difficulties for any high school seeking to prepare students to gain entry to any one of a broad array of colleges. The premise underlying the CEEB system was that by making the standards for college admission clear, and by using these standards to create a common college entrance examination, high schools with good teachers could reliably prepare diligent students for admission to selective Ivy League colleges. This same premise—that good teaching and student diligence rather than extraordinary talent or privilege are the essential prerequisites for academic success—is an axiom of modern educational policy. Under the CEEB system, however, children from wealthy families had an additional advantage, as paid exampreparation tutors could help ready students for college entrance examinations.

The CEEB system contained many features of interest to today's reformers. The College Board developed a novel and vibrant process for creating and continually revising the standards on which its examinations were based. These standards were delineated in annual publications called the "Definitions of the Requirements," and represent the result of often intense debates about "what students should know and be able to do." The College Board also created a reli-

---

[6] Examination papers had eight main headings, and each answer was to be structured in a highly prescribed manner and limited to fewer than 700 characters.

able process for turning standards into examinations. Of special power were the readings, a practice in which college faculty and, especially in the later years of the system, high school teachers, convened to grade the examinations. This practice became an exemplar of effective professional development for teachers.

From its earliest days, critics and even members of the College Board were concerned that the college entrance examination system was exerting too large an effect on the high school curriculum. Further, the rapid advances of modern psychology and the social sciences in the first decades of the 1900s, and the broad use of intelligence testing during World War I, led the College Board to explore the use of intelligence testing as a tool for college admissions. The result was the Scholastic Aptitude Test, a precursor to today's SAT, which was first administered in 1926 to 8,040 students (Lemann, 1999). In the 1930s, the rapid advance of psychology, which then held that intelligence was largely innate and easily measured, and the fears of class warfare during the Great Depression led to the rapidly increasing use of the SAT. Elite colleges were seeking to broaden the socioeconomic diversity of their student bodies and needed a mechanism to identify unpolished talent. Support for the SAT grew among college officials as a replacement to the CEEB examination system.

On December 7, 1941, immediately after learning of the attack on Pearl Harbor, the admissions directors of Harvard, Yale, and Princeton, who were meeting about College Board issues, decided that candidates for admission to their campuses would not take the June CEEB. Instead, they would take the April SAT, so that students could start taking courses in the summer rather than having to wait for the fall (Valentine, 1987). Other colleges quickly followed suit, and the College Board cancelled the June CEEB examinations, effectively ending the program. The SAT remained, and until the creation of the American College Testing Program (ACT) in 1959, was the only national examination used for college admissions.

Historians view the SAT as a primary instrument in bringing about the diversification of American higher education, at least for Catholics and Jews. Donald Stewart, a former president of the College Board, has long argued that under affirmative action the SAT was also instrumental in diversifying the ethnic and racial makeup of American higher education. Certainly, for at least three decades beginning in 1960, the SAT and the ACT were used by selective public and private colleges and universities to identify minority students who they believed, by virtue of their test scores, had the potential to succeed. In places where affirmative action policies in college admissions have been ended, it can conversely be argued that the SAT is now a hurdle to minority access to higher education because, as described above, relatively few minority students receive high scores on standardized tests. More broadly, the question of which approach to testing best advances equity—one, like the SAT, that purports to identify unvarnished talent, or one, like the CEEB, that purports to test mastery of a defined curriculum—remains contentious and unresolved (Atkinson, 2001).[7]

The compensatory education movement of the mid-1960s to the early 1980s provides a powerful example of using testing to shape educational practice. This movement was focused explicitly on raising the academic performance of poor children and on reducing the gap in test scores between minority and non-minority students. The instructional focus of the movement was on reducing illiteracy and innumeracy and, more generally, on ensuring that all students learned basic skills as measured by national norm-referenced tests. Federal legislation, particularly the Elementary and Secondary Education Act (ESEA), provided great impetus to the testing movement by requiring regular testing in exchange for federal funding for disadvantaged students. Tests, textbooks, and teacher professional development in high-poverty communities were mutually reinforcing. Many states adopted minimum competency testing and, going beyond federal requirements, included such testing as part of their high school graduation requirements (Texas Education Agency, 1996). The use of testing in Title I of ESEA provided a model for the use of testing in state education reforms of the 1990s (Ravitch, 1995).

The compensatory education movement did, in fact, help increase the test scores of minority and economically disadvantaged children. Because the test scores of relatively advantaged children were comparatively stable during this period, the disparities in scores were dramatically reduced (O'Day & Smith, 1993). NAEP data show that from 1971 to 1988, achievement gaps between African-American and white students were reduced by 30% to 60%, depending on the subject tested. There is some dispute, however, about how much of this performance narrowing was the result of instruction and how much was the result of significant reductions in the percentage of children living in poverty—an issue of fundamental concern to both researchers and policy analysts (O'Day & Smith, 1993).

A LOOK AT THE DATA

National Assessment of Educational Progress

The primary resource for tracking changes in students' academic performance is the National Assessment of Educational Progress, also known as NAEP,

---

[7] Concerns about the SAT and similar exams have now so permeated American society that the University of California system, among others, is wrestling with the question of whether the tests have become too dominant a force. The concern is that the tests are limiting the curriculum to such an extent that they are harming the education of children. The president of the University of California system has recommended that the university system no longer require the SAT I. A complete description of University of California president Richard C. Atkinson's views on the SAT I are in the 2001 Robert H. Atwell Distinguished Lecture which he delivered at the 83rd Annual Meeting of the American Council on Education.

or the "Nation's Report Card." Established in 1969, NAEP now includes a variety of assessment programs designed to measure changes over time in students' competence in basic skills as well as in the content defined by important national standards documents (such as that published by the National Council of Teachers of Mathematics[8]). Especially important to evaluating systemic reform efforts is a state NAEP testing program begun in 1990, which allows sophisticated and multidimensional comparisons of state academic performance. Data from this NAEP assessment can be used to compare student performance from state to state at grades 4, 8, and 12. This NAEP data set can also be used to estimate the learning gains of cohorts of students as they move, for example, from the fourth to the eighth grade.

To illustrate how NAEP supports complex analyses of state performance, we examine data from two states with roughly similar student populations, California and Texas. In Figure 1, we report the states' fourth and eighth grade average mathematics scale scores in 1992 and 1996, the most recent years for which NAEP data are available. In a cohort analysis—comparing the scores of 1996 eighth graders with those of 1992 fourth graders—California appears to have done a slightly better job than Texas in supporting ongoing student mathematics learning. If, however, one compares state scores at fixed grade levels—i.e., 1992 fourth graders with 1996 fourth graders and 1992 eighth graders with 1996 eighth graders—it appears that Texas has done a better job in supporting student learning. Note that the absolute differences in the performance of Texas and California students are strikingly large—20 points in 1996 at the fourth-grade level and 7 points at the eighth-grade level. A difference of about 11 points corresponds to one year of learning (Loveless & Diperna, 2000).

NAEP allows the disaggregation of a state's performance data by major ethnic or racial subgroup, a crucial fact for its contributions to analysis of performance. As one example of the power of this capacity, we report in Figure 2 the average scale scores of participating states[9] on the 1998 eighth-grade NAEP writing assessment. African-American students in Texas score as well as or bet-

California	4th Grade	8th Grade		Texas	4th Grade	8th Grade
1992	208	261		1992	218	264
1996	209	263		1996	229	270

FIGURE 1 1992 and 1996 NAEP Mathematics Scores for California and Texas
SOURCE: NAEP 1996 Mathematics Report Card for the Nation and the States.

---

[8] These standards are available online at http://standards.nctm.org/.

[9] Currently, state NAEP assessments are voluntary, but the great majority of states choose to participate.

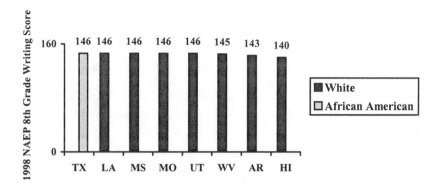

FIGURE 2 1998 NAEP 8th Grade Writing for Texas African-American Students and White Students in Seven Other States.
SOURCE: National Center for Educational Statistics and The Education Trust.

ter than white students in seven other states. (These various analyses of the data dispel the myth that the demography of a state determines the outcomes of its educational system. After all, it is the adults in the system, not the children, who determine its outcomes.)

As described above, NAEP data show that nationally, between 1971 and 1988, the gap in scores between African-American and white students closed significantly. Figure 3 shows the closing of the gap in NAEP reading scores. There was also a substantial closing of the gap between the scores of middle class children and those of poor children. There is no evidence, however, that these gaps have closed further in the 1990s. Rather, the unhappy finding is that nationally the gaps, especially in reading, are growing (Barton, 2001). The positive news is that there have been gains in average scores for all the major subgroups tested; even so, nationwide these gains can be fairly described as being small to modest (Barton, 2001). The data clearly indicate that younger students have made significantly greater progress than have older students (Loveless & Diperna, 2000).[10] Indeed, the increases in reading and mathematics learning gains from grades 8 to 12 are about one-third the gains from grades 4 to 8.

---

[10] One of the few findings about which there is broad agreement is that learning gains decrease as students move through the American education system. This deceleration of learning gains once students reach high school has profound consequences for equity in and access to mathematics- and science-based careers.

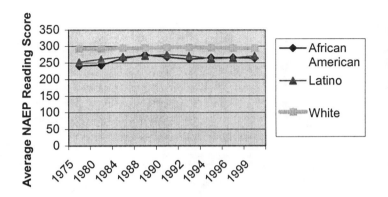

FIGURE 3 Gap in NAEP Reading Scores for 12th Graders.
SOURCE: U.S. Department of Education, National Center for Educational Statistics and The Education Trust.

Of course, analysis of NAEP data alone cannot tell us how much of the observed gain in student performance in a state is the result of that state's systemic reform strategy. In the 1980s and 1990s, states implemented a broad array of policies addressing what were believed to be important opportunities for improving learning. These included state initiatives to lower class size (especially in the early grades), to raise teacher and administrator salaries, to strengthen teacher licensing requirements, to create mentoring programs for new teachers, and so on.

In their analysis of NAEP mathematics gains, David Grissmer and Ann Flanagan controlled for the most common of these strategies and still found that modest progress—at least in mathematics—can be attributed to state systemic reform policies (Grissmer & Flanagan, 1998). Grissmer and Flanagan found that Texas and North Carolina, early adopters of standards-based reform, show the largest gains.

In a separate study, Grissmer and Flanagan used census figures to adjust NAEP data that rely on student reports of key variables—such as family income—about which children may be poor judges (Grissmer & Flanagan, 2001). Grissmer and Flanagan then disaggregated adjusted state NAEP data by geographic locality—urban, suburban, and rural—to see the breadth of effect that state policy has on student learning gains. The researchers hypothesize that "achievement gains within states should occur in all localities within the state . . . if statewide reforms are effective" (Grissmer & Flanagan, 2001). Using this test and their adjusted data, they find that only three states meet this criterion of broad geographic effect—Michigan, North Carolina, and Texas.

These three states agreed to participate along with ten others in TIMSS-R,[11] a benchmarking project conducted as part of the 1999 Third International Mathematics and Science Study (Jerald, 2001). In Table 1, we show data on the relative performance of these states, as well as explicit benchmarking data relevant to high performance. The data show that Michigan and Texas have the highest average TIMSS scores; Texas also has the highest percentages of students scoring at the top reported levels of performance. Note that, as can also be seen in Table 1, Texas had substantially higher proportions than did other states of minority and low-income test takers.

A natural extension of the disaggregation idea is to examine student learning gains not only by geographic locality, but also by the race or ethnicity of students and by subject matter (for example, gains in reading versus mathematics). If policy was the primary driver of improvement, then Grissmer and Flanagan's argument would suggest that performance would be somewhat uniform across these three policy relevant variables. Subject matter is important as a check on the effects of state policy because mathematics and reading are typically treated with equal or nearly equal weight in state policy frameworks and testing programs. Ethnicity and locality are both important because they illuminate a canonical legislative process—that is, any legislature's need to balance the competing interests of rural, urban, and suburban constituencies, as well as ethnic and racial constituencies. Finally, disaggregation by ethnicity is especially important because the *raison d'etre* of systemic reform is to achieve equity in the educational system.

A look at state NAEP data in the 1990s shows that no state at any grade level has shown statistically significant gains across all academic subjects, ethnic and racial groups, and localities. Grissmer and Flanagan were surprised by the apparent near statistical independence of these variables. Between 1992 and 1998, 13 states made statistically significant gains on the fourth-grade NAEP reading assessment; between 1992 and 1996,[12] 16 states made statistically significant gains on the fourth-grade NAEP mathematics assessment (Grissmer & Flanagan, 2001). Only six states showed statistically significant gains in both subjects.

If we examine NAEP reading data for differences by locality—that is, rural, urban, or suburban—only Connecticut made statistically significant gains in two of the three localities. No other state made gains in more than one locality. Of

---

[11] This is the Third International Mathematics and Science Study-Repeat.
[12] Each time NAEP is administered it does not test students on every academic subject; thus, the variation in dates for reading and mathematics.

TABLE 1 1999 TIMSS-R 8th Grade Mathematics Scores

Average Math Score		Students Scoring in Top 10% Internationally		Students Scoring in Top 25% Internationally		Minority Student Test Takers		Low-Income Student Test Takers	
Michigan	*517*	*Texas*	*13%*	*Texas*	*37%*	*Texas*	*53%*	*Texas*	*48%*
Texas	*516*	Connecticut	11%	*Michigan*	*33%*	Maryland	45%	South Carolina	45%
Indiana	515	Illinois	10%	Oregon	32%	North Carolina	38%	North Carolina	44%
Oregon	514	Massachusetts	10%	Connecticut	31%	South Carolina	37%	Idaho	37%
Massachusetts	513	*Michigan*	*10%*	Massachusetts	31%	Illinois	35%	Missouri	34%
Connecticut	512	Oregon	10%	Indiana	30%	Connecticut	26%	Oregon	33%
Illinois	509	South Carolina	10%	South Carolina	30%	Massachusetts	26%	Illinois	31%
Pennsylvania	507	Indiana	9%	Illinois	29%	Missouri	22%	Pennsylvania	30%
South Carolina	502	Pennsylvania	9%	Pennsylvania	28%	Pennsylvania	22%	Massachusetts	28%
North Carolina	495	Maryland	8%	Maryland	27%	Oregon	20%	Maryland	28%
Idaho	495	North Carolina	7%	North Carolina	25%	*Michigan*	*18%*	Indiana	25%
Maryland	495	Idaho	5%	Idaho	24%	Idaho	17%	Connecticut	20%
Missouri	490	Missouri	4%	Missouri	20%	Indiana	17%	*Michigan*	*17%*

SOURCE: International Study Center and The Education Trust

Grissmer and Flanagan's top tier of states, Texas showed statistically significant gains in reading only for rural students; no locality in North Carolina or Michigan showed statistically significant gains.

NAEP also reports proportions of students in each state who score at the four NAEP-defined levels: below basic, basic, proficient, and advanced. The data show that in no state in either 1992 or 1996 did more than 3% of students score at the advanced level. The data for minority students are even worse—almost no minority students in any state score at the advanced level. Journalist and researcher Richard Rothstein has pointed out that NAEP levels are set arbitrarily, so that low percentages of students (regardless of ethnicity) scoring at the advanced level may be an indication of unrealistic level-setting (Rothstein, 1999). Regardless, the fact that low numbers of minority students are achieving at very high levels is a special problem for the development of minority leaders.

In overview, then, we find little hard evidence that state systemic reform policies have had their intended effects. Nonetheless, there is some supporting evidence for attributing gains in mathematics learning in Texas, Michigan, and North Carolina to their state policy frameworks. There is also evidence that gains in minority achievement in Texas can be at least partially attributed to the use of disaggregated data in its accountability system (Treisman & Fuller, 2001). To examine educational performance in Texas, we turn to data from the Texas Assessment of Academic Skills (TAAS), the principal state testing instrument.[13]

Texas Assessment of Academic Skills

Texas has a comparatively long history with systemic reform and has made an unusually large investment in collecting data on school and school district performance, including student test performance (Texas Education Agency, 1996). Moreover, because of a recent high-profile legal challenge to the state's testing system,[14] and a Texan's prominence in the 2000 presidential election race, these Texas data have received careful scrutiny.

In Figures 5 and 6, we examine differences in TAAS passing rates of white and African-American students and of white and Hispanic students on both the mathematics and reading portions of the TAAS. As the data clearly show, there has been a marked decrease in the performance gaps in the elementary school years. Note that state reading results are far less impressive, mirroring the na-

---

[13] The TAAS measures the statewide curriculum in reading and mathematics at grades 3–8 and 10; in writing at grades 4, 8, and 10; and in science and social studies at grade 8. Satisfactory performance on the TAAS 10th grade tests is a prerequisite to a high school diploma. TAAS scores are also used to rate individual schools and school districts.

[14] See *GI Forum et al.* v. *Texas Education Agency et al.* at 87 F. Supp. 2d 667. The issue in this case was whether the use of Texas' high-stakes exam as a requirement for high school graduation unfairly discriminated against Texas minority students or violated their right to due process. The court found that it did neither. Uri Treisman served as an expert witness for the Texas Education Agency in this case.

tional pattern, despite considerable political attention and substantial state funds dedicated to improving reading performance. Similar data exist for the middle school years. It is important to note that these analyses are possible because Texas has required TAAS data to be disaggregated by ethnic and racial group.

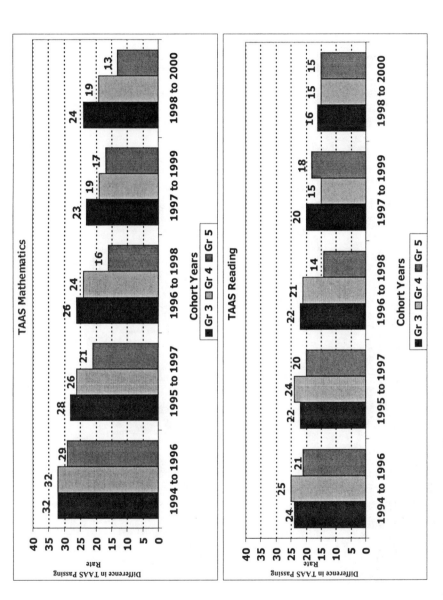

FIGURE 5 Cohort Analysis of Performance Gaps on TAAS Between Texas White and African-American Elementary Students.
SOURCE: Texas Education Agency and Edward J. Fuller

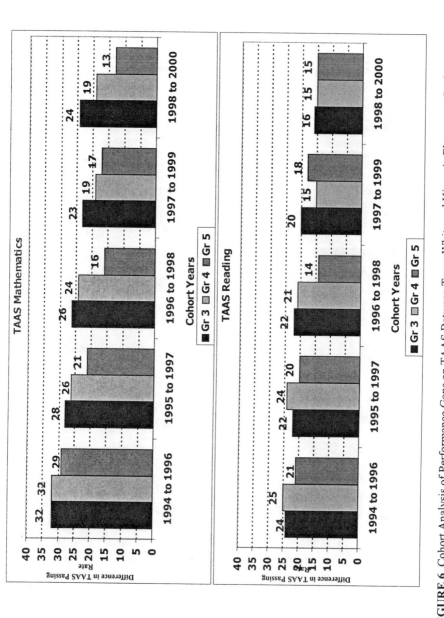

FIGURE 6 Cohort Analysis of Performance Gaps on TAAS Between Texas White and Hispanic Elementary Students.
SOURCE: Texas Education Agency and Edward J. Fuller.

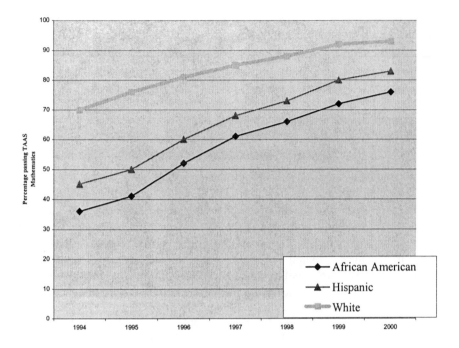

FIGURE 7 Students passing TAAS Mathematics Grades 3–8 and 10.
SOURCE: Texas Education Agency.

We see in Figure 7 that ceiling effects on the testing instrument may be responsible for some of this decrease in the performance gaps.

A close look at Texas education between 1980 and 2000 suggests that for systemic reform to have its intended effect, schools and school systems need to have certain capacities and supports (Treisman & Fuller, 2001). In Texas, a series of successful court challenges to the state's system of financing education addressed massive inequities in local capacity to offer the kind of education envisioned in the state's standards.[15] Rural and urban schools, as well as schools with high proportions of poor children, received large increases in state aid that allowed them to create "opportunities to learn." Further, a broad-based coalition of business leaders heavily engaged in strengthening Texas education through a standards-based approach counterbalanced the natural legislative tendency to

---

[15] In the case of *Edgewood Independent School District et al. v. Kirby et al.* (777 S.W.2d 391), the Texas Supreme Court ruled that the Texas school financing system was unconstitutional under the Texas constitution, which makes education a fundamental right for each child. A series of cases were generated around this issue.

enact short-term solutions to long-term problems (Treisman & Fuller, 2001).[16] In addition, a broad-based mathematics education leadership, by taking an ecumenical approach to curriculum and pedagogy, prevented the dissipation of teacher energy associated with the politicization of the curriculum (Treisman & Fuller, 2001). It would be hard to argue that policies concerning standards, testing, and school accountability alone are responsible for observed improvements in Texas's mathematics education.

LOOKING TO THE FUTURE

Perhaps the systemic reform movement, with its powerful armamentarium of explicit performance standards, tests tied by law to these standards, and systems of rewards and sanctions for schools and districts, can, under the best circumstances, significantly reduce the low achievement that has been endemic in schools serving largely minority and poor populations. But, if high achievement is to become a common outcome of our educational systems, we must develop comprehensive policies that make such achievement a priority. These policies must be supported by substantial federal, state, and local investments so that the accident of where children attend school does not determine the academic opportunities and challenges that they can pursue. Developing such policies, and the wherewithal to fully implement them, will require the support of leaders in all of those sectors that, in the end, determine the priorities of government spending and of local action.

To sustain a system that produces high achievement, we will need to develop better mechanisms for measuring and reporting such achievement and for using that information to strengthen our schools. We must pay special attention to support systems for teachers and administrators, so that the nurturance of their students' intellectual and artistic passions becomes central to the curriculum. We must invest in building the extracurricular institutions that have produced so many of today's senior professionals (College Entrance Examination Board, 1999), and we must charge these institutions with building a generation of professionals that reflects our increasingly diverse population.

American educational policy need not choose between the elimination of low achievement and the promotion of high achievement. We have in our history learned how to achieve both of these goals. The imperative now is to attain them simultaneously.

---

[16] An important state policy that is beyond the scope of this paper is Texas' strategy of incremental improvement. Originally, the standards for the educational system were set at a relatively low level so that most schools could meet them with only modest increases in resources. The standards were then "ratcheted up" over time.

REFERENCES

Atkinson, R. (2001 February 18). Standardized Tests and Access to American Universities. Robert H. Atwell Distinguished Lecture presented at the 83rd Annual Meeting of the American Council on Education. Washington, DC: American Council on Education. [Online]. Available: http://www.ucop.edu/ucophome/pres/comments/satspch.html.

Barton, P. (2001). Raising achievement and reducing gaps: Reporting progress toward goals for academic achievement. Commissioned paper. Washington, DC: National Education Goals Panel.

Borman, G., Stringfield, S., & Rachuba, L. (2000). Advancing minority high achievement: National trends and promising programs and practices. New York: College Entrance Examination Board.

Bowen, W., & Bok, D. (1998). The shape of the river: Long-term consequences of considering race in college and university admissions. Princeton, NJ: Princeton University Press.

College Entrance Examination Board. (1999). Reaching the top: A report of the National Task Force on Minority High Achievement. New York: College Entrance Examination Board.

Gandara, P., & Maxwell-Jolly, J. (1999). Priming the pump: Strategies for increasing the achievement of underrepresented minority undergraduates. New York: College Entrance Examination Board.

Grissmer, D., & Flanagan, A. (1998). Exploring rapid score gains in Texas and North Carolina. Commissioned paper. Washington, DC: National Education Goals Panel.

Grissmer, D., & Flanagan, A. (2001). Searching for indirect evidence for the effects of statewide reforms. Brookings Papers on Education Policy 2001. D. Ravitch (Ed.). Washington, DC: Brookings Institution Press, 2001.

Guthrie, J., & Rothstein, R. (2001). A new millennium and a likely new era of school finance. S. Chaikind & W.J. Fowler, Jr. (Eds.). Education Finance in the New Millennium. Larchmont, NY: Eye on Education.

Jerald, C. (2001). Real results, remaining challenges: The story of Texas education reform. Commissioned paper. Washington, DC: The Business Roundtable.

Lemann, N. (1999). The big test: The secret history of the American meritocracy. New York: Farrar, Straus and Giroux.

Loveless, T., & Diperna, P. (2000). How well are American students learning? Focus on math achievement. The Brown Center Report on American Education, Volume I, Number 1. Washington, DC: The Brookings Institution.

National Science Board. (2000). Science and engineering indicators 2000. Washington, DC: National Science Foundation.

O'Day, J., & Smith, M.. (1993). Systemic reform and educational opportunity. In Designing coherent education policy: Improving the system, S.H. Fuhrman, (Ed.) San Francisco: Jossey-Bass Publishers.

Ravitch, D. (1995). National standards in American education: A citizen's guide. Washington, DC: Brookings Institution Press.

Rothstein, R. (April 12, 1999). NAEP gets failing grade on grading. The American Prospect. [Online]. Available: http://www.epn.org/idea/columns/ro981021.html.

Rothstein, R. (2001). Comment by Richard Rothstein. In Brookings papers on education policy 2001. D. Ravitch, (Ed.) Washington, DC: Brookings Institution Press.

Texas Education Agency. (1996 April). The development of accountability systems nationwide and in Texas. Statewide Texas Educational Progress Study, Report No. 1. Austin: Texas Education Agency.

Treisman, U., & Fuller, E. (2001). Comment by Philip Uri Treisman and Edward J. Fuller, 2001. Brookings Papers on Education Policy 2001. D. Ravitch (Ed.). Washington, DC: Brookings Institution Press.

Tyack, D. (1974). The one best system: A history of American urban education. Cambridge, MA: Harvard University Press.

Valentine, J. (1987). The College Board and the school curriculum: A history of the College Board's influence on the substance and standards of American Education, 1900–1980. New York: College Entrance Examination Board.

Sustaining Minorities in Prehealth Advising Programs: Challenges and Strategies for Success

Saundra Herndon Oyewole
Trinity College, Washington, D.C.

Dramatic racial and ethnic changes in the demographics of the United States make increasing the diversity of the health professions workforce a pragmatic as well as a moral imperative. Yet, despite years of concerted effort, African Americans, Hispanics, and Native Americans continue to be underrepresented in the health professions (CGME, 1998; AADS, 2000; AAMC, 2000a,b). Addressing this persistent problem requires proactive, systemic approaches at all levels of the educational process. Whether the metaphor used is the "pipeline" or Bowen and Bok's *Shape of the River* (Bowen & Bok, 1998), the educational system loses many minority students during the undergraduate years. This is especially the case for minority students who enter colleges and universities expressing an interest in the health professions, regardless of their intellectual abilities (Bowen & Bok, 1998; CB, 1999; Gandara, 1999). Attention to the undergraduate years of academic preparation and personal growth is, therefore, essential to achieving the goal of a health professions workforce that reflects the racial and ethnic diversity of this country.

The pervasive inequities in education that leave many underrepresented minority students ill prepared for the rigors of advanced education have been well documented. These inequities severely limit the pool of students entering colleges and universities (NCES, 1998; NSF, 2000). Therefore, it is imperative that undergraduate institutions provide the programmatic and personal support necessary to ensure the persistence of minority students to the baccalaureate. With respect to the health professions, effective undergraduate prehealth advising programs play a unique and important role in the successful advancement of underrepresented minorities to careers in the health professions.

Understanding the root causes of the underrepresentation of minorities in the health professions will facilitate the development of effective strategies for remedying the problem. For example, poor academic performance in science and math courses often impedes the advancement of minority students to health professions schools. Because the factors influencing their performance in rigorous science and mathematics courses are complex, the solutions must be equally creative and multifaceted to have an impact. Several studies on the persistence of minority students to the baccalaureate in all majors, particularly in science and math, illuminate the complexity. These studies move the discourse from anecdote to data, giving direction to those committed to increasing the diversity of the health professions workforce, and contributing persuasive evidence of the need for aggressive action by educational institutions, governmental and private funding agencies, and society at large.

The prehealth advising program is a key element in the success of students pursuing careers in the health professions. The quality of prehealth programs is greatly influenced by the level of institutional commitment and external support. The review of successful prehealth advising programs included in this paper is presented in the context of general aspects of the undergraduate experience, with special emphasis on findings related to the performance of underrepresented minorities in science and math. An analysis of health professions advising cannot be uncoupled from an examination of core elements of the undergraduate experience, particularly math and science education. This is important because the majority of minority student applicants and matriculants to health professions schools major in one of the sciences, most often biology (AADS, 1999; NSF, 2000; Van Houten, 2001).

Anecdotal evidence suggests that a significant number of minority students have expressed dissatisfaction with the academic and/or prehealth advising they received at their undergraduate institutions. Many have perceived their advisors to be unsupportive. Indeed, there are successful health professionals who give accounts of advisors or faculty members who advised them to give up their goal of a career in a health profession (AADS, 1999). It is difficult to know the number of students who were not able to overcome this discouragement. A survey of minority students attending a Student National Medical Association conference was designed to provide a data-based analysis of student perceptions of the undergraduate prehealth advising programs at their home institutions.

An overview of prehealth advising programs and studies on factors affecting the persistence of minority students to the baccalaureate and entrance into health professions schools follows. The paper concludes with recommendations that are a synthesis of the research studies and the recommendations of the participants in the "Sustaining Minorities in Prehealth Advising Programs" workshop at the Symposium on Diversity in the Health Professions in honor of Herbert W. Nickens, M.D. Without question, effective prehealth advising is important to the successful advancement of all students to health professions schools. However, it is especially critical to the success of minority students.

OVERVIEW OF PREHEALTH ADVISING PROGRAMS

Prehealth advising programs vary greatly, reflecting the variety of institutional types in the United States. For example, the prehealth advisor may be a faculty member—often in the sciences—whose primary responsibility is teaching, a member of the academic dean's office who oversees all academic advising, or a staff member of the institution's career center who specializes in prehealth advising. Of the respondents to a 2000 survey of the members of the National Association of Advisors for the Health Professions (NAAHP), the percentage of advisors who reside in academic departments versus dean's offices was 43.8% and 33.7%, respectively (Klein, 2000). The academic department affiliation was most often biology. Only 34.6% of the respondents participated in minority student programs. Although the respondents represented only 58.6% of the NAAHP membership, these data provide some indication of the balance between faculty and administrative affiliations.

The student-to-advisor ratio also varies widely among prehealth advising programs, which can have a major impact on the accessibility of the advisor. The most successful advising programs are those that have developed mechanisms for ensuring access regardless of the size of the institution. At large institutions, underrepresented minority students—especially those who are not assertive—are often at the greatest risk of being lost. This is not to suggest that problems do not exist at smaller institutions as well. Often, budget constraints and heavy teaching loads impede the professional development of prehealth advisors at resource-poor institutions. Consequently, the advisor might find it difficult to stay abreast of all the information necessary to be effective. Advisors at smaller institutions often have less difficulty in getting to know their prehealth students. A number of advisors teach one of the prerequisite courses, which is especially advantageous when it comes time to write informed letters of recommendation to health professions schools. Effective advising systems at larger institutions have developed mechanisms for providing informed and personalized evaluations from faculty members who have worked closely with the candidates.

The level of institutional support varies among institutions. At smaller institutions, prehealth advisors are not compensated for their work as advisors. Instead, their work as prehealth advisors may be recognized as service to the college. There is often no budget for prehealth advising and a faculty member's office is the site of prehealth advising. At larger institutions there are usually multiple advisors with support staff. As will be seen later, many successful prehealth advising programs are well funded, from both institutional and external sources. Most institutions probably fall between these extremes of funding and staff support.

Technology has played a major role in narrowing the gap between the well-funded institutions and those with less funding. Valuable information about such things as admissions requirements, entrance examinations, the application process, enrollment patterns, and career opportunities is now available on the websites of health professions schools and health professions organizations, as well as pre-health advising programs. A number of prehealth advisors have sophisticated websites with links to all of the relevant sites. Members of NAAHP and its regional affiliates, along with some representatives of health professions schools and organizations, are linked by a Listserv, which has become a major resource for quick feedback on issues related to prehealth advising. A concern is that many disadvantaged students do not have easy access to the Internet (CB, 1999) and will, therefore, not have easy access to information provided through this medium.

Effective advisors are student-oriented and committed to assisting students in achieving their goals. They are knowledgeable, supportive individuals whose role is to provide information and guidance as students make academic, personal, and career decisions. Cecilia Fox of Occidental College was the first prehealth advisor honored by the Association of American Medical Colleges (AAMC) Group on Student Affairs-Minority Affairs Section (MAS) with a Herbert W. Nickens, M.D., Special Recognition Award for her outstanding work in advising underrepresented minority students interested in careers in medicine. In honoring Cecilia Fox at the AAMC Annual Meeting in 2000, the MAS acknowledged the importance of prehealth advising to the success of minority students interested in careers in the health professions. Fox exemplifies a prehealth advisor at a small institution who has been especially effective. She tailors her advising to the individual—recognizing that each student's situation is unique—and advises students in a manner appropriate to their specific needs. Her first contact with prehealth students begins at freshman orientation, if not before. She considers this crucial (personal communication, C. Fox, Occidental College, January 12, 2001). She has helped to create networks on and off campus among students and with admissions officers at health professions schools, especially the University of Southern California School of Medicine and its Health Education Prep Program. This program provides summer enrichment activities for minority students the summer before the freshman year and for two additional summers. The students take science and writing classes, and gain exposure to college juniors and seniors who tutor them as well as to medical school students and faculty. In addition, Occidental prehealth students benefit from special programs organized by the Chicano Medical Student Association and other minority medical student organizations (personal communication, C. Fox, Occidental College, January 12, 2001).

Given that prehealth advising is not the primary responsibility of many faculty who serve in that role, professional development opportunities are especially important. Such opportunities are provided by the National Association of Advisors for the Health Professions (NAAHP) and its regional affiliates—the Central, Northeast, Southeastern, and Western Associations of Advisors for the Health Professions (CAAHP, NEAAHP, SAAHP, WAAHP, respectively). NAAHP is the only national organization concerned exclusively with the needs of prehealth professions advisors and their students. NAAHP and its regional affiliates provide professional development opportunities to advisors through national and regional meetings and through electronic and print communication. Collaborative relationships with representatives of health professions schools and their professional organizations have facilitated communication and cooperation among those most important to forming bridges between undergraduate institutions and health professions schools.

In response to concerns about the quality of prehealth advising for minority students, the NAAHP Board of Directors recently formed a Committee on Minority Affairs charged with developing programs for enhancing prehealth advising of underrepresented minority students. The committee has identified a range of issues which must be addressed. These issues include:

- recognizing and encouraging competitive underrepresented minority students;
- promoting the persistence of minority students through the undergraduate program;
- advising minority students who experience early academic difficulty;
- recognizing prospective applicants with potential to succeed in the health professions;
- clarifying the role of the health professions advisor: gatekeeper vs. advocate;
- presenting and reporting admissions statistics for students from minority groups;
- advising rejected students;
- advising under-prepared students;
- encouraging advisors to be open to professional development in this area;
- educating faculty on institutional prehealth advisory committees on issues of affirmative action and minority access to the health professions;
- developing principles and guidelines for the review and evaluation of underrepresented candidates;
- addressing constraints, such as limited resources and workload, that impede efforts in this area;
- increasing membership of advisors from institutions with large African-American, Hispanic/Latino, and Native American populations.

The implementation of this agenda will require collaboration among advisors, undergraduate institutions, health professions schools, and funding agencies. Fortunately, a number of important collaborative relationships have already been established. Developing and implementing strategies that will significantly increase the number of underrepresented minorities entering the health professions will require intentional and sustained effort.

In developing advising programs to meet the needs of underrepresented minority students, it is a mistake to ignore their diversity—diversity in race, ethnicity, academic preparation, socioeconomic background, and cultural background. To assume that all minority students have the same needs is to ignore their individuality and, ultimately, to fail them. The ability of advisors to advise minority students effectively can be enhanced by a better understanding of the factors affecting their achievement and persistence to the baccalaureate. Understanding the challenges faced by underrepresented minorities and implementing the strategies demonstrated to lead to a successful transition of minority students to health professions schools are essential to effective advising programs. Advisors at selective institutions must also pay attention to these issues, because there is compelling evidence that minority students with competitive grade point averages (GPAs) and SAT scores do not perform as well as their majority counterparts in these institutions (Bowen & Bok, 1998). Academic ability is not the issue. Because these students are in fact the ones with the greatest potential for success in entering the health professions, we cannot afford to lose them because of a lack of understanding of the factors that affect their performance. A review of factors influencing access, enrollment patterns, retention and graduation, and high achievement of minority students follows.

PERSISTENCE TO THE BACCALAUREATE

Statistics on the persistence of minority students to the baccalaureate dramatically reflect the high attrition rates of underrepresented minorities (NCES, 1998; NSF, 2000). Simply put, Blacks, Hispanics, and Native Americans are less likely than Whites to graduate from college. Among those who were ages 25–29 in 1998 and who had completed high school, 18% of Blacks, 16% of Hispanics, and 34% of Whites had earned bachelor's degrees or higher (NCES, 1998). Black and Hispanic students are also less likely to complete a bachelor's degree within 5 years. While 48% of white students and 47% of Asian students who entered a bachelor's degree program in 1989 had earned their degree by spring 1994, only 34% of black students and 32% of Hispanic students did so (NCES, 1998). Thirty-seven percent of both black and Hispanic students, compared with 27% of white students and 26% of Asian students, had earned no degree and were no longer enrolled in a bachelor's program in 1994. As is often the case, there was too small a sample size of Native Americans to allow for a similar analysis during the period studied (NCES, 1998).

A number of studies have tried to identify the factors responsible for the higher attrition rates of minority undergraduate students (NCES, 1998; NSF, 2000). Some of the factors identified were age at enrollment, enrollment status (full-time vs. part-time), socioeconomic status, parents' education, level of first institution (2-year vs. 4-year), and financial resources. Those students entering undergraduate institutions at a younger age, enrolling full-time, beginning at 4-year colleges, and having parents with a 4-year degree or higher, and a higher income were more likely to complete a bachelor's degree in 5 years (NCES, 1998). Additional factors that influence persistence to the baccalaureate are presented below.

RELATIONSHIP OF MATHEMATICS TO BACHELOR'S DEGREE ATTAINMENT

Answers in the Tool Box (Adelman, 1999), an analysis of course taking between 1982 and 1993, revealed that mathematics was the most powerful predictor of ultimate completion of bachelor's degrees. It was determined that of all the components of curriculum intensity and quality, none had a more obvious and powerful relationship to ultimate completion of degrees as the highest level of mathematics studied in high school. This relationship existed for all students, regardless of race/ethnicity, demonstrating that underrepresented minority students can succeed, given high-quality preparation in high school. Unfortunately, minority students are less likely to attend schools that offer advanced math courses that will increase the probability of their earning bachelor's degrees (Adelman, 1999). Although socioeconomic status is generally one of the most powerful predictors of students' academic achievement (CB, 1999), the correlation with completion of degrees was stronger with math courses taken than with socioeconomic status.

The author of *Answers in the Tool Box*, Clifford Adelman, was able to develop a "math ladder" correlating the highest math course taken with the percent of high school graduates earning a Bachelor of Arts degree (B.A). The percentages of students earning a B.A. by course taken were: calculus, 79.8%; precalculus, 74.3%; trigonometry, 62.2%; algebra II, 39.5%; and algebra I, 7.9%. Unfortunately, during the period studied, only 23.6% of students entering college in the high school and beyond/sophomore 1982–1993 cohort reached trigonometry or a higher level of math in high school.

STATUS OF MINORITIES IN SCIENCE, ENGINEERING, AND TECHNOLOGY

An important study commissioned by the U.S. Congress gives greater definition to the magnitude of the problem of underrepresentation of minorities in the majors most often selected by prehealth students. The Commission on the Advancement of Women and Minorities in Science, Engineering, and Technology (CAWMSET, 2000) was mandated to analyze and describe the status of women, underrepresented minorities, and persons with disabilities in the science, engineering, and technology pipeline. The final report, *Land of Plenty: Diversity as America's Competitive Edge in Science, Engineering, and Technology* (CAWMSET, 2000), addresses some of the issues in higher education that have an impact on minorities. Specifically, the report addresses the issue of access, questioning whether the educational system is the "gatekeeper" or "door to the future" for those underrepresented in science, engineering, and technology. The reasons for the higher attrition rates for minorities were found to include financial difficulties, poor pre-college preparation, low expectations from faculty, poor quality of teaching, and an inflexible curriculum (CAWMSET, 2000). This study is relevant to the issue of preparing students for the health professions because of the large percentage of minority prehealth students who choose science as their undergraduate major.

The commission concluded that members of underrepresented groups exit in large numbers at different transition points in the mathematics and science pipeline. At the transition from high school to college, a large percentage of highly capable underrepresented minority students is forced out of the pipeline because of a lack of high-quality science and mathematics preparation in high school. The commission identified a need for better articulation between 2-year and 4-year colleges. Rising costs of college tuition and the inadequacy of scholarships and grants available to students have reduced the prospect of a college education, especially for low-income students. The commission recommended that federal and state governments significantly expand financial investment in support of underrepresented groups in science, engineering, and technology higher education through funding to both students and institutions. The commission explicitly recommended that financial support for students should include scholarships, fellowships, and internships, rather than loans. The commission also recommended that expansion of support to institutions include institutional awards, research assistantships, traineeships, and the expansion of proven programs (CAWMSET, 2000).

UNDERGRADUATE INSTITUTIONS ATTENDED BY MINORITY STUDENTS

For many minority students, persistence to the baccalaureate degree involves transition from a 2-year college to a 4-year college or university. The number of students in this pool is very high, yet formal prehealth advising programs are typically absent from 2-year institutions. Over 40% of African-American students (46% in 1996) and over 50% of Hispanic (54% in 1996) and Native American (52% in 1996) students are enrolled in community colleges (NSF, 2000). Socioeconomic barriers and/or academic deficiencies often influence the decision to enroll in a 2-year institution. Because only a very small percentage of these students continues to the baccalaureate, this is a major untapped pool of minority students. Given that 40–50% of these students take their first prehealth-prerequisite science courses at a community college, it is essential that strategies for improving prehealth advising for minority students be disseminated to community colleges as well as 4-year colleges and universities.

Asians are more likely than other groups to enroll in Research I institutions—21% of Asian undergraduates versus 7–12% of other racial/ethnic groups. Black and Hispanic undergraduates are enrolled in Research I institutions in the lowest percentages. Higher percentages of black and white undergraduates are enrolled in comprehensive and liberal arts institutions than other racial/ethnic groups. American Indian and Hispanic undergraduates, as indicated earlier, are the most likely of the racial/ethnic groups to enroll in 2-year institutions (NSF, 2000).

The AAMC report, *Minority Graduates of U.S. Medical Schools: Trends, 1950–1998* (AAMC, 2000a), provides valuable longitudinal data about the undergraduate institutions attended by minority graduates of U.S. medical schools. Although Xavier University of Louisiana has been ranked first among undergraduate institutions sending African Americans to medical school in recent years, Howard University ranked first over the 1950–1998 period, followed by Morehouse, Fisk, Harvard, and Xavier, respectively. The data presented in the report document the effects of desegregation on attendance patterns. Approximately 57% of Blacks attending medical school in the 1950s and 1960s attended historically black colleges and universities (HBCUs) as undergraduates; however, that percentage dropped to just under 22% by the 1980s and 1990s. For the entire 1950–1998 period, however, nearly 29% of all black medical school graduates attended HBCUs as undergraduates.

During the 1950–1998 study period, approximately 21% of all minority graduates of U.S. medical schools came from just 10 undergraduate institutions: the University of Puerto Rico-Rio Piedras, the University of California-Berkeley (UC-Berkeley), Howard University, the University of California-Los Angeles (UCLA), Stanford, Harvard, the University of Michigan-Ann Arbor, Northwestern University, the University of California-Irvine, and the University of Texas-Austin. Interestingly, the top five undergraduate institutions varied for different minority groups. For Asians, the top five were UC-Berkeley, UCLA, Stanford, Northwestern, and the University of Michigan-Ann Arbor, respectively. For Hispanics, the top five schools were the University of Puerto Rico-Rio Piedras, the University of Puerto Rico-Mayaguez, the University of Miami, the University of Texas-Austin, and UCLA, respectively. For American Indian/Alaska Natives, the top five were the University of Oklahoma-Norman, Pembroke State University, UC-Berkeley, UC-Davis, and the University of North Dakota-Main Campus, respectively. An assessment of the prehealth advising programs at these and other institutions sending large numbers of underrepresented minorities to health professions schools would provide useful information for developing and disseminating effective strategies for advising minority students. It would be particularly valuable to examine those programs with demonstrated success in preparing Native Americans for the health professions, because statistically valid data from national databases are limited by the small sample size of Native Americans in the pools studied.

PREMEDICAL EDUCATION AT HISTORICALLY BLACK COLLEGES AND UNIVERSITIES

There are little empirical data to illuminate the factors that influence the persistence of underrepresented minority students through the undergraduate years to admission to health professions schools. However, some insight can be gained from data collected by various organizations. Of particular interest is a study that focused on nine HBCUs with respect to the number of their graduates entering medical school (Atkinson et al., 1994). Completed in 1991 by the Division of Disadvantaged Assistance, Bureau of Health Professions, Health Resources and Services Administration within the Public Health Service, the study was motivated by the decline in the number of black applicants and matriculants to medical school from HBCUs. During the mid-1980s, nearly 30% of all black applicants to medical schools received their degrees from HBCUs (AAMC, 2000a).

The nine schools studied were divided into two groups based on medical school acceptance rates, one group higher-ranked and the other group lower-ranked. The medical school acceptance rates for participating HBCUs ranged from about 14% to 58%. Interestingly, all of the higher-ranked and two of the lower-ranked institutions had Health Careers Opportunity Programs (HCOP), programs designed to increase the pool of underrepresented minorities and other disadvantaged students successfully entering and completing health professions training programs. Comparisons of data on the schools from the two cohorts revealed factors that might be related to the difference in acceptance rates.

An assessment of the curricula of both cohorts revealed little difference between the types of courses required for premedical students at the HBCUs in each group. Although the courses were the same, there was a difference in the pattern of course taking and curriculum design. Institutions with higher acceptance rates reduced course loads in the freshman and sophomore years. At two of the institutions with lower acceptance rates, students took biology, chemistry, and mathematics in the freshman year. There was also a notable difference in course content. Science faculty at four of the five institutions with higher acceptance rates did not tailor their courses specifically for premedical students; however, faculty at the lower acceptance rate institutions tended to tailor their curricula to the needs of premedical students, with some gearing their courses to the Medical College Admission Test (MCAT). With respect to teaching, introductory biology and chemistry courses at institutions with lower acceptance rates were more likely to belong to a single faculty member. At the institutions with higher acceptance rates, a team-teaching departmental approach was common.

Interestingly, MCAT scores or grade point averages could not explain the difference in acceptance rates between the two cohorts. However, medical school admissions officers considered the premedical programs at some of the institutions with higher acceptance rates to be very strong, based on their experience with graduates and premedical advisors of those institutions, and not necessarily on knowledge of the curriculum or programs at the schools. This points to the importance of the relationships that are established between prehealth advisors and admissions officers and to the effect that performance of admitted students has on the success of future applicants from the same undergraduate institution.

Not surprisingly, the more successful institutions were found to have more resources, including larger faculties. In addition the more successful institutions had larger numbers of students interested in medicine and other health professions, even though the total student enrollment was small. There were more biology majors (12–27%) at the institutions with higher acceptance rates, with an average of only 5% at the institutions with lower acceptance rates. These findings reflect the recurring theme that resources enhance the quality of prehealth advising programs and also suggest that students benefit from having a community of students with common interests. The two factors might be linked in that the distribution of financial resources, both internal and external, is often linked to enrollment.

Among the factors thought to contribute to the success of the higher-achieving programs were positive relationships with medical schools, summer internship and work programs, clinical and research experiences, visits to hospitals, and interactions between medical school and undergraduate faculty members. All of the institutions had academic enrichment programs, but the higher-achieving schools had more. In addition, the institutions with higher acceptance rates had more externally sponsored enrichment programs, such as NIH-funded Minority Biomedical Research Support Programs, Minority Access to Research Careers Honors Undergraduate Research Training Programs, and Howard Hughes Medical Institute Undergraduate Biological Sciences Education Initiative Grants.

Although all nine of the participating institutions believed premedical advising to be a strength of their program, three of the five institutions with lower acceptance rates had no funds for an institutional or departmental premedical component. These institutions did not provide support for the premedical advisor. Given these findings, it is not surprising that the advisors from the institutions with higher acceptance rates were more likely to belong to the National Association of Advisors for the Health Professions (NAAHP) or the National Association of Medical Minority Educators (NAMME) and their regional affiliates. Advisors from the institutions with higher acceptance rates were also more likely to participate in other professional organizations and attend professional meetings. Only one of the four institutions with lower acceptance rates had an advisor who was active in these organizations.

An important recommendation coming out of this study with respect to pre-health advising programs was that advisors need "backing from the institution to continue to make their programs flourish." The premedical advisor was shown to be the dominant force in successful premedical training programs. In institutions with higher acceptance rates, outstanding premedical advisors made the system work regardless of the amount of support received from the institution. This suggests that exceptional advisors can compensate for limited support through their own personal efforts. However, sustaining a national effort to ensure quality prehealth advising for all students requires institutional commitment and support.

Xavier University of Louisiana

Xavier University of Louisiana's success as a source of black applicants to health professions schools deserves a closer look. Xavier, the only historically black Catholic university in the country, has an exemplary premedical advising program that has received national attention. There are lessons to be learned from Xavier's success. Xavier has ranked first in the number of African-American students placed in medical school since 1993. The number of black U.S. medical school graduates who attended Xavier University as undergraduates increased dramatically from 1950–1998, from 15 during the period of 1950–1959, to 98 from 1980–1989, and 210 from 1990–1998 (AAMC, 2000a).

J.W. Carmichael, Jr., Ph.D., the chief health professions advisor at Xavier University, was interviewed for this paper in January, 2001. During that conversation he revealed his passion and systematic approach to preparing students for the health professions. Much of what he shared is clearly evidenced on the Xavier premedical program website, which has been developed and maintained by staff and students in Xavier's Premedical Office. The website reflects the attention to detail and comprehensive approach to advising that characterizes the Xavier program.

There are a number of elements that contribute to Xavier's success. First, Xavier's advising program is highly structured and begins in the freshman year. Xavier provides a great deal of academic support in the freshman-level courses (Carmichael et al., 1993). Carmichael believes that important continuity of instruction is provided by a departmental approach to science and math courses, which includes ongoing assessment and modification of courses to enhance student learning. A core of faculty from different disciplines meets one hour per week to review and develop course materials (personal communication, J.W. Carmichael, Xavier University, January 19, 2001). This is an excellent example of interdepartmental cooperation. Strong institutional support is evidenced by the one-fourth release time given to the faculty members on the prehealth advising team.

In addition to the sciences, Xavier's program also stresses systematic building of general vocabulary. Students must learn 40–80 new vocabulary words each week during the academic year. Emphasis is also placed on developing problem-solving skills. It should be noted that Xavier not only excels in placing African-American students in health professions schools, but also has been very successful in placing African-American students in graduate programs in the physical and biological sciences (Carmichael et al., 1993).

Providing academic support without lowering standards is key to ensuring high academic performance. Students are encouraged in the freshman year to visit the tutoring center several times a week. The tutoring program is coupled with peer mentoring. The Xavier program operates under the assumption that the fraction of students who will be successful in preparing for science careers without support is extremely small. Data reported by Xavier indicate that African Americans who enter Xavier are more likely to gain admission into allopathic medical school than are their peers nationally with similar academic ability (Carmichael et al., 1988). The same pattern was observed for osteopathic medicine, veterinary medicine, dentistry, optometry, and podiatry.

Xavier's prehealth advising program is more than a 4-year program in that Xavier actively recruits high school students, especially those with an interest in the health professions. Xavier's summer science and math programs for high school students serve as a very effective recruiting tool (Carmichael et al., 1993). Xavier students are given class-specific guidance with many checkpoints to ensure that they stay on-track. Students are provided with information about research and summer programs targeted to prehealth students and strongly encouraged to participate in them. To assist students in accessing their potential for successful admission to medical school, the administration generates profiles of accepted Xavier students showing the percentage of Xavier students in various GPA/MCAT categories who have been accepted into medical school. This information is posted on the website for easy access by all students.

A feature at Xavier uncommon to most prehealth advising programs is parental involvement. Parents are informed of what their children should be doing at each step of the preparation process. For example, Xavier sends multiple letters to parents in August and September to inform them of whether their children are meeting established deadlines. This elicits parental pressure to keep students on task, and also educates parents unfamiliar with the process of preparing for a career in the health professions.

STRATEGIES FOR PROMOTING
HIGH ACADEMIC PERFORMANCE

Two exceptionally in-depth studies have focused on high academic performance of minorities: *The Shape of the River: Long-Term Consequences of Considering Race in College and University Admissions* (1998) by William Bowen and Derek Bok, and *Priming the Pump: Strategies for Increasing the Achievement of Underrepresented Minority Undergraduates* (1999) by Patricia Gandara. Bowen and Bok's study focused on the academic, employment, and personal histories of more than 45,000 students of all races who attended a set of academically selective colleges and universities. Their study provides an empirical base for evaluating the impact of race-sensitive admissions policies on students of different races, particularly on Whites and African Americans. The Gandara study, commissioned by the College Board's National Task Force on Minority High Achievement, focused on 20 programs seen as exemplars of effective efforts toward increasing the number of high-achieving underrepresented minority students eligible for graduate and professional study. The study focused on programs with students with a wide range of abilities, but excluded programs that were remedial in nature. The majority of the programs studied focused on the physical and biological sciences, engineering, and technology.

Five major components of successful programs were identified in *Priming the Pump*: 1) mentoring, 2) financial support, 3) academic support, 4) psychosocial support, and 5) professional opportunities. Financial support was found to be the least common feature, although inadequate financial resources have been shown to contribute to higher minority attrition rates (CB, 1999).

The programs and students studied by Gandara and Bowen and Bok have relevance for all prehealth advisors, but particularly those at selective majority institutions. Underrepresented minority students at majority colleges and universities generally do not earn grades that are as high as the grades of white and Asian students with similar high school GPAs and SAT scores (Steele, 1997; Bowen & Bok, 1998; CB, 1999). Bowen and Bok provided extensive confirmation of this pattern. In their study, African-American students at 28 selective colleges and universities graduated with significantly lower GPAs, on average, than their white counterparts with similar SAT I scores. Among these African Americans were many students who were well prepared academically for selective institutions and who were from middle and high socioeconomic status families. The Hispanic students in the study also had lower GPAs than white students with similar scores.

There is compelling empirical evidence that the underperformance of black students may be caused by the fear of confirming the stereotype that they are intellectually inferior, in spite of their competitive SAT scores and high school grades upon entry. This phenomenon has been referred to as "stereotype threat" (Steele, 1997). Fear of confirming negative stereotypes also prevents some minority students from taking advantage of academic support systems, which means that health professions advisors must be proactive in encouraging minority students to understand that all students can benefit from using academic support services. Gandara points out that close supervision of students' academic progress and decision making is necessary because many minority students lack the "cultural capital" that provides familiarity with strategies for navigating suc-

SUSTAINING MINORITIES IN PREHEALTH ADVISING PROGRAMS 295

cessfully through college and career decisions. Many of the successful programs have socialized students to a set of high expectations that the students internalized (Gandara, 1999).

The programs that have been successful are concerned with both the academic and social development of participating students. In summary, programs with demonstrated success in improving academic performance of underrepresented minority students were found to:

1. stress scholastic excellence;
2. encourage each student to do his or her best;
3. emphasize helping students succeed in freshman year;
4. focus on mastery in foundation courses;
5. help students build strong academically-oriented peer groups;
6. build strong student/faculty relationships;
7. focus on providing good ongoing academic advising services;
8. encourage participation in research;
9. provide strong support beyond the freshman year; and
10. provide students with sufficient financial aid to concentrate fully on their studies.

In addition, the following broader categories have been found to be strongly associated with student educational outcomes: 1) economic circumstances; 2) level of parents' education; 3) racial and ethnic prejudice and discrimination; 4) cultural attributes of the home, community, and school; and 5) quality, amount and uses of school resources (CB, 1999). To be effective, prehealth advisors must also consider these factors when designing programs to assist minority students in preparing for health profession schools.

SURVEY OF STUDENT OPINION

Understanding student perceptions of their prehealth advising programs must be a part of the effort to improve prehealth advising programs. In the fall of 2001, a survey developed by the author to assess student perceptions of their prehealth/premed advising programs was administered at the Student National Medical Association (SNMA), Region IX Symposium "Critical Choices: Overcoming the Medical Pipeline Challenges." The conference was organized by SNMA members and members of the Minority Association of Pre-Health Students (MAPS). SNMA is the nation's oldest and largest organization focused on the needs and concerns of medical students of color. Its membership includes medical students, premedical students, residents, and physicians. MAPS is targeted towards undergraduate pre-medical students and aims to increase the matriculation of underrepresented students into health professions-related programs through partnerships with local SNMA chapters. The partnership primarily serves as an academic support system by providing information on how undergraduates may establish themselves as competitive candidates for medical school early in their undergraduate careers. The students attending the conference were from undergraduate institutions in the Northeast/Mid-Atlantic region, and some of them were accompanied by prehealth advisors and parents.

The purpose of the survey was to reconcile the analysis of prehealth advising programs with the perceptions of minority undergraduate prehealth/premedical students. It is a small step toward providing more than anecdotal evidence about the quality of prehealth advising for minority students. Assessment of prehealth programs must be influenced by both student perceptions and outcomes.

Survey Design

Students identified their institutions by the following descriptors: 1) community college, 4-year college, university; 2) private, public; 3) student enrollment; 4) HBCU, minority-serving (more than 50% minority), majority. Students were asked to describe their prehealth advisors as: 1) a single faculty member (scientist or non-scientist); 2) committee of faculty; 3) committee of faculty and non-faculty; 4) non-faculty; 5) team of non-faculty advisors. Questions were also asked about the time of first contact with the prehealth advisor and the frequency of contact. Students were then asked to evaluate their advisors' attitudes toward them.

Using a scale of 1–5 (1-Poor, 2-Fair, 3-Good, 4-Very Good, 5-Excellent) and not applicable (N/A), the students rated their premedical advising program, the personal support received, and the quality of programs tailored to the needs of minority students. There were opportunities for additional open-ended responses to each of these questions. The students were then asked to rate the quality of information provided on the following topics: summer programs for minority students, academic support services, premedical requirements, allopathic medical schools, osteopathic medical schools, other health professions programs, internships, post-baccalaureate programs, exams (MCAT, DAT, VAT), the admissions process, and profiles of competitive minority students. These were aggregated into a category called "information provided." Finally, students were given an opportunity through an open-ended question to share additional thoughts on factors that influenced their persistence toward their goal of becoming a doctor. The surveys were analyzed using SPSS. All correlations were significant at the 0.05 level (2–tailed).

Results and Discussion

Seventy-one students completed the survey. Of the 71 students, three were medical students and all but one were undergraduates from 4-year colleges or universities with enrollments that ranged from under 2,000 students to over 10,000. One percent attended a community college, 37% attended a 4-year college, and 54% attended a university. Thirteen percent reported attending an HBCU, 10% reported attending a minority-serving institution, and 20% reported attending a majority institution. Fifty-seven percent of the students did not respond to this question. This was possibly due, in part, to their difficulty in distinguishing between a minority-serving institution and a majority institution. Regarding the structure of the prehealth advising program, 41% had a single faculty member, 38% had a committee of faculty, 10% had a committee of faculty and non-faculty members, and 10% had a team of non-faculty advisors.

The results showed that students at the SNMA symposium had mixed opinions about their prehealth advising programs. Twenty-seven percent of the students gave their programs a "good" rating, 24% gave their programs a "very good" rating, and 6% gave their programs an "excellent" rating. Although this means over half of the students were pleased with their advising programs, a significant proportion of the students considered their programs fair (20%) or poor (20%). Four percent responded "not applicable" when asked to rate the quality of their prehealth advising program. Unfortunately, we cannot be sure, nor can we assume, that N/A means that no such programs exist at the institutions attended by these respondents.

The students expressed a similar range of opinions when asked about the quality of the personal support they received from their institutions. Twenty-six percent rated the support they received as good, 22% very good, and 12% excellent. But again, a significant proportion of the students gave ratings below good: 15% fair, 18% poor, and 7% N/A. The increase in excellent ratings between this question and the question about advising programs may be an indication that students found specific advising programs or activities lacking, but found personal attention from advisors more beneficial.

Another item on the survey asked students to rate specific programs tailored to the needs of minority students. In response, 19% indicated their programs were good, 16% indicated they were very good, and 13% of the students thought the programs that met minority needs were excellent. In contrast to the previous questions, this left more than half of the students who rated their programs as less than good. Fourteen percent rated minority programs fair, 19% rated them poor, and 19% responded N/A. Due to the large difference between the N/A responses for the two questions about general prehealth advising programs and the N/A responses for a question about programs specifically for minorities, we can speculate that minority programs are absent from some of the institutions the students attend. Such speculation is also based on some open-ended responses in which students stated a lack of minority programs at their institutions.

In order to get a sense of how early advising begins for underrepresented minorities, the students were asked to indicate when they first met their prehealth advisors. Fourteen percent of the students first met their advisors before matriculation, 16% during freshman orientation, and 19% during the freshman year. The remaining 51% percent of the students did not meet their advisors until their sophomore year or later: 30% in sophomore year, 16% in junior year, and 4% in senior year. It may seem that a large proportion of students met their advisor when they were well into their undergraduate education; however, this may be a function of when some students decide to pursue a career in a health profession. Some may not decide until after their sophomore year. Nevertheless, this may limit the impact of prehealth advising, as there is evidence supporting the importance of early identification and support in ensuring high academic achievement by minority students (Gandara, 1999).

Further analysis of the survey results examined the relationships between different items. For example, a negative relationship was found between the size of the institution the students attended and the students' ratings of minority needs programs and personal support received. That is, students at larger institutions were more likely to have lower ratings of minority programs and personal support. They also gave lower ratings to the quality of information provided on various programs, types of medical schools, and medical school admissions procedures. Students who responded with higher overall ratings of advising programs were more likely to give higher ratings of the personal support they received, the quality of minority needs programs, and the quality of information their advising programs offered.

One might expect that students who met with their advisors more frequently would have higher ratings of the support they received. However, students who met their advisors more often were more likely to have lower ratings of the personal support their institutions provided. This is an interesting observation that requires further exploration.

There was one community college student among the respondents. She made a plea that programs such as the one organized by SNMA be offered at community colleges. She made the point that there are many minority students at her community college. Data presented earlier strongly support the importance of addressing the needs of minority students interested in the health professions who begin their undergraduate education at community colleges.

In summary, it is evident that the students' perceptions of their prehealth advising programs were mixed. While it is encouraging that many of these students found their programs to be good to excellent, a significant number rated the programs at their home institutions as poor or fair. Conversations with individual students suggested that the survey approach should be supplemented with student interviews to obtain more detailed information about which aspects of advising programs should be strengthened. Certainly all prehealth advising programs would benefit from periodic assessment with the goal of continued improvement. Understanding and being responsive to the reasons for student perceptions, both positive and negative, will strengthen advising programs.

Challenges and Strategies for Success

Without question, minority students face many challenges as they prepare for careers in the health professions. To be effective, prehealth advisors must be aware of and sensitive to these challenges. Increasing the number of minority students advancing to health professions schools requires special attention on the part of advisors. Fortunately, there are many advisors who are doing an excellent job; however, inadequate guidance and information specific to the academic, experiential, and personal development of minority students is a barrier to success.

It is essential that all prehealth advisors be well informed about the admissions profiles of competitive minority matriculants to all health professions schools. Often advisors are fearful that poor grades in the freshman year are a forecast of failure, and believe that they are acting in the student's best interest when they counsel them out of prehealth advising programs in their freshman year. With the appropriate academic, financial, and/or personal support, many of those students can overcome the deficit in their academic record. Fortunately, some of these students later enroll in postbaccalaureate programs, once they have regained their confidence (CGME, 1998).

Advisors are an important component of the evaluation process for admission to health professions schools, and they therefore influence the number of minority students applying to health professions schools. Striking the balance between advocate and evaluator can be challenging. More comprehensive information from the health professions schools on profiles of competitive minority applicants would facilitate a more appropriate assessment of minority students. Many advisors are advising based on published average test scores and GPAs of all students admitted to various health professions schools without an appreciation for the range of scores of admitted students. It is important that advisors' letters of recommendation for applicants to health professions schools be culturally sensitive and free of cultural stereotypes. The letters must also give insights into the personal characteristics and life experiences of individual students that complement test scores and GPAs.

Personal attributes, sometimes referred to as "non-cognitive skills," certainly factor into the admissions process, but they are not easily quantified. Many have argued that the focus on numbers is a major disadvantage for minority students who have the skills to become successful health professionals, but lack competitive numbers. Breaking the hold of the meritocracy of numbers will continue to be a challenge, especially as opponents of affirmative action continue to use numbers to justify their position. There is a need for longitudinal studies documenting the success of minority health professionals whose numbers alone would not have gained them admission to medical school. In the absence of such a research base, the emphasis on numbers will continue.

Features of effective prehealth advising programs have been shown to include most, if not all, of the following features:

1. early identification of students interested in the health professions;
2. pre-matriculation activities;
3. proactive academic support;
4. early identification of academic problems;
5. academic skills development;
6. study skills workshops;
7. time management workshops;
8. formation of study groups;
9. four-year advising plan specific to preparation for health professions schools;
10. peer mentoring;
11. special interest student groups; and
12. advice on summer enrichment programs and research opportunities.

Many of these strategies contribute to the recruitment, retention, and high achievement of underrepresented minority students. Academic support services and other student services, such as financial aid, are essential elements for success. What follows is an elaboration on some of these strategies, which includes a synthesis of the discussion at the "Sustaining Minorities in Health Professions Programs" workshop at the Symposium on Diversity in the Health Professions in honor of Herbert W. Nickens, M.D. One important recommendation from the workshop is that minority high school students interested in careers in the health professions should consider the quality of the prehealth advising program for minority students when selecting a college or university.

Early Intervention

Early interventions with proactive academic and personal support have been shown to be effective strategies. During the first semester of the freshman year, many underrepresented minority students experience their first academic difficulty. Therefore, assessing the readiness of students for a rigorous academic program is very important. Frequent feedback, especially positive and encouraging feedback, in spite of deficiencies, is essential. This does not mean that deficiencies should not be addressed honestly. Strategies for early intervention are: 1) tutoring by a faculty member, learning center staff member, or a peer; 2) reducing the number of science courses taken in one semester; and/or 3) aligning course schedules with academic preparation, for example, additional math and English courses might be needed before taking biology. Many minority students require assistance in becoming acclimated to the academic culture. In some cases, it is simply that very intelligent students have not been challenged in their high schools and have underestimated the effort required to earn the As that came with little effort in high school. The issue of lower grades may not be related to intellectual ability, but may reflect poor time-management skills and poor study skills.

Access to undergraduate education without support often leads to failure. Although many prehealth advisors are members of the science faculty, many others are members of an advising staff, with limited influence as to what goes on in the classroom. It is imperative that faculty members teaching the "gateway courses" understand the importance of early and consistent intervention to ensure high achievement among minority students in their classes. Academic support must go beyond remediation and include the support necessary to enhance the performance of high-achieving minority students.

Identifying best practices will be of little value if those practices are not disseminated widely and implemented. Their implementation will require both human and financial resources. In addition, professional development opportunities for those professionals involved in the preparation of undergraduate students for entry into health professions schools must be provided.

Chilly Climate and Stereotyping

As stated earlier, it is absolutely essential that the individuality of each minority student be recognized, and that stereotyping not interfere with appropriate and competent individualized advising. Many minorities, regardless of their socioeconomic background or level of academic preparation, are plagued by ongoing racial and ethnic stereotyping. There must be an institutional commitment to creating a welcoming climate. Prehealth advising programs can assist by offering appropriate co-curricular programming, promoting the formation of student groups focused on the health professions, and providing opportunities for students to work one-on-one with faculty.

Building a Critical Mass

Finding ways to build a critical mass of minority prehealth students may involve establishing partnerships among small colleges and encouraging students to form student organizations that focus on minority students interested in the health professions. Such strategies can help to minimize isolation. Advisors at small institutions often feel it is an imposition to invite admissions officers to their campuses to meet a small number of students. Forming local and regional networks is an effective solution to this problem.

Financial Support

Providing students with sufficient financial aid to allow them to concentrate fully on their studies is important. Minority students from disadvantaged socioeconomic backgrounds often have parents who have difficulty with financial aid forms, and they may therefore need assistance from financial aid officers at the undergraduate institution. Prehealth advisors can help by directing students to the appropriate resources.

Too many students end their undergraduate years with both educational and consumer debt. It is important that students understand the importance of a good credit rating to ensure eligibility for the loans necessary to pay for a medical education. Students must also be made aware of the possibility of fee waivers for those who qualify and how to plan for all the expenses associated with the application process, including the cost of traveling to interviews.

It is also essential that financial support be provided for prehealth programs designed to ensure high academic achievement by minority students. Committed individuals can do great things with limited resources; however, institutional support is essential to sustaining programs. Many of the programs recognized for their documented success have benefited from external funding.

Mentoring

Mentoring has been demonstrated to be an important component of effective advising programs. Successful mentoring programs use a variety of formats and components to meet the differing needs of individual students. Programs that provide a continuous structure and offer ongoing reinforcement, encouragement, and support are most helpful. Upper-level undergraduate and graduate students can be effective mentors for students. Effective mentoring programs reduce isolation and facilitate acclimation to the undergraduate institution.

Summer Enrichment Programs and Post-Baccalaureate Programs

Summer enrichment programs have been shown to significantly benefit minority students interested in the health professions (AAMC, 1999). One of the most successful is the Minority Medical Education Program (MMEP) of the Robert Wood Johnson Foundation and the Association of American Medical Colleges. MMEP programs are located at 11 medical schools around the country. For a number of students, these programs provide academic advising specific to the needs of underrepresented minority students.

Postbaccalaureate programs are especially valuable for students who choose to pursue a degree in the health professions after completing a bachelor's degree. There are a number of programs designed for underrepresented minority students. These programs may consist of upper-level science courses. Others offer master's degrees in physiology and biophysics. These programs are typically 1-year programs.

The Application Process

Effective prehealth advising programs give students very specific guidelines on a 4-year time line for preparing for admission to health professions schools. According to a number of admissions officers, many minority students do not submit applications by the deadline or believe that merely making the deadline is sufficient. Students must be made aware of the implications of the rolling admission process. Given that many minority students are first-generation college students and that most are first-generation health professions students, they may not have a family network of academic support and advice. The advice must come from the prehealth advising program or from the academic advisor.

Professional Development for Prehealth Advisors

Evidence presented earlier supports the value of participation in professional organizations focused on developing advising skills. Many prehealth advisors work in isolation and have few opportunities for professional development. Organizations such as the National Association of Advisors for the Health Professions (NAAHP) and the National Association of Medical Minority Educators (NAMME) can play a major role in providing such professional training. The goals of the newly established NAAHP Committee on Minority Affairs were described earlier. Collaboration between key partners in the recruitment, retention, and acceptance of underrepresented minorities into undergraduate prehealth programs and health professions schools is essential. Short meeting sessions are helpful, but not sufficient to provide the in-depth training needed. Resources will be necessary to support this effort. On many campuses, prehealth advising is not a priority. Therefore, efforts must be made to impress upon administrators at undergraduate institutions the importance of strong institutional support for prehealth advising programs. Most successful programs benefit from such support.

Finally, attention to the undergraduate prehealth experience must be a major part of the portfolio of strategies designed to increase the number of underrepresented minorities entering the health professions. The strategies for success presented here must be implemented nationwide to have a significant impact. The dynamic and evolving nature of the health professions requires continued expansion and modification of the programs that prepare future health professionals. The success of the effort will depend on the development of strong partnerships and programs that are student-centered. Minority students must not be denied the personal and professional rewards of careers in the health professions. Furthermore, this nation cannot afford to waste their considerable talents and promise as contributing members of the nation's health professions workforce.

REFERENCES

American Association of Dental Schools. (1999). Opportunities for minority students in United States dental schools: 2000–2002, 3rd Edition. Washington, DC: AADS.
Association of American Medical Colleges (AAMC). (1999). Special theme issue: Educational programs to strengthen the medical school pipeline. Academic Medicine 74 (4):305–460.

AAMC. (2000a). Minority graduates of U.S. medical schools: Trends, 1950–1998. Washington, DC: AAMC.

AAMC. (2000b). Minority student opportunities in United States medical schools 2000. Washington, DC: AAMC.

Adelman C., (1999). Answers in the toolbox: Academic intensity, attendance patterns, and Bachelor's degree attainment. Jessup, MD: U.S. Department of Education, Education Publications Center.

Atkinson, D.D., Spratley, E., & Simpson, C.E. (1994). Increasing the pool of qualified minority medical school applicants: Premedical training at historically black colleges and universities. Public Health Report 109(1):77–85.

Bowen, W. & Bok, D., (1998). The shape of the river: Long-term consequences of considering race in college and university admissions. Princeton, NJ: Princeton University Press.

Carmichael, J.W., Jr., Bauer, J., Hunter, J., Labat, D., & Sevenair, J. (1988). An assessment of a premedical program in terms of its ability to serve black Americans. Journal of the National Medical Association 80(10):1094–1104.

Carmichael, J.W., Jr., Labat, D., Hunter, J., Preivett, J., & Sevenair J. (1993). Minorities in the biological sciences—The Xavier success story and some implications. Bioscience 43(8):564–569.

College Board. (1999). Reaching the top. New York: National Task Force on Minority High Achievement/College Board.

Commission on the Advancement of Women and Minorities in Science Engineering and Technology Development. (2000). Land of plenty: Diversity as America's competitive edge in science, engineering and technology. [Online]. Available: http://www.nsf.gov/od/cawmset/report [accessed May 17, 2001].

Council on Graduate Medical Education. (1998). Twelfth Report. Rockville, MD: U.S. Department of Health and Human Services.

Gandara, P. (1999). Priming the pump: Strategies for increasing the achievement of underrepresented minority undergraduates. New York: National Task Force on Minority High Achievement/College Board.

Klein, J. (2000). Results from the Advisor Survey 2000. The Advisor 20(4):50–66.

National Center for Education Statistics. 1998. The Condition of Education 1998, NCES 98–013, by Wirt, J., Snyder, T., Sable, J., Choy, S.P., Bae, Y., Stennett, J., Gruner, A., and Perie, M. Washington, DC: U.S. Government Printing Office.

National Science Foundation. (2000). Women, minorities, and persons with disabilities in science and engineering: 2000. Arlington, VA: National Science Foundation.

Nickens, H.W., Ready, T.P., & Petersdorf, R.G. (1994). Project 3000 by 2000: Racial and ethnic diversity in U.S. medical schools. New England Journal of Medicine 331(7):472–476.

Steele, C.M. (1997). A threat in the air: How stereotypes shape intellectual identity and performance. American Psychologist 52(6):613–629.

Van Houten, P. (2001). A retrospective look at premedical students' majors. The Advisor 21(2):31–33.

Rethinking the Admissions Process: Evaluation Techniques That Promote Inclusiveness in Admissions Decisions

Filo Maldonado
Texas A&M Medical School

This paper discusses current debate regarding the medical school admissions process, in light of attacks on affirmative action and the subsequent exclusion, in many jurisdictions, of race or ethnicity as factors in admissions decisions. Within the work of admissions committees, some perspectives can be narrow with regard to the consideration of students with broad educational backgrounds, varied interests, and substantial accomplishments, particularly among medical schools. Hence, a discussion is timely and necessary as to the efforts and practices exercised by some to venture creatively and methodically beyond prevailing criteria and processes. These new approaches should be be characterized as concerted efforts to responsibly adapt to the mandates of law, as well as to effectively respond to the changing demographic trends, diversity, population increases, and health needs of the citizens of burgeoning minority groups.

The dismantling of affirmative action in Texas[1] has compelled its public institutions to rethink the process of selecting applicants. It has also evoked new and creative perspectives that can be used to examine unique attributes of applicants and to better understand how applicants' unusual or special life circumstances effect admissions decisions. The loss of affirmative action has also forced Texas institutions to explore how they can best select individuals who will become competent, humanitarian health care providers and who will most likely serve the health care needs of the communities from which they come, and provide direction and inducement for recruitment and retention strategies.

---

[1] *Hopwood* v. *University of Texas*, 78 F.3d 932 (5thCir.,1996), cert denied, 116 S.Ct. 2580 (1996).

The common criteria among Texas' health-professions institutions in identifying and selecting underrepresented or disadvantaged applicants are:

1. Economic, social, and/or educational background;
2. Relationship to school alumni;
3. Parents' level of education;
4. Whether the applicant would be the first generation of the applicant's family to attend or graduate from an institution of higher education;
5. Cultural factors such as bilingual or multilingual proficiency;
6. Employment or other responsibilities, such as assisting in the raising of children or being legally responsible for other people as a parent or guardian, while attending school;
7. Region of residence;
8. Whether the applicant is a resident of a rural, underserved, or health professions shortage area of the state;
9. Performance on standardized tests in comparison with the performance of other students from similar socioeconomic backgrounds;
10. Personal interview; and
11. Admission to a comparable accredited out-of-state institution

My goal in this discussion is to address the question of how we proceed in identifying and selecting applicants who have the potential of becoming positive health professionals in light of the attacks on affirmative action and the use of race-neutral processes. I have provided an overview of some of the literature that indicates the importance of studying the relationships between traditional cognitive determinants and non-cognitive factors in selecting applicants and in predicting success in the health professions education environment. It is apparent among the authors cited that success in a health professions school is dependent not only on varied and balanced factors—some with stronger correlations than others—but also on an institution's commitment to advise prospective applicants and provide support services for students perhaps considered vulnerable.

My discussion centers on the methods used and issues faced by health professions schools in developing race-neutral admissions processes. I believe that there can be merit in such approaches, provided that there is a change in criteria and in the process of evaluation, as well as an institutional culture that places value on the uniqueness of an applicant.

BACKGROUND

What can be said about the relevance of non-cognitive variables in identifying and selecting underrepresented minority and disadvantaged applicants? Many medical school admissions committees take the position that an applicant who is motivated and has knowledge of the profession through experience; the skill to lead; resilience, especially in the face of adversity; and a propensity for community service will most likely succeed as a medical student and medical professional.[2,3,4,5,6,7,8,9] Most medical schools attach significant value to such traits when making selection decisions.[10] According to the studies of Mavis and Doig,[8] Tekian,[9] Elam, Andrykowski, and Johnson,[10] and Elam, Studts, and Johnson,[12] the relationship of cognitive and non-cognitive variables to performance in medical school is significant. However, it remains difficult to determine which of the many noncognitive variables to measure and, then, how to measure or draw parallels from these attributes.[8, 9, 10, 12,13]

Although noncognitive factors are important, it has become apparent that applicants admitted to some medical schools with strong noncognitive features may possess modest grade point averages (GPAs) and Medical College Admission Test (MCAT) scores.[8, 9] This has compelled many medical schools to track how these students perform in medical school and whether they are succeeding. Madison's[14] research on medical school admission and generalist physicians suggests that it is useful to look back at these admitted students and examine the outcomes in order to determine the relationship of cognitive and noncognitive factors considered in the admissions process.

Elam et al.[11] conducted this type of retrospective study to determine which cognitive and noncognitive variables among admitted at-risk applicants at the University of Kentucky College of Medicine contributed to their success in the first two years of medical school. After an extensive review of the summary

---

[2] Mitchell, K.J. Traditional predictors of performance in medical school. Acad Med. 1990;65:149–158.

[3] Shen, H., Comrey, A.L. Predicting medical students' academic performance by their cognitive abilities and personality characteristics. Acad Med. 1997; 72: 781–6.

[4] Sedlacek WE, Prieto DO. Predicting minority students' success in medical school. Acad Med. 1990;65:161–6.

[5] McGahie WC. Qualitative variables in medical school admission. Acad Med. 1990;65:145–9.

[6] Walton HJ. Personality assessment of future doctors: Discussion paper. J R Soc Med. 1987;80:27–30.

[7] Mavis B, Doig K. The value of noncognitive factors in predicting students' first-year academic probation. Acad Med. 1998;73:201–3.

[8] Tekian A. Attrition rates of underrepresented minority students at the University of Illinois at Chicago College of Medicine, 1993-97. Acad. Med. 1998;73:336–8.

[9] Elam CL, Andrykowski MA, Johnson MMS. Assessing motivation to learn: A comparison of ratings assigned by premedical advisors and medical school interviewers. The Advisor 1993;14(1):2–6.

[10] Elam CL, Wilson JF, Johnson R, Wiggs JS, Goodman N. A retrospective review of medical school admission files of academically at-risk matriculants. Acad Med. 1999, October; 74(10 Suppl):S58–S61.

[12] Elam CL, Studts JL, Johnson MMS. Prediction of medical school performance: Use of admission interview narratives. Teach Learn Med. 1997;99:181–5.

[13] Tekian A, Mrtek R, Syftestad P, Roley R, Sandlow LJ. Baseline longitudinal data of undergraduate medical students at risk. Acad Med. 1996;71(10 Suppl): S86–S87.

[14] Madison DL. Medical school admission and generalist physicians: A study of the class of 1985. Acad Med. 1994;69:825–31.

statements made by admissions committee members regarding the students' strengths and the concerns about the students' potential performance, they concluded that the successful at-risk students (those who passed both the first and second years of medical school and Step 1 of the United Stated Medical Licensing Examination [USMLE]) were identified as 1) being scant on service, (2) more likely to be focused on their academics, and (3) less likely to scatter their attention while in medical school. On the other hand, the unsuccessful at-risk students (those who attained GPAs below 2.75 in the first and second years of medical school and repeated either the first year or the first and second years or failed Step 1 of the USMLE) were more likely to have had cognitive weaknesses, stronger personal characteristics, and fitting exposure to the profession. Table 1 presents the findings with regard to the frequency and consistency data for the summary statements regarding concerns about students' projected performances.

However, Elam et al.[11] noted two critical limitations to the current study. First, the study was limited by the eccentricities of the students at one institution with a small number of minority students, and second, the study confined itself to the scrutiny of only preclinical variables. In addition, other perplexing factors such as the students' perceptions of the learning environment and their efforts to obtain tutoring or other forms of academic support were not measured. In view of these findings and limitations, Elam et al.[11] encouraged further examination of how "too much service in medical school" (p. S60) functions as a distraction and a predictor of poor performance among at-risk students. Since the findings showed that MCAT scores were predictive of success for at-risk white students but not for at-risk African-American students, it was recommended that this finding be replicated and that the dynamics of the relationship between MCAT scores and noncognitive variables be explored. These findings provide very useful information about the relative contributions of noncognitive variables and academic abilities in predicting academic success, and medical school admissions committees should use these findings to develop or augment programs to advise prospective applicants and provide intervention or support services for students considered at risk.

A study from the Texas A&M College of Medicine extended the concept of the relevance of noncognitive variables in the selection of underrepresented or disadvantaged applicants and evaluated the effects on the acceptance or rejection of these applicants when giving different weighting to academic and interview scores. The study was an attempt at examining another means of achieving the goal "to produce doctors who will practice where they are needed most,"[15]

---

[15] Edward JC, Maldonado FG, Calvin JA. The effects of differently weighting interview scores on the admission of underrepresented minority medical students. Acad Med. 1999, January; 74(1);59–61.

TABLE 1 Summary Statements of Concerns Related to Performances of At-Risk Students at the University of Kentucky College of Medicine (1991–1994)

Concern	Frequency*			Consistency†		
	Successful	Unsuccessful	p Value	Successful	Unsuccessful	p Value
Lack of service and leadership	73.5	23.5	.001	1.20	.47	.014
Lack of motivation or purpose	67.6	52.9	NS‡	1.00	.59	NS
Lack of exposure to medicine	50.0	23.6	NS	.79	.24	.008
Negative personal characteristics	50.0	11.8	.008	.56	.12	.008
Cognitive weaknesses	76.4	94.1	NS	1.23	1.95	.017
Lack of adversity in life	20.5	23.5	NS	.25	.25	NS
Presence of distractions	8.8	35.2	.019	.15	.35	NS

* Percentage of students who had this concern listed by at least one file reviewer (out of a total of 3).
†Average number of file reviewers who listed this concern per student (range = 0–3).
‡NS = not significant; p _.05

which in this case were the underserved areas of Texas. Although the study concluded that increasing the weights on the interview scores consistently produced positive changes in the number of accepted underrepresented minority applicants, the numbers were nonetheless small. The study also set the stage for exploring whether different weighting of the interview score had an effect on the admission of problem students (those students who may require a disproportionate amount of faculty time and effort).[15] Using the different weighting on the interview score to compare the numbers and different types of problem students may provide a glimpse at the issues facing problem students and the means of rendering support services for these students in crisis. Table 2 depicts the results, assuming the 70%/30% formula, which weighted the interview score 70% and the academic score 30%.

TABLE 2 Demographics and Academic Information About 439 Applicants to Texas A&M University College of Medicine Who Would Have Been Affected by a Change in the Admission Process Weighting Formula, 1996–1997.*

	Those Who Would Have Gained Acceptance	Those Who Would Have Lost Acceptance
Underrepresented minorities	3	0
Asian Americans	6	4
Caucasians	9	10
Disadvantaged students [†]	3	0
Average MCAT scores	9.67	10.81
Average interview scores	8.31	5.20
Average number of acceptances to other medical schools	1.22	1.29

* Applicants were offered or denied admission based on a score that weighted their academic and interview scores at 50% each. The changes shown on this table would have occurred if the formula had instead weighted the academic scores at 30% and the interview scores at 70%.
† Two of the three disadvantaged applicants were underrepresented.

Since admissions committees do not consider MCAT scores in isolation, it is difficult to predict the power of MCAT scores in conjunction with preadmission criteria. There are a number of studies that have examined the predictive relationships of MCAT scores across different variables and different populations. Wiley[16] found a comparability of relationships between MCAT and the USMLE Step 1 scores for students who repeated the MCAT. His results showed no differences in predictive validity associated with use of the first set of scores as the predictor versus use of retest scores as the predictor. Koenig et al.[17] studied the relationship between MCAT scores and basic science grades and USMLE Step 1 scores, which resulted in no difference for men versus women, and slight tendencies for over-prediction of performance for African Americans, Hispanics, and Asians. After investigating the predictive relationships for students taking a commercial review course against those who did not, Huff and

---

[16] Wiley A. Predicting Medical School Performance with the MCAT: Does Retesting Make a Difference? Paper presented at the Annual Meeting of the American Educational Research Association, New York, NY, 1996.
[17] Koenig JA, Sireci SG, Wiley A. Evaluating the predictive validity of MCAT scores across diverse applicant groups. Acad Med. 1998;73:1095–106.

Koenig[18] found no difference among examiners. Similarly, Koenig and Swanson[19] found no difference when comparing the predictive relationships between medical schools implementing problem-based curricula and those using traditional curricula and modes of instruction. More recently, Huff et al.[20] investigated the predictive power of MCAT scores with performance in third-year clerkships, as well as the extent to which MCAT scores predict differences in performance among racial and ethnic groups. The results proved the usefulness of the MCAT in predicting clerkship grades, which accounted for at least 1/5 of the variance in clerkship grades, and demonstrated a reasonable predictive consistency across the racial and ethnic groups studied. When MCAT scores were considered with preadmission data, particularly science GPA, prediction was improved, especially among African Americans and Hispanics.

All in all, results from the above studies punctuate the significance of using multiple factors in making admissions decisions and the stability of the predictive relationships across different population groups. The observations stemming from these studies indicate a need for future research into the use of additional variables that may predict success in medical school, such as diligence, motivation, communication skills, study habits, and other relevant characteristics.[20]

HOW THE USE OF RACE-NEUTRAL PRINCIPLES ACHIEVES DIVERSITY

Why is it so compelling for us in medicine to achieve a diverse student body?

Medical education has an obligation and a social contract to better prepare physicians to deal with the issues of disease and disability afflicting many Americans.[21, 22] According to Cohen,[21] medical schools in the past have not adequately focused their attention on matters of health promotion and disease prevention. He pointed out that this shortcoming, along with the scant attention paid to behavioral determinants of ill health in medical school curricula and the lack of a research agenda that emphasizes ways to modify unhealthy human behaviors

---

[18] Huff KL, Koenig JA. The impact of commercial review courses on the validity of MCAT scores for predicting performance on USMLE Step 1 (work in progress).

[19] Koenig JA, Swanson DB. Examination of MCAT's Ability to Predict USMLE Step 1 Scores and Students Trained with Problem-Based Instructional Programs. Paper presented at the 1996 Annual Meeting of the American Educational Research Association, New York, NY.

[20] Huff KL, Koenig JA, Treptau MM, Sireci SG. Validity of MCAT scores for predicting clerkship performance of medical students grouped by sex and ethnicity. Acad Med. 1999, October;74(10):S41–S44.

[21] Cohen JJ. Missions of a medical school: North American perspective. Acad Med. 1999, August;74(8):S27–S30.

[22] Schroeder SA. Doctors and diversity: Improving the health of poor and minority people. The Chronicle of Higher Education. 1996 Nov 1;B5.

might all contribute substantially to improving the lifestyle choices and health habits of Americans. Cohen[21] believed that this situation can be augmented by "producing a greater stress on population-based health care and strengthening emphasis on disease prevention, health promotion, and the competency of the physician to treat patients from various cultural backgrounds" (p. S29).

Another alarming problem in U.S. medicine is inadequate access to health care across population groups. According to the National Center for Policy Analysis,[23] the problem of inadequate access stems largely from the fact that 41.4 million Americans, which by Census Bureau statistics comprises 17.7% of the non-elderly population, have no health insurance. Just as worrisome is the additional problem that many Americans who live in inner-city or remote rural areas have no access to health care, despite being insured.

One compelling reason for this phenomenon may be an erosion of trust between patient and doctor. The development of commercialized approaches to managing health care in the country seems to be evolving into a system characterized as impersonal and untrustworthy.[24] According to Cohen,[21] the fact that physicians are encouraged to become more cost-effective in the practice of medicine is a principal reason threatening the fundamental ethic of medicine.[21] He describes the fundamental ethic of medicine as one centering on altruism— "holding paramount the best interest of one's patients, not oneself" (p. S30).

How can medical education scale back the erosion of trust in the doctor? One important part of the solution is that medical schools must try and select students into the study of medicine who possess the essential traits of altruism, compassion, honesty, and integrity.[21] Cohen[21] also believed that medical education cannot single-handedly solve the dismal problem of lack of access, but is nevertheless "responsible for addressing those aspects of the problem that it can influence" (p. S29).

One issue high on medicine's agenda is making certain that the medical profession mirrors the growing diversity of the American population. The evidence clearly shows that the numbers of underrepresented minority medical students (African Americans, Mexican Americans, Native Americans and Mainland Puerto Ricans) continue to be disproportionately low.[25, 26] Despite sufficient data proving that physicians from underrepresented minority groups tend to practice in medically underserved communities, white males continue to make

[23] National Center for Policy Analysis. Explaining the Growing Number of Uninsured. Brief Analysis No. 251. 1998 January 12.

[24] Mechanic D, Schlesinger M. The impact of managed care on patients' trust in medical care and their physicians. JAMA. 1996;275:1693–7.

[25] Nickens H., Ready T, Petersdorf R. Project 3000 by 2000: Racial and ethnic diversity in U.S. medical schools. N Engl J Med. 1994;331:472–6.

[26] Petersdorf R, Turner K, Nickens H, Ready T. Minorities in medicine: Past, present and future. Acad Med. 1990;65:633–70.

up a high ratio of practicing physicians in this country.[21,22,27,28,29] Therefore, to ensure that the healthcare needs of minority and indigent communities are met, physicians from underrepresented minority groups should be in these communities practicing medicine. Unfortunately, physicians from underrepresented minority groups continue to be scarce in the medical profession. In 1996, for example, Schroeder[22] reported that African Americans and Hispanics represented only 4% and 5%, respectively, of the nation's physicians.

Another important piece of evidence supporting the need for more physicians from underrepresented minority groups is the extent to which physicians from specific racial and ethnic groups practice in communities with high proportions of black and Hispanic residents and uninsured patients. Studies by Komaromy et al.[26] and Cantor et al.[27] revealed that black and Hispanic physicians were much more likely to care for patients who were not only from their respective minority population groups, but who were uninsured or on Medicaid and that physicians who treated many minority, poor, and Medicaid patients were motivated to do so because they valued helping the disadvantaged more than making lucrative salaries or using the latest medical technology. In fact, black and Hispanic physicians derived about 25% of their salaries from Medicaid fees in comparison with 15% for white physicians. Another finding showed that black and Hispanic physicians were more likely to treat patients of underserved groups, particularly if the physicians' parents had low incomes or less than a high school education.

Therefore, the need is great. Medical schools, according to Schroeder,[22] are producing a national resource. By enrolling more qualified underrepresented and disadvantaged applicants, medical schools have the opportunity to promote better access to health care—and in all probability, improved health—and to help fulfill medicine's obligation to serve society's needs.

Can We Achieve a Diverse Student Body Using Race-Neutral Principles?

It is obvious that American society has become more multicultural and racially and ethnically diverse. The evidence shows that the need to close the diversity gap in the medical profession has become increasingly urgent. For approximately 30 years, many medical schools have undertaken efforts to increase opportunities in medical education for qualified members of underrepresented groups.[25] However, the current pressure to eradicate affirmative action policies

---

[27] Komaromy M, Grumbach K, Drake M, et al. The role of black and Hispanic physicians in providing health care for underserved populations. N Engl J Med. 1996;334:1305–10.

[28] Cantor J, Miles E., Baker L, Baker D. Physician service to the underserved: Affirmative action in medical education. Inquiry 1996;33:167–80.

[29] Minority Students in Medical Education: Facts and Figures. 10th ed. Washington, DC: Association of American Medical Colleges, 1997.

in conjunction with recent litigation has prompted many medical schools, particularly in Texas and California, to rethink how they select applicants from racial and ethnic population groups.

Over the last five years, Texas A&M College of Medicine—along with the other seven Texas medical schools[*] and three dental schools[†]—has taken significant steps to develop an admissions process that is race-neutral in nature. This action was in response to the decision by the Fifth Circuit Court of Appeals in the *Hopwood* v. *State of Texas* case in 1996. In sum, the Fifth Circuit Court[2] ruled:

> The use of race to achieve a diverse student body whether as a proxy for permissible characteristics, simply cannot be a state interest compelling enough to meet the steep standard of strict scrutiny. These latter factors may, in fact, turn out to be substantially correlated with race, but the key is that race itself not be taken into account. Thus, that portion of the district court's opinion upholding the diversity rationale is flawed.

The *Hopwood* decision has posed a challenge to the College of Medicine's efforts to enroll significantly more underrepresented minority students. Although the admissions committee attempted to modify its use of algorithms throughout the process of evaluation and selection, a new plan went into effect in 1998 that altogether eliminated the algorithm at the time of selection.

The new plan called for:
1. a mindfulness of the vision and mission of the institution in assessing and selecting students;
2. a more inclusive approach in assessing cognitive abilities;
3. a broad-minded scrutiny of applicants' non-cognitive characteristics at the pre-interview and interview phases of the evaluation process;
4. enhanced interview techniques;
5. improved protocol for admissions committee deliberations; and
6. frequent self-monitoring.

The admissions committee embarked on its new plan by first taking into consideration the Health Science Center's (HSC) and the College of Medicine's (COM) mission and institutional goals when assessing the relative importance of applicants' MCAT scores, academic records, and various personal and experiential qualities. This mission, along with the institution's goals, became the philosophy by which the admissions committee guided and directed the admissions process. An important factor comprising this transition included the formation of three highly focused admissions committee task force groups to study criteria for interviewing applicants, the interview protocol, and admissions committee deliberations. With this focus, the admissions committee then im-

---

[*] Texas Medical Schools: Texas A&M, Texas Tech, UT-Southwestern, UTMB-Galveston, UT-Houston, UT-San Antonio, Baylor, U North Texas-Texas College of Osteopathic Medicine

[†] Texas Dental Schools: TAMUS Baylor-Dallas, UT-Houston, UT-San Antonio

plemented a system by which to weigh MCAT scores and grade point averages (GPA) and to sort applicants in a way that would jeopardize neither the integrity of academic criteria nor the breadth of choice of qualified applicants. The equal weightings given to the MCAT (50%) and the overall GPA (50%) produced an "Academic Score," which was based on the admissions committee's judgment as to how well the knowledge and skills tested by the exam corresponded to the requirements of the medical school curriculum. This method was adopted in large part because of the findings of the AAMC's Predictive Validity Research Study,[20] which utilized performance data of the 1992 and 1993 entering classes from 14 participating medical schools. The outcomes showed a strong correlation between undergraduate GPA and performance in medical school and between MCAT scores and performance in medical school. For example, the study showed that 34% of the variation in cumulative medical school GPA could be explained by medical students' undergraduate GPAs; 41% of the variation in cumulative medical school GPA could be explained by medical students' MCAT scores; and that 58% of the variation in cumulative medical school GPA could be explained by MCAT scores and undergraduate GPA. The study also revealed that 42% of the variation in medical school grades was not explained by students' MCAT scores and undergraduate GPA. In fact, some of the variability in medical school performance might be attributed to or explained by other academic or experiential factors, such as:

1. major grades in honors or graduate courses or additional degree (graduate or baccalaureate) ;
2. extraordinary educational achievements or experiences;
3. community service activities;
4. leadership experiences; and
5. character and motivation of the applicant.

Mindful of the importance of non-cognitive factors in 1) facilitating the selection of students, 2) remedying the serious lack of diversity in the student body, and 3) abiding by the *Hopwood* Decision, the admissions committee implemented some extraordinary changes. First, the committee made the decision to widen the range of applicants considered for interview via the academic score and to screen a sizable number (900–1,000) of applicants. This decision was based largely on careful consideration of the distribution of academic scores for the 1997–1998 application years and the need to make better-informed decisions based on information provided by a new screening instrument rather than using solely an algorithm.

For example, academic scores (raw scores from 1–1,000 points) within the range of 800–1,000 showed that approximately 20% of applicants (286 from a pool of 1,419) had GPAs and MCATs averaging 3.81 and 27, respectively. The committee, therefore, decided to give these applicants an automatic or high-priority interview (without screening), ensuring that the best of the applicants, based on grades and standardized test scores, were seriously considered. Second, after carefully examining the distribution of the academic scores, the committee again determined how deep they should go to consider applicants for screening. The range was set at academic scores of 799 on the top end and 651 on the bottom end. The number of applicants within this range was sizable, numbering 959 (68%) of the total pool. The academic scores in this middle of the pool group showed that these applicants had GPAs and MCAT scores averaging 3.45 and 26, respectively, ensuring that the committee would screen and interview a broader and larger range of applicants with varying credentials and circumstances (17.3% disadvantaged and 11.8% underrepresented). Finally, the distribution of academic scores at 649 and below revealed that a small number of applicants (174 [12%]) had GPAs and MCAT scores that were considered dangerously low. These applications also revealed a host of academic problems ranging from GPAs below 2.00 to MCAT scores well below 5 in the sub-tests and multiple retakes of the MCAT. The committee unanimously agreed that this was a particularly high-risk group of applicants and should not be considered further unless they were self-proclaimed disadvantaged. These applicant files are typically reviewed by the assistant dean for admissions to determine the genuineness of the applicants' disadvantaged circumstances. Tables 3, 4, and 5 depict the applicants by race and ethnicity and provide a more detail breakdown as to the ranges of academic scores, GPAs, and MCAT scores.

TABLE 3 1997–1998 Application Year (1,419 Total Applicants)
High Academic Applicants—286 (Academic Scores of 800 and above)

Applicants by Race & Ethnicity	# High Academic Applicants	% of Total Applicants	# High Academic Disadvantaged	% of Total Applicants
American Indian/ Alaskan Native	0	0	0	0
Asian Americans	62	4.40%	1	< 1%
African Americans	11	0.78%	1	< 1%
Hispanic	26	1.80%	1	< 1%
White/Caucasians	164	11.60%	6	< 1%
Other	23	1.60%	0	0
Total High Academic (HA) Applicants	286	20.20%	9	0.63%

(continued)

Avg. MCAT scores for HA applicants:	VR–9	PS–9	BS–9
MCAT score range for HA applicants:	VR 6–13	PS 7–13	BS 8–14
Average U-GPA for HA applicants::		3.81	
GPA range for HA applicants:		3.10–4.00	
Avg. Academic Score-HA applicants:		836	

TABLE 4 1997–1998 Application Year (1,419 Total Applicants)
Middle of the Pool Applicants—959 (Academic Scores of 799 to 651)

Applicants by Race & Ethnicity	# Middle of Pool Applicants	% of Total Applicants	# Middle of Pool Disadvantaged	% of Total Applicants
American Indian/ Alaskan Native	8	0.56%	0	0
Asian Americans	207	14.60%	61	4.3%
African Americans	27	1.90%	2	< 1%
Hispanic	72	5.10%	12	0.85%
White/Caucasians	567	40.00%	87	6.1%
Other	78	5.50%	4	< 1%
Total Middle of Pool (MP) Applicants	959	68.00%	166	11.7%

Avg. MCAT scores for MP applicants:	VR–9	PS–9	BS–8
MCAT score range for MP applicants:	VR 3–13	PS 4–13	BS 4–13
Average U-GPA for MP applicants::		3.45	
GPA range for MP applicants:		2.39–4.00	
Avg. Academic Score-MP applicants:		733	

TABLE 5 1997–1998 Application Year (1,419 Total Applicants)
All Other Applicants—174 (Academic Scores of 650 and below)

Applicants by Race & Ethnicity	# All Other Applicants	% All Other Applicants	# All Other Disadvantaged	% All Other Applicants
American Indian/ Alaskan Native	0	0	0	0
Asian Americans	51	3.6%	6	< 1%
African Americans	4	< 1%	2	< 1%
Hispanic	18	1.3%	11	0.78%
White/Caucasians	84	5.9%	18	1.3%
Other	17	1.2%	2	< 1%
Total All Other (AO) Applicants:	174	12.3%	39	2.7%
Avg. MCAT scores for AO applicants:		VR–6	PS–6	BS–7
MCAT score range for AO applicants:		VR 2–11	PS 3–11	BS 2–11
Average U-GPA for AO applicants:			3.05	
GPA range for AO applicants:			1.80–3.95	
Avg. Academic Score-AO applicants:			598	

These simple data illustrated a consistent contrast in how the applicants were compartmentalized and revealed the complex workload to be undertaken in the screening process. After analyzing the academic scores and post-interview committee scores, it became apparent that we were correct in expanding our hunch to expand our efforts to the middle of the pool. Our analyses also showed that while a substantial number of our middle-of-the-pool applicants enrolled in the medical school, at most, only 19% of our high-academic applicants did so. We found this compelling, and, hence, increased our efforts to give close attention to the middle range of applicants. We were also encouraged by the high number of qualified underrepresented and disadvantaged applicants (nearly 12%) in the middle-of-the-pool group compared with the other two groups.

The data provided a number of compelling reasons to scrutinize and screen in greater depth the middle-of-the-pool group and to interview more of these applicants. One of the most pivotal reasons was the increased likelihood of interviewing more underrepresented and disadvantaged applicants. The screening instrument became the key element in our endeavor not only to interview more qualified and potentially acceptable applicants but also to interview more qualified and potentially acceptable underrepresented and disadvantaged applicants without factoring in race or ethnicity. All members of the committee agreed that screening, although time-consuming, was a fairer way to judge our applicants than simply using the quantitative algorithm.

The next challenge was to create a screening instrument that would widen our field of vision even further. A brief study was conducted by three people on the committee (the associate dean for student affairs and admissions, the assistant dean for admissions, and the chair of the admissions committee) to examine existing and new screening criteria as well as the process used to evaluate applicants of the 1997–1998 cycle.[30] The results of the study were presented to a subcommittee of the admissions committee, who in turn discussed all facets of the instrument and made some revisions. The instrument was subsequently sent to full committee and was adopted unanimously as the screening instrument for upcoming application cycles.

The final version of the screening instrument had four categories (with space for comments) whose scores totaled to a maximum of 100 points. Table 6 depicts the *M.D. Admissions Screening Evaluation Form*.

---

[30] Edward JC, Maldonado FG, Engelgau,GR. Beyond affirmative action: One school's experiences with a race-neutral admission process. Acad Med. 2000, August; 75(8);806-815.

TABLE 6 Screening Evaluation Form–2000

Applicant _____ SSN _____ Date		
Screener _____ Signature		
Score each factor between the range of points given, then provide a total not exceeding the maximum score.		
ACADEMIC PERFORMANCE AND INTELLECTUAL CAPACITY	**Score Between 0–10 Points**	
Quality of Educational Institution Most Competitive–10; Highly Competitive–9; Very Competitive–8; Competitive–7; Less Competitive Texas–6; Less Competitive Out of State–5; Non-Competitive Texas–4; Non-Competitive Out of State-3 or less. (See Barron.)		
Academic Achievements Overall & Science GPAs, GPA for last 45–60 credit hours, Rigor of Major, Graduate courses or degree, Grades in premedical course requirements, MCAT.		
Extraordinary Educational Achievements or Experiences Academic scholarship(s), Academic recognition awards, Research fellowship(s), competitive internships, EMT certification, Paramedic.		
TOTAL SCORE (MAXIMUM 30 POINTS) =		
COMMENTS:		
HUMANISM, DEDICATION TO SERVICE, AND CAPACITY FOR EFFECTIVE INTERACTIONS	**Score Between 0–8 Points**	
Participation in Community Human Service Activities or Altruism Active in improving the community or society in which he/she lives.		
Leadership in School Organizations or Projects Holding positions of leadership or taking a lead in projects in school or community.		
Clinical or Health Care-Related Experiences Volunteer or job-related experiences–Shadowing, providing ancillary support as a staff employee or volunteer of a hospital, clinic, mission outreach program, etc.		
Quality of Personal Statement Genuine, original, well organized, coherent, and substantive.		
Motivation for Medicine as a Career Focus for the most part is on the humanistic concern for others.		
TOTAL SCORE (MAXIMUM 40 POINTS) =		
COMMENTS:		

SPECIAL LIFE EXPERIENCES	Score Between 0–5 Points
Circumstances Indicative of Some Hardship or Adversity Financial difficulties; A death in the immediate family; Personal illness; Educational disadvantage; Family illness; Disability; A medical condition; Other condition of suffering or extraordinary responsibility* *As a student, applicant was responsible for other people as a parent or guardian.	
Need to Work, and Impact on Life or Educational Circumstances Steady job(s) while attending school necessitating a consistent 20 or more hours per week to meet financial obligations or to alleviate financial burden.	
First-Generation College Student and Educational Level of Parents First-generation college student and parents have a high school or less education.	
TOTAL SCORE (MAXIMUM 15 POINTS) =	

COMMENTS:

OTHER COMPELLING FACTORS	Score As Shown Below
Supportive Letters of Evaluation from (primarily) Professors and Others Health professions committee or individual letters from professors and others: Supportive; Strongly supportive; Problematic	¨ 6 points
Areas of Interest in Medicine (Refer to Secondary Application, Item 9) *Evidence* of interest in a practice in: Primary Care; Rural Medicine; Underserved Area	¨ 3 points
Area in Which Applicant Lives (Refer to Secondary Application, Items 3 and 3B): Rural; Medically Underserved; Low-Income	¨ 3 points
Awareness and Knowledge of Cultural Factors as They Impact on Health Care *Evidence* of experiences or skills (e.g., foreign language) sensitizing applicant to other cultures and the human condition.	¨ 3 points
TOTAL SCORE (MAXIMUM 15 POINTS) =	

COMMENTS:

GRAND TOTAL (Maximum 100 Points) =	

¨ Second Screen Required because score is less than a total of 55 points.
¨ Second Screen Requested for other compelling reasons (Comments Required)

COMMENTS:

At the end of his or her evaluation, the evaluator (one of 19 members of the admissions committee or the assistant dean for admissions) could recommend an interview or decide not to interview an applicant, regardless of the number of points given. The number of points set for granting an applicant an interview was 55. This number was determined by one standard deviation (9.8) below the mean of the distribution of screen scores (64.3). The assistant dean for admissions and chair of the admissions committee could slide this score up or down depending upon the distribution of screen scores and the standard deviation during the screening process, but they rarely exercised this option. Instead, they opted to make any adjustment to the screen score cutoff point only after studying the results of the previous year(s), then applying it to the next application season, if necessary. Although a screen score cutoff point was set, an evaluator could exercise his or her discretion to recommend that an applicant not be interviewed and have the application screened by a second person. Applications with scores in the range of two standard deviations below the mean would automatically be screened by a second person. This broad-minded scrutiny of applicants' academic and non-cognitive characteristics at the pre-interview level allowed us to:

• identify a broad range of acceptable applicants regardless of race or ethnicity;

• make judgments about the suitability of each applicant to carry out the mission of the medical school; and

• evaluate more deeply character, motivation, and life circumstances.

If we are to select applicants who will fulfill the complex health care needs of our society and reach out to the wider human community, we must make significant investment of both our emotional and our cognitive selves. This investment extends itself well into the interview process and committee deliberations. There is, therefore, a substantive process in interviewing and deliberating about applicants. In fact, applicants often leave the interview encounter knowing that they have been closely observed and that we have formulated any number of assumptions about them. Our perception of them often depends on how they measured up as people and how they might measure up as professionals.

One way we felt we could improve the admissions committee's ability to broaden its selection of qualified applicants was to change how we deliberated about post-interview applicants during committee meetings and how we ranked applicants. For example, in committee deliberations, the admissions committee was principally charged with evaluating applicants selected for interview and making recommendations for admission to the dean of the College of Medicine. Based on the interview scores (using a scale of 1–10) the committee was called by the chair to exercise nine steps in decision making:

1. Vote as a committee (with no discussion) to *accept* applicants whose interview scores average *9.0 or better.*

2. Vote as a committee (with no discussion) to *reject* applicants whose interview scores average *6.9 or less.*
3. Discuss and rate applicants who received interview scores that average in the *7–8.9 range.* (Committee members rate individually the applicants based on the information provided during discussion, which includes the interviewers' evaluation, record of college work, MCAT performance[s], and other pertinent details.)
4. Discuss and rate applicants who have received interviewers' scores with a discrepancy of three points or more. (Again, committee members rate individually the applicants based on the information provided during discussion.)
5. Vote as a committee (with some discussion) to recommend applicants for the M.D./Ph.D. program whose interview scores average 8.0 or better.
6. Vote as a committee (with some discussion) to reject M.D./Ph.D. applicants whose interview scores average 6.9 or less.
7. Present applicants using the following protocol:
   - *Avoid superfluous information in individual presentations* such as hometown, school, major, GPA, and MCAT scores. (This information is already provided in the Biographical and Academic Profile Sheet included in the committee packet.)
   - *Present only the most salient points or observations* derived from the interview, outlining briefly the strengths and/or weaknesses within each category of the Interview Evaluation Form.
   - *Keep the total presentation to approximately three minutes.*
   - *Score the applicant* (using the 1–10 scale) on a ballot sheet (which is considered secret and confidential).
8. Rate applicants on the ballot sheet as each applicant is presented and discussed.
9. Submit ballots to the assistant dean for admissions for computer tabulation and ranking of applicants.

This approach allowed for greater focus and discussion on the applicants with acceptable interview scores in the range of 7–8.9, which was the range of scores received by the majority of those interviewed. The committee also gave itself the flexibility to present and discuss any applicant who was accepted or rejected by vote.

Each week, committee scores for each applicant interviewed were calculated by simply determining the average from the ballots submitted by each committee member. Using the committee score in this way gave greater weight to the interview evaluations and committee deliberations. As each week of interviews elapsed, applicants were rank ordered based on the committee scores. Applicants with committee scores were further distinguished by ranking them on three standards in the following sequence: (1) committee score, (2) overall GPA, and (3) total MCAT score. All in all, changing from a process that was largely quantitative to one involving more extensive evaluation and deliberation of non-cognitive factors accomplished two important goals: 1) the criteria as set preserved a sound basis of academic qualifications, and 2) the measures as set allowed for broad-minded scrutiny of applicants' non-cognitive characteristics at the pre-interview and interview phases of the evaluation process.

Table 7 presents some descriptive data about the applicant pool and the enrolled entering classes from 1995 through 2000.

TABLE 7 Texas A&M University System Health Science Center College of Medicine—Entering Classes of 1995–2000

Progression Through the Admissions Process	1995		1996		1997*		1998		1999		2000	
	No.	%	No.	%	No.	%	No.	%	No.	%	No.	%
All Applicants	1518	100	1576	100	1412	100	1419	100	1442	100	1782	100
URM† Applicants	154	10	156	10	140	10	141	10	151	11	265	15
All Interviewed	486	32	401	26	438	31	480	34	553	38	486	27
URM† Interviewed	67	14	63	15	25	6	32	7	42	8	44	9
All Accepted	165	34	200	50	208	47	192	40	208	38	168	35
URM† Accepted	31	19	30	15	9	4	18	6	19	9	23	14
All Matriculated	64	100	64	100	64	100	64	100	78	100	64	100
URM† Matriculated	6	9.4	10	15.6	5	8	4	6.3	6	7.7	2	3

* First class affected by the *Hopwood* decision. † Underrepresented minorities.

The data clearly show the effect the *Hopwood* decision has had on the College of Medicine's enrollment of underrepresented minority applicants. One can assume that the decrease in the numbers of underrepresented minority applicants interviewed and enrolled in 1997 were affected by the *Hopwood* decision. Since the admissions committee increased its efforts to commit more time and to contemplate more deeply the admissions process for the entering classes of 1998, 1999, and 2000, more underrepresented minority applicants are being interviewed and have been accepted. However, the number of underrepresented minority applicants who enroll, despite the substantive changes in the evaluation process and the increased efforts to select applicants who fit the mission and ethos of the College of Medicine, still remains alarmingly low. Although it is encouraging to see the admissions committee making such strides, the trend is far below the rate necessary to produce physicians who will meet the needs of the burgeoning minority population in the state of Texas.[30]

Like Steven Schroeder, President of the Robert Wood Johnson Foundation, we hope that efforts like making substantive changes in the admissions criteria and process, coupled with more efforts to recruit applicants from disadvantaged backgrounds, will result in achieving greater racial and ethnic diversity in the medical profession. And as we approach the fruition of this goal, we will simultaneously improve access to health care—and, in all probability, achieve better health—for a large number of Americans.[22]

WHAT HAVE WE LEARNED?

Developing and implementing a race-neutral admissions process can indeed challenge an institution's comfort with rigid algorithms, unquestioned admissions criteria and processes, and aloofness from both public and legislative scrutiny. In fact, under these circumstances, the institution may have to engage in practices it deems uncommon and uncomfortable, including 1) frequent self-monitoring, 2) a more inclusive approach in assessing cognitive abilities; 3) a broad-minded perspective of applicants' non-cognitive characteristics; 4) increased workload; 5) a constant mindfulness of the mission of the institution; 6) accountability; and 7) learning to act in concert to develop legal and effective criteria and processes for selecting applicants who will fulfill the complex needs and issues of the future.

It is painstaking work to change a medical school perspective from one that is insular and narrow in seeking students with broad educations, varied interests, and substantial accomplishments to one that examines unique attributes of applicants in new, creative, and effective ways. The work is often characterized by frustration and discouraging results. However, successful agents for change at a medical school usually connect or partner with forces outside of the institution, such as high schools, colleges and universities, other medical schools or health professions, community agencies, and legislators—all of which can spur action and facilitate institutional change.

The paramount challenge to any medical school committed to achieving diversity is to honestly assess itself and address the modifiable causes of rigid, laissez-faire practices. Because those underlying causes are passive and narrow, such a medical school must invest in redesigning its admissions processes and recruitment of members of minority groups to select applicants who fit the mission and ethos of the institution *and* who will likely care for patients from rapidly growing minority groups.

How Do We Retain Minority Health Professions Students?

Michael Larimer Rainey
SUNY Stony Brook School of Medicine

"In the competition to recruit minority students, most medical schools relaxed their admissions standards . . . On the other hand, no school relaxed its graduation requirements. Even as affirmative action spread, schools remained bound by their fiduciary duty to society to graduate only competent physicians. Accordingly, schools accepted the fact that some students would require extra help and additional time." (Ludmerer K. 1999)

There is a wealth of published information on efforts to increase the preparation for, admission of, and education of historically underrepresented minority (URM) students in allopathic medical education. This paper will focus on retention of Blacks, American Indian, Mexican-American, and Mainland Puerto Rican (URM) students compared with non-minority (white) medical students. A third group, "other minorities" (Asian/ Pacific Islander, other Hispanic, and Commonwealth Puerto Rican), will not be included in this analysis.

In the ensuing discussion, it is hoped that representatives from other health professions can contribute, since little data is published for these health professions schools. It is also recognized that students in the other minority categories as well as foreign students and non-traditional students may also experience problems with retention similar to the problems discussed in this paper.

THE CHALLENGE

In 1999, 4,181 underrepresented minority students applied to 126 allopathic medical schools. A total of 2,041 (49%) matriculated. URM students represented

328

10.9% of the applicant pool and 12.1% of the entering class for the 1999–2000 academic year (AAMC, 1997). Using the best available retention data, by November 2000, we can predict that about 3% (61) of this group of URM students are already off schedule for graduation with their class in 2004.

Ultimately, at graduation day in May/June 2004, the model predicts that 38.9% (814) of URM students admitted in 1999–2000 will not be on stage with their original classmates receiving the M.D. degree, being hooded by the faculty and shaking hands with the dean. In contrast, 14.6% of non-minority (white) students would be predicted not to graduate with their class that day. This difference in graduation rates reflects very different patterns of attrition, promotion, remedial strategies, intervention, and retention between these two groups of medical students.

Historically, the primary strategy to increase URM representation in medical education has been to increase the number of minority students admitted to medical schools. It is time to take a closer look at the retention rates of accepted URM applicants. Why are URM medical students three times more likely to experience academic problems that result in changes in academic status and delayed graduation than their non-minority classmates?

Either URM students are not as well prepared as non-minority students to succeed in medical school or medical schools do not provide a learning environment conducive to the success of URM students. Or both! What are the barriers and what can be done to lower, or better yet remove, these barriers and maximize URM retention and on-time graduation rates?

EFFORTS TO INCREASE THE "URM PIPELINE" TO THE MEDICAL PROFESSION

In 1970 when the enrollment of underrepresented minority (URM) students in U.S. medical schools was 2.8%, the AAMC initiated a task force to expand educational opportunities in medicine for Blacks, Hispanics, and American Indian/Native Alaskan students in the medical profession. The stated goal was an enrollment of 12% URM students by 1975 or 1976 (AAMC, 1970).

One strategy employed by some medical schools was to start post baccalaureate or special reinforcement programs using medical school resources. Early examples of these programs were Wayne State (1965), the University of Illinois (1969), SIU (1972), and New Jersey (1972).

In the late 1980's the AAMC concluded that there needed to be a renewed effort directed at the fundamental cause of minority underrepresentation. "...Too few minority young people are both academically prepared for and interested in the health professions..." (Nickens & Ready, 1999). Medical schools also began to admit URM students with academic credentials that were lower than the school's usual cut-off levels. Non-academic factors, such as extracurricular activities, leadership, and inter-personal skills which could be discerned from the application and through a personal interview, were also used to make admissions decisions. The focus was on non-cognitive factors which would help schools to identify URM students who had the potential to be successful medical students even if their grades and MCAT scores were lower than non-minority students. These same factors were also used to accept women, non-science majors, rural applicants, and older applicants. This was a period of great diversification of the medical school student body, especially women and non-traditional students, but URM students did not benefit as much through these efforts as did other groups.

Despite good intentions and considerable effort, first-time enrollment of URM students did not reach 12% until the 1994–1995 academic year, and total URM enrollment did not reach 12% until the 1996–1997 academic year. From 1975 to 1989, the proportion of minorities in the population increased by 22%, while the proportion in medical school increased by only 12% (AAMC, 1997).

In 1991, Dr. Robert Petersdorf, in his presidential address at the Annual Meeting of the Association of American Medical Colleges, challenged United States allopathic medical schools to matriculate 3,000 underrepresented minority students by the year 2000 (Petersdorf, Turner, Nickens, & Ready, 1990). This highly promoted initiative highlighted a renewed interest on the part of the AAMC and the medical schools to increase the number of medical students from historically underrepresented minority groups—Black, Hispanic, and American Indian/Alaska Native. At the time Project 3000 by 2000 was announced in 1991, the total number of first-time URM applicants to medical school was 2,854 and 1,584 of these URM applicants joined the 1991–1992 class of medical students.

Medical schools, historically the passive benefactors of the college pre-medical applicants, began to explore ways to directly increase the size and quality of the URM applicant pool. In contrast to the short-term strategy of post baccalaureate programs, a long-term strategy was also explored. Many medical schools joined in educational partnerships with elementary and secondary schools and community groups at the start of the pre-medical pipeline and then at various later stages with colleges and universities.

These initiatives involved medical school faculty and administrators directly interacting with potential applicants before and during the application process which made it possible for these minority youths to have an opportunity to have first-hand exposure to the medical school culture, medical students, faculty, and administrators. Using a variety of different templates, collaborative efforts were made to increase the draw, flow, and output of the pipeline to maximize the quality and quantity of URM students who applied to and were accepted by medical schools. The April 1999 issue of *Academic Medicine* is devoted to descriptions of 12 K–12 programs and 14 College and Medical School Programs (Nickens, & Ready, 1999).

The pipeline approach focused on convincing young minority students and their parents that medicine was a desirable and realistic career goal. Once students entered the pipeline, the focus was on improving their overall science education and retention, and reinforcing their motivation to seek out careers in the health professions, especially medicine. It was assumed that if more qualified and motivated minority applicants applied to medical school, more URM students would be accepted at predominately white medical schools. Once accepted, presumably the hardest part, they would progress satisfactorily through the medical school curriculum, graduate in four years, complete residency training, and enter the practice of medicine, hopefully helping the poor in underserved areas.

In summary, starting in the 1960s the AAMC and most medical schools began serious efforts to increase the number of enrolled medical students from historically underrepresented minority groups. In 1960, black, Hispanic, and American Indian/Alaska Native students represented 1% of the graduating seniors. For many medical schools, that represented none or one person of color on stage receiving the M.D. degree. In 1970 the percent of URM students had increased slightly to 1.3%. In the 1970s the numbers began to noticeably increase and by 1980, 8.4% of the graduating class were members of a URM group. In 1990 the percentage had increased modestly to 11.7% (AAMC, 1997).

During this 40-year period, the number of medical schools increased and the overall enrollment increased from 5,553 to 15,398 students. In other words, the almost 12-fold increase in minority enrollment did improve both in absolute numbers and compared with the overall 3-fold increase in medical student total enrollment. Meanwhile, the minority population from which these students were drawn and the minority patient population continued to grow at a significantly higher rate.

By 1999 there were 4,181 URM applicants to medical schools, a decline of 6.8% from the previous year. Of these, 2,041, or 49%, matriculated. URM applicants represented 10.9% of the total applicants in 1999 and 12.1% of the accepted students starting in the 1999–2000 academic year.

For purposes of comparison, the URM applicant pool for the 1998 entering dental school class included 9.5% URM applicants and the entering class consisted of 8.7% URM students. In the 1996/1997 academic year, URM students comprised 11.1% of the entering dental class (American Dental Association, 1999. *Dental Practice.* [Online]. Available: www.ada.org/prof/ed/careers/factsheets/dentistry.html). In baccalaureate nursing schools in fall 1999, black students represented 10.8% of the enrolled students, American Indian or Alaska Native represented 0.7% and Hispanic 4.5%. In graduate nursing programs URM students represented 12.4% of students in masters programs and 8.1% in doctorate programs. (American Association of Colleges of Nursing and the National Organization of Nurse Practitioner Faculties, 2000. *1999–2000 Enrollment in Baccalaureate and Graduate Programs in Nursing.* [Online]. Available: www.aacn.nche.edu and www.nonpf.com). In clinical laboratory education programs, a cohort study published in 1999 reported URM enrollment of 14.7%. This was the only health professions study outside of medicine that I was able to find which reported attrition data. Of the 272 URM students in the study, 25 voluntarily withdrew and 61 were dismissed, for an overall attrition rate of 31.7% (Laudicina, 1999). In fall 1998 a total of 33,090 students enrolled in schools and colleges of pharmacy in pursuit of their initial professional pharmacy degree. Of these, 12.3% were described as minority students (no definition of "minority" was provided.). In 1999, in a study of first professional degrees conferred in pharmacy, 9.8% of the graduates were black, Hispanic, and Native American. (American Association of Colleges of Pharmacy, 2001, *Pharmacy Education Facts and Figures*. [Online] Available: www.aacp.org/students /pharmacyeducation.html).

Recent anti-affirmative action initiatives and judicial decisions in the latter part of the decade have had a negative impact on the number of URM students who applied to and were accepted by medical schools. The medical school class that matriculated in 1999–2000 contained 1,923 URM students. The breakdown of URM students in this cohort is 7.9% black, 0.7% Native American, and 2.8% Mexican American.

Clearly, much more work needs to be done to expand the draw, flow, and output of the pipeline, both in terms of the quantity and quality of URM applicants applying to medical schools. But this is only part of the equation. The other part is to decrease the "leakage" of URM students once admitted to medical school. As we will see, too many URM students, deemed to have potential to succeed in medical school, are not being retained or graduated on time at the same rate as non-minority students. Why?

URM ATTRITION AND RETENTION

Starting in 1992, the AAMC conducted a cohort study of all students admitted to U.S. medical schools. Data is presented, year by year for URM students (Black, Mainland Puerto Rican, American Indian/Native Alaskan), nonminority (white), and Asian Pacific and other Hispanic. Data is presented on withdrawals, leaves of absence, dismissals, graduation, and still in school. For this paper I have chosen only to look at the URM and non-minority (white) student cohorts (AAMC, 1998).

TABLE 1 Academic Progression of 1992 Underrepresented Minority (URM) Matriculants[1]

Status	1992		1993		1994		1995		1996		1997	
	Number	Percent	Number	Percent	Number	Percent	Number	Percent	Number	Percent	Number	Percent
Withdrawal	4	0.2	10	0.5	26	1.4	41	2.2	46	2.5	51	2.8
Dismissal			13	0.7	28	1.5	49	2.7	57	3.1	62	3.4
On Official Leave	13	0.7	28	1.5	61	3.3	69	3.8	46	2.5	38	2.1
In School	1,804*	99.1	1,772	97.2	1,708	93.7	1,664	91.3	560	30.7	228	12.5
Graduated									1,114	61.1	1,444	79.2

*All remaining Number columns add up to 1823. This column adds up to 1821.
SOURCE: AAMC (1998). Minority Students in Medical Education: Facts and Figures XI, 1998. Washington, DC: AAMC.

TABLE 2 Academic Progression of 1992 Non-Minority Matriculants[1]

Status	1992		1993		1994		1995		1996		1997	
	Number	Percent	Number	Percent	Number	Percent	Number	Percent	Number	Percent	Number	Percent
Withdrawal	17	0.2	66	0.6	110	1.0	129	1.2	137	1.2	142	1.3
Dismissal			18	0.2	28	0.3	41	0.4	52	0.5	60	3.2*
On Official Leave	53	0.5	120	1.1	337	3.0	304	2.7	215	1.9	178	9.5*
In School	11,083	99.4	10,949	98.4	10,678	95.7	10,666	95.6	9,523	85.4	396	21.2*
Graduated									13	0.1	10,377	93.0

[1]Based on enrollment status as of November of each year.
Note: Racial/ethnic categories do not include foreign students.
*These figures would seem to be in error. They should be corrected as follows: 3.2 should be .5; 9.5 should be 1.6; 21.2 should be 3.6.
SOURCE: AAMC (1998). Minority Students in Medical Education: Facts and Figures XI, 1998. Washington, DC: AAMC.

MEDICAL STUDENT RETENTION

As shown in Table 1, in 1992 1,821 URM students were admitted to medical school, and 11,157 non-minority students were admitted:

- 1,114 URM students graduated in four consecutive years. This is a four-year on-time graduation rate of 61.2%. This compares with a four-year on-time graduation rate of 85.4% for non-minority (white) medical students.
- A total of 707 URM students were either dismissed, withdrew, or were placed on an extended educational program. If the non-minority graduation rate is applied to the URM cohort, only 273 URM students would have failed to graduate on time. This means that there was an "excess" of 434 URM students who did not graduate on schedule.
- The overall four-year graduation rate for this cohort of students (including other minorities) is 18%. Using this figure we would expect 328 minority students not to graduate in four consecutive years, which gives us an "excess" of 399 students if the same non-graduation rate was used for all students.
- In November of the second year 97.2% of URM and 98.4% of non-minority students were still enrolled although not necessarily promoted.
- A few months into the third year, 93.7% of URM and 95.7% of non-minority students were still enrolled.
- The percent of URM students who have withdrawn or been dismissed by the beginning of the junior year is 4.3%, twice the rate of non-minority students at 2.1%. In addition, 5.6% of the URM students have been granted a leave of absence (LOA) compared to 4.6% of the white students.
- At the start of the fourth year the percentages of students still enrolled were 91.3% (URM) and 95.6% non-minority. At this juncture, 8.7% of the enrolled URM students are not likely to graduate on time, compared with 4.5% of the non-minority students.
- In November of the fifth year following a May/June graduation, 30.7% of the URM students were still enrolled and had not graduated with their original classes. This compares dramatically with 11% of the non-minority students. In other words, on graduation day URM students are roughly three times more likely to find themselves *not* receiving the M.D. degree than their non-minority counterparts.
- By the end of the cohort study, the URM students had accumulated a total of 242 leaves of absence, or about 1 instance for every 7 students. The non-minority students accumulated a total of 1,207 LOAs or 1 per every 9 students. Leaves can occur multiple times and may extend from one academic year to the next.
- By the start of the sixth year, 79.2 % of URM students had graduated compared with 93% of non-minority students, and 14.6% of the URM students

were still enrolled or on an official leave of absence. In contrast, 5.2% of the non-minority students were still enrolled or were on an official leave of absence. Put another way, after more than five years in medical school, 379 minority students, 20.8% of the original cohort who matriculated in 1992, either had not received their M.D. degree or were at high risk of never receiving it. This compares with 776 white students (7%) who also matriculated in 1992.

• Overall, URM students were dismissed six times more frequently than white students, withdrew three times more frequently, were somewhat more likely to take a leave of absence, and were three times more likely to still be enrolled in medical school at the start of the sixth year of school.

This cohort data reports events, but it does not report reasons for the status changes. We do not know why the students' status was changed. Was a student dismissed for failing one course, two courses, or more? Did the student withdraw to avoid a termination? Why were some students placed in extended programs? Why did a student take a leave of absence? There is a multitude of reasons why a student might graduate late, ranging from earning an advanced degree, to an illness, to multiple academic problems.

Using AAMC individual student records, Huff and Fang were able to answer some of these questions (1999). They used data for only 13,118 students for whom there was complete data, versus the 16,289 students whom they reported matriculated in 1992. The AAMC table reports a total of 16,053 students started medical school in 1992. The AAMC reported that overall, 82% of the students for whom they had complete data in this cohort eventually graduated. Their data is not broken down by racial groups. The following gives data about the first reported events which resulted in a change of academic status:

• 537 (4%) of the students in the cohort experienced academic difficulty, which caused graduation to be terminated or delayed.

• Other known reasons why students did not graduate on time, or never graduated, include 555 students engaged in research (4%), 117 (<1%) for health reasons, three (<1%) for non-academic dismissal, nine (<1%) students died, and four (<1%) students experienced financial difficulties.

• 768 (5.8%) students graduated late or not at all for "other" documented reasons.

• In addition, 407 (3%) students graduated in more than four years without documented reasons.

In general, we see that URM students were 97% more likely than were their counterparts in the referent group to experience academic difficulty, controlling for the effects of all other variables.

Academic problems are the primary reason why students experience a change in academic status. However, the 768 students who were terminated or graduated late for "other reasons" and the 407 students who graduated in more than four years without documented reasons, highlight a major problem in using this data. For about 9% of the cases, the medical schools did not provide sufficient information to determine the reasons for the status change.

Based on my 30 plus years of experience in medical education I am admittedly jaded about the veracity of medical student transcripts and the quality of the information which schools communicate to the AAMC. Especially when it concerns minority students. I seriously question that only 3 of over 13,000 students were dismissed for non-academic problems. Or that only four students had financial problems which delayed graduation or caused them not to graduate. I believe that the numbers in these categories are much higher and are buried in the "other" category or in the "voluntary withdrawal" category as a face-saving strategy on behalf of the particular student and/or the medical school.

I am also uncomfortable saying that the students who graduated on time (82%) did not have any academic problems. Undoubtedly, some of these students failed individual course exams, some may have received unfavorable clinical evaluations in their chosen field although they passed the clerkship, or some received low grades in courses in which they expected to excel. There are schools with academic policies that would allow a student to fail a course, remediate it quickly, and not have this failure reported on the transcript, in a dean's letter, or to the AAMC database.

Another problem with this data is that a single event, a course failure, or failure on a NBME Step exam would trigger different responses from different schools based on their academic policies. Along the same lines, the threshold for multiple problems might produce different actions based on academic policy or the actions of a school's "promotions committee" or "academic standing committee."

Based on the Huff and Fang data, we now know that of the 1,449 leaves of absence given to an unknown number of individual students (a student could have more than one LOA over a six-year period), 555 were for research. Thus, there were probably about 900 leaves of absence granted for academic and personal reasons. If we eliminate the 126 reported instances of death or illness we might reduce the number of leaves to slightly less than 800. Again, a leave of absence could well be granted to a student who has an academic problem compounded by a personal or health problem. The student could be granted a leave of absence as a way to avoid failing a course that would result in a dismissal or to discourage the student from withdrawing from medical school.

In my experience, many medical schools under-report academic and personal problems encountered by their students. Confidentiality, paternalism, poor record keeping, concerns about lawsuits, unwillingness to disclose problems with the school's academic policy, and enforcement of policy are underlying reasons.

Finally, there is the issue of when these problems arise. Huff and Fang reported, "The evidence also highlights the critical time periods for encountering problems. Students with lower mean MCAT scores and lower undergraduate science GPAs tended to experience academic problems throughout the first three years of medical school, as did URMs, whereas older students tend to have problems only in the first two years. Overall, students already identified by their scores as being at risk experienced the majority of problems during the first year." (1999, p. 459.) The bottom line is that about one of three minority students encounters significant changes in academic status during medical school, most often beginning in the first year, which result in leaving medical school or graduating late with a troublesome transcript. Why is this the case?

WHY DO URM STUDENTS HAVE MORE ACADEMIC AND RETENTION PROBLEMS THAN THEIR NON-MINORITY CLASSMATES?

The following are five problem areas that need to be explored: Admissions, Curriculum, Faculty, Support Services, and Remedial Strategies. At the conclusion of this paper I will make specific recommendations for improvement of medical school URM student retention.

Admissions

For several decades, medical school deans have strongly articulated the desirability of a diverse medical student body that reflects the composition of the patient population to be served. It is the medical school admissions committee, the gatekeeper to the medical profession, that plays the major role in increasing the number of minority students enrolled in medical schools. Unfortunately, deanships of U.S. allopathic medical schools have been experiencing significant turnover in recent years. Of the 125 deans who were in office on August 1, 1999, in either a full or interim capacity, 22 (18%) were no longer occupying those positions on July 31, 2000 (Barzansky, Jonas, & Etzel, 2000). High turnover and short tenure of medical education leadership do not bode well for strong and consistent support for the increasing admission and retention of URM students in our medical schools.

In general, underrepresented minority students apply to medical school with lower average grades and lower average MCAT scores than members of the admissions committee feel are needed to predict success in their medical school. Sometimes these cut-off numbers are based on national or school studies. But often these cut-off numbers are really used to reduce a large applicant pool down to a manageable interview size, given limited faculty time to interview applicants. We know that average grades and MCAT scores are reported rather than the range of grades and MCAT scores because there are many students, minority and non-minority, with scores below the cut-off values who are interviewed, accepted, matriculate, and graduate on schedule.

Admissions committees seem to believe that they are the final gatekeepers to the medical profession, that everyone they admit ultimately graduates. They see their decisions as "high stakes" decisions protecting society from medical school graduates who are ill-suited to the practice of medicine and the medical profession. Therefore it is their duty to admit only students with acceptable grades and MCAT scores who also impressed the interviewers.

Ironically, it is the students themselves who, by their acceptance or rejection of a medical school's offer, actually determine the composition of the first-year class at each medical school in the fall. A school with one hundred places in the class reviews several thousand applications, interviews hundreds of pre-screened applicants, selects a few hundred acceptable candidates, and offers acceptances on a rolling basis. The actual overall composition of the class on the first day of classes is determined by the students who show up, not by the committee.

For the 1992 retention study cohort of students previously presented, the following table contains information about their average MCAT scores and grade point averages:

TABLE 3 Academic Profile of 1992 Matriculants by Status as of November 1997

URM	Graduated	Enrolled[1]	Withdrew[2]	Dismissed[3]
BCPM GPA	2.97	2.89	2.83	2.78
AO GPA	3.32	3.27	3.38	3.19
Total GPA	3.12	3.04	3.07	2.96
Biological Sciences	7.8	6.8	6.3	6.4
Physical Sciences	7.3	6.9	6.1	6.3
Verbal Reading	7.8	7.1	7.6	6.8
Writing Sample (median)	O[4]	O	O	N
Non-Minorities	**Graduated**	**Enrolled[1]**	**Withdrew[2]**	**Dismissed[3]**
BCPM GPA	3.44			
AO GPA	3.56	3.50	3.52	3.32
Total GPA	3.49	3.57	3.65	3.47
		3.53	3.58	3.37
Biological Sciences	9.5	10.2	8.9	8.3
Physical Sciences	9.3	10.1	8.8	8.8
Verbal Reading	9.6	10.0	9.6	8.8
Writing Sample (median)	O	O	O	O

[1] "Enrolled" includes those who are on official leave of absence.
[2] "Withdrew" category denotes voluntary withdrawal for academic, financial, health, and other reasons.
[3] "Dismissed" category covers those dismissed from medical school for academic or non-academic reasons.
[4] "O" and "N" are MCAT scores (range is from J to T).
NOTE: Racial/Ethnic categories do not include foreign students.
SOURCE: AAMC (1998). Minority Students in Medical Education: Facts and Figures XI, 1998. Washington, DC: AAMC.

Academic information about these students shows that the non-minority students across the board had higher average college grades and higher average MCAT scores than did the URM students. URM students who graduated on time had higher average grades and higher average MCAT scores than did URM students who were dismissed, withdrew, or took more than four consecutive years to graduate. In the case of non-minority students, this same pattern holds, with two exceptions. The white students who withdrew or delayed graduation had higher grades and MCAT scores than did the students who were dismissed, withdrew, or took more than four consecutive years to graduate. No information was provided to explain this anomaly. Perhaps they were students who left medical school to pursue master's or Ph.D. degrees.

It should be remembered that these are average scores for each group. Clearly, for both groups of students, there will be students with high grades and high MCAT scores who do not graduate, and students with low grades and low MCAT scores who do graduate on schedule with no academic difficulties.

Many medical schools, seeking out the most academically qualified URM applicants, typically offered acceptances to the same subset of the entire URM applicant pool. Many schools were not willing to give strong consideration to URM students with lower academic credentials. It is easy for the chair of the admission's committee to say, "We recruited, interviewed, and accepted enough URM students to do our part to meet the goal of 3000 by 2000, but less than a handful actually matriculated to our school. We did our part. Don't blame us. We tried." For the 3000 by 2000 challenge to be achieved, however, given the current rate of acceptance, there need to be at least 6,000 minority applicants in the pipeline. This has not happened yet.

There is a growing body of literature regarding non-academic or non-cognitive factors which may be useful in predicting academic success in college and professional schools. Since the typical URM applicant has college grades and MCAT scores below the cut-off levels, admissions committees have become interested in non-cognitive factors which can be derived from the application or the interview process that would be helpful in selecting URM and non-traditional students with the greatest chances of academic success in medical school.

After reviewing the literature, particularly with respect to students in the health professions, I am not convinced that anyone has found a combination of academic and non-cognitive factors which highly predicts success in all phases of medical education. In fact, it is even questionable if the MCAT and GPA, separately or in combination, are reliable predictors. Tucker suggests several factors which are believed to be helpful in promoting successful college transition: vision, the image which students hold for their future, and a sense of community in which a student feels a sense of belonging to a new educational environment. (Tucker, 1999). Sedlacek and colleagues suggest a number of factors including positive self-concept or confidence, realistic self-appraisal, understanding and dealing with racism, preferring long-range goals, successful leadership experience, demonstrated community service, and knowledge acquired in the field (Sedlacek & Prieto, 1990). Cariaga-Lo and colleagues, in their study of medical student attrition, reported that non-cognitive characteristics that influenced students' chances of academic difficulty were "being more norm-favoring, less self-realized, lower tendency for achievement via independence, age (generally older), gender (women) and race (nonwhite)." (Cariaga-Lo, Enarson, Crandall, Zaccaro, & Richards, 1997).

In 1999, Greg Strayhorn put together a very useful literature review of non-cognitive variables and research (Strayhorn, 1999). There is much food for thought in this line of research. These variables have the potential to be useful in screening URM students whom otherwise would not be considered, and in looking for clues to help the student in academic difficulty to identify underlying problems and to seek solutions. Non-cognitive factors probably play a role in how well students interview, how well they adapt socially to the new environment of medical school, how well they cope with racism and other stressors, and how well they are able to function in the clinical setting.

I have worked with medical students from a variety of different backgrounds, who perform below their own and/or the school's expectations. I believe that there are additional factors, discoverable as part of the admissions process, that are predictive of success in medical school. These include the students' knowledge of their own most efficient and effective learning strategies, willingness to try new ways of learning, appropriate use of learning strategies, openness to seek out help, appropriate use of time management skills, feelings of being "imposter" medical students, family support, adequate financial support, lack of role models and mentors, and inability to cope with stress and failures. At one time or another many medical students, even successful students, wonder if they have made a serious career choice mistake.

Anyone who has served on a medical school admissions committee knows that selecting applicants to medical school is a demanding and difficult task. Is a 3.1 science GPA from a selective college a better predictor of success in medical school than a 3.4 from a less selective school? Will a student with a very high verbal reasoning score and only average biological sciences and physical science scores perform better than an applicant with an average verbal reasoning score and above-average physical science and biological science MCAT scores? Will an older student with impressive life experiences be a stronger clinical student than a 21-year-old right out of college with impressive grades and no extracurricular accomplishments?

The database used to admit or deny a novice student entry into the profession of medicine includes: 1) a four-page application/transcript, 2) an essay which may or may not have been written by the applicant, 3) the results of a one-day multiple choice exam, 4) a few carefully crafted, positive faculty letters of recommendation, and 5) one or two hour-long interviews. Admissions committee meeting discussions about each applicant are often relatively short.

Committees often have little or no information about how well students they have accepted in the past have performed in medical school, or how well students they rejected did in the medical school which they subsequently attended. As anyone who has served as a member of an admissions committee knows, selecting successful medical students is more an art form, less a science.

The selection of URM students most likely to succeed is compounded by the problem that medical school admissions committees typically have few URM faculty members. In 1989, for example, URM faculty represented only 2.9% of the clinical faculty at U.S. medical schools (Petersdorf, Turner, Nickens, & Ready, 1990). Kondo and Judd reported in 2000 that on average, there were 4.1 URM members (16%) per admissions committee. Physicians with URM status comprised 8% of committee membership. Half (51%) of medical schools had one or no URM representatives (Kondo & Judd, 2000).

This means there are usually few URM faculty with whom interviewing URM students can identify. In committee deliberations, there are few URM faculty, even fewer with senior rank, who can provide insight about life experiences of URM students, have knowledge about the colleges they attended, and can provide insight into non-cognitive factors which might be helpful in selecting successful URM candidates.

Prediction studies provide us with clues about which applicants might encounter academic problems. However, since no medical school openly admits to conducting controlled admissions experiments, it is unlikely that we will ever know with exact precision what personal and academic characteristics most accurately predict academic performance. The absence of a published controlled study is ironic given that most members of a typical medical school admissions committee consider themselves to be scientists, or physicians who practice medicine scientifically.

The Curriculum

Medical research and technology have significantly increased the fund of knowledge medical students must master in four short years of medical school. The content of the medical school curriculum is under constant change as new discoveries are made. But the way this content is delivered to medical students has changed relatively little since the Flexner Report in 1910 (Flexner, 1910). GPEP, ACME-TRI, and, more recently, the AAMC Milbank Study of Curricular Change all point to tremendous internal resistance to changing the format of curriculum delivery in both the basic sciences and clinical years. (AAMC, 1984; AAMC, 1999; AAMC & Milbank Memorial Fund, 2000). There is resistance to moving away from focusing on content delivery to focusing on student learning. A cutting-edge lecture presentation, which results in no learning on the part of the audience, is not education. In particular, there has been a reluctance to replace the lecture format as the primary method of presenting core material to students. Small groups and the use of computers, for example, have made relatively little inroad into curriculum delivery. Labs have virtually disappeared in medical education with the exception of the gross anatomy dissection labs, which may soon be replaced with computer simulations. In an environment where the emphasis is on hours of lecture delivered, rather than knowledge acquired, it is the weakest and least-prepared student who will suffer the most.

Nowhere in the curriculum is this more evident than in the first semester of the first year. The typical college "pre-medical curriculum" at best prepares medical students for the content of the first several weeks of the medical school curriculum. It does not prepare students well for the culture of medical education or for the profession of medicine. It does not prepare students adequately for the pace of the curriculum, for the volume of material to be mastered, and for the detail-oriented questions on multiple-choice exams. Many students typically are not facile with the learning tools needed to survive in the medical school environment. It has been my observation that medical students are usually so smart that they often have not learned how to learn effectively and efficiently. When strategies acquired in high school and college start to fail them, they are clueless about what to do. They tend to put in more hours studying using their customary strategies rather than consider trying different, and potentially more effective, strategies. Seeking help is a strategy of last resort.

URM students, by and large, are at greater risk, given their diverse backgrounds, of not thriving in the unfamiliar, fast-paced environment of medical school, especially during the first semester. The retention cohort data presented earlier suggests that many academic problems that result in attrition start in the first semester and are compounded in the second semester. By the second year, students who are not performing well have either left medical school or have already been placed on a remedial plan, allowing them more time to learn the material.

The first semester of the first year at most medical schools consists of a gross anatomy course and a biochemistry and/or molecular biology course, plus perhaps one or two smaller courses. There is a "boot camp" mentality operative during the first several months of medical school. Faculty create an environment where the workload increases dramatically and the early exams are designed to produce relatively low scores.

The curriculum during the first semester is delivered primarily in a lecture format. Last year's lectures are read again by the faculty and students follow along reading the photocopied notes from the previous year. The pace is fast, there is no time for questions, and it is a good day when the AV equipment works properly. Anatomy lab is scheduled for three hours but there are five hours of expected dissection work. The tests use the multiple-choice format with a heavy emphasis on the recall of detailed information. The pace is so fast that comprehension and long-term retention are nearly out of the question for many students. Memorization is the most common strategy and cutting one class to cram for a test in another course is the norm. The word "survival" is common when students talk about the first semester. Learning is secondary.

There are two possible explanations for this behavior on the part of course directors. One is that many faculty think it is their job to weed out those students who should not be in medical school; that is, to correct admissions committee errors. The other is to create a boot camp environment to toughen up the students, focus their attention on academics, and motivate (scare) them into giving 110% to learning the material in their course. Within a few weeks, even the students with very strong science backgrounds are starting to flounder and non-science majors are wondering if they have made a horrible error in career choice.

The medical school basic science faculty are researchers and content experts. Teaching medical students is something they do in order to be able to hold a faculty appointment in the medical school with its rich research resources. Many do not feel that they will be promoted or given raises based on their teaching performance. They would rather teach graduate students who also work in their labs, and who will also be their proteges. Faculty are expected to deliver an expanding body of knowledge, in an organized way, in a pre-set number of hour-long lectures. Typically medical students have little input into faculty promotion and tenure decisions. They either are not asked or their comments are given little or no consideration. After all, there is only one anatomist on staff who can teach the medical student gross anatomy course. If she is not promoted and given tenure, who will teach the course? Course directors and primary lecturers in courses are typically not members of an underrepresented minority group.

Medical school faculty tend to look at lecturing, reading, and testing as the only ways students can learn the material and the only ways that mastery of their knowledge can be tested. Faculty equate "teaching" with "student learning." They have been resistant to any form of small-group teaching, especially problem-based learning (PBL). Even in the anatomy lab, the groups of four to five students assigned to each cadaver are regarded as dissection or work groups, not as learning groups. What would happen, for example, if the group was tested as a team and all received the same grade? This would encourage all members of the group to make sure that they were, as a group, well prepared for the test. Perhaps the "gunner" in the group would be less likely to come into the lab after hours to do additional dissection so he will get a better grade on the next exam, while depriving his partners of a learning experience.

For many beginning medical students, the test scores they receive in the first semester are lower than they expected. Many report they are the lowest test scores they have ever received. They wonder how they have suddenly become so "stupid." They typically do not share these scores with classmates, nonmedical student friends, spouses, partners, or family. Since the grade distribution is announced in class, it is known that 20% of the class failed the exam. Students who failed, or almost failed, the exam tend to isolate themselves so that classmates will not ask them how they did on the exam. And unfortunately, many students in the class believe incorrectly that *all* the minority students are in the group that failed.

Medical school faculty, by and large, assume that every student learns the same way that they learn. UMR students, by and large, are at greater risk, given their lower grades and MCAT scores, of not thriving in the educational culture of medical education. One study has suggested that perhaps URM students prefer a different learning style compared with their non-minority classmates. Taylor and Rust suggested white students are "assimilators" and prefer the lecture format, while URM students tend to be "convergers," "divergers," or "accommodators" and are at a disadvantage when more interactive styles of teaching methods are not used (Taylor & Rust, 1999).

Another possibility is that a URM student may have an undiagnosed learning disability that may not be recognized because of the presumption that URM students always perform at a lower level than non-minority students. A URM student who suspects a problem may also choose not to submit to testing because she lacks the funds to pay for it. She may also be reluctant to be labeled as "disabled."

Most medical schools conduct an orientation program prior to the official start of the first year. For the most part, this program is an orientation to the medical school facility. With the exception of a talk by the dean and a White Coat ceremony, it is not an orientation to the profession of medicine. Other than handing out textbook lists and the class schedule, there is little attention given to helping students manage the curriculum and navigate through the first semester. The students are more likely to be given information about the best student-friendly bars in the area than information on how to prepare for medical school lectures, how to take notes, how to read medical textbooks, how to study for and take multiple-choice exams, and other learning strategies which might be useful in the fast-paced, content-rich medical school curriculum. They receive no advice about being effective adult learners. The sophomores who are invited back early to "orient" new students or to tutor first-year students are typically those students who did extremely well academically the previous year. They probably have little understanding of the problems some classmates experienced. Many do not even know why they themselves were successful.

It has also been my experience that minority students often do not participate actively in the orientation programs. They often need the orientation week to take care of housing and financial aid. I have, in the past, attended workshops conducted by Leon Johnson, the former president of National Medical Fellowships (NMF), for minority students preparing for medical school. He makes a strong case regarding minority students who have become too dependent on easy-to-obtain, high-interest credit cards for daily living expenses. Students who do not pay off credit cards on time develop poor credit histories which make it very difficult for them to qualify for financial aid, to obtain credit, to open bank accounts, and to pass credit checks for apartment leases and utilities hookups. As a result they often miss portions of the orientation program so that they can take care of "life" problems which non-minority students in the class were able to take care of weeks ahead of time. Some students with high consumer debt try to secretly work part-time while in medical school just to pay off their debts. This usually leads to poor academic performance, missed classes, and lack of sleep.

Medical schools that do not devote time and resources to preparing students for the medical school curriculum are missing an opportunity to improve the quality of life for students during the first year. This information can help to level the academic playing field for URM and non-traditional students. The money "lost" on scholarships and financial aid given to students who do not graduate and default on loans would more than pay for the cost of providing more support services for students in academic difficulty.

A study recently published by the AAMC and the Milbank Memorial Fund takes a close look at curricular change at 10 medical schools. "The good news is that many medical educators are implementing curricular changes that are responsive to the latest advances in biomedical science, to the social and policy sciences relevant to medical practice, to the burden of disease, to the organization and financing of health care, and to the changing demography of the American population." (AAMC & Milbank Memorial Fund, 2000, p. v). Northwestern was the only medical school featured in the report which specifically addressed the issue of diversity of its student body. The Northwestern report stated, "Finally, we will be working to further increase the cultural diversity of our medical classes and to enhance the 'cultural competence' of each individual student . . . "Nevertheless, we still fall far short of our goals for enrollment of underrepresented minority students . . . With respect to each student's skills in working with patients from other cultures . . . We are creating a new program to ensure that every student has the opportunity to learn basic medical Spanish and increasing opportunities for clerkship experiences in ethnic neighborhoods." (AAMC & Milbank Memorial Fund, 2000, p. 146).

Other than this one exception, I did not find acknowledgement of the increasing diversity of the medical student body or that URM students had higher levels of attrition than non-minority students. There was an occasional comment that faculty needed to know more about adult learning, and that perhaps it would be beneficial to increase small-group learning formats, such as PBL.

Few medical schools have elements of the curriculum which involve cultural competency. Typically this term is used to describe curricular efforts to inform future practitioners of different cultural values, norms, and beliefs as they apply to birth, life, growing up, puberty, pregnancy, illness, old age, and death. Ideally, the curriculum would include language training sufficient for a student to do a basic physical exam in two languages, but the term could also be applied to helping students understand the backgrounds of other members of their class. URM students could share their own knowledge and experience with other members of the class as discussion group leaders and participants, helping to teach physical diagnosis language courses and being available to the hospital as translators and patient advocates.

Curriculum accountability is an area that has attracted considerable attention in recent years. At many medical schools there is no curricular authority and no central education budget. Departments own most of the courses except for a few interdisciplinary "dean's" courses. The curriculum committee primarily schedules classes, adjudicates disputes about course hours and use of lecture halls and labs, and determines exam schedules. Lip service is often given to evaluating the curriculum, the quality of individual courses, faculty educational efforts, and overall student performance. If a large number of first-year students fail biochemistry, for example, would this be the province of academic affairs or student affairs? Would the promotions or academic standing committee focus on the course or on the failing students? Typically, student failure of a course is considered to be the fault of the student, not the instructor or the course itself. Who would have jurisdiction if all 12 students who failed were URM students?

Faculty

Basic science and clinical faculty with medical school appointments have come under increased pressure to "earn their keep" through funded research projects and clinical practice revenue. As noted earlier, teaching medical students is not valued or rewarded when tenure is granted or salary increases are determined. Medical schools and associated research and clinical facilities are expensive to operate. Tuition pays only a fraction of the total cost of medical education. Medical students are transitory "visitors" to the medical school campus. Faculty stay forever.

There is a severe shortage of URM faculty teaching core courses. "Although African Americans, Native Americans, Mexican Americans, and Mainland Puerto Ricans make up almost 25% of the U.S. population, they account for less that 8% of all practicing physicians. Only 3% of medical school faculty members belong to one of these minority groups." "First, minority faculty, by virtue of their small numbers in a given medical school, is disadvantaged by comparative isolation within the academic community. Second, minority faculty often feel disproportionately obliged to serve on time-consuming committees, to mentor students with complicated nonacademic problems, and to participate in community service activities that are not typically career advancing. There is even a term that has been coined for these contributions, the black tax. Third, attainment of senior faculty rank by minority faculty is tantamount to crashing a long-running party at which a relatively circumscribed group of invitees has had privileged access to the trappings of power" (Cohen, 1998).

A study published in 1998 reported faculty in each ethnic group working similar hours, but black faculty spent more time in clinical activities and less time in research. More black and Hispanic faculty felt pressure to serve on committees due to their race or ethnicity, although they actually did not spend more time in hours per month on committee-related activities than the other faculty groups. They also reported that controlling for age, URM faculty were substantially less likely to have attained senior rank than white faculty. URM faculty were also found to have a greater debt burden than other faculty, which may explain more time spent in clinic and less time engaged in research (Palepu, Carr, Friedman, Amos, Ash, & Moskowitz, 1998).

The medical school faculty is predominately composed of white males, particularly persons in positions of educational leadership and administration. URM students are marginalized in this environment. They do not encounter faculty with whom they can identify. They have difficulty finding faculty who overcame the same problems that they are now encountering. How could a faculty member who never needed to study hard, never failed a course, and did not have to borrow large amounts of money understand what a URM student, who is at risk of flunking out of medical school, is going through on a day-to-day basis?

Because URM faculty tend to hold lower rank and to experience difficulty gaining promotion and tenure, they do not have much time to mentor minority students, provide them with survival strategies, be advocates for them with deans and promotions committees, provide career advice, or help with applying to residency programs (Fang, Moy, Colburn, & Hurley, 2000). The absence of URM faculty decreases the chances that a URM student can find a faculty mentor, someone who has "walked the same path" and can serve as a guide. The increasing diversity of medical school classes will, in the next 10 to 20 years, begin to diversify the predominately white male faculty of medical schools, especially the clinical faculty. In 1989 URM faculty represented only 2.9% of the clinical faculty at U.S. medical schools (Petersdorf, Turner, Nickens, & Ready, 1990).

In the AAMC's 2000 Medical School Graduation Questionnaire, seniors anonymously responded to a wide range of questions about their experiences at their school. Each school received their own aggregate results as well at national results. When asked to what degree the racial and ethnic diversity of the school's student body positively fostered professional growth and development, only 34.2% of the students said it was a moderate or strong influence. When students were asked if they had been personally mistreated during medical school, 20% of the almost 14,000 respondents said yes. When this 20% were asked if they were denied opportunities for training or rewards because of their race ethnicity, 12% said one or more times. When asked if they had been subjected to racially or ethnically offensive remarks/names directed at them personally, 15.8% said one or more times. Asked if they felt they had received lower evaluations or grades based solely on their race or ethnicity rather than performance, 12.3% said one or more times. When asked the source of this mistreatment, faculty in the clinical setting and interns/residents were cited as the most common sources of mistreatment. While the numbers are small, these instances of racial discrimination or harassment loom large in the eyes of the medical student victims, especially when the perpetrators are physicians who are also their teachers, mentors, and professional role models. These behaviors are perpetuating harassment from one generation to another (AAMC, 2000).

Support Services

I recently conducted a small study of the minority affairs officers listed in a publication called *2000–01 Diversity of American Medical Education* published by the AAMC (AAMC, 2001). This publication listed the names, degrees and titles of all persons identified as each school's minority affairs officer. Of the 120 predominately white medical schools (excluding Meharry, Howard, Morehouse, and the three schools in Puerto Rico) there were 69 (57%) schools who listed a minority affairs officer. Of these, 38 persons (55%) were physicians and 37 (54%) held the title of associate dean or higher. Half the schools had a minority affairs officer at some administrative level, but only one-quarter of the schools had a minority affairs officer at the senior level of administration. Race was not identified in the publication, but based on my own knowledge, a large percentage of these minority affairs officers are members of an underrepresented minority group.

According to the current issue of AAMC Medical Schools Admissions Requirements, every medical school lists a contact person for URM applicants. A total of 101 (78%) persons listed held the title of Dr. (although it was not specified whether it was a M.D. or other earned doctorate). A total of 68 persons (53%) held some variation of the title minority affairs officer. A total of 52 (40%) held the title of associate dean or higher. Overall, only 26 (20%) persons listed had a doctorate degree, the title of associate dean, and the title of minority affairs officer (AAMC, 2001).

Overall, while a majority of predominately white medical schools list a minority affairs officer, only about one in four has one with a Ph.D. or M.D. who holds senior rank in the administration. This is not to say that a minority person with an M.S. in degree counseling and the title of director could not be an effective advisor, counselor, and advocate for minority students. However, a person without an advanced degree and a senior-level administrative title is less likely to be a voting member of the admissions, academic standing or promotions committee, or the curriculum committee, and is less likely to have access to the dean.

A relatively recent addition to the administrative staff of some medical schools is a learning assistance specialist. I found no resource that provides data on learning assistance specialists at medical schools or that specifies that they are readily available to medical students on the university's main campus. I suspect that most were initially hired because of problems that minority students were encountering. Once in place, they provide service to a wide variety of students who wish to perform academically at a higher level. A few even have linkages to faculty development programs for medical school faculty. The availability of these specialists increases support resources available to medical students. More are needed.

Even if support resources are available to URM students, they still may have to seek help for personal or academic problems. It has been my experience that URM students, like most medical students, are reluctant to ask for help. The students, when asked, are aware of the services available, but are less likely than non-minority students to make appointments or to respond to offers of assistance. Denial, fear of exposure, concerns about confidentiality, lack of trust, pride, the possible high out-of-pocket cost of diagnostic testing are all possible reasons. The fact that most of the persons providing assistance are not URM faculty or staff is an additional contributing factor to explaining poor utilization.

A high percentage of URM students come from economically disadvantaged backgrounds and cannot afford the high cost of medical tuition and living expenses without assistance. Most need loans and scholarships to attend medical school. It has already been mentioned that some of these students or their parents have credit rating problems, which preclude loans. Scholarships are often used by the admissions committee to attract URM students with high academic credentials. URM students, for example, receive about 6% of the cost of medical education from their families, compared with 20% for non-minority students. URM students are considerably more dependent on loans and scholarships for their medical education (AAMC, 1998). They are also more likely to come to medical school with a higher undergraduate debt than non-minority students. Many URM students often contribute some of their financial aid to help their parents or siblings.

However, virtually all forms of financial aid assume that the student is in good academic standing. If a student has to repeat a year, she or he may lose a scholarship or may not be eligible for a loan. During the repeat year the student may have difficulty finding financial aid and will have to seek employment while also attending medical school or studying for a remedial exam. Students who need more than four years to graduate may find expensive loans or work part-time while doing clinical rotations. None of these options are desirable and they may significantly interfere with the student's ability to recover academically. The financial aid officer needs to be an involved member of the support team capable of dealing with the difficult financial issues which many of the URM students face, especially when they encounter academic problems. Failure to obtain adequate financial support during periods when they are experiencing academic problems, are in a remedial mode, or are on leave of absence, can contribute to eventual dismissal or withdrawal from school.

Remedial Strategies

There is the temptation to identify students at risk of academic and/or personal problems in medical school, and to attempt to intercede, either by requir-

ing them to attend a special pre-orientation program or to see a coun-
selor/advisor soon after classes start. There are several problems with these
strategies. First, these strategies run the risk of stigmatizing the student doing
poorly and of increasing his or her already high level of anxiety. Often, the student refuses to participate in special programs and/or resists preventive advisement appointments. He or she firmly believes that all that is needed is to "study
more" and things will be fine.

Some medical schools have experimented with "lightened load" programs
in which students spend three years completing the first two years of medical
school. While this strategy may help some students who have non-academic
problems which may limit their ability to fully participate in the curriculum at
full pace (for example, a mother with a young child), in most cases these programs can be stigmatizing, making the participants feel like second-class citizens. In some schools, students who get into early academic difficulty are forced
into lightened load programs without giving them the chance to succeed on their
own. Overall, I have not been a proponent of obligatory or forced lightened load
programs. While they may lighten the load, they do not help students develop
requisite survival skills and, too often, they stigmatize the participating students.

One option is to encourage faculty to give a test one or two weeks after the
start of classes which does not count heavily toward the final grade, but is constructed just like a real exam with the same level of difficulty. Then conduct a
post mortem. It would be helpful if the faculty can provide information about
questions that students missed. Was this information they should have known
from college or was it new material? Did the students make careless errors suggesting they did not read the question carefully? Did they change right answers
to wrong answers? Did the students finish the exam? Providing this information
to the students and to the learning assistance specialist opens up an opportunity
for each student and counselor to discuss study skills and testing strategies. This
is important because the counselor may not be a content expert. Waiting until
the sixth week before the first test results are available is often too late for initial
feedback because it allows relatively little time for corrective action to occur
before the mid-term exam. The early first exam score gives the student a "ticket"
to seek help and the counselor/advisor a specific reason to call the student in for
a counseling session.

If a medical student fails a first-year course, there is typically a six- to
eight-week break between the first and second years which the student can use
to study and take a remedial exam or take a summer course at one of a dozen
medical schools which offer remedial courses. After the second year there is
usually a month before the junior year starts and at most medical schools, students are encouraged or required to take the Step 1 exam before they start clinical rotations. The last two years of medical school run almost continuously with
periodic week-long breaks and end one or two months before graduation. In this
extremely compressed curriculum, the only mechanism for allowing a student to

remediate a failed course is to derail the student from normal progress and give the student extra time to deal with the course failure.

This basic strategy of giving more time is fundamentally flawed. First of all, if a student could not learn in a supervised, structured environment the first time through, why is it assumed that she can learn better in an unsupervised, unstructured environment? If the student is using inappropriate learning techniques, additional time is a waste of time. Counselors need to work with the student to determine why she is failing and help her acquire strategies that will assure success in the future. Support, not time, is what is needed more.

Unfortunately, a common strategy is to give the student a leave of absence, either to study the material for a make-up test or to take a time out and wait for the course to be offered again. Another strategy is to tell the student that he or she has to take a make-up test at the end of the summer before the next year starts. Unless the student has access to financial resources, this means that the student often has to return home. This removes the student from sources of academic support from faculty, tutors, classmates, learning assistance specialists, and administrators. Faculty, who are already complaining about too much work, are reluctant to advise or tutor remedial students and often do nothing more than provide the student with a generic reading list. Over time the "banished" student will feel estranged from the school, will be less likely to seek help, and be less inclined to return to medical school to try again. Instead, every effort needs to be made to keep the student on campus, in contact with resources and, if possible, in the classroom.

In the absence of health or personal problems that require the student to leave campus, I would strongly support remedial strategies that would keep the student in an academic environment. Often there are untapped resources in the form of medical students in M.D./Ph.D. programs who would be interested in tutoring a student, which in turn helps them to review material prior to resuming their own medical training. Junior faculty, who someday will be teaching themselves, could help a struggling student as part of their own professional development. Other URM students who have been successful could collectively organize tutorial or help sessions for struggling URM students. A list of URM faculty who would be willing to serve as tutors, or coaches, or just someone to talk with should be readily available to struggling students.

Another approach is to ask classmates who are doing well in the course to provide assistance, either on a voluntary basis or with compensation provided by the dean's office. Rather than use the "best" students in the class, it might make more sense to identify students with prior teaching experience or students with master's degrees.

A student who will have to repeat first semester will still profit by sitting in on, or auditing, second-semester courses. No one in the class needs to know that the student did not pass all first-semester courses. This allows the student to see what is coming, may help him or her to put first semester material into perspective, and allows him or her some degree of dignity to stay with his or her class-mates and friends. This approach will necessitate creative ways to finance the student's living expenses for the year.

Intervention should be coordinated between the student affairs, minority affairs and academic affairs staff, the learning skills specialist, and the course director of the failed course. This will also alert the academic affairs dean in cases where a large number of URM students are failing the same courses. This information should also be provided to the admissions dean and the admissions committee.

It has been my experience, at several medical schools, that in some first-semester courses the content "ramp" is too steep. Too little time is taken by faculty to review material which they assume all students should have learned prior to starting medical school. A summary of the academic records of the class should be made available to first-semester faculty. For example, how many students had biochemistry courses in college, how many have advanced science degrees, how many students were non-science majors. The pace of first-semester courses is often too fast, causing most students to very quickly fall behind. A few questions at the start of a lecture might help the lecturer to determine if the pace is appropriate and if key concepts from the previous lecture have been understood.

There is nothing sacred about the first semester concluding before the December holiday period. Giving students a block of time to study in December might improve overall learning and exam performance. Scheduling first-semester exams after the holiday season would also help decompress the first semester. There is also nothing sacred about giving medical students a month or two break at the end of the first year. While this is a prime time for remedial efforts, perhaps a few extra weeks should be added to the end of the semester to review basic core concepts before the final exam. All of these strategies would allow all students more time to learn the material and result in fewer failures during the critical first year.

Once a student experiences an academic failure that results in a projected delayed graduation date, there appears to be a cumulative effect that significantly increases the chances the student will never graduate. The student no longer has the support of friends and classmates. She has increased financial problems. She believes that her failures are common knowledge. She may believe that future faculty will know she has failed a course and will pre-judge her. And, of course, her transcript may keep her from getting desirable electives at other hospitals. Residency program directors are less likely to grant her an interview with a flawed transcript and graduation in more than four years.

Early identification of academic failure, swift and intense efforts to provide assistance by faculty and administration, making every effort to keep the student on schedule, and providing continuing and adequate financial aid are essential elements of a successful remedial strategy, especially for first- and second-year academic problems.

SUMMARY

Project 3000 by 2000 and prior initiatives increased the size and quality of the URM medical school pipeline and probably the number of URM candidates for admission to the other health professions as well. The application credentials of the URM candidates for admission to medical school increased and so did the interest in identifying non-cognitive factors which would predict success in medical training.

However, one of three accepted URM medical students still fails to graduate on time. Most academic problems begin in the first semester of the first year and are not resolved, causing delays in graduation or a failure to graduate. Admissions committees need to continue to look beyond grades and MCAT scores for indicators of academic success among URM applicants, and the faculty need to take a close look at elements of the medical school curriculum, especially the first semester, which may be causing avoidable academic failures.

Faculty need to explore other instructional methodologies than lecture, to create a more hospitable and effective learning environment for URM students. This should also include a curriculum which promotes cultural competence. URM faculty are few in number and struggle to be successful in their own careers and also be available to help future URM faculty succeed in medical school. It should be recognized that when a URM student gets into academic difficulty, it is not a good practice to just give the student more time without supervision and structure. The student needs to stay on campus with adequate financial support and with access to all available support services. Minority affairs officers, in conjunction with other deans, need to be aggressive and vigilant advocates for URM students. The financial challenges facing students who need additional time to complete their medical training must be met by the medical school. The school needs to actively preserve the financial, as well as professional, investment which they have made in the students accepted by the admissions committee.

RECOMMENDATIONS

With limited sources, limited time, and an uncertain political climate, which strategies would have the greatest bang for the buck and the greatest probability of success? Below are 34 specific recommendations to improve retention of URM medical students that would also be applicable to students in the other health professions.

Admissions

1. The word "diversity" should be part of the mission statement of every medical school accredited by LCME.

354 THE RIGHT THING TO DO, THE SMART THING TO DO

2. Schools should continue to recruit, interview, and accept URM students to meet a new AAMC goal of 20% URM enrollment by the year 2010.
3. Medical schools should get more directly involved in their own URM pipeline which would involve increasing the numbers of URM students on campus prior to the start of the admissions process.
4. Deploy senior URM faculty, residents, and students to serve on the admissions committee as recruiters, interviewers, and voting committee members.
5. Track the progress of admitted students in the curriculum and use both cognitive and non-cognitive factors to determine the success profile for a school consistent with (1) above.
6. If scholarships and loans are available, commit resources for no less than five years without a requirement of academic progress.
7. Encourage URM applicants to attend classes, labs, make return visits, and to come to the entire extended orientation program.

Curriculum

1. Orientation should be at least two weeks long and should include an orientation to the curriculum, learning styles, testing strategies, and small-group work as well as an introduction to the medical school and the community.
2. During the extended orientation program some classes should be held covering prerequisite material. Material presented should be tested in the same way that first-semester courses are tested. Feedback which identifies areas of strength and weakness, should be provided to students.
3. Students who are identified as potential risks during orientation should be involved in on-going coordinated assistance immediately.
4. Decompress, slow the pace, and extend the length of the first year, especially the first semester. Lower the entry ramp a few degrees.
5. Increase URM faculty representation in every year of the curriculum. URM clinical faculty could, for example, provide clinical correlates, present patients, and discuss cases as part of first-year courses.
6. The curriculum committees should mandate that lectures be significantly reduced and replaced with small-group learning experiences and other alternate methodologies. There are a variety of ways in which an electronic curriculum would foster diversity in educational modalities.
7. Learning assistance specialists should work with faculty on courses, presentations, and tests.
8. The structure of the course should reflect the learning styles of the students in the course.
9. Cultural competency components need to be added to all phases of the curriculum starting in the first semester. This can be done using small-group-based courses, which focus on social, psychological, economic, and professionalism issues in medical practice.

10. Medical students at the end of the second year should be able to do an acceptable patient examination in two languages. This should be an LCME standard and tested by USMLE.
11. Decrease dependence on MCQ exams, especially in the first year. Use computers to test students, employing a variety of testing formats.
12. Offer early systematic academic support to students during the first semester.

Faculty

1. Explore ways to help URM faculty earn tenure and promotion at the same rate as non-minority faculty.
2. Find ways to involve URM faculty in the curriculum design and delivery, especially in the first year.
3. Strategically deploy URM faculty to student and education-related committees.
4. Address the issues of clinical faculty and resident/intern discrimination and harassment directed at URM students in the school.

Support Services

1. The office of minority affairs should be staffed with high-ranking, visible, and available staff and should have resources to provide support services to URM students.
2. Deans of student, academic, and minority affairs should work together to eliminate attrition in the first year.
3. Learning assistance support should be available within the medical school and work in conjunction with the offices of minority, student, and academic affairs.
4. Implement strategies to make students and faculty aware of differences in learning styles, and alter the curriculum and support services to maximize learning for all students.
5. Find alternative remedial strategies which are not based on "time out." Students in academic difficulty should be on campus, working with faculty, fully supported, and able to continue their education, even if they are in a remedial mode.
6. Increase available financial aid funds for URM students and guarantee support for a minimum of five years.
7. Find creative ways to encourage URM students to seek help when they encounter academic or personal problems. Find ways to reduce further stigmatizing students who are already coping with the prospect of academic failure.

Miscellaneous

1. Medical schools should keep detailed records of reasons why URM students experience academic difficulty, evaluate remedial strategies employed, and document outcomes. They should publish results of this research.
2. Attention should be given to both cognitive and non-cognitive variables and academic problems which are linked to specific courses.
3. Feedback should be provided to the admissions, academic standing and curriculum committees as well as to the office of academic affairs, student affairs, minority affairs and the dean's office.
4. The AAMC should start another, more detailed cohort study.
5. LCME should take a close look at accreditation standards relative to improving retention of URM students and on-time graduation rates.

REFERENCES

American Association of Colleges of Nursing and the National Organization of Nurse Practitioner Faculties. (2000). 1999–2000 Enrollment in baccalaureate and graduate programs in nursing. [Online]. Available: www.aacn.nche.edu and www.nonpf.com [accessed December 12, 2000].

American Association of Colleges of Pharmacy. (2001). Pharmacy education facts and figures. [Online] Available: www.aacp.org/students/pharmacyeducation.html [accessed January 14, 2001].

Association of American Medical Colleges (AAMC). (1970). Report of the Task Force on Expanding Educational Opportunities for Blacks and Other Minorities, 1970. Washington, DC: AAMC.

AAMC. (1984). Physicians for the twenty-first century, The GPEP Report. Washington, DC: AAMC.

AAMC. (1997). Minority students in medical education: Facts and figures XI, 1997. Washington, DC: AAMC.

AAMC. (1998). Minority students in medical education: Facts and figures XI, 1998. Washington, DC: AAMC.

AAMC. (1999). Educating medical students: Assessing change in medical education—The road to implementation. ACME-TRI Report. Washington, DC: AAMC.

AAMC. (2000). LCME graduation questionnaire. Washington, DC: AAMC.

AAMC. (2001). 2000–01 Diversity of American medical education. Washington, DC: AAMC.

AAMC. (2001). Medical school admission requirements United States and Canada 2001–2002. Washington, DC: AAMC.

AAMC & Milbank Memorial Fund. (2000). The education of medical students: Ten stories of study of curricular change. New York: Milbank Memorial Fund.

American Dental Association. (1999). Dental practice. [Online]. Available: www.ada.org/prof/ed/careers/factsheets/dentistry.html [accessed December 18, 2000].

Barzansky, B., Jonas, H.S., & Etzel, SI. (2000). Educational programs in U.S. medical schools, 1999–2000. Journal of the American Medical Association 284(9):1114–1120.

Cariaga-Lo, L.D., Enarson, C.E., Crandall, S.J., Zaccaro, D.J., & Richards B.F. (1997). Cognitive and noncognitive predictors of academic difficulty and attrition. Academic Medicine 72(10 suppl.):S71.

Cohen, J.J. (1998). Time to shatter the glass ceiling for minority faculty. Journal of the American Medical Association 280(9):821.

Fang, D., Moy, E., Colburn, L., & Hurley, J. (2000). Racial and ethnic disparities in faculty promotion in academic medicine. Journal of the American Medical Association 284(9):1085.

Flexner, A. (1910). Medical Education in the United States and Canada. New York: Carnegie Foundation. Bulletin 4.

Huff, K.L., & Fang, D. (1999). When are students most at risk of encountering academic difficulty? A study of the 1992 matriculants to U.S. medical schools. Academic Medicine 74(4):454–460.

Kondo, D.G., & Judd, V.E. (2000). Demographic characteristics of U.S. medical school admission committees. Journal of the American Medical Association 284(9)1111–1113.

Laudicina, R.J. (1999). Minority student persistence in clinical laboratory education programs. Journal of Allied Health 28(2):80–85.

Ludmerer, K. (1999). Time to heal. New York: Oxford; p. 251.

Nickens, H.W., & Ready, T. (1999). A strategy to team the "savage inequalities." Academic Medicine 74(4):310–311.

Palepu, A., Carr, P.L., Friedman, R.H., Amos, H., Ash, A.S., & Moskowitz, M.A. (1998). Minority faculty and academic rank in medicine. Journal of the American Medical Association 280(9):767.

Petersdorf, R.G., Turner, K.S., Nickens, H.W., & Ready, T. (1990). Minorities in Mmdicine: Past, present and future. Academic Medicine 65(11):663–670.

Sedlacek, W.E., & Prieto, D.O. (1990). Predicting minority students' success in medical school. Academic Medicine 65(3):161–166.

Strayhorn, G., (Ed.) (1999). Literature review on non-cognitive variables. Chapel Hill: University of North Carolina, Fall.

Taylor, V., & Rust, G.S. (1999). The needs of students from diverse cultures. Academic Medicine 74(4):302–304.

Tucker, J.E. (1999). Tinto's model and successful college transitions. Journal of College Student Retention: Research, Theory & Practice 1(2):163–175.

DISCUSSION CASE STUDY

Angela is a 22-year-old Hispanic student in her first year of medical school. She was a psychology major at State College. She earned a 3.0 GPA overall, 3.1 in BCPM, and 7s on the MCAT. She was accepted by two medical schools, and chose this medical school because a classmate from State was also accepted.

She was late arriving to freshman orientation because she had car trouble driving to the school 300 miles from her home. She missed the White Coat Ceremony and the presentations by the administration. When she went to the financial aid office she discovered that her parents had not submitted the necessary tax forms in time and she would not be receiving her financial aid package. Tuition payment was deferred until the end of the month.

In the first semester, she was quickly overwhelmed by both the gross anatomy and biochemistry courses. She had taken only the basic pre-medical curriculum at her school. She received 50% on the first gross anatomy test and 45% on the biochemistry test. The class average in both exams was in the low 70s. For the rest of the semester Angela focused on gross anatomy because she felt she had a better chance of passing it, especially because she did very well (85%) on the practical exam. She passed gross anatomy but failed biochemistry by five points.

Angela was allowed by academic policy to take second-semester courses knowing that she would have to take and pass a remedial exam in biochemistry during the summer after her first year. She did better in the second semester, passing all courses with grades in the low 70s.

Lacking financial resources to live near campus during summer, she went home to study for the biochemistry make-up exam. She worked part-time in the local library. A few weeks later her mother suffered a mild heart attack. Her parents are divorced and Angela spent a lot of time with her mother at the doctor's office, translating what the doctor said. At home she helped her mother take care of her two younger sisters and the house.

Angela only had few weeks during the summer to intensively study biochemistry. She returned to medical school the week before classes, took the remedial exam, and failed it by one point. Angela reviewed the exam and challenged two answers which the instructor had marked wrong. He refused to consider her petition to reconsider her answers, saying, "You are a marginal student. It would do you well to repeat the year. Maybe you will study harder." She sought help from Dr. Green, the Assistant Dean for Minority Affairs. Dr. Green is a relatively young, black physician in the Department of Family Medicine who works part-time as the Medical School's Minority Affairs Officer. She reviewed the entire exam with Angela. She was quite surprised to see several very poorly written questions on the exam, including the two that Angela had challenged. Dr. Green called the biochemistry instructor, who reluctantly agreed to meet with her that afternoon.

Dr. Green pointed out the poorly worded questions. After 20 minutes of somewhat heated discussion, the instructor finally agreed that one of the questions Angela had challenged should be thrown out. He pointed out, however, that after throwing out the question and recalculating the grade, Angela still received a failing grade of 69.7%. His printed rule is that the final exam grade must be at least a 70% to pass his course. Dr. Green then went to the associate dean for academic affairs and explained the situation. A week later, and several days after second-year classes had already started, Dr. Green told Angela that her grade had been rounded up to a 70 by the chair of the biochemistry department and that she has been promoted to the second year. Angela began attending second-year classes at the start of the second week.

In the third semester she failed the pharmacology course. According to academic policy, failure of a second course results in a "invitation" to meet with the academic standing committee. She explained to the committee that she did not have a strong science background, that she is not strong in memorization, and that she was preoccupied by her mother's continuing health problems.

She was put on probation, told to find a tutor, and to keep in close touch with her instructors. She was also told to attend more of the help sessions offered in the evenings by graduate students. She was warned that, should she fail another course, she would be dismissed. She had to use loan money she budgeted for her food to pay for a tutor. She also went to the learning assistance specialist and discovered that she was a slow reader and employed a poor strategy for taking multiple-choice exams. By mid-semester she was "just" passing all courses.

A month later she received a note from the associate dean for student affairs, asking her to come in for an advisement appointment. She made the appointment, but did not keep it. Terrified that she was going to be dismissed, she started staying up very late at night, studying pharmacology and other third-semester courses. She managed to continue passing exams, but began to experience severe headaches. She thought she might need glasses but did not have the time or the money to get the glasses. She did manage to pass all third-semester courses.

In her fourth semester she did extremely well in the physical diagnosis course. She received very positive reviews about her ability to conduct a competent patient interview in both English and Spanish, and helped to organize a physical diagnosis Spanish course for classmates. However, she had a great deal of difficulty passing the organ systems course exams. On most exams she passed by only a few points. At the start of the class, the instructor told the students, "Students who can't pass my course never pass Step 1."

Afraid that she might fail pharmacology and later Step 1, she went back to Dr. Green and asked for help. If you were Dr. Green what would you advise?

- What are Angela's options?
- What are the advantages and disadvantages of each option?
- What could the medical school have done differently in Angela's situation?

Addendum

Symposium on Diversity in the Health Professions
in Honor of Herbert W. Nickens M.D.
Sponsored by the Association of American Medical Colleges,
the Institute of Medicine,
and the Association of Academic Health Centers

March 16 and 17, 2001

National Academy of Sciences
2101 Constitution Avenue NW, Washington, DC

March 16, 2001

7:30–8:15 am   Registration and Continental Breakfast
8:15–8:45 am   Welcome and Overview of Conference
                Fitzhugh Mullan, M.D., Health Affairs/Project Hope
                Welcome to IOM
                Kenneth Shine, M.D., President, Institute of Medicine
                Memorial to Herbert W. Nickens
                Jordan J. Cohen, M.D., President, Association of
                American Medical Colleges

8:45–9:45 am   Keynote Address: Diversity in Health Professions: Why It
                Matters to Everyone
                Introduction: Roger J. Bulger, M.D., President, Associa-
                tion of Academic Health Centers
                Benefits of Diversity in the Health Professions
                Mark Smith M.D., M.B.A., President and CEO, Cali-
                fornia Health Care Foundation
                Diversity as a Means of Promoting Educational Equity
                Lee Bollinger, J.D., President, University of Michigan

9:45–11:00 am   Making the Case for Diversity

361

1. Addressing Health Disparities Through Diversity in Health Professionals
   Raynard Kington, M.D., Ph.D., Associate Director of NIH for Behav-
   ioral and Social Sciences Research
   David Carlisle M.D., Ph.D., Director, Office of Statewide Health Plan-
   ning and Development, State of California
   Diana Tisnado Ph.D., AHRQ Postdoctoral Fellow, UCLA School of
   Public Health
2. The Role of Diversity in the Training of Health Professionals
   Lisa Tedesco, Ph.D., Vice President and Secretary, University of
   Michigan

Question & Answer: Lauro Cavazos Ph.D., Professor of Family Medicine
   and Community Health, Tufts University School of Medicine

11:00–11:15 am   Break

11:15–12:00 noon   Redefining Achievement

3. Admissions Decisions That Meet Broader Social Needs: An Examination
   of Merit and Non-Cognitive Variables
   Michael Nettles, Ph.D., and Catherine Millet, Ph.D., Center for Study
      of Higher and Postsecondary Education, University of Michigan

Question & Answer: Susan Scrimshaw, Ph.D., Dean, School of Public
   Health, University of Illinois Health Science Center

12:00 noon–1:00 pm Lunch (box lunch provided)

1:00–1:30 pm   Afternoon Keynote Address: Building Human Capi-
                    tal: From South Africa to North America
                       Alan Herman, M.D., Ph.D., Dean, National
                       School of Public Health, Medical University of
                       Southern Africa

1:30–2:45 pm   Trends in Admission, Enrollment and Matriculation of
                    URM Students in the Health Professions Training
                    Pipeline

4. Trends in Applications, Acceptance, Matriculation, Graduation of URM
   Students in the Health Professions Programs
   Kevin Grumbach, M.D., Chief, Family and Community Medicine, San
      Francisco General Hospital/Community Health Network

5. Trends of URM Student Representation at Different Points Along the
   Educational Continuum
   Patricia Gandara, Ph.D., Division of Education, University of Califor-
   nia, Davis

Question & Answer: T.B.A.

2:45–3:00 pm   Break

3:00–4:15 pm   Policy Context

6. What Is The Current Legal Status of Affirmative Action Programs?
   Thomas Perez, J.D., Assistant Professor, University of Maryland
   School of Law

7. Current Policy Initiatives That May Affect URM Participation in Health
   Professions
   Marta Tienda, Ph.D., Director, Office of Population Research, Prince-
   ton University

Question & Answer: Sam Shekar, M.D., M.P.H. Associate Administrator,
   Bureau of Health Professions, HRSA, DHHS

4:15–5:15pm   Future Directions—Moderated Panel /Roundtable
                  Convener: Lauro Cavazos, Ph.D., Tufts University
                     School of Medicine
                  Panelists:
                     Michael Bird, Ph.D., President, American Public
                        Health Association
                     Caswell Evans D.D.S., Office of the Director,
                        NIDCR, National Institutes of Health
                     Vanessa Northington Gamble, M.D., Ph.D., Vice
                        President, Division of Community and Minority
                        Programs, Association of American Medical
                        Colleges
                     Beverly Malone, Ph.D., former Deputy Assistant
                        Secretary for Health, Office of Public Health
                        Services, DHHS
                     Peter Vaughan, Ph.D. Dean, School of Social Serv-
                        ices, Fordham University

5:30–6:30 pm   Wine & Cheese Reception

Saturday, March 17, 2001

8:00–8:30 am   Continental breakfast/Registration

8:30–8:50 am   Opening Session: Recaps Key Themes of Day One
                    Clyde Evans, Ph.D., Vice President and Director,
                        American Network of Health Promoting Universities,
                        Association of Academic Health Centers

8:50–9:50 am   Keynote Presentation: Successful Teachers—Successful
                        Students: The Algebra Project
                        Robert Moses, Ph.D.

9:50–10:00 am   Break

WAVE ONE SMALL GROUP DISCUSSIONS: Raising Minority
Achievement in Grades K–12

10:00–10:30 a.m. Paper presentation
10:30–11:15 a.m. Discussion
11:15–11:30 a.m. Recap and consensus

1. What Are the Barriers or Challenges Facing Us as We Raise Minority
    Achievement?
    Linda Darling-Hammond, Ph.D., Charles E. Ducommon Professor of
        Education, Stanford University School of Education
    Discussion leader: James Hamos, Ph.D., University of Massachusetts
        Medical School

    How and When Do We Intervene to Raise Minority Achievement?
    Sam Stringfield, Ph.D., Center for Social Organization of Schools,
        Johns Hopkins University
    Discussion leader: Maxine Bleich, President, Ventures in Education

    High Stakes Standardized Tests—Steppingstone or Hurdle?
    Uri Treisman, Ph.D., Professor of Mathematics and Director, Dana
        Center, University of Texas, Austin
    Discussion leader: Catherine Millett, Ph.D., School of Education, Uni-
        versity of Michigan

11:30–12:00 noon Large Group Meets to Recap Wave One
                    Facilitator : Lauro Cavazos, Ph.D.

12:00–1:00 p.m.   Lunch (box lunches provided)

WAVE TWO SMALL GROUP DISCUSSIONS: Improving Minority Recruitment and Retention—High School and Beyond

1:00–1:30 p.m.   Paper presentation
1:30–2:15 p.m.   Discussion
2:15–2:30 p.m.   Recap and consensus

4. Sustaining Minorities in Prehealth Advising Programs
   Saundra Herndon Oyewole, Ph.D., Dean of the Faculty, Trinity College
   Discussion Leader: Susana Morales, M.D., Department of Medicine,
   Weill Medical College of Cornell University

5. What Makes a Great Health Professional—Rethinking the Admissions
   Process?
   Filo Maldonado, Assistant Dean for Admissions ,Texas A&M Medical
   School
   Discussion Leader: Richard Valachovic, D.M.D., M.P.H., Executive
   Director, American Association of Dental Education

How Do We Retain Minority Health Professional Students?
   Michael Rainey, Ph.D., Acting Associate Dean for Academic Affairs,
   SUNY Stony Brook, School of Medicine
   Discussion leader: Joseph Betancourt, M.D., M.P.H., Associate Director, and Center of Multinational and Minority Health, New York
   Presbyterian Hospital

2:30–3:00 pm   Large Group Meets to Recap Wave Two
                    Facilitator: Lauro Cavazos, Ph.D.

3:00–3:15 pm   Break

3:15–4:15 pm   Wrap Up Session: What Have We Learned? What
                    Will Go Home with Us?
                    Fitzhugh Mullan, M.D., Health Affairs/Project Hope

This Symposium is sponsored by:

The Association of American Medical Colleges
The Institute of Medicine
The Association of Academic Health Centers

And supported by generous contributions from:
The Robert Wood Johnson Foundation
The Henry J. Kaiser Family Foundation
W.K. Kellogg Foundation
Bureau of Health Professions, Division of Health Professions
Diversity, HRSA
Bureau of Primary Health Care, HRSA
Office of Minority Health, U.S. DHHS